Pornography and Prostitution in Canada

Report of the
Special Committee on
Pornography and Prostitution

Volume 2

Canada

Minister of Supply and Services Canada 1985

Available in Canada through

Authorized Bookstore Agents

and other bookstores

or by mail from

Canadian Government Publishing Centre
Supply and Services Canada
Ottawa, Canada   K1A 0S9

Catalogue No. J2-55/2-1985E

ISBN 0-660-11813-0
     0-660-11809-2 (Set)

Canada: $37.95 (Set)
Other Countries: $45.55 (Set)

Price subject to change without notice

Reprinted 1986

REQ. 66525-5-09096

TABLE OF CONTENTS

Volume II

Part III

Prostitution

Section I

Prostitution as a Social Issue

Chapter 27

Views from the Public Hearings

1. Introduction

If one thing became clear during the public hearings across Canada, it was that there is no consensus on the subject of prostitution in this country. Many of the hundreds of organizations and individuals who presented briefs at hearings in 22 different centres across the country were concerned about prostitution, often for different reasons, but their proposed solutions ranged all the way from those who would have the law eliminate prostitution entirely to those who would legalize or decriminalize it.

The types of groups presenting briefs on prostitution tended to be somewhat different from those who presented briefs on pornography. Most of the briefs on pornography were from women's organizations and church groups, with a smaller number from community organizations, educational associations and civil liberties groups. The briefs on prostitution, on the other hand, came primarily from police and municipal officials such as mayors and aldermen of affected cities, community and business associations in affected areas of cities and a smaller number of women's groups, gay groups, prostitutes' associations, churches and social work associations.

Many women's groups said that while they recognized the importance of the problem of prostitution and would have liked to contribute to the discussion on it, they had been so involved in researching and campaigning against pornography that they simply did not have the time or the resources to prepare an adequate brief on prostitution.

The focus of the briefs varied according to the type of group making the presentation. The police, civic officials and community associations tended to favour tougher laws designed to drive prostitutes off the streets, with very little discussion as to where they might go. Women's groups, social work associations and some churches were primarily concerned with the welfare of the prostitutes themselves, who they considered to be victims, rather than criminals.

This dichotomy was more pronounced in the views expressed on how prostitution was affecting individuals, families and communities.

2. Prostitution and its Effects

2.1 Effect on Communities

The cities most seriously affected by prostitution, according to the views expressed at the hearings, were Vancouver, Toronto, Montréal, Calgary, Halifax and Niagara Falls. Community groups, particularly in Vancouver, Toronto and Halifax, where street prostitution had moved out of commercial and industrial sections of the city and into residential areas, presented the most vivid descriptions of the effect prostitution was having on their communities.

> What you see in the West End [of Vancouver] is the total disintegration of a neighbourhood and a social impact as well as an economic impact on its residents, which extends from seniors to school children. *Pat Carney, MP, Vancouver Centre*

> There is no fixed place for this service. It is practised in many public places like cars, in back lanes, in parking lots and underground parkades of apartment buildings. *Rental Housing Council of B.C., Vancouver*

> ...the tenants suffer a serious decline in the quality of their living conditions and environment. Tenants are faced with the problem of prostitutes working from very early in the morning to catch the going to work crowd, right through the noon and dinner hours to catch the "quickies", and then all-night traffic which will continue to four and five o'clock in the morning. This kind of activity is repugnant, at best, to the average resident in the community. In addition to this kind of activity, there is...continual verbal harassment of residents, prostitutes, and customers alike, all through the day and night. *The West End Tenants Association, Vancouver*

> [Sex in itself isn't bad, but] the hatred and violence generated as a result of street prostitution certainly is bad. The pimps hate the girls, the girls hate the pimps, the girls hate one another and hate themselves. They all certainly hate us, the homeowners out of whose neighbourbood they work, and we hate them. The relationship of pimps and girls and tricks is apparently a perfect growing medium for outright violence at the worst of times and minor skirmishes of aggravation at the best of times.

> I illustrate the severity of the problem in our neighbourhood by just one anecdote. Not so long ago one of the girls, stationed in front of my house and several months pregnant, was stabbed in the belly by her pimp in some disciplinary move. She bled profusely through her hands, he casually watched as we pleaded in vain for her to get into an ambulance. When we finally drew off in defeat he threw her into the back seat of his car and drove away.

> Such nightlife affects my life. The situation in my neighbourhood has become one of the forced sharing of not just our sidewalks but of my OWN DOORSTEP with half a dozen girls between the hours of 8 p.m. and the early morning. *Jill Robinson, Halifax*

> [There is] congestion on the sidewalks, high noise levels, increased vehicular traffic, with disregard of laws, harassment of our members while walking on the street, many with canes, walkers or wheel chairs, increased litter, and lack of safety in the evening. Night after sleepless night, [we] suffer from a barrage of squealing tires, breaking bottles, screaming, laughing, cursing, crying. *The West End Seniors Network, Vancouver*

Our streets are already sex ghettos, with prostitutes as commodities. What a terrible effect on the [residents] of a neighbourhood ... no rational society can ever permit what we see happening daily in our neighbourhood: juvenile prostitutes enslaved by their pimps, offering themselves for sale on public streets... Will the neighbourhood residents no longer have safe and free access to their streets for fear of the transient and migrant prostitute population? We want our streets returned to us.
Homewood Residents Association, Toronto

As we will discuss in Chapter 28, it is difficult to get accurate and reliable estimates on the number of street prostitutes, and thereby, some assessment of the potential disturbances to neighbourhoods.

Estimates of the number of street prostitutes working in major Canadian cities were given to the Committee in general briefs from police officials and social workers. In Montréal, the Fraternité des Policiers de la Communauté urbaine de Montréal Inc. estimated that as many as 5,000 juvenile prostitutes work in the greater Montréal area. In Toronto, police estimated that 600 full-time prostitutes work in that city, but the Canadian Organization for the Rights of Prostitutes, Toronto, claims that when the "irregulars" are added, the total is at least 1,000. The police estimate for Vancouver was 600, with the Vancouver Multicultural Women's Centre estimating that one-half of them are visible minority women.

In Halifax, it is estimated that between 30 and 40 prostitutes work in a downtown area that has traditionally been their venue, but as middle-class renovators have moved into the area, the number of complaints to police has increased. In addition, the Nova Scotia Association of Social Workers reports that there is a good deal of activity aboard ships, as there is no provincial or local statute controlling this activity, as there is in Newfoundland.

On the prairies, where most of the prostitutes are young native women, Calgary police say they have a prostitute population of approximately 100, with the number increasing to about 150 in the summer. Most are under the control of about 75 pimps. They work in a downtown commercial area, with the result that the police receive numerous complaints from businesses, restaurants, hotels and apartment dwellers.

Winnipeg reports 400 to 500 prostitutes, with about half of them working on the street, while Regina police report 40 habitual street level prostitutes, only two of whom are not native women.

In Niagara Falls, police reported about 80 to 100 American prostitutes regularly work near the Whirlpool Rapids, with 15 to 20 on view at any one time. Most of them are controlled by pimps. The prostitution trade at the local hotels has been controlled for the past three years by members of a local motorcycle club.

Given the variation in the number of prostitutes on the streets, it is apparent that not all cities are equally affected by the presence of prostitutes and their activities. Indeed, while many of the briefs from community groups and police insisted that the prostitutes were totally to blame for the disruption to the neighbourhoods in which they worked, some of the briefs from women's organizations and social workers took a different view. Women Against Pornography, Victoria, believes that the public nuisance effects are not caused by the prostitutes, but by clients and on-lookers. Vancouver Status of Women believes that the prostitutes are being "scapegoated for noise and traffic problems caused by others". Other groups argue that:

> [The current concern over prostitution involves] a police campaign to try to toughen the solicitation laws, as well as the manipulation by the police and moral conservatives of legitimate concerns by residents of [affected] neighbourhoods... These concerns have been organized into a campaign to criminalize prostitution and further clamp down on street prostitutes.
> *Pink Ink, Toronto*

> There is little street prostitution in most urban centres outside of Vancouver, Calgary, Toronto and Montreal. ...prostitutes have unjustifiably been focused upon by powerful urban lobby groups and the media, who have ignored other street populations which are equally problematic.
> *The Elizabeth Fry Society of Kingston*

Women's groups also placed considerable emphasis on the fact that many of the prostitutes first started working the streets as teenagers and that they should be regarded as victims, rather than as criminals.

> The prostitutes ...come from a very disadvantaged background. They are victims. There's very little hope for them to break out of that cycle and, certainly, they are getting younger and younger every year. They're not 19 to 25. They are kids, and they've got no place to turn, and they're runaways, and they're drug-dependent; and they are victims.
> *Nova Scotia Advisory Council on the Status of Women, Halifax*

2.2 Effect on the Family and Individuals

The effect of prostitution on all members of the family, including women, children and the family member who uses prostitutes, was of particular concern to some of the church and other groups who presented briefs at the public hearings.

> [Prostitution] is contrary to everything that constitutes a healthy marriage where life-long commitment and mutual love and respect are the basis for good family life.
> *REAL Women of Canada, Toronto*

> [The public is] intimidated from using streets and public places...because of the number of persons seeking to buy or sell sexual services on the street.
> *David Butcher, social worker, Vancouver*

> The West End prostitution scene has as its primary victims the women residents of the area, who for financial reasons cannot afford to move out. These are largely senior citizens and single mothers.
> *Concerned Residents of the West End, Women's Committee, Vancouver*

348

It's been three years since I've been able to walk the half block from my home to the corner store, because of the looks and comments from cruising cars whose drivers assume that *any* female walking in my neighbourhood is a prostitute.

How can I make you understand the feeling of vulnerability I have when walking on the streets of a city where I've felt safe for 20 years before the prostitutes appeared?

How can I make you understand the fury I feel when I hear that prostitution is a victimless crime, when I feel I am a victim!

How can I make you understand the intimidation I feel when I see and hear a pimp parked five feet from my kitchen window, or the revulsion that I feel when a man purchases sexual services in a car parked under my bedroom window and then to have a judge say that the law is powerless to stop him.

How can I make you understand my frustration at the simplistic solutions of de-criminalizing or the like put forward by those who have no experience or understanding of this offensive and intimidating scene.
Elizabeth J. McNutt, Halifax

The effect on young children of seeing prostitutes plying their trade on the streets near their homes and schools was of particular concern to community groups.

In the West End, two elementary schools and one day-care centre are confronted by the presence of street prostitutes. Children go to school in the morning often to find hookers working their school sidewalks. And by the end of the day, the sale of sex just outside the school yards is busy and distracting.

It is disturbing to watch young children stare at this activity as it flourishes around them.... The lack of any action to stop this activity clearly suggests to our children that selling their bodies anywhere is totally acceptable and obviously condoned by our society. Why else would it be taking place so freely?
Concerned Residents of the West End, Children's Committee, Vancouver

And finally, the effect on the user of prostitutes' services:

It provides sexual satisfaction at the high cost of guilt, sexual deviation, the loss of respect of other human beings, and often the loss of family and friends.
The Pentecostal Assemblies of Canada, Toronto

The beauty of human relationships is destroyed as the buyers of sexual favours see people and sexuality as a commodity for use and discard, rather than a developing relationship.
St. Andrew's-Wesley Church, Vancouver

2.3 Effect on Prostitutes

Many of the groups expressed a strong sympathy for the plight of prostitutes, pointing out that contrary to popular opinion, being a street prostitute is not a desirable life. "At best it is degrading... At worst, it is dangerous," according to the Elizabeth Fry Society of Kingston, an organization which works with women prisoners.

... the public should be aware of the dark side of prostitution such as violence towards prostitutes by pimps and clients. Prostitution is decidedly not a crime without a victim.

[According to the sociological data surveyed, once a person has entered into prostitution] they are caught in a trap, with little choice but to continue.
Faculty of Law Students, University of Western Ontario, London

They have been and will continue to be subject to attacks by the customers and their pimps. National figures show that instances of drug use and addiction are inordinately high among street prostitutes, so much so that between violent death and drug overdose their mortality rate may be forty times the national average.
City of Regina

[The] illegality of prostitution traps them in the life, and makes them more vulnerable to violence, pressure from pimps and police, and harassment from men... By stigmatizing women as prostitutes, and by giving them criminal records through arrests for prostitution, it makes it even harder for them to get out of the life when they are ready.
Calgary Status of Women Action Committee, Calgary

In trying to change their lifestyle, these women are vulnerable, not only to societal censure but also to the vengeance and control of the pimps. Our staff is working with a young woman who has tried and is still trying to leave prostitution... One former pimp broke her nose and ribs when she wanted to opt out and, most recently, another pimp had her severely beaten because she would not join his stable.
The Children's Home of Winnipeg

2.4 Effect on Morals

Prostitution as a moral issue brought forth a variety of responses:

Of all the girls that we encountered, they regard themselves without exception, merely as "working girls". They don't consider themselves immoral. They suffer no embarrassment by being prostitutes, as they regard it as strictly a business deal and they truly feel that they provide a service to society.

It is interesting to note, however, that although they do not regard being a prostitute as bad, they will go to extreme lengths to keep this information from their families...None of them use their real name on the street. They all have street names or nicknames.
Niagara Regional Police Force, Niagara Falls

[We do] not feel that prostitution is an indication of...some sort of moral slide in our society... What it is, is the overt expression of the oppression of women in our society...
The Feminist Research Group, Regina

It is the responsibility of the religious community to speak out against the human degradation that is part of prostitution and street soliciting. The effects on attitudes toward sexuality, relationships and community...[are] devastating.
Group of Clergy, Vancouver

3. Causes of Prostitution

3.1 Introduction

The issue of what causes prostitution produced many theories and opinions, almost all of them from women's groups. With one or two exceptions, the community associations, police and civic leaders who were anxious to force prostitutes from the streets of their cities, said very little when it came to a discussion of the root causes of the phenomenon of prostitution.

Most of the women's groups believed that women's involvement in prostitution was primarily the result of the desperate economic plight in which many women find themselves. They also attributed prostitution to the socialization of women who are brought up to believe that their bodies are their only valued asset. The National Action Committee on the Status of Women pointed out that "the selling of our bodies does not take place only in Vancouver's West End or other strips. It takes place [in various media] all across Canada every day."

Several groups also cited new sociological research, particularly from the United States, which is finding a correlation between incest and sexual assault of young girls and their later involvement in prostitution. The use of drugs, the fact of having run away from home (sometimes to escape abuse), and the prevalence of pornography were also blamed for the increase in prostitution.

> The true causes of prostitution are social and economic and it is only through social and economic change that the prostitution problem can be solved... Women do not want to sell their bodies. For the most part, women enter prostitution because they have learned that their bodies are saleable commodities and feel they have nothing else to offer...
> *National Action Committee on the Status of Women, Toronto*

> [Prostitution and soliciting] must be understood as stemming from both short-run and long-run causes. A society that continues to define women as sexual objects and allows men to act as if women are fit to be the recipients of male aggression cannot be surprised when women accept that definition of themselves and market themselves as a commodity when their other limited economic resources fail.

> The shorter-term cause is that in times of high unemployment, hard economic times, and increasing social pressures, many women must earn money any way they can.

> [In both analyses, however, the fact that] society has labelled one party to the transaction as 'bad' and 'criminal' and the other party as entering an economic transaction for the provision of services in a legitimate way is indefensible rationally, logically or morally.
> *The Elizabeth Fry Society of Kingston*

> ...pornography and prostitution are symptoms and particularly graphic symbols of oppression and objectification of women in our society, revealing the violence directed towards women and the merchandising of that violence. Pornography and prostitution are institutions which reinforce and mirror the daily abuse of women by men. This daily abuse of women takes many forms such as rape, battering and harassment. But this abuse and bullying is not

only perpetuated by individual men; in the areas of reproductive choice, family-law and economic inequities in the workplace, the subservience of women to men is sanctioned and institutionalized, by governments, businesses and religious organizations. These institutions further contribute to the cheapening and devaluing of women's labour in society.... It is clear that it is men who are to blame for the institutions of pornography and prostitution...
Men Against Sexism, Winnipeg

[Prostitution] is a form of domination and nothing else. The existence of both pornography and prostitution depends on the availability of a population of disadvantaged women. If women were not disadvantaged, if they had true equality under the law, if they had proper access to education, and training, if they had access to experiences which build self-esteem, it would not be possible for either of these things to take place...
Le Comité de la Protection de la Jeunesse, Montréal

3.2 Sexual Abuse and Incest

Many of the social work organizations which work with prostitutes reported to the Committee that they are finding that many prostitutes were sexually abused as children. (See Part IV on Children for a discussion of this view). The Elizabeth Fry Society of Kingston, for example, estimates that one third of the women in the federal penitentiary were sexually abused as children. The Children's Home of Winnipeg, which works with troubled children, told the Committee that up to 80 percent of the young people in one of their training programs were sexually abused as youngsters.

As we delved into the literature in the area, we discovered....that our observations were consistent with experts in the field who have acknowledged that teenage prostitution is a point on a continuum of an early destructive sexual experience. One recent case in which we were involved was that of a young woman who used to obtain her allowance for performing fellatio on her father; for her it was a natural progression to move on to other forms of selling sex.
The Children's Home of Winnipeg

The association of child abuse with prostitution appears to be gaining increased recognition by researchers. In one recent study, detailed life histories were collected on 200 prostitutes. Former prostitutes working with Delancy Street Foundation, a self-help residential facility known for its work with prostitutes, criminals and drug addicts, conducted this survey. Their results clearly link abuse as juveniles and prostitution as adults. This particular study found that:

60 per cent of the prostitutes became so when 16 or younger; the youngest was a mere child of 10;

65 per cent came from families of middle or higher income;

60 per cent had been sexually exploited as juveniles; in 63 per cent of the cases, the abuser had been the father or surrogate father;

only 10 per cent had been abused by strangers;

in 81 per cent of the cases, some sort of force was used and almost all reported that the sexual abuse caused severe physical harm: cuts, bruises, broken bones, venereal disease;

17 per cent ran away from home to avoid the abuse; and

2 per cent had attempted to commit suicide.
Government of Saskatchewan, Regina

3.3 Economic Conditions

The economic plight of women, particularly young, poorly educated women who are unable to find employment, was cited by many groups as the major cause of prostitution. They pointed out that in times of economic hardship and high unemployment, those who lack schooling, training or work experience may have no choice but to turn to prostitution to provide the basic necessities for themselves and their dependents. They also pointed out that Canadian women earn, on average, 60 cents for every dollar earned by men. Their low income is even more graphically illustrated by the fact that in 1981, 75 per cent of all minimum wage earners were women.

> Prostitution [must] be understood as a crime of poverty. As long as there is demand for purchasable sex, and a combination of high unemployment and low-paying jobs, we should realize the prostitutes are driven by hunger and frustration to fill the supply of that demand.
> *Concordia [University] Women's Collective, Montréal*

> The recent increase in street prostitution in the Halifax Metro area directly corresponds to the downturn in the economy, the increase in exhausted rates of Unemployment Insurance, and restraints and tightening up of welfare budgets. This correlation is extremely important.
> *Nova Scotia Association of Social Workers, Halifax*

> In Regina the majority of street walkers are young native teenage women, one of the groups with the highest unemployment rates in the country.
> *The Feminist Research Group, Regina*

The Ontario Advisory Council on the Status of Women emphasized the need for economic reforms to alleviate the problem of women and girls turning to prostitution because they have few other available options. Their recommendations, designed to improve the economic status of all women in our society, encourage both federal and provincial governments to introduce:
1) legislated affirmative action programs;
2) contract compliance;
3) better enforcement of the employment standards legislation;
4) improved child care facilities;
5) re-training programs for women to assist them to enter the higher paying non-traditional jobs;
6) extension of benefits to part-time workers on a pro-rated basis with full-time workers;
7) changes to social benefits legislation in order to allow women to adequately support their families.

3.4 Other Causes

Three other causes of prostitution which were mentioned at the public hearings were the problems of runaways who fall into prostitution as a last resort, the use of drugs and the effect of pornography. It was pointed out that large urban cities have become refuges for thousands of homeless people, many of whom are juveniles escaping from abusive families or provincial juvenile homes.

> While one researcher documented that 96 percent of teenage prostitutes were runaways, this phenomenon is often mistakenly assumed to be the problem, when actually it is largely a symptom of a pattern of victimization which begins for most prostitutes when they are young children at home.
> *Faculty of Law Students, University of Western Ontario, London*

> Three quarters of juvenile prostitutes interviewed at Kingston Penitentiary were escaping from families which subjected them to sexual abuse.
> *The Elizabeth Fry Society of Kingston*

While no statistics on drug use and addiction by prostitutes were available, some social workers and civic officials described the use of drugs by prostitutes as being much higher than for the population as a whole. On the other hand, the Committee was told in a private meeting with prostitutes in one major city that some prostitutes use drugs and alcohol to help them to endure their work, but that the majority do not because the dangers of their job require that they be constantly alert.

Pornography was also cited by some as a cause or a contributor to prostitution. The prevalence of pornography reinforces the view that women are sexual objects available for men's pleasure. Others believe that for the consumer of pornography, the prostitute is the most available person to engage in the sexual acts portrayed in pornography. One promises, the other delivers.

4. The Present Law and its Enforcement

4.1 The Law

The public hearings revealed that there are two distinct, and diametrically opposed, schools of thought regarding the present law on prostitution. On one side, one tends to find the police, mayors, municipal officials and community groups representing areas affected by prostitution, as well as conservative church groups. On the other are organizations such as women's groups, civil liberties associations, social workers, some churches and gay organizations.

On the basis of the briefs presented to the Committee, it would appear that the first group is convinced that the only solution to the problem of street prostitution is the introduction of stronger federal laws, similar to those proposed by the Standing Committee on Justice and Legal Affairs in 1983, but with a wider definition of street soliciting. Briefs from the second group indicate that the present laws, both in their substance and in their administration, have been unfair and unworkable because they have had the effect of punishing the prostitute and not the customer. In addition, they believe that these laws discriminate chiefly against street prostitutes, who tend to be poor, disadvantaged, and from visible minorities. These groups believe that the only solution to the problem of prostitution has to be a long-range one, based on social and economic programs designed to keep young people out of prostitution, rather than harsher laws to punish those already in it. They tended to favour decriminalization of prostitution.

Some examples of the views of the first group, who favour stronger controls, follow:

> To put an end to the problems caused by prostitution and to allow citizens to move about freely in the streets of Canada as a whole, the Criminal Code must define the notion of solicitation as any person who through words, gestures or otherwise offers oneself, proposes oneself or in any way demonstrates that he or she is available for purposes of prostitution.
> *Service de Police de la Communauté Urbaine de Montréal*

> ...whatever changes are made to the Criminal Code, it should be amended to remove the uncertainty as to whether clients are liable to prosecution.

> ...a new offence [should] be added consisting of the offering or acceptance of an offer to engage in prostitution in a public place...

> ...the definition of public place [should] be amended to include vehicles in public places, and private places open to public view.
> *Mayor Ron Wallace, Halifax*

> [The Hutt decision] has virtually rendered the existing [soliciting] legislation useless...[Now] a police officer must virtually witness a prostitute 'putting a half nelson on' or 'wrestling a client to the ground' in order to obtain a conviction. Consequently, local police have laid but one soliciting charge in the past two years and it was then thrown out of court.
> *Patrick Cummings, Acting Mayor, Niagara Falls*

The proposals, made by women's groups and civil liberties associations, that other laws, such as those designed to control nuisance, traffic, and noise, could be used to prevent the most disturbing aspects of street prostitution, were dismissed as unworkable by police and many community groups.

> Evidence required for the enforcement of Sections 171 (creating a disturbance) and 193 (keeping a bawdy house) are so onerous as to make them virtually useless. ...while the potential of indirect controls exists, the reality, as seen in inner-city communities, is that they have not been or cannot be effectively used.
> *West End Community Advisory Council, Vancouver*

> ...increased police foot patrols in the North Jarvis area and the study of possible traffic modifications to deter customers, can only curtail street soliciting a small degree, and for only a short term.
> *Mayor Art Eggleton, Toronto*

> ...[these] regulations are stop gap measures that add to the inconvenience of citizens in the affected neighbourhoods; the only solution is the adoption of the Justice Committee amendments.
> *Toronto Residents on Street Soliciting*

The views of the women's groups, civil liberties associations and gay groups were diametrically opposed to those of the civic officials and community groups.

The supposed legal activity of prostitution is indirectly criminalized because of the effect of Sections 193 [bawdy houses] and 195 [living on the avails]. In the case of the soliciting section, a further effect is to protect men from the undue solicitations of women...[while] women receive no such equivalent protection from unwelcome and persistent solicitations, nor is society at large protected from the solicitations of politicians, street hawkers, religious advocates or others plying their wares. Section 195.1 [soliciting] is clearly discriminatory and criminalizes the behaviour of only one group of people who solicit, prostitutes who work the street.

In more serious nuisance cases, other Criminal Code provisions such as causing a disturbance, indecent exposure, or intimidation, could be utilized instead of the soliciting section.
Vancouver Status of Women, Vancouver

...increased use of Section 169 (causing a disturbance), and Section 171 (public indecency) [could be used] to counter prostitution-related crime.
B.C. Civil Liberties Association, Vancouver

[The] present law deprives the prostitute of husband or mate and stable family life; any man living with a prostitute can be charged with 'living on the avails'... Bawdy house laws force her to work on the run.
Canadian Organization for the Rights of Prostitutes, Toronto

The debate on amending the Criminal Code dealing with prostitution centers on two issues: the right of adult gays to have sex in gay institutions such as steambaths, and the provision of sexual services for financial reward. At present, the criminalization of gay prostitutes under the bawdy house sections is used by the police to harass gays and reinforce the prevailing social mores of stigmatizing and persecuting gays.
Right to Privacy Committee, Toronto

4.2 Police Practices

Police practices with regard to the enforcement of laws against prostitution came under attack from two different directions. First, police were criticized by aldermen in some cities for their failure (since the Hutt decision requiring pressing and persistent behaviour made it more difficult to arrest prostitutes) to use other laws to curtail the activities of street prostitutes. Secondly, they were criticized by women's groups for their harassment of prostitutes.

...police will not increase foot patrols, which in the past substantially reduced the problem of street soliciting, because of their inability to obtain arrests; an attitude that appears to be part of a stratagem to obtain the passage of the tougher Criminal Code amendments.
Alderman Jack Layton, Toronto

If the spirit is there, the police could control many of the public nuisance factors under the current legislation.
Elizabeth Fry Society of Toronto

There has been a great public campaign by the police and the prosecutors to obtain new anti-prostitution laws by not enforcing the existing statutes.
Alderman Harry Rankin, Vancouver

The harassment of prostitutes by police was described in some of the briefs from women's groups.

> The criminalization of solicitation for the purposes of prostitution is a difficult offence for the police to charge, and yet they are expected to deal with it. This can, and does, allow for harassment of women who work as prostitutes by the police. For example, in Winnipeg, open and surreptitious photographic surveillance of the women is done routinely by the police. Common tactics reported are frequent drug searches without warrants, being taken off the street and held for questioning, etc.

> There is no special training for police officers who work in this area. They learn 'on the job', and they are picked for their ability to have a 'good rapport with the girls'. So it is not surprising the unenlightened attitude of law enforcement officers towards women on the street.
> *Manitoba Action Committee on the Status of Women, Winnipeg*

> Perhaps many of the problems surrounding prostitution, such as physical and psychological harassment by police, may be the result of the law.
> *Manitoba Advisory Council on the Status of Women, Winnipeg*

> Enforcement of existing legislation has proved troublesome, costly in money and police personnel, prosecution efforts and court attention and ineffective in deterring recidivism. Furthermore, enforcement patterns are often selective and discriminatory. The use of undercover agents posing as prostitutes or clients is questionable and tends to bring the administration of justice into disrepute.
> *Association Nationale de la Femme et le Droit, Montréal*

5. Recommendations for Change

5.1 The Law

The recommendations for changes to the law fall into four categories, which are described in detail in Chapter 36. This section will attempt to provide only a cross-section of the views expressed at the public hearings.

The four categories of changes proposed to the Committee were:

a) The criminal law should be strengthened in an effort to control street prostitution more effectively, or, in the view of a small minority, to do away entirely with prostitution of all types;

b) Prostitution-related activities should be decriminalized, that is removed from the control of the criminal law, unless other forms of criminal conduct are involved;

c) Prostitution should be legalized and controlled by regulation;

d) The prostitution activities of prostitutes should be decriminalized, but those of customers and pimps should be criminalized, a blending of criminalization and decriminalization.

a) Strengthen the Present Law

The majority of those who believed that stronger laws were the solution to the problem wanted to make it possible for the police to control street prostitution more effectively and to secure convictions more easily. This view was put forward by the police in most cities, as well as by mayors and councils, community and commercial groups and individuals in major cities in which street prostitution was creating problems. These groups supported the 1983 recommendations of the House of Commons Standing Committee on Justice and Legal Affairs which recommended: the addition of a new offence of offering or accepting an offer to engage in prostitution; the application of the law to both prostitute and customer; and the redefinition of "public place" to include a motor vehicle in a public place.

> In any amendments to the *Criminal Code* it [must] be made abundantly clear that if any person solicits any other person in a public place for the purposes of prostitution in any manner that person is guilty of an offence.
> *Calgary Police Commission, Calgary*

> Section 195.1 [soliciting] must be amended to overcome the pressing and persistent problem. The amendments proposed by the Justice Committee will be unenforceable while police are still left with the need to prove that solicitation is "pressing and persistent."
> *Mayor Art Eggleton, Toronto*

The extreme view, that prostitution should be eliminated entirely, was held by only a very small proportion of those making submissions.

> The government should pass laws prohibiting the practice of prostitution in any form.
> *Christian and Missionary Alliance of Churches, Regina*

> ...favours criminalizing all forms of prostitution, as well as all associated activities. To meet this objective, the Hutt decision should be specifically overruled by provisions of the Criminal Code; clients of prostitutes should be made equally liable to prosecution; ... consideration should be given to including private places as well as public places in any prohibition on soliciting.
> *REAL Women of Canada, Toronto*

b) Decriminalize Prostitution

The proposal that prostitution should be decriminalized was made by the majority of women's groups which presented briefs on prostitution, by individual prostitutes and prostitute organizations, gay rights organizations, social workers, civil liberties organizations, some church groups and a small minority of municipal politicians.

These briefs advocated: the removal of street soliciting from the *Criminal Code*; the repeal of the common bawdy house provisions, or at least changing them to allow small numbers of prostitutes to work out of their own premises; and the use of other *Criminal Code* provisions, along with provincial legislation and municipal by-laws to deal with the nuisances associated with street prostitution.

Those who favoured decriminalization of prostitution told the Committee that prostitutes are essentially victims of a sexist society, and should not be treated as criminals. Although they did not condone prostitution as a way of life, they believed that it could be eliminated only through long-term social and economic measures, not through legal restraints.

> Given that no legal changes, in and of themselves, can eliminate prostitution, decriminalization seems to afford the fairest, least costly and most effective choice, and to offer the most opportunity for options for prostitute women.
>
> Prostitution, like water, can be dammed in one place, but will simply find another outlet. Prostitution may change its form but it will not disappear so long as society creates and fosters conditions where it must prevail."
> *National Action Committee on the Status of Women, Toronto*

The National Action Committee on the Status of Women, Toronto, made a detailed proposal outlining how the law should be changed to decriminalize prostitution. Similar proposals were put forward by the B.C. Civil Liberties Association and by regional women's groups such as the Manitoba Action Committee on the Status of Women, the Vancouver Status of Women, and the Feminist Research Group, Regina. The NAC proposals are:

1. Section 195.1 of the *Criminal Code*, Soliciting for the Purposes of Prostitution, ought to be repealed.

2. In the alternative, Section 195.1 ought not to be amended with a view to cancelling the effect of Hutt. It is doubtful, and we doubt, that soliciting which is pressing and persistent is sufficiently harmful to properly constitute a crime; however, it is clear that soliciting which is not pressing and persistent is not sufficiently harmful, and should not constitute an offence.

3. Section 193, Keeping a Common Bawdy House, ought to be repealed. Alternatively, S. 193 should be amended to make it possible for prostitutes to use their own homes for the purposes of prostitution.

4. The problems raised by the phenomenon of street prostitution, insofar as they would remain if recommendation 3 were adopted, should be regarded as problems of public order. They are properly dealt with by legal remedies other than criminal sanctions aimed specifically and exclusively at the prostitutes. For example, police and concerned citizens should be urged to make use of the following types of legislation:

    (a) Existing provincial residential tenancy legislation which protects the right to quiet enjoyment of one's residential premises. In the event that Section 193 is repealed, this legislation, along with well developed common law, is available to deal with any nuisances arising from the operation of bawdy houses.

    (b) Motor vehicle legislation, municipal zoning by-laws and similar regulatory legislative controls can be used to control any nuisance problems resulting from street prostitution.

    (c) Insofar as serious nuisance problems that amount to criminal behaviour manifest themselves, enforcement of existing sections of the *Criminal Code* can be relied upon. Specifically, Section 171 (Causing a Disturbance, Indecent Exhibition, Loitering, etc...), Section 169 (Indecent Acts), Section 305 (Extortion), and Section 381 (Intimidation) could be used.

National Action Committee on the Status of Women, Toronto

The Canadian Advisory Council on the Status of Women put forward a slightly different proposal which recommends a form of partial decriminalization of selected prostitution-related offences while retaining sanctions against all offensive solicitors. The Council recommends the abolition of the present 'soliciting' provision in s. 195.1 of the *Criminal Code* and its replacement with a new offence wherein the pressing or persistent solicitations of anyone, for *whatever purpose* in a public place, would be liable to penalty.

The Council also proposed that the definition of a common bawdy house in s. 179 of the *Criminal Code* be amended to allow up to three persons to use premises for the purpose of their own prostitution.

The decriminalization option was also the most popular with organized groups of prostitutes, Alliance for the Safety of Prostitutes in Vancouver and the Canadian Organization for the Rights of Prostitutes in Toronto.

> The [decriminalization] option represents the only viable and socially just alternative. It would allow women:
>
> - the option of working indoors and ... methods [other than street soliciting] of securing business, alleviating much of the existing problems on the street;
>
> - increased security for the prostitutes by reducing the potential for exploitation by customer, police and pimp;
>
> - a sense of dignity and self worth.
>
> *Canadian Organization for the Rights of Prostitutes, Toronto*

Gay groups presenting briefs in several cities also supported the decriminalization of prostitution, especially the bawdy house sections.

> We wish to comment only on a few aspects of the issues of prostitution, pending a full study of this very complex subject. Since the decriminalization of consensual sodomy between two adults, bawdy-house statutes, along with obscenity statutes, have provided the most common legal pretexts to police and the courts for the politically motivated persecution of gay people. Indeed, they have replaced the sodomy statutes as the legislative means of criminalization of gay people, and been used systematically against gay institutions, meeting-places, and even private homes, where no monetary transactions were ever proven to have taken place.
>
> We demand the immediate repeal of all bawdy-house statutes that may be interpreted to apply to any situation other than strictly defined prostitution. Furthermore, we demand the removal of the categories of "gross indecency" and "buggery" from the *Criminal Code*, undefined terms which are systematically defined by the police and our other political enemies in such a way as to selectively prosecute gay people and criminalize our valid sexual practices.
>
> Finally, in view of recent tendencies of the law to invade our private space and criminalize our lives by extending the definition of public space, we urge the commission to consider the proposed definition of automobiles as public space with extreme caution. If approved this revision will be used selectively by police as one more means to criminalize our private lives as gay people: heterosexual teenagers parked in "lovers' lanes" will continue unimpeded as

before, while the gay equivalents will continue to be subjected to the full force of legal terrorism with increased legislative justification.
Emergency Committee of Gay Cultural Workers Against Obscenity Laws, Montréal

Those opposed to decriminalization predicted dire consequences if such a change were introduced.

If this option were chosen... thereafter the downtown streets of major Canadian cities would be literally clogged with prostitutes from all over North America lured to Canada by the lax laws. Decriminalization would, in effect, be a giveaway of our downtown areas over to the prostitutes and their pimps.
Mayor Art Eggleton, Toronto

...this option [decriminalization] exists now. Simple soliciting is not a criminal act, and those who argue for decriminalization are simply arguing for maintaining the present unpleasant situation.
Downtown Halifax Residents Association, Halifax

c) Legalize Prostitution

The view that prostitution should be legalized and regulated was presented to the Committee by only a few individuals, including a few municipal politicians. Some wanted licensed brothels, and licensing and compulsory medical examinations of prostitutes. Others suggested red light districts.

Legalization, with appropriate control mechanisms, would be a better situation than we have today... Then maybe we can start to discuss the control mechanisms, the zoning, the licensing, the income taxes, the hours of operation, the age limits, the types of sexual services that are authorized for sale, and all of the other governmental controls that are involved with 'legalized prostitution.' Legalization does not mean uncontrolled prostitution, as the prostitutes would like to have.
Downtown Halifax Residents Association, Halifax

I firmly believe that controlling prostitution and allowing it to proceed within the framework of strict regulation is the only way to eliminate its harmful and unpleasant effects. [However], I do not believe that establishing "red-light districts" will solve the problem. European cities which have done this are experiencing very high levels of criminal activities in these areas.

I do believe, however, that by limiting the number of licences issued, by allowing business operators to accept or refuse an application by a prostitute to operate on their premises, and by allowing prostitutes to work in all areas zoned exclusively for commercial use, we can prevent a high concentration of this kind of activity in any one area.

The licensing provision would enable law enforcement officials to get many of the young prostitutes off the streets and place them in the care of juvenile authorities, where they may receive medical attention, [and] counselling...
Alderman Anne Johnston, Toronto

While there were only a few suggestions for legalization of prostitution, many presenters expressed strong opposition to the imposition of any such regime. Mayors and community associations, as well as women's groups and the prostitutes themselves were all opposed to legalization.

...the state would, in effect, become the pimp and benefit, through taxes, from an activity that is regarded by many in our society as exploitative of women. There are also some practical drawbacks to legalization. It has been suggested that only a certain number of licensed prostitutes be allowed to solicit on designated streets...or that a red light district be created... There would be an immediate outcry from residents and businesses, "not on my street!"
Mayor Art Eggleton, Toronto

...legalization raises three problems. First, politicians are seen to condone prostitution; secondly, the government becomes the pimp; and thirdly, it retains prohibitions and a system of enforcement that duplicates the current provisions of the *Criminal Code* in order to control 'free-lancers'.
West End Community Advisory Council, Vancouver

...by licensing, you would be ensuring that the most vulnerable, the young, would be put in the hands of the pimps and the underworld.
Elizabeth Fry Society of Toronto

The real disadvantage of legalization would be the danger of enslavement and ghettoization of prostitutes through their being registered.
First United Church, Vancouver

d) Penalize only the Customer

The proposal that the law should penalize the customers, pimps and procurers, but decriminalize the behaviour of the prostitutes was made by Professor Constance Backhouse and a group of law students at the University of Western Ontario, London. This view was supported by some women's groups as well.

The law students made three proposals for reforming the *Criminal Code*: that a partial decriminalization approach be taken that would repeal the existing sections used against prostitutes; that criminal sanctions against exploiters be tightened; and that emphasis be put on the client's offer to purchase sexual services. It also proposed that the bawdy house sections should be amended to deal solely with keepers and owners, not inmates or found-ins, in order to deter those who profit from the prostitution of other persons.

Their argument is that prostitution should not be accepted without question. The law should attempt to deal with the root cause, which is the demand by men for sexual services. It is this male attitude which creates the need for prostitutes and the situation which allows other males, in particular the procurers and pimps, to exploit them.

The major criticism of this approach, which would create a law which distinguishes between buyers (almost entirely men) and sellers (mostly women) of sexual services, is the possibility that it would be open to a challenge under the equality provisions (Section 15) of the Charter of Rights.

362

6. Rehabilitation Programs

The groups which addressed the need for rehabilitation programs to prevent women from entering prostitution, and to assist those in the field to find other means of employment held the belief that the present social and economic inequalities of women in our society are responsible for driving disadvantaged women into prostitution. They pointed out that the government, if it is truly committed to reducing solicitation, must look at the conditions that lead women into prostitution and at the nature of our society which perceives women as sexual objects to be bought and sold.

They took the position that the root causes of prostitution could be eradicated if the social and economic inequalities faced by women were addressed. They urged the provision of improved services for women, such as interval houses, community living alternatives, 24-hour day care centres, employment and career counselling and training, drug and alcohol counselling, the implementation of affirmative action programs and the enforcement of equal pay for work of equal value regulations.

> Economic independence is the key to resolving the problem of prostitution, as it is the key to resolving most of the issues taken up by feminists: child care, women's wages and job ghettos, discrimination and devaluation. Prostitution is but one symptom of the pervasive inequalities condoned by our society vis-à-vis women and children.
> *Saskatoon Committee Against Pornography, Saskatoon*

> Until women have equality of opportunity and treatment, there will be those who endure the censure, arrest, harassment and punishment of prostitution in order to make a living wage. For those who are already involved in prostitution we must provide services in re-training, life skills and assertiveness training, and affirmative action in all areas.
> *Manitoba Advisory Council on the Status of Women, Winnipeg*

> It may or may not be possible to prevent prostitution, but it should certainly be possible to make alternatives more possible to women and children. Services to abused or distressed women and children are "under the gun" at this time, just when the problem of these groups is being addressed.
> *First United Church, Vancouver*

> If we are to resolve the prostitution problem, we must begin by preventing child abuse, by refusing to condone the use of women's bodies as a sales incentive in advertising and their abuse in violent pornography, by providing alternatives to children and women now involved in prostitution in the form of alternative housing arrangements, social services and employment training programs.
> *National Action Committee on the Status of Women, Toronto*

The most detailed proposals for services which would help women to get out of prostitution and assist those now in it were made by the Alliance for the Safety of Prostitutes in Vancouver. They proposed:

1. Drop-in store front centres should be set up to provide health care, family planning information, legal services, court advocacy and welfare appeals.

2. The incidence of prostitution could be reduced if some or all of the following services were available to ease the financial burden for single women and sole support mothers:

- day care, so that single parent prostitutes could get a regular job;

- student grants to allow prostitutes to improve their education or job skills;

- co-operative housing, to reduce the cost of living for single parents or single women;

- an increase in welfare payments so that welfare women would not have to resort to prostitution on the last few days before their next cheque arrives;

- an increase in the minimum wage so that low income women would not have to resort to prostitution to make ends meet;

- special training for social workers and police who do not presently know how to deal with prostitutes.

Alliance for the Safety of Prostitutes, Vancouver

7. Research

Many groups commented on the fact that research on the subject of prostitution is almost non-existent in Canada, and that the little that has been done has concentrated almost entirely on street prostitution. Very little is known about the other types of prostitution, such as call-girls, escort services and massage parlours. Even less is known about the customers of prostitutes.

> ...a thorough and professional study [should] be undertaken to uncover the roots of prostitution and to document to what extent the economic plight of young women and sexual exploitation of children play substantial roles in leading women into prostitution.
> *Manitoba Action Committee on the Status of Women, Winnipeg*

> ...the federal government should allocate a sum of money for an in-depth, national study of the needs of prostitutes. Such a study must include such aspects as: the involuntary or voluntary nature of their participation; reasons for participation, if voluntary; perceived needs vis-à-vis safety, medical services, etc.; ...and ways of aiding, through training programs, employment opportunities, etc. those who wish to leave the field.
> *The Feminist Research Group, Regina*

8. Conclusion

The public hearings were a very important aspect of the work of the Special Committee. The careful and thoughtful briefs, presented by groups and individuals in every region of Canada and representing a wide diversity of opinion, were an invaluable contribution to the body of information the Committee collected on this issue. In conclusion, the Committee would like to thank all of the participants who devoted many hours of their time to writing their briefs, presenting their views and participating in the development of legal and social reform.

364

Chapter 28

Prostitution in Canada Today

1. Introduction

Briefs presented at the public hearings were an invaluable source of information about Canadians' views and experiences with prostitution activities. Many presentations included information about prostitution in particular cities and towns and made reference to research studies. In this chapter, we will consider in more detail what published studies say about prostitution so that our subsequent recommendations are based on as comprehensive a view of the issue as is possible.

Historical and empirical information about prostitution in Canada is largely absent from the available research literature. Perhaps the major reason for this state of affairs is that only recently have researchers turned their attention to the study of this issue. When they do begin to investigate the context and manifestations of prostitution, they realize that the research area is a very difficult one. Not surprisingly, therefore, our information is relatively incomplete. While we do find the occasional study or reference to prostitution in Canada, only rarely do we have multiple or comparable studies such that the information reported in one source can be checked against another set of findings, and thus we can be confident that we have a reliable body of information.[1]

This lack of good, comprehensive research does not mean, of course, that people have been unaware of the business of prostitution or that people do not have firmly held views about the profession, and its causes and consequences. Indeed, one can see in the history of legislation which has been passed to control prostitution, that certain views and ideas about it are reflected in changes to the legal codes. However, these changes do not necessarily mean that people and politicians had a thorough or accurate understanding of the issues with which they were dealing. Rather, a partial knowledge, coupled with periodic waves of moral fervour, convinced various Parliaments to take action.[2]

In the 1980s, it is our belief that policy makers, politicians and the general public look for a more complete understanding of social issues before implementing or changing legislation. While previous generations may have striven for this goal as well, the means to accomplish this end are more available to us now, and the possibilities for conducting research into an issue as difficult and complex as prostitution have increased. The accuracy of information may also be perhaps, more significant to us today, given the involvement of the state in all aspects of our lives. If the state is to set so many of the parameters within which we will live, then we must be sure that the principles and bases from which action is taken, are ones with which Canadians agree and ones which are legitimate and defensible.

Typically, we believe that unless we understand the phenomenon we are seeking to control, our efforts towards that end will not be overly successful. For example, we must have a good understanding of the harms, if any, resulting from prostitution as it currently operates before we can determine what action may be necessary. Similarly, when we seek to implement social policies, we will be more successful if they are specifically targeted at certain categories of people. This again assumes that we know the characteristics and number of people involved in the issues we seek to address, otherwise our policies may be inappropriate and special facilities over- or under-utilized.

Part of the task of the Committee, therefore, has been to gain as full an understanding of the business of prostitution as is possible. As indicated earlier, most people have views about the issue, but may not be very clear about the basis for their views, and certainly have varying degrees of knowledge based on personal experiences. Through its public hearings, the Committee received submissions from a variety of Canadians who had information to bring to our attention.

This information typically came from people who had had direct contact with prostitution either as members of the public who were inconvenienced by the business, as members of the various professions who from time to time had prostitutes as clients or as members of police forces. In addition, the Committee held private meetings with them whenever prostitutes requested the opportunity to present their views in private. The Committee also heard from people who, although they may not have had any direct contact with prostitution, had specific beliefs about it.

While briefs, submissions and interviews from concerned individuals and groups constituted one source of information for the Committee, an additional source was the program of research undertaken by the Department of Justice, which was designed to assist the Committee in its deliberations. There were three major components to the research on prostitution: 1) five regional studies, 2) a national population survey, and 3) a review of prostitution and its control in selected countries outside Canada.

The five regional studies were undertaken in order to learn as much as possible about who the prostitutes are and how they work, current control practices, social programs and the need for changes in our current legislation. The regional studies were conducted in Vancouver, the Prairie provinces (essentially Winnipeg, Saskatoon and Calgary), Ontario (primarily Toronto but with some information from Niagara Falls, London, Timmins, Sudbury, Hamilton, Ottawa, Windsor and Cornwall), the province of Québec (focusing on Québec City, Montréal and Trois-Rivières) and the Atlantic region (with Halifax and St. John's being the focus).[3] The researchers were operating under very tight schedules since the Committee needed the information as quickly as possible for its deliberations. The shortness of time was particularly problematic for research such as this, since the quasi-legality of the business means that researchers have to establish their credibility and reliability with those involved before people are willing to talk about what they do. Establishing this credibility, of course, takes time. For these reasons, the researchers could not cover all aspects of prostitution, but had to concentrate their efforts on certain aspects of the business. Because of public concern about the most visible aspects of prostitution, the researchers were asked to focus on prostitution which is carried out on the street and in public places, and to do all they could to investigate the other forms of the business. In addition, the researchers were to concentrate, if possible, on the customers (who they are and their motivations) and those who procure and maintain people in the profession (i.e. pimps). Although we now have more information about prostitution in Canada than we have ever had before, it must be stressed that we still know about only certain parts of the business and, as will be apparent in the discussion of the research findings, there are whole areas about which we still know virtually nothing.

The second component of the Department of Justice's research program was the National Population Study on Pornography and Prostitution.[4] This survey included 2,018 Canadians over 18 years of age who were interviewed during June and July, 1984 on the issues of pornography and prostitution. Because the sample is representative of Canadians over 18 years of age, and in all parts of the country with the exception of the Yukon and Northwest Territories, we are able to draw conclusions about Canadians' knowledge of prostitution, their attitudes towards it, and similar issues of interest. The study was designed to learn about "Canadians attitudes towards, knowledge and perceptions of pornography and prostitution."[5] This is the first time that such a large-scale study has been conducted in Canada. While the study has given the Committee some interesting information on Canadians' views, use and exposure to pornography and prostitution, it should be remembered that this is the first such foray into this area of research, and everyone involved with it would do it somewhat differently if the study were to be repeated. For example, questions would be reworded and some of the conceptualization on which the survey is based requires further thought and elaboration. In addition, it must be stressed that social surveys such as this can give us only a very partial and somewhat superficial understanding of the issues with which we are concerned. Constraints on the time it takes respondents to answer the questions mean that each facet of the topic cannot be pursued in depth. Therefore, very complex issues are simplified and respondents may be answering questions on issues to which they have given very little thought, and to which they would give different answers if they were to reflect more thoroughly on their own views and attitudes. The National Population Survey should, therefore, be seen as a good, first effort to explore Canadian's perceptions about pornography and prostitution, but not as a definitive statement on the issues. As will be discussed later in the Report, it gives us more descriptive information about Canadians' views on the issues than we have had to date, but still leaves us with many unanswered questions which need to be the subject of further research.

A final set of studies looks at prostitution in other countries.[6] The research involved an analysis of the current legislation, published studies discussing aspects of prostitution or the public's views for the country in question, and interviews with selected officials whenever this was possible. Although such research does not provide the detail given in the five regional studies it is invaluable in indicating the trends in legislation and the major advantages or disadvantages to particular approaches of the issue.

Apart from these major research initiatives, smaller studies were completed which dealt with specific topics, for example, sexually transmitted diseases and the media coverage of prostitution-related news.[7] The Committee's Director of Legal Research and individual Committee members were also involved in particular aspects of the overall research effort, in relation to such issues as the current state and effectiveness of Canadian criminal law on prostitution-related activities, the relevance of provincial law, municipal by-laws and the impact of the *Charter* on proposed changes to the *Criminal Code*.

Apart from the studies specially commissioned by the Department of Justice or the Committee, we have, of course, made use of published studies and reports whenever possible. As indicated earlier, these are not very numerous when dealing specifically with Canadian experiences, but there is some material available. In particular, the Committee was able to draw on information from the recently published report of the Committee on Sexual Offences Against Children and Youth's (Badgley Report).[8] Although the primary focus of our Committee was on adults, children were included in our mandate and consequently, it was important for us to understand their involvement in prostitution. Other studies gave us some information about prostitution prior to the most recent research in Canada, and studies conducted in other countries provided information which at least allowed us to ask the questions of how and why the Canadian experience would be different from that reported elsewhere. By inference, therefore, we may be able to reach a better understanding of prostitution within the Canadian context.

Although it may be too obvious and trite an observation, we must state that we are not dealing with a new phenomenon in Canadian society. While some may wish to challenge the old cliché that prostitution is the oldest profession, it is apparent that prostitution has been practised in Canada from the time of white contact, and, depending on the precise definition of prostitution, in native societies prior to European settlement.[9]

As Canadian society has changed, however, so has the practice of prostitution. Certainly by the nineteenth century, we find a pattern which is repeated in many western countries of visible street prostitution and known houses of ill-repute often found in conjunction with military establishments and commercial areas, such as ports and frontier settlements.[10] Whether prostitution was also being practised in the smaller towns and rural areas of the country and in less visible forms, is an unanswered question. But the questions and dilemmas about prostitution which we can discuss in the 1980s were certainly familiar to earlier generations of Canadians.

Then, as now, we are asking "How many prostitutes are there?" "How many customers?" "Who becomes a prostitute, and why?" "Why do men use the services of prostitutes?" and "What are the characteristics of these men?" "What are the perceptions of prostitutes about their work and the context in which it takes place?" "Does the public at large have views about the practice of prostitution and its effect on society?" "What should be the response of society to prostitution?" These and similar questions have concerned segments of our society for generations. The work of this Committee is simply the latest attempt to consider these problems in the light of our current situation, but from everything we have learned, it certainly will not be the last.

The remainder of the chapter will present an overview of prostitution in Canada, drawn from information collected at the public hearings and the research studies outlined above.

2. The Incidence of Prostitution

On the basis of the specific research studies conducted for the Department of Justice, and from information given at the public hearings or in private meetings, it is safe to say that prostitution is an identifiable activity in all mid-sized and large cities in Canada, and is certainly not unknown, although perhaps less visible, to the average citizen in smaller cities and towns across the country. On the basis of the National Population Survey, 55% of the respondents were not aware that prostitution was taking place in their community. Thus, although prostitution is a widespread activity in terms of geographical distribution, and as such, has the potential to affect people in each of the provinces and territories, it is by no means a phenomenon with which all Canadians are familiar. The extent to which it does affect people is, of course, related to the actual number of people working as prostitutes and the manner in which they work.

The reliability of estimates about the number of prostitutes in any city is certainly questionable. While it is possible to have some idea of the number of prostitutes on the street at any one time, it is more difficult to know the extent to which the same people are involved in the business over several months and years, and the turnover rates or the movement of people in and out of the profession. It becomes virtually impossible to answer such a straight-forward question as "Are there more prostitutes today than there were 10, 15 or 50 years ago?"

In Montréal, Toronto and Vancouver, for instance, the number of active street prostitutes may vary between 50 and 500, depending on whether only full-time and not part-time prostitutes are included, on the weather, on economic conditions and on police enforcement patterns. Similar fluctuations in figures would be found in all cities where street prostitution occurs. Despite the difficulties of assessing precise numbers, however, there has undoubtedly been an increase in the number of prostitutes working the streets in the past few years in some, though not necessarily all, cities. Whether this represents an increase in total prostitution activities rather than a displacement of prostitutes from private to public areas, and thus a restructuring of the business, is, however, unknown.

The difficulty in answering the question "How many prostitutes are there?" is even more apparent when one considers that street prostitution represents an unknown proportion of all prostitution activities. Some prostitutes work in taverns, bars and lounges, in escort services, massage and body-rub parlours, or advertise that their services are available in private apartments. At this time we have no information and no estimates about the number of people who offer prostitution services in these ways.

In some cities, for example, Fredericton, Saint John and Moncton, non-street forms of prostitution are likely to account for the major part of the business. In other cities, it is apparent that street prostitution is a significant part of the trade, in addition to prostitution provided through other organizational set-ups. Researchers conducting the regional studies in Vancouver and the Atlantic area analysed the advertisements for massage parlours and escort services in the Yellow Pages of Vancouver, Halifax and St. John's. In Halifax and St. John's, the Yellow Pages were analysed from 1925-84. For Vancouver, the study involved both the Yellow Pages and advertisements in selected newspapers, from 1970 onward.

While it has to be remembered that not all advertisements for massage or escort services are fronts for prostitution activities, the increasing explicitness of some advertisements leaves little room for doubt about the exact nature of the services available. Thus, one business has moved from advertising a massage service to a massage hotel service; another advertisement for an escort service shows a couple embracing, bordered by a telephone number which includes the digits "6969"; a third states "All muscles are massaged."[11] There seems little doubt therefore, that off-street prostitution is an important element in the total picture, although we have no information on the numbers of women and men who are engaged in these forms of the business. A reasonable conclusion, however, is that off-street prostitution has increased significantly from the mid-70s onward and may have escalated even more in the past three to four years. Indeed, Lowman suggests that despite the increases in street prostitution in Vancouver, off-street prostitution is likely to have had a higher level of increase, although we have no information on the actual numbers involved.[12]

It is, therefore, extremely difficult to calculate the total number of people in prostitution in any city and the Committee is unable to advance any reliable estimates. The experience of Gordon, writing about Halifax in 1862, is all too familiar:

> According to the Police Returns made some two or three years ago the number of common prostitutes was five hundred. According to an estimate made by a Clergyman at a later date there were six hundred. Afterwards another Clergyman of the City stated, in a public meeting, that there were as many as five hundred, but many thought the statement extravagant. Subsequently, one or two gentlemen of unquestionable authority, who had unusual facilities for ascertaining as nearly as was practicable the actual number, gave, as their opinion, that there were no less than double that number. Then we may put the number of the fallen women of this City at ONE THOUSAND.
>
> In addition to the public, it is undeniable, though not generally known, that there are many private Brothels. Of course the purse-proud and the would-be-thought-to-be-somebody, would not care to meet on common ground Jack Tar and Red Coat.[13]

The difficulties of those attempting to estimate the number of prostitutes in the 1860s are no less real for the researchers of the 1980s. At best, counts of prostitutes on the streets are supplemented by the educated guesses of police, social agencies and other people who have observed the situation over time. Consequently, any assessment of the magnitude of the problem with which we are concerned, at least in relation to the numbers of people offering sexual services, is highly speculative.

3. Characteristics of Prostitutes

Prostitution is overwhelmingly a female occupation. Reports of increases in male homosexual prostitution appear to be reasonably reliable, although not very precise. In terms of adult prostitution, the ratio of female to male prostitutes is estimated to be at least four to one, although there appears to be a variation in this overall figure among cities.

The following account of a young male hustler from the Atlantic region appears to be fairly typical of male prostitutes.

Charles

Charles is a nineteen year old street prostitute, born in New Brunswick and now living in Dartmouth, N.S. He is single and describes himself as bisexual. He does part-time body-work in a garage and lives with his mother, who pays the rent.

His childhood was spent in Dartmouth. He was the second in a family of three children. His father was a vending machine repair man and his mother worked on a fish and chip truck. When he was seven his parents separated and he stayed with his mother.

His strongest childhood memories are of hating school and of his father hitting him with a belt. He ran away from home once but soon returned home again. His first sexual experience was oral sex with a girl at school. He was 13 at the time.

His introduction to prostitution was through a friend who was also a "hustler" on the street. Charles was eighteen and made $80.00 from his first transaction.

Some of the hazards he describes on the street are: "fag beaters", loud prostitutes and rude comments by detectives. He would prefer the privacy and convenience of the telephone/escort system of prostitution but says no such service for males exists at this time.

He works two to three hours a night and sees about two customers. He estimates their average age as thirty-five and that most of them are professionals. Though they are married, he feels that they are "closet" homosexuals. Oral sex performed on him by the customer is the most requested act. He will give anal sex but will not receive it. He has also performed unusual requests such as, ejaculating in the customer's face and allowing his body to be squirted with lotions while the customer masturbates.

Charles has been physically assaulted by customers who do not want to pay for extra services, but he himself, has admitted to stealing money and drugs from customers. He does not drink while working in order to be in control. However, he does take drugs after working saying, "I'd live on acid if I could".

He finds the work enjoyable "when the customer is good-looking". He goes to Dartmouth General Hospital for check-ups every two months.

He charges $30.00 for oral sex and $50.00 for anal sex on the customer. A good night's financial intake would be $70.00 which he spends on food, clothing and V.C.R.'s.

He has no criminal record. His contact with the police is limited to rude comments on their part and their telling him to "move on".[14]

Most street prostitutes are in the 18-24 age group. Although juvenile prostitutes are sometimes an identifiable group within a particular location, prostitutes are typically adults. There is also reason to believe that prostitutes working from places other than the streets, are somewhat older and less likely to be juveniles than the street prostitutes. Such a situation seems probable because prostitutes in these circumstances are more likely to be subjected to scrutiny with respect to their age by employers, bar staff or hotel personnel, in order to minimize any potential legal problems for the establishment from which the prostitute is working.

While most prostitutes are adults, it is clear that many of them started in the business as juveniles. While there is evidence that some prostitutes started as young as 10 or 12, this appears to be exceptional and it is more likely that young people engage in the business from the age of 15 or 16 on. Prostitutes' careers on the streets are certainly not long term. For males, their term in the business is typically finished by the time they are in their early 20s as they are no longer competitive with the new and younger hustlers. Women can operate for a longer time, but there is a tendency for women, as they move into their late 20s and 30s to have to take the less desirable work areas. Thus, with increasing age they, too, become less competitive and move down the hierarchy within the profession.

In looking at the social backgrounds of prostitutes, there is no clear pattern which could be considered a predisposing influence on the decision to become a prostitute. Both the Badgley Committee's and the Department of Justice's researchers met prostitutes from all socio-economic levels and from a wide variety of family situations. Nevertheless, there is support for the contention that prostitutes disproportionately come from homes where there are tensions and problems, for example, alcohol and drug abuse and continuous fighting, although these may not be a result of poor economic circumstances or lead to the break-up of the family.

It also appears that street prostitutes are more likely to come from families of relatively low economic means than from the more affluent homes. Whether prostitutes working in other circumstances come from different social backgrounds remains an open question because of our very limited information on this part of the business. The Ontario study does suggest that call-girls may well be somewhat older than the typical street prostitute, more articulate, better educated and likely to have an occupation in addition to prostitution. Such factors may be an indication of social backgrounds which are not as economically disadvantaged as those of street prostitutes.

A further issue relating to the family milieu is the question of sexual abuse of prostitutes as children. Reports from the United States indicate that prostitutes have experienced much higher levels of sexual abuse as children than the population in general.[15] Research in Canada on this issue is considerably more rudimentary and tentative but on the evidence currently available, we would not conclude that the Canadian experience mirrors that of the U.S. The most comprehensive study on this issue is that undertaken by the Badgley Committee.[16]

Results from a national population survey conducted for the Badgley Committee indicate that 53.5% of women respondents and 22.3% of male respondents had been the victims of unwanted sexual acts. These figures appear very high, given that it has usually been assumed that such activities would only be experienced by a very small minority of people. Some child welfare groups and women's associations have agreed, however, that the extent of child sexual abuse is far greater than society has been willing to admit, and these figures certainly support that contention since the majority of victims were between the ages of 12 and 18 years when the unwanted sexual acts occurred. When we conclude, therefore, that prostitutes do not appear to have higher levels of being sexually abused as children, it is not because they are unlikely to have been abused, but because it appears to be such a common phenomenon in our society that the chance of any woman reaching adulthood without being the victim of an unwanted sexual act is approximately one in two. What we do not know, however, is the extent to which prostitutes, as children, may have been the victims of more serious sexual abuse. The figures from the Badgley Report represent a variety of sexual acts, some of which are much more serious than others. The acts range from exposing the sexual part of his body to unwanted touching and forced sexual relations. When prostitutes indicated to the researchers that they had been sexually abused as children, (a considerable number of them did indicate this), the tendency is to assume that they were victims of serious abuse, although this is not usually elaborated upon. However, we do not know whether the levels of serious sexual abuse of prostitutes when they were children is different from the level of the general population.

There is a further note of caution about this whole issue. As indicated in the description of the National Population Study of Pornography and Prostitution, the investigation of such complex issues through large-scale survey research is in its infancy, and this applies equally to the investigation of sexual abuse. The whole topic thus requires considerably more attention before we can feel really confident in speaking of the experiences of the public in general, and prostitutes in particular.

While the public perception of prostitutes may be that they are young and single, this view is most applicable to male prostitutes. As indicated previously, women prostitutes are not uniformly young nor are they uniformly single. It appears that some 20 to 25% of female street prostitutes are married or have been married, and that some of them have children to take care of. Information from the United Kingdom suggests that women find prostitution well-suited to working around the hours when the children are away from home,[17] but how prostitutes accommodate both work and family in Canadian cities, is something about which we know very little. Information from the Prairies suggests that prostitutes rely on the help of various family members for child care arrangements, a pattern which would seem to be the most likely and is indeed very common for all women in the labour force who have children.

Most prostitutes have a criminal record. Although this record may not be for prostitution offences, but be for such activities as shoplifting, prostitutes do run afoul of the law because of the business they are in. They are for instance, charged with such offences as soliciting in the streets or being a found-in in a bawdy house. The quasi-legality of the business may attract women and men who already have criminal records, and it certainly increases the probability of eventually acquiring one. In Ontario, 69% of the prostitutes interviewed had been arrested at least once, 25% of them for prostitution-related offences. Figures for the Maritimes were 62% with a criminal record, with 19% of the offences being related to prostitution. In Vancouver, 67% had a criminal record, the majority being charged with non-prostitution offences. There is, therefore, a similarity to the pattern of offences across the country. Again, we do not know the whole picture in terms of the relationship between being a prostitute and having a criminal record. Particularly, we do not know whether having such a record may bring a prostitute into contact with people who can facilitate her entry into the business, or whether the record is acquired subsequent to the decision to move into prostitution. Certainly a prior criminal record could be a factor in making it difficult to acquire employment in the regular way.

Prostitutes report using alcohol and drugs as part of their lifestyle, but there is no evidence whether they use alcohol to a greater or lesser extent than other people in their age group. Similarly, the use of soft, as opposed to hard, drugs is characteristic of prostitutes, but we do not know whether their patterns of use are different from other members of our society. The notion that prostitutes are on the street in order to earn the large amounts of money necessary to support a serious drug habit, does not find significant support from the research. There are some prostitutes who are in this position but they appear to be a very small part of the business and not at all typical. While some use alcohol and drugs in order to be able to cope with their work, the majority are not heavy users and do not use these substances while working because they do not want to lower their levels of awareness. In what is often a violent business, prostitutes need to keep all their wits about them. Many of the issues discussed above are reflected in the following case history:

Laura

Laura is a 19 year old ex-prostitute. She worked the streets for seven months, but is now attending the Dartmouth Work Activity Program through Probation services, where she is upgrading her clerical skills in order to get a job. She is separated, has no children and lives by herself in a rooming house.

Born in Halifax, her early childhood was spent in a rural setting. From the time she was eight years old she lived in Halifax and Darmouth, spending the summers in the country. During this period she was adopted, for reasons unknown to her, into a very large family, where the father was a building superintendent. The mother, who was an invalid, was described by Laura as "her best friend". She recalls arguments between her adoptive parents, at which time she would physically defend her mother against her father. She also remembers being sexually abused at the age of ten when her eighteen year old nephew threatened to beat her up if she did not have intercourse with him. This was her first sexual experience. Her adoptive mother was supportive by banishing the nephew, following the sexual assault. However, Laura felt that both parents were very restrictive and this is the reason she gave for constantly running away.

It was during one of these escapades that she met Pimp No. 1 on Gottingen Street (the pimp numbers refer to case studies elsewhere in the Report). "He knew I was scared and had no place to go. He asked if I was hungry and if I needed a place to sleep. So I said O.K." She lived at his girlfriend's house and was forced to earn her keep by prostituting. Pimp No. 1 initiated and then encouraged her dependency on drugs to keep her working for him. She was 14 when she turned her first trick.

Laura worked on the street with all the hazards inherent to that type of prostitution. She remembers being "hassled" by several pimps, being physically abused by a customer who wanted more than he had paid for and having treament for gonorrhea at a community clinic.

She would work for an average of five hours a night. During this time she would see six or seven customers who were predominately "white collar" workers and whose average age she estimated at fifty years. At one point she had ten or twelve regular customers. The act that was most requested of her was oral sex. On occasion she was called up to perform unusual acts, for example, spatting (defacating on the customer) and various S and M acts. She had also posed nude for photographs for a customer for $150.00. Laura did not like her work; she was continuously stoned on speed, mescaline or cocaine in order to forget what she was doing.

She was expected to make at least $150.00 per night for Pimp N
turned it over nightly. In return for money she was given cigar
drugs.

After some time on the street, Pimp No. 1 sold Laura to Pimp No.
this, she "... fell in love with him". One night, when she held back s
money from Pimp No. 4, she was locked in the living room, beaten
no food for a long period of time.

Laura commented about Pimp No. 4 who was in jail at the ti
interview; "I was scared to death of him and his violence. If he com
Halifax, he's coming for me".

Laura has a criminal record for such offences as: shoplifting, distu
peace and impeding other persons.

After a severe beating when Pimp No. 4 broke her nose and ribs and '
bullet in the wall above her head", she decided (with encouragemer
another prostitute) to charge and testify against him. She remembers the
Halifax morality officers as being very supportive. The support she received
from the other prostitute and the police enabled her to leave prostitution.[18]

As indicated elsewhere in the report, most of our information relates to
street prostitutes. Information on call-girl operations, for instance, is much
more haphazard and incomplete. From the information which can be pieced
together, however, it appears that call-girls are somewhat older than street
prostitutes, better educated and not so reliant on prostitution because they
often have other employment. Information about men who work in escort
services or women in massage and body-rub parlours is simply not available.

4. Why Prostitution?

Overwhelmingly, prostitutes cite economic causes as the reason they are
on the streets.

"Money. I got involved to make money and because the man I was head-over-heels in love with wanted me to."

"I became a whore for the money. I needed to eat. I had left my old man and I wasn't making enough money, so I became a whore."

"I got to Canada and couldn't find a job. I needed money to live, so I became a prostitute."

"I needed the money, but my family needed extra funds."

"I was in a locked setting for youths. Some of the girls there were involved in prostitution. They told me about it, so I went out and did it. I was on the run and needed money to eat."

"I got started because I wanted the money. A friend of mine always had money and clothes and I asked her how she did it. She told me - took me down to the agency she worked at and I got started in the business. Once I got started and making the money, it didn't seem like such a big deal. People do worse things for a living."

376

"I got involved with prostitution because I wanted the finer things in life. I recognized I could get paid and paid well for providing well-off men with sexual services." (This respondent ended up as a call-girl after starting as a street-hooker.)

Comments from prostitutes
in the Prairies[19]

The precise nature of the economic motivation, however, obviously varies among prostitutes. Juveniles who are run-aways may end up prostituting themselves because they have no money, typically have no skills and wish to avoid authorities who might help, in case they are sent back home. In addition, of course, the fact that they are so young may mean that it is unlikely that they can find more usual forms of employment. Adult prostitutes may have similar experiences, having been unable to find alternative work, especially in times of high unemployment. Some groups of prostitutes face very particular problems. Trans-sexuals who are prostitutes report being on the street because of the reluctance of employers to hire them once they know of their change in sexual identity. Other prostitutes undoubtedly move into the business at the urging of friends or acquaintances, on the understanding that it is a lucrative business and free of many of the constraints on more run-of-the-mill occupations. Thus, it is seen as a good way to earn a living. Whatever the individual motivation, prostitution is a means of making a living; that is why people move into the profession and that is why they stay.

The regional studies indicate that prostitutes have relatively low levels of educational attainment in comparison to the general population and consequently, are less competitive in the search for jobs. The Maritime study found that 84% of street prostitutes had not completed high school, and the lowest figure across the country was in Québec where of those interviewed, 68%, had less than high school graduation. Some of the problems prostitutes face in finding other forms of employment are certainly substantiated, but we are unable to answer the question of why, in a group of people in virtually identical circumstances, some choose prostitution and others do not. Perhaps the deciding factor is that prostitutes already know someone in the business who encourages them and who can facilitate their entry.

Once in the business, it may be difficult to move out. Some prostitutes, particularly women, may be coerced into continuing in the profession, but it is probably the more indirect pressures which prove so difficult to overcome. In particular, prostitutes face the problem of explaining why they have no employment record, especially if they are single and cannot hide behind the possibility of having run a houschold and raised children. Prostitutes have no previous experience they can put before employers, and are unlikely to stress the skills they have acquired from being in the business. In a time of high unemployment, when employers have many people from whom to select for a job, prostitutes seeking to move into other occupations will likely appear to be poor prospects. Thus, the conditions that got them into the business in the first place may well keep them there after they wish to leave.

Despite the difficulties of giving up the business, however, it is apparent that most of them do. As indicated, most street prostitutes are young and have left the streets by their mid to late 20s. What happens to these women and men, and what is a normal career in prostitution, are questions to which we do not have answers. The small amount of evidence we have on call-girl operations suggests that street prostitutes do not move into these operations and prostitutes working in bars and night clubs are, again, typically young. It is reasonable to argue, therefore, that most prostitutes are out of the business by their mid 20s, but we do not know about their lives subsequent to their careers in prostitution. "What forms of employment do they take up;?" "Do they marry or maintain long term relationships in a manner similar to other people in society, and does prostitution have any long term effects on the well-being of ex-prostitutes?" These and similar questions require further research since we have no systematic information on these crucial issues.

5. The Business of Prostitution

Prostitution is a complex business and, as indicated earlier, one in which it is difficult to obtain comprehensive and accurate information. Based on the five regional studies, however, one has to conclude that the way in which street prostitution is currently carried out, results in a profession which is often dangerous, especially to the prostitute, but also to the customer at times. Certainly it is dehumanizing and fraught with potential and actual conflict between those in the business and people who wish to go about their own daily lives, and between the prostitutes and the police. Based on the evidence we have, it is impossible to believe that anyone can find the existing situation satisfactory.

Although it is very difficult to collect complete and accurate information, it would appear that most prostitutes are independent operators, that is, they are not organized or managed by any one other than themselves. While there are considerable variations both within and between cities in the organization of the business, we found no evidence to suggest a link between prostitution and organized crime. That is, there is no large-scale or interconnecting organization which in a highly organized way recruits, controls or moves women and men through prostitution circuits. Certainly, some street prostitutes are controlled by pimps and some call-girls are subject to the strict regulations of the madam for whom they work, but this sort of organization appears to be small-scale and each operation in a city is typically independent of the others. In some cities, notably Vancouver, the prostitutes themselves have attempted to organize their own business. The Alliance for the Safety of Prostitutes has attempted to improve the working conditions of prostitutes by increasing the understanding of the problems of the various parties affected by the business (prostitutes, general public, customers, police) and by publishing a "Bad Tricks" sheet. This publication describes customers who have behaved violently towards prostitutes and who should, therefore, be avoided. It would be accurate to say, however, that this attempt to organize prostitutes has not been very successful. Indeed,

378

the problems the Alliance for the Safety of Prostitutes encountered probably parallel the problems other agencies face, in that prostitutes are independent people who prefer to organize their own work and their own lives.

Some prostitutes are, however, undoubtedly under the control of other people with respect to their work and typically, with respect to their lives outside the actual working situation. "For many of the prostitutes, the whole world is 'this man, and making money'. They don't want to think about the future. They're crazy."[20] The extent to which prostitutes are controlled by pimps is, of course, difficult to estimate. Prostitutes who are in what can be considered to be the stereotypical pimp-prostitute relationship, that is, a coercive and exploitative one, are unlikely to want to talk about their situation because of the violence that is likely to result when their pimps learn that they had been talking about the relationship. These women (there is no evidence that adult males are pimped) work for men who set quotas for the daily earnings, with $200.00 to $300.00 being the most common figure, or who take from 40 to 100% of the prostitutes' daily revenues. "At first I paid everything to a pimp. Then I got smart and started holding out at least one trick for myself. At the end, I held it all back for myself."[21] It appears that pimps do not run large "stables" of prostitutes but usually control two to six women within a well-defined territory. Pimps, along with customers, are the major source of violence against prostitutes. Women who would talk about their pimps indicated that physical violence, forced acts of sexual degradation and subtle forms of coercion, were used by the pimps to keep them on the streets. In some ways the relationship is most closely analogous to slavery. Prostitutes have no control over their lives, they are subject to constant exploitation and there are accounts of prostitutes being traded to another pimp to pay off debts or for money.

As it is illegal for pimps to operate, it is not surprising that prostitutes were reluctant to talk about this aspect of the business, especially when the threat of physical violence from the pimps is so likely to be realized. A further problem arises, however, because the current definition of pimp is so broad. While the stereotypical pimp-prostitute relationship, is that of a violent and abusive exploiter, prostitutes are aware that the husband or lover with whom they live in a genuinely voluntary and supportive relationship may be seen to be pimping his wife or girlfriend, especially if he is unemployed and living on the earnings his companion makes from prostitution.

> In any situation that you are involved with a person, on the personal level you are going to share things and they're going to share what they have; it's just a give and take type of thing, sometimes they might not have something and you help them or they help you when they have it and you don't, and they look after you when you are sick and keep you company.[22]

Knowing the ambiguous status of their men, prostitutes are unwilling to talk about their relationships with men who are not customers.

In each of the five studies, very few women admitted to being pimped. Cities such as Montréal, Québec, Trois-Rivières and St. John's appear to have very few pimps operating. In a city such as Vancouver, it is apparent that in some areas prostitutes work independently, whereas in other areas pimps appear to be in greater control. In some cities, Halifax and Winnipeg being notable examples, street prostitution is virtually controlled by pimps. These pimps are likely to fight each other for territory with the most powerful pimps controlling the best women (those young and very attractive) and the best areas in which to meet customers. As with many other illegal activities, one tends to find socially disadvantaged groups over-represented in the ranks of those known to be involved in pimping. In the Prairie provinces, for instance, men of native ancestry typically run native prostitutes, whereas in Halifax, it is evident that some notorious pimps come from local black families which have had a long history of problems and involvement in criminal activities. Indeed, it is unusual for pimps not to be involved in other illegal activities such as drug-dealing and gambling. The common understanding of pimps being engaged in a variety of illegal activities and living off the frailties of others in a violent and exploitative milieu can be substantiated, although how representative of pimps such men are is unknown. Only when prostitutes have suffered extreme abuse and their lives appear to be endangered are they likely to testify against their pimps. Police action against pimps is, therefore, very difficult and unlikely to result in a conviction unless a prostitute is willing to testify about the relationship. Consequently, police officers may simply resort to making life as difficult as possible for those men who they know are pimps, since they see these men as operating beyond the legal and moral boundaries of society, but are unable to lay charges.

The following account of a pimp illustrates the issue we have discussed:

Pimp No. 4

Pimp No. 4 was 24 years old at the time of the trial. He is a black resident of Halifax. He was charged with "living on the avails of prostitution" (Sec.195(1)(j)). No. 4's criminal background included sixteen prior convictions on various offences including "trafficking of narcotics". He had already been incarcerated for 2 1/2 year period. No. 4 lived on the earnings of 17 year old Barbara from January to June 1982. During the six month period Barbara earned approximately $15,000. She worked six hours a night, 7 days a week, and earned between $150 and $200 a night, which she always turned over to No. 4. With this money, No. 4 paid for food, rent and her meagre clothing. The surplus was spent on his car, drugs and alcohol.

Barbara testifed that she was often physically abused by No. 4. He would beat her if she did not earn enough money. She reported four particularly severe beatings in which No. 4 whipped her legs with a leather belt, hit her in the face, kicked her in the ribs and caused her nose to bleed. Barbara finally went to the police because she was afraid of further beatings and wanted to get away from No. 4.

Throughout the trial, No. 4 maintained that he had not been living with Barbara and that he had his own income from "junking". No. 4's mother gave supporting testimony that he had not been living with Barbara. The judge, however, noted that he "thought the mother was lying". The Court's decision that No. 4 was guilty of "living on the avails of prostitution" was based on stronger evidence that he indeed was living with her and had no other source of income. No. 4 was sentenced to 2 1/2 years in Federal penitentiary.

One social worker who was personally familiar with No. 4 provided background information for this case study. She stated that No. 4 came from a family of known "women haters". Several of his brothers and uncles had been pimps also. His father hated women and taught his son to call all women by derogatory names such as "whore", "cunt" and "bitch". No. 4's mother was beaten regularly by her husband and her sons. They lived in an apartment building in a poverty stricken area of Halifax where they often went without heat and food.

No. 4's pimping tactics involved "hanging out at roller skating rinks, bowling alleys and shopping centres, preying on young children, most often with behavioural problems and unstable family backgrounds". The social worker further stated that she had treated female children who had been physically abused by No. 4. He had in the past brought children as young as eleven years old to a room where he was known to conduct his beatings. These children continued to live in fear of being brought there even after communication was broken with him. In some cases he prostituted the same children and even went as far as to bring the customers to his apartment to avoid the children being seen in public in the prostitution areas of Halifax.[23]

It is apparent that the question of pimps and their part in the business of prostitution, is by no means a simple or uniform occurrence across the country. While some women are controlled through entirely illegal and totally unacceptable relationships, others are able to work independently or work within a more acceptable (i.e. less violent and exploitative) business relationship. Still others would argue that they have no pimps, although a strictly legal interpretation of their relationships would conflict with the prostitute's statement.

The concern about pimps is understandable when one considers that the stereotypical view of them is taken to be the norm. It would appear, however, that the most highly organized segment of the prostitution business is the escort service operations. Public concern in this area is that the operations are controlled by organized crime, and that the prostitutes are treated simply as commodities to be moved around at the whim of the manager. We do not know the extent to which organized crime may be involved in such operations. We do know that some businesses are truly independent operations. Nevertheless, some of the more established operations have links to each other in different cities and there is evidence of circuits on which the prostitutes circulate. As the interviews with call-girls were with women who worked in the smaller operations, we have no information about the perceptions and opinions of call-girls working in the larger businesses. Whether they feel exploited or a lack of personal freedoms and independence are open questions. It should also be noted that women appear somewhat more likely to own and operate call-girl operations than other types of prostitution businesses. Evidence suggests that these women are independent operators and not fronts for organizations run by men, which are connected to various other illegal activities. The situation with regard to body-rub and massage parlours is not nearly so clear.

Street prostitutes are able to pursue their business because there are identifiable areas within cities and towns where those seeking to buy sexual services can go. Without defined territories for prostitution, street prostitutes would find it very difficult to contact potential customers and customers would find it equally difficult to find prostitutes.

Because of the need to be in identifiable areas and the fact that some locations are more advantageous than others, competition for space on the streets can be fierce.

> You start standing somewhere and if nobody kicks you off it's yours. If they kick you off it's theirs.

> You get there first. It's usually by seniority. The number of years a certain person has been around working at that corner and usually to work that territory you have to get in good with that person first of all then you've got to prove yourself; prove your worthiness. In other words if nobody likes me I'd be working down on Granville Street if I was lucky. Quite a few know me in the area so I'm allowed to work where I work. I'm sure if one of the trannys decided they didn't want me working around there I'm no match for a big tranny. I'm sure that I'd lose it but nobody's done that so far. In fact I have people I don't even know asking me to work with them. I say no because I'm o.k. where I'm working. It's not my territory, it's not anybody's territory, it's a combined group that works there.

> When I went down there I had to stand up to everybody; it's a test of guts. If you've got the moxy to stand up to them they will leave you alone. You may take a few shit kickings but if you can't fight back or don't fight back then they will walk all over you. It depends on how you establish yourself and then you establish your territory by being there saying that's my spot and you work away from me. Most of the girls that are down there now know me and they stay away from me. If I tell them to move, they move or I'll move them.
>
> *Vancouver*
> *prostitutes* [24]

Most areas of street prostitution (strolls) are located in downtown areas of cities and usually in the business or commercial areas. These are the areas large numbers of people pass through and where the bars and hotels are located. Prostitutes are thus operating in areas where they are most likely to meet the men who will buy their services. At the same time, this allows the customers anonymity because they are away from their home districts and because of the large numbers of people moving about in the downtown areas.

The most obvious exception to this pattern was Vancouver prior to June, 1984, where one of the three major areas for street prostitution was primarily a residential area in the West End section of the city. This part of the city had not always been a prostitution stroll but became so as prostitutes were pushed out of the nighclubs, bars and hotels of the downtown area. Given its proximity to the downtown region, this residential area was a convenient location to which the prostitutes could gravitate. In Toronto and Halifax, some street prostitution also takes place in areas where residents live. Prostitution strolls in these areas are not so clearly an invasion of established residential areas. Rather prostitutes and residents claim areas which are now being refurbished and becoming desirable residential locations.

The reasons street prostitutes pursue their business in these areas are because they are close to downtown areas, allow customers easy access by car and are not so uniformly residential that customers would be extremely visible and perhaps intimidated. It is not surprising that the greatest conflict over street prostitution occurs in these areas, because the activities associated with prostitution quite clearly conflict with the lifestyle and atmosphere that residents want for their neighbourhoods.

> I imagine some people complain about the activity. When it gets noisy, yes they complain which I don't blame them for doing, the police come down and say who's making the noise or whatever and they keep it down and if that continues they come and park their car on the corner so people eventually have to leave.[25]

Street prostitution increases traffic and impedes the flow of traffic as potential customers and simple onlookers cruise the streets. It increases the noise in neighbourhoods, particularly in the early morning hours, as car doors are slammed or altercations occur between the various parties to the business. Although prostitutes are rarely pressing and persistent in their solicitation of customers, most prostitutes have at some time approached someone they thought was a potential customer, but who, in fact, was not looking for sexual services. Similarly, women walking through these areas have sometimes been approached by men who thought they were prostitutes. Such instances of mistaken identity are understandably very aggravating and annoying for the person who is not, and does not want to be, involved in the prostitution business in any way whatsoever.

The fact that these mistaken approaches do occur points to the difficulty of prostitutes and customers identifying one another. Although working in defined areas, prostitutes are not particularly identifiable by their style of dress in most instances, but rather by their stance on the sidewalk and their willingness to make eye contact with male passers-by. Operating under these conditions, it is not surprising that people unconnected to the business are sometimes solicited. Perhaps what is surprising is that the incidences of mistaken identity are as few as they seem to be.

The problem of making contact only with interested parties is compounded by the fact that prostitutes are on the streets when there are also present a lot of people who are not looking for sexual services. While working hours vary from city to city, and according to the season, it is typical to find some prostitutes starting work at about 11:00 a.m. in time for what may be termed the "lunch-time customers". More prostitutes will be on the streets by 3:00 p.m. and most will be working from early evening through to midnight, with some continuing to the early hours of the morning. The number of hours worked in a week primarily depends on the financial needs of the prostitute, the demands of pimps and the level of competition among prostitutes for the customers. Prostitutes certainly work much less in the winter months and at all seasons generally prefer Wednesday to the end of the week as days to work. On a good day, prostitutes may have three or four customers but on bad days may have only one, and may even leave the street because no customers are willing to buy their services. Prostitutes also report exceptional days, however, when as many as ten customers are serviced.

It appears that the transaction is initiated as often by the customer as by the prostitute. A prostitute will try to settle all the details with regard to price and the services to be bought, before moving away with the customer. Although not generally the case, a number of prostitutes do work in pairs. In this way, they note who their friend has gone with, perhaps taking down the number of the car licence plate and alerting other prostitutes or the police if their friends are absent for an unusually long time, or if a customer is violent or does not pay the price negotiated.

The sexual acts most frequently requested are oral sex and sexual intercourse. The sexual transaction usually takes place in the customer's car, or in a hotel room selected by the prostitute. It is unusual for a sexual transaction to take more than 20 to 30 minutes from the time the customer and prostitute start to negotiate to the prostitute being back on the street. Quick, impersonal sexual relations are the norm. Only rarely are sado-masochistic acts requested or are invitations to produce pornographic material issued. In both these instances, prostitutes rarely accept the invitations, and if they do, may try to ensure that one of their friends is also included to give them greater safety.

Prostitutes are very aware of the dangers of sexually transmitted diseases (STDs) and the reputation prostitutes have for the spread of such diseases. (It should be noted that this reputation is unsubstantiated by epidemiological researchers, see page 395). Consequently, prostitutes virtually always require their customers to use condoms. Many prostitutes also practise other forms of birth control, so that the requirement for condoms is not to prevent conception. Rather, it is a precaution against contracting an STD and a barrier between the customer and the prostitute, so that the prostitute does not feel that she has allowed the customer to touch the most intimate parts of her body.

> All of my dates have to wear safes. Also, I do not let them kiss me or go down on me. If a safe breaks, I don't do anything with anyone until I know I'm all right. Some of the girls out there aren't that careful, though. ... I go for regular check-ups with my own doctor, but if I just want to check for something specific I will go the clinic. They are really polite there and don't make any comments about what I do. If a date doesn't want to use a safe I just explain to him what could happen - taking something home to his wife."[26]

Although street prostitution may appear to be quite unorganized and indeed, a chaotic business, the power of informal organization is reflected in the uniformity of prices charged for services, in the definition of territories and in the attempts to control what are seen to be the worst aspects of the business, for example, customer violence or the presence of very young prostitutes.

> A thirteen year old girl is working on Jervis Street right next to that corner and nobody is kicking them off. 13/14/15 year old girls that are getting into the D.A. (a drug) and they're undercutting. They're doing $20-$30 blow jobs but nobody kicks them off. (Q. Why do you think nobody kicks the other people off?) Because nobody's bothered and because they'll come back again. There used to be a lot more unity in the streets. I've been working down here for 8 years now off and on and people have really known me for about 3 1/2 years and about 6 months ago I was kicked off Jervis Street by someone I've never met before, by some big bitch and I turned around and said help me out

here and everybody kicked her off. The new girls think that if they're bigger and stronger they can come down and kick everybody off which is not true. But nobody wants to help anyone else out because they're so worried about getting their fix or their goddamn rent paid they're not worried about the other people running around the street trying to get their rent paid and they're doing cheaper dates. Then all of a sudden everyone falls back down, going where's the money going to? How come we're not making any money? They're really fucked.[27]

That some level of organization does take place among the prostitutes is shown in the uniformity of prices charged for services within a city. Information is passed on to the new prostitutes, and they may not be allowed to work in a certain area or on a certain corner if the prostitutes already there consider the new person to be too disruptive to the existing patterns of business. Although many prostitutes report lowering their prices when they really needed some money, they are aware that such a practice is problematic and may result in confrontation with other prostitutes. If someone is known to be generally undercutting the accepted prices, prostitutes are likely to pressure that person to conform to the standards, or may push the person out of the area through continual harassment.

Right now everybody is undercutting, I don't. Well I do sometimes, seriously. It's $80 for a lay and $100 for a half and half. I charge $70 - $90 and if I can $80 - $100. $70 - $90 is really not undercutting, but it's the lowest you're supposed to go. I don't compete that much and have quite a few regulars and it's just whoever stops, stops. It takes longer to catch a trick these days.[28]

Despite some minimal level of organization, prostitutes' incomes are much lower than sensationalist accounts may have led people to believe. The income structure of prostitution mimics the income structure in other forms of employment: women typically earn less than men and employees earn less than managers. In the prostitution hierarchy, madams of the larger escort services make the most money followed by pimps, escort service prostitutes, male street prostitutes, female street prostitutes and those working bars and taverns, and juveniles. This hierarchy is quite rigid so that street prostitutes and those working in bars and taverns rarely move into the higher paying escort services. As suggested earlier, street prostitutes may well be the most socially disadvantaged as well as the most economically disadvantaged of prostitutes.

Income levels are difficult to calculate because the numbers of days a week worked and the number of weeks a year, are not documented. Researchers have to rely on the recall of the prostitutes themselves. Similarly, there is a considerable fluctuation in the number of customers and it is difficult to recall the level of activity from several months previously. Researchers estimate income on the basis of several assumptions, and in doing so make educated guesses about the number of customers a prostitute may have during an average day or week. The best estimates put the net income of a female street prostitute at $12,000 to $15,000 per year. Although prostitutes can legitimately claim deductions for business related expenses such as tips to intermediaries, clothing, condoms, legal fees and meals, if they obtain the necessary receipts, few prostitutes do this. Nevertheless, these can be seen as expenses associated with the business and have been taken into consideration when calculating a net income. Prostitutes with pimps see very little of their income since they are likely to turn over anywhere from 40 to 100% of their earnings.

> The more you make, the more you throw away. The first few years are your best, and those you lose - can't tell the girls that their money is going to drop when they're making $300 - $500 a night. It only lasts so long ...[29]

Perhaps a further indication that prostitution is not as rewarding as believed is that prostitutes appear to accumulate very little in the way of assets. Thus, the belief that a prostitute can easily make a fortune on the streets would appear to be very exaggerated and seems to come from newspaper reports that provide little in the way of evidence to support their claims. While some prostitutes may have relatively high incomes (the Committee heard reports of prostitutes whose gross incomes were over $40,000 a year), it appears that the majority do not earn anything close to such an amount, but that they live on relatively modest levels of income.

Male prostitutes can earn higher incomes because the prices they charge are typically somewhat higher than those of the women, and they keep the money they earn since they have no pimps. Call-girls would appear to have even higher levels of income, despite turning over a percentage of their earning to the organization. It appears not uncommon for call-girls to pay 40% of their fee from the client to the management. The fees they charge, however, are several times higher than those of street prostitutes and so despite not keeping all the money they earn, call-girls are likely to have substantially higher incomes than women working on the street.

Prostitutes appear to start in business in the city closest to them, or if it is a large city, in the city where they were brought up. However, some movement does occur between cities. In the west, prostitutes are likely to move on a circuit from Winnipeg to Vancouver, while a corresponding eastern circuit stretches from St. John's to Toronto. Although these circuits are the common ones, it is not unusual to find that prostitutes move from one end of the country to the other. Prostitutes also move backwards and forwards over the U.S.A. and Canada border, particularly in the Maritimes, Ontario and British Columbia. The major part of this movement results in women from the U.S.A. coming to Canada to work because it is easier to be a prostitute in Canada, or because they follow the convention trade into the larger Canadian cities. The movement of prostitutes within Canada usually results from there being a bad market in one area, from an attempt to escape a pimp, or from police harassing or seeking a particular prostitute.

Concern that there may be a revival of an international white slave trade appears unfounded. Prostitutes within Canada generally make their own decisions to move, and the researchers found virtually no evidence that women were moving across international boundaries (except the U.S.-Canada border) with the express purpose of continuing or starting in prostitution. Only in the Prairies was there any suggestion that women were being brought into Canada (in this case from Asia) for a short time period for the purposes of prostitution, and this report is somewhat tentative.

6. Customers

The one category of individual about whom it is virtually impossible to obtain first hand information, and yet without whom none of this often complex and unsavoury business would function, is the customer. Prostitutes indicate that a majority of their customers are married men between the ages of 30 and 50. These men come from all social and economic backgrounds, but there is some indication that street prostitutes service blue collar workers, and some white collar workers while escort services are frequented by men with somewhat higher incomes. We know virtually nothing of the motivations of these men who buy the services of prostitutes, and we are really able to only speculate about their behaviour. Prostitutes indicate that men are sometimes looking for sexual acts in which their wives will not participate. Further, prostitutes with regular customers indicate that these men generally describe unsatisfactory sexual relations within their marriages. We do not know, however, whether these accounts are representative of the reasons why men use prostitutes.

> Men buy sex for all kinds of reasons. Their wives won't do what they want them to. I don't know. If I had a lot of money I might even pay for it. It avoids a lot of hassle. I've been hurt in a lot of relationships so I know what it is. It's just like purchasing a movie and watching it. You enjoy it for the length of time and then you return and that's all there is to it. There's nothing else to it. Just the discreetness of it and that's all they want out of it is the immediate satisfaction and nothing more or it's either that generally or they're really lonely. They're really lonely and they don't know how to make friends or they don't know how to go out and meet anybody.

> I'd say 50% of them is out of curiosity because the women down there are supposed to be thought of as sexy and all that sort of stuff and a lot of them really aren't. 25% are getting something that they don't get at home which is, for example, the S & M trips. Husbands who want blow jobs, but they don't get them at home, buy them. The other 25% are just lonely people that are very unsuccessful with women.

> They're just men that need to get something and they can't get it for free and everybody needs it once in awhile. They're not bad people, some of them are good people, some of them are bad.

> Men who go to prostitutes go to prostitutes (and I've been hooking for 19 years) because it's a power trip. They pay the money, they get to call the shots. They own you for that 1/2 hour or that 20 minutes or that hour. They are buying you. They have no attachments, you're not a person, you're a thing to be used.

> I have no idea why gay men buy sex. I think it's pretty stupid. I don't know why. I think that they can just go to any of these gays bars around here, and find some cute little guy or some older guy or whatever they want for nothing. I think they enjoy paying for it.

Quotes from Vancouver
prostitutes[30]

Single men tend to stress the ease of buying sexual needs without building any long term commitments. Depersonalized sex is indeed what they want and what they buy. Male prostitutes suggest that their customers are a mix of men who are relatively open in the fact that they are homosexual and men, often married, who would not want it known that they had homosexual preferences. At this stage, the conclusion would be that those who use the services of female prostitutes are a cross-section of ordinary Canadian men, with the exception that they buy sexual services.

Based on the results of the National Population Study, four percent of men have bought the services of a prostitute at least once. Most of those respondents used such services five times or fewer but there appears to be a smaller category for whom the buying of sex is a regular activity. This suggests that there may be two broad categories of customers: those who use prostitutes' services just a few times and perhaps out of a curiosity to try different sexual acts, and those for whom prostitutes constitute a major means of satisfying their sexual needs. The possibility of such different categories of customers, an understanding of their motivations and their personal and social characteristics, are all areas in need of substantial research.

Customers are the primary source of sexual violence against prostitutes and may be the cause of most of the violence the prostitutes experience, depending on the prevalence of pimps. The majority of prostitutes have been sexually assaulted at least once by a customer, and have had money stolen from them or withheld despite the provision of services. Although it appears to be less common than customers assaulting prostitutes, customers are also subject to violence and theft by prostitutes or pimps.

7. Control Practices

In considering the problems associated with the current legal system and its control of prostitution-related activities, prostitutes themselves are only too well aware of the problems they encounter. The special laws in the *Criminal Code* that deal with activities relating to prostitution, mean that prostitution is not regarded as a normal business to be regulated by the usual provincial and municipal schemes. Rather, prostitution is seen as something extraordinary which requires unique legislation. Laws which are designed to control activities such as extortion, fraud, blackmail, or intimidation in normal businesses, are seen to be inadequate with respect to prostitution. Instead we have a series of special laws. This legislation reflects the thinking of earlier generations which saw prostitution and related activites as immoral, the people engaged in these activities as truly depraved or of sub-normal intelligence, and always, the danger of innocent women being seduced into the business. Special legislation to counter such unacceptable behaviour was seen as necessary, remembering that then, as now, there was a certain level of hypocrisy involved in the whole business. Although prostitution was decried by many people, many others used the services of prostitutes and argued that prostitution was necessary and would always be with us. Attitudes towards prostitutes themselves h? been ambiguous and complex, and remain so today.

Relations between police and prostitutes can be characterized as uneven at best. While police officers must and do protect prostitutes who have been assaulted, it is clear that an ambivalent attitude prevails with respect to dealing with them. On one hand, prostitutes are entitled to be treated like any other citizen, but on the other, the police will argue that prostitutes are in a violent and quasi-legal profession and should not be surprised when they are mistreated. Their close connection to other illegal activities in some instances, makes them subject to pressure from the police when information about offences is being sought.

The unevenness of the prostitute/police relationship is reflected in the following statements:

> I have a pretty good relationship with the police. I don't do anything illegal so they have nothing really to bother me about. I keep to myself.

> Some relationships I have with police are very good, some of them are very fatherly, some are nice, I find the older policemen that have seen years of service, tend to understand life, lifestyles, life trends, whatever you want to call it, and they just - well age teaches you everything and they don't react as violently to things as younger officers. Some young policemen, fresh on the force, can be complete assholes in the sense that I'm wearing a badge so I can say or do anything I want to do.

> Some of them can be alright, some of them can be pricks. Depends on what cop it is. There's good and bad in everything.

> A couple of girls jacked me up one night as I was standing on the corner, and oh thank God there was a cop coming around the corner. I was scared shitless. The funny thing is that I had been extra mouthy with this one cop just 15 minutes before - he must have thought "Oh, that mouthy little cunt." I guess he just saw that there was something wrong and he pulled right over and just sat there and watched. And then he says "Hey, you, come here." I went over, shaking, and he said "What's the matter?" It was really great - he got me out of there. The more you're nice to them, the more you find they are nice to you. If you're a real little bitch, they kind of let you have it.

And in the case of another woman:

> This one cop ran two blocks to get this pimp off my back. He intervened and got this guy out of there. And yet when he first came downtown he was a real jerk but he learned more or less the law of the street, not the law of the street but the ambience of the street. He had the intelligence to deal with it properly and not go around being an asshole.
>
> *Quotes from prostitutes*
> *in Vancouver,*[31]

A police officer in the Prairies made the following comments:

> If there are any criminal acts against them they have the right to complain ... just because she's a prostitute, doesn't mean people can kick her ass around. I don't agree with what they do, but it doesn't give me the right to tell them they don't deserve help. I mean, a guy goes around beating up girls he thinks

are prostitutes, some time he might beat up someone who isn't. I've heard guys (other than police) who don't want to help because they feel they're scum and they deserve what they get.[32]

Prostitution laws are probably no different from other morals laws with respect to their enforcement. Nor is control by the police of undesirable, although not necessarily illegal prostitution activities different from the control of other activities deemed to be a problem. Control practices are both formal and informal. Arrests are made and charges are laid because participants in the business of prostitution are thought to have contravened specific sections of the *Criminal Code*. In addition, the police seek to control prostitution activities through means other than laying charges: by the selective patrolling of the streets, accumulating information on prostitutes, and generally making it more difficult for customers and prostitutes to meet. As in other areas of the law, the relatively powerless are controlled, accused and convicted and the relatively powerful are ignored, excused and acquitted.

Female street prostitutes are more likely to be arrested and convicted of prostitution-related crimes than any other category of person involved in the business. Pimps and customers are the least likely to be charged and convicted. Thus the enforcement pattern is uneven with respect to gender and occupation. It should be noted, however, that the low level of charges and convictions against pimps does not appear to be the result of biased law enforcement on the part of police forces, as much as a reflection of the difficulty of accumulating sufficient evidence on pimps' activities.

The reasons that customers are so rarely prosecuted, however, may not be so clear cut and is certainly a contentious issue with many people and organizations. Because it takes both a prostitute and her customer to participate in the activity, there seems to be no reason why the buyer should receive preferential treatment at the expense of the seller. There appear, however, to be several reasons why the buyers of sexual services have been treated differently from the sellers. In some instances, the law has dictated this differential treatment. Street solicitation laws, for instance, typically allow charging of prostitutes, but not customers. In other instances, the different treatment of prostitutes and customers is caused by the decision to apply the law in a particular way. Customers could be charged for being an inmate of a bawdy house, for example, but are sometimes released in exchange for assistance in prosecuting the owners of the establishment. It is also undoubtedly the case that some police officers felt sympathetic towards the customers and were less likely to press charges, the belief being that the customer was sufficiently scared about losing his good name and was unlikely to buy a prostitute's services again. Such a line of action does, however, assume that the police understand the motivation of customers and this seems unlikely, given the little we know about them. Perhaps more importantly, it underplays the role of men as customers in the whole business of prostitution and leaves the belief that if we control the behaviour of prostitutes we will have solved the problems of prostitution.

390

Attitudes towards customers and control of their actions are revealed by statements from the police in the Prairies:

> We search them (pimps) all the time since a number of them are in the drug trade. We don't as often search the girls. Sometimes we take them in and search them. It takes them (the women) off the street and interrupts their business flow. If we see a guy talking to a prostitute, we'll stop and converse with them. They usually get nervous and drive away when we pull up. If we see them in a parking lot with a guy, we may approach and talk to them. Run the client's name for warrants. Maybe give them a parking violation. A lot of them know we can't do much, but the average person gets embarrassed and leaves. If they get offensive, we try to embarrass them and dissuade them from returning. We make it clear to some people that we don't want them back. We tell them they'll get in trouble from prostitutes or us. We say 'who knows what will happen in a dark alley', and let them draw their inferences from that. If they do come back, nothing happens. Sometimes it works. Sometimes it doesn't.

> We spot-check clients. We ask for two things, a driver's licence and hospitalization card. That way we can tell if he has a wife and kids. If he does, we tell him if we see him down there one more time, his wife will be getting an anonymous phone call telling her where her husband is. We do this if we see the guy enough. These guys backtrack like you wouldn't believe, even don't take the girl back to where they pick her up, to miss us. The department (police) would rake us over the coals if they ever found out we did this.

> Clients are used for statements. They're usually scared of publicity so they'll give a statement if they're gotten to right away. We don't usually charge clients.

> The clients aren't charged. Instead we use them to get statements and then subpoena them to court to do our bawdy house charges. We have to have the customers. They show up.

We never charge customers because we use them.[33]

Efforts to control prostitution are directed almost exclusively towards the prostitute, rarely at the customer and occasionally at those who run or control certain aspects of the business. It is apparent that prostitutes do indeed change their behaviour in response to both legal changes and informal control practices. Although they do not necessarily have a complete understanding of the legal intricacies surrounding the issue of street solicitation, most prostitutes appear to be aware that they have to be fairly circumspect in their approach to customers. Similarly, they are aware that the activities of pimps are illegal and that difficulties surround the use of certain locations for the completion of the sexual transaction. Control of some of the undesirable activities associated with prostitution through the law is certainly evident to a degree.

> The brass deal with the laws. As street cops, we deal with people as people in our area. We deal with our safety, their safety, and other people's safety.[34]

On a day to day basis, however, it is the more informal control methods which bring the police and the participants in prostitution into contact. The decision to patrol the prostitution strolls more actively usually results in a decrease in activities, as customers, in particular, become wary of being identified. In this way, the police in many cities are able to keep prostitution within confined areas and at levels that are reasonably tolerable to the community. By discouraging customers, it is possible to retain some control over the number of prostitutes on the street and their location.

> We can screw up their whole day, just by standing there. It puts the clinch on and takes money away from them. Clients leave. I think they think (the clients) we can do a lot more about it. They leave because they're embarrassed. Who'd want to say they took a hooker and had to pay for it. The girls show their displeasure. They come up and tell us or wave us away. Our 'standing around' is our way of saying we want to find something out, or we are getting pressure from the brass (police administration), or the community, all that bureaucratic bullshit. That's why the beatmen are on the street. It's good for public relations to have beatmen walking around because it makes them (the women) go indoors and keeps them out of the public eye.[35]

The fact that we have special laws surrounding prostitution does not, however, result in curtailing all of the worst aspects of the business, or in affording prostitutes the same protection as other members of the public. Indeed, because there are special laws, this seems to result in prostitutes being categorized as different from other women and men, less worthy of protection by the police, and a general attitude that they are second-class citizens. The police and the public act towards prostitutes in ways that they would not with other women or men. The police in some cities take photographs of the prostitutes, with or without their consent, to keep on file. These files are justified on the grounds of wanting to be able to identify prostitutes if they are missing and a serious crime is suspected, but more importantly, they allow the police better control over the prostitutes' behaviour through increasing documentation on who they are and what they have done. The police files are an illustration of the ambiguity of their response towards prostitution: on the one hand they may help prostitutes, but on the other, they control them in ways they would not use for other citizens.

Prostitutes in Vancouver gave accounts of their experiences with picture taking:

> They've always said I would like to take your picture so sure I go along with it and you never know, something might happen to me and I might be in such shape that I'm unidentifiable and that might just help. I find that the people that use their camera more forcibly are the press more than the police and there's always the little boys running around clicking off their camera. The press are the people that are exploiting the picture thing, not the police. They usually come up and ask you, usually quite polite about it because the ones that are doing it I find are the police that have been around for a while.

> Yes they took my picture very sneakily. They drive by when you're not looking and I thought that was illegal. I told the girls don't, if they come up to you, say no, I'm not doing it, and if they insist, say no I don't have to, it's against the law, which it is. It's a harassment thing.

> Not forcibly but they said we have to have your picture taken and they took my picture. It's not like they pinned me down and took my picture but they said we'll get it one way or another. The ones that took my picture were actually quite nice about it.[36]

From the Prairies the police explained their actions and reasons:

> We talk to them, try to find out who they are and where they a
> them who we are and explain what we can do for them if they decn
> off the street. Then take their photo and fill out an identification sheet. .
> them that the I.D. process will help us to notify next of kin if anything
> happens to them. They are generally pretty co-operative.

> We find out who she is, whether she has a record. Then fill out an
> information sheet for Vice. We circulate the news to other guys. If Vice asks,
> we get a picture. Usually walk up to the girl with a polaroid and say "Smile".
> If they won't let us take their picture, we play word games with them. Tell
> them we think they must have done something wrong or look much like a
> person who committed an offence and we need to take the picture to pass
> around and see if it really is the person. We run them on CPIC also to see if
> they're violent.

> We stop and do a check. Then we put them to the attention of vice. They take
> her picture if they haven't already. Vice is usually right on top of that. The
> women know that if they want to work out there, they'll let us take their
> picture. They'll be convinced, "advised", that they should follow the
> procedure. We tell them it's in case we have any complaints about them or in
> case we find them 'upside down' (dead). Most go along with it. Sometimes if
> they don't we park our car in front of her for a week until she does.[37]

The public's attitude towards prostitutes is similarly ambiguous. Some customers appear to feel little compunction about assaulting or stealing from prostitutes. Other people feel entitled to abuse prostitutes verbally, to throw things at them and to indicate that they have no right to be on the streets. At the same time, the public appears reluctant to tackle the issue in a systematic and logical manner. Rather, there is an insistence that prostitution be moved out of an area but little concern for what will happen to other areas or for the prostitutes themselves.

The current special status of prostitution in the *Criminal Code* does not appear to have given society the protection it seeks from the harmful consequences of prostitution, nor to have given prostitutes the right to dignity and equal treatment in society. Information from the public hearings and the Department of Justice's research program, leads to the conclusion that the current law and its practice is unsatisfactory from virtually everyone's point of view: prostitutes, public and police. Opinions clearly differ, however, about proposals for change and these are reported more fully in subsection 9 of this Chapter. It is worth noting here, however, that those most affected by changes, prostitutes and police, do not espouse only one solution. Although police officers have a vested interest in maintaining control of street activities and being able to easily discover linkages between prostitution and illegal activities, not all police forces and not all officers within any particular force believe that tougher laws are the appropriate way to deal with prostitution. Police opinion is not unidimensional nor unambiguous. Interviews with police officers in the regional studies indicate that many would prefer some form of decriminalization of prostitution activities. What they ask for is that there be clear legislation and clear government policy based on their belief that prostitution will always be with us.

Prostitutes echo these sentiments. They see the current laws as pure hypocrisy. Prostitution is not illegal, but it is virtually impossible to practise it anywhere but in the streets. Working on the streets then leads to conflict with the public and the police. Prostitutes argue that they should be allowed to work out of their apartments or other establishments, which within the present context of the law, calls for revisions to the sections on bawdy houses. As with others who have expressed their views, prostitutes are by no means unanimous about the necessary legal changes. Although virtually all would wish to carry out their work free from legal restrictions, some have argued that it is safer to work on the streets where one is visible, than behind closed doors.

The current system of prostitution clearly assigns to the prostitute a disproportionate part of the responsibility for the activities. While there are others who suffer, it is the prostitute who is most severely harmed. This is the case whether one looks at the more abstract question of prostitutes' status in society and their standing in the law, or at their daily experiences where it is apparent that they suffer enormous indignities and violence.

> Why do we turn so much away from the straight life? Because we're not even considered part of society. For example, to rent a place, you need to put down your occupation. You can't get a bank loan, buy a car... You need to come up with stories. So you live in a world that is strictly cash ... When you leave the business, you have to start at the bottom again. People ask what you've been doing the last five years. Society is what shapes how girls get out of the business. The minute you try to do anything like open a business with money, the government is down your back. You have to fight the whole world. You try to make it back into the system, get fired, and then people ask, 'Why didn't you make it'.[38]

> For years I had a very low self esteem. Society's attitudes makes one feel different about themself. The reinforcement that you're a whore, that you're nothing, that you're a low life does have an impact on how you feel about yourself. If you're constantly being told that given the same message for years and years and years by society, by the social agencies, by the police force, by your family, you can't help but have a low self esteem and it's only in the last couple of years that I've started feeling good about myself. For years I didn't.

> Now I feel good about myself. For awhile I was really confused. I didn't know how I felt about myself because people, they treat you a lot differently when they know you're a hooker. They really talk down to you or treat you as a lesser being. Now I say fuck you, you think you're so high and mighty, I probably fucked your old man and he paid me good. Now it's like, you're no better than I am. I'm probably better than you are because I can face up to life and not ignore things that you ignore but before it was like I didn't feel as good about myself as I do now. I've come to accept it.[39]

Prostitutes agree that life on the street is a "hell hole". Virtually all women prostitutes have been sexually assaulted, and some of them as often as three or four times a year; pimps are violent towards their prostitutes and prostitutes are violent towards each other. The competition to be on the street and to earn some money is fierce. And, perhaps as a consequence of our attitudes towards prostitutes, very little attention is paid to their specific needs in relation to social services.

8. Social and Health Services

Prostitutes appear to use very few social services. Some prostitutes do use the provincial welfare systems and survive financially through a mixture of government financial aid and prostitution. On the whole, however, it appears that prostitutes are on the streets as an alternative to living on welfare and only move to such programs when business is extremely poor or they are unable to work for some reason or other. Apart from a sporadic use of welfare systems, prostitutes also use legal aid and medical clinics, both services being closely related to some consequence of being in the business.

While the use of legal aid clinics is perhaps easy to understand, the relationship between sexually transmitted diseases (STDs) and prostitution is not so readily apparent. Certainly, a majority of prostitutes do contract an STD at least once during their time on the streets. Most however, are very well aware of the problems associated with STD's, visit medical clinics regularly and take precautionary measures, usually requiring customers to use condoms. Adult prostitutes also stop working when they are infected because word about their state spreads quickly. An infected prostitute not only finds that business stops, but that it has a harmful effect on others' business in the same area. Pressure to stop working is, therefore, likely to be intense.

Although prostitutes do contract STDs, the public's strongly held belief (held by 69% of the survey respondents) that prostitutes are a major cause of the spread of such diseases, is not substantiated. Epidemiological studies indicate that prostitutes are not a prime factor in the spreading of STDs. This occurs as a consequence of sexual mores changing throughout society and cannot be seen as the result of the behaviour of one relatively small group of people. As indicated, prostitutes, of all people in society, have a real interest in seeing that they are not infected.

Recent public concern about STDs has probably been influenced by accounts in the media of homosexual men who have contracted AIDS (acquired immune deficiency syndrome). At this time, this is a highly-charged issue and subject to very intensive research efforts. Our understanding of its causes and the manner in which it is passed from one person to another is incomplete. Nevertheless, it appears that high levels of sexual activity with a variety of partners is a greater factor in the spread of the disease than is prostitution. In addition, the view that the disease was confined only to homosexual men is being challenged. As more information becomes available, it may be necessary to reconsider our conclusions, but at this time, any notion that prostitutes play a decisive role in the spread of the disease, is unsubstantiated.

9. Public Opinions and Perceptions

The public opinions and perceptions reported in this section are based on the National Population Study on Pornography and Prostitution. While some people may question the extent to which one can gain an understanding of the public's views on such a complex issue as prostitution in a relatively short interview, we consider the results of the survey important to report. In the first instance, they may suggest lines of research which had not previously been considered. Secondly, they suggest areas where there is a need for public debate and efforts at public education. Thirdly, we believe that they do indeed give a good indication of the public's knowledge and some of their views on the subject of prostitution.

It is evident from the survey results that prostitution is not a major problem or concern for the majority of Canadians. While for some, the issues have become overwhelmingly significant, most Canadians do not encounter any of the activities associated with prostitution, and for them it is not an important issue. Fifty-five percent of the respondents indicated that they did not know of any places in their towns or cities where prostitution was occurring. In addition, approximately three-quarters of those surveyed thought that street soliciting was not occurring in their residential neighbourhoods or in the areas where they shopped. Given these results, it is apparent that most Canadians do not have a first hand knowledge of the problems associated with prostitution and street solicitation in particular. This view is confirmed by the fact that only four percent of the respondents, all men, indicated that they had ever bought the sexual services of a prostitute. Fifteen percent of respondents did, however, know someone who had accepted money in exchange for sex and twenty-one percent knew someone who had paid for sexual services. It is perhaps not surprising, given the nature of the business, to find that respondents in larger communities, men, younger people and those who are single, are most aware that prostitution is being carried on or know someone who has bought or sold sexual services.

On the basis of all these figures, one can conclude that most Canadians' views on prostitution have not been moulded by their own experiences or observations. Instead the information about prostitution which people have is likely to have come from the mass media, and to supplement any orientation to the issue that might have been learned through religious teachings or the educational system. Much, and in some cities most, of the newspaper coverage given to prostitution during the past five years, has dealt with the problems of enforcing the current street soliciting legislation and called for stricter laws. Coverage of prostitution-related issues has not been particularly comprehensive and it is not surprising, therefore, that the public, depending on the mass media for its information, is not particularly well informed or knowledgeable about the current situation.

Prostitution is defined by 90% of the respondents as the exchange of sex for money. This high level of agreement over the definition suggests that there is little ambiguity in the public's mind about the activity. Indeed, a somewhat more complex notion of prostitution that would imply providing sexual services for material gains other than money, is supported by somewhat less than three-fifths (57%) of the respondents. Women are considerably more likely than men to believe that sex in exchange for non-monetary items is also prostitution.

Many, but by no means all Canadians, find prostitution morally unacceptable. The exchange of sex for money is considered morally wrong by 62%, but this figure drops to 53% when sex is exchanged for other benefits. Men and residents of larger communities are the most accepting of prostitution.

These figures indicate that there is a considerable diversity of opinion in Canada and that proposed responses to some of the issues will not be universally acceptable.

There is a very high agreement, however, on the question of street solicitation. The various forms of prostitution differ with respect to the extent to which people will tolerate them, with prostitution on private premises being most acceptable (45% in favour of allowing this form of the business), followed by escort and call-girl services (43%), brothels (38%), all forms of prostitution but in designated areas (28%), and street solicitation (11%). Clearly, prostitution which takes place on the street is decried by overwhelming numbers of Canadians. Women and older citizens, in particular, are offended by street solicitation. Perhaps contrary to what one might expect, those who have had most exposure to prostitution, find it more acceptable than those who have had no personal familiarity with how prostitution is actually carried out.

Although prostitution is unacceptable to many respondents, only 51% thought the business degrading to prostitutes, and 46% believed it degrading to customers. Thus, although prostitution is morally unacceptable to many Canadians, they do not necessarily consider the participants in the transaction to have lost status.

Beliefs about the actual operations of prostitution lead 60% of the respondents to maintain that organized crime is a major factor in the business, and that most prostitutes have pimps. On the basis of our other information, we would suggest that the public's perceptions are incorrect. Similarly, the belief held by 69% of those surveyed, that prostitutes are a major cause of the spread of sexually transmitted diseases, is not confirmed by the available research.

Differences of opinion about the reasons why people become prostitutes are also evident. Slightly over half of the respondents (52%) suggest that economic reasons account for adults being prostitutes, whereas prostitutes themselves cite such reasons with much greater frequency. Based on other data, it also appears that the public has an inflated view of the income of many prostitutes.

With regard to the responses given to questions on controlling prostitution and related activities, again there is a high degree of agreement on some issues and a diversity of opinion on others. Sixty-four percent of the respondents, and especially those in British Columbia, thought that the legal system does not deal adequately with prostitution. For some, (32%), the solution would be to legalize or decriminalize prostitution, whereas others (40%) would suggest more stringent legislation. Whereas, Alberta and British Columbia residents were most likely to support the former alternative, residents of Atlantic Canada and francophones opted for the latter solution. As indicated, opinions again varied over how and where prostitution should be carried out, with 72% of respondents wanting tougher laws to allow the police more control of street soliciting, since the street is the least acceptable place for the business.

The survey results present an intriguing view of the public's thinking about some of the issues surrounding prostitution. What it may demonstrate most clearly is the need to better understand the public's responses to the phenomenon of prostitution, and the diversity of opinion on all issues. This diversity does not, however, reflect a view that the existing system should remain unchanged. Indeed, perhaps the most compelling reason to develop a more satisfactory system for all those affected by prostitution, is the fact that 92% of the respondents, and by inference, 92% of Canadians, think that prostitution will always be part of our society.

Footnotes

[1] See *Prostitution in Canada*, Canadian Advisory Council on the Status of Women (1984), for a bibliography of recent research on prostitution which highlights Canadian studies.

[2] *Ibid.*, c. 1.

[3] N. Crook, *A Report on Prostitution in the Atlantic Provinces* WPPP#12; J. Fleischman, *A Report on Prostitution in Ontario* WPPP#10; R. Gemme, A. Murphy, M. Bourque, M.A. Nemeh, and N. Payment, *A Report on Prostitution in Québec* WPPP#11; M. Lautt, *A Report on Prostitution in the Prairies* WPPP#9; J. Lowman, *Vancouver Field Study on Prostitution* WPPP#8.

[4] Peat Marwick and Partners, *National Population Study on Pornography and Prostitution* WPPP#6.

[5] *Ibid.*, at 1.

[6] C.H.S. Jayewardene, T. Juliani and C.K. Talbot, *Pornography and Prostitution in Selected Countries* WPPP#4; J. Kiedrowski and J.M. van Dijk, *Pornography and Prostitution in Denmark, France, West Germany, The Netherlands and Sweden*, WPPP#1; D. Sansfaçon, *Pornography and Prostitution in the United States*, WPPP#2, and *United Nations Conventions, Agreements and Resolutions on Prostitution and Pornography* WPPP#3.

[7] M. El Komos, *Canadian Newspaper Coverage of Prostitution and Pornography* WPPP#5; M. Haug and M. Cini, *The Ladies (and Gentlemen) of the Night and the Spread of Sexually Transmitted Diseases* WPPP#7.

[8] Report of the Committee on Sexual Offences Against Children and Youth, Ottawa: Supply and Services, 1984.

[9] N. Burley and R. Symanski, "Women Without: An Evolutionary and Cross-Cultural Perspective on Prostitution," in Richard Symanski, ed., *The Immoral Landscape: Female Prostitution in Western Societies* (Toronto: Butterworths, 1981) at 239-73.

[10] See J. Fingard, "The Social Evil in Halifax in the Mid-19th Century", Department of History, Dalhousie University, Halifax, N.S., unpublished paper; B. Senioc, *British Regulars in Montreal* (Montreal: McGill Queen's Press, 1981); J. H. Gray, *Red Lights on the Prairies* (Toronto: MacMillan, 1971).

[11] Crook, *A Report on Prostitution in the Atlantic Provinces* WPPP#12

[12] Lowman, *Vancouver Field Study of Prostitution* WPPP#8

[13] James Douglas Gordon, *Halifax - Its Sins and Sorrows* (Halifax: Conference Job Printing, 1862).

[14] Crook, *op. cit.* at 48.

[15] James and Meyending, "Early Sexual Experience and Prostitution", (1977) 134 *Am. J. of Psych.* 1381.

[16] Badgley Report, vol I, 175-193.

[17] McLeod, *Women Working: Prostitution Now* (London: Croom Helm Ltd., 1982).

[18] Crook, *op. cit.* at 46.

[19] Lautt, *Prostitution in the Prairies* WPPP#9 at 45-47.

[20] *Ibid.*, at 94.

[21] *Ibid.*, at 95.

[22] Lowman, *op cit.* at 195.

[23] Crook, *op. cit.* at 81.

[24] Lowman, *op. cit.* at 190-2.

[25] *Ibid.*, at 209.

[26] Lautt, *Prostitution in the Prairies* WPPP#9 at 86-7.

[27] Lowman, *op. cit* at 190.

[28] *Ibid.*, 190.

[29] Lautt, *op. cit.* at 91.

[30] Lowman, *op. cit.* at 216-8.

[31] *Ibid.*, at 199 and 205.

[32] Lautt, *op. cit.* at 29.

[33] *Ibid.*, at 38 and 13.

[34] *Ibid.*, at 31.

[35] *Ibid.*, at 38.

[36] Lowman, *op. cit.* at 204.

[37] Lautt, *op. cit.* at 34.

[38] *Ibid.*, at 91.

[39] Lowman, *op. cit.* at 246.

Section II

Prostitution and the Law

Summary

In Section II, the Committee examines the law relating to prostitution in Canada. Chapter 29 begins with a short introduction to the historical evolution of the criminal law surrounding this form of conduct and is followed by an analysis of the current *Criminal Code* provisions on prostitution-related activity. Attention is directed in Chapter 30 to the more general provisions of the criminal law and their impact on prostitution. Chapter 31 addresses the control and regulation of prostitution by provincial and municipal law. The actual and potential impact of the *Charter* on the law relating to prostitution is examined in Chapter 32, and international conventions and agreements on prostitution, and Canada's position in relation to them, in Chapter 33. The Section closes with Chapter 34 in which consideration is given to recent legislative proposals for changes in the law relating to prostitution in Canada.

Chapter 29

The Prostitution-Related Offences in the Criminal Code

1. Introduction

The earliest provisions in Canadian criminal law relating specifically to prostitution dealt with bawdy houses and street walking.[1] The bawdy house provisions which were "received" from England made it an offence to "keep" a bawdy house (typically a brothel). However, unlike the parallel English law, they also embraced both being an inmate of or one "found in" (a customer in) a bawdy house. The law on streetwalkers which developed from more general provisions on vagrancy made it an offence to be a prostitute or streetwalker "not giving a satisfactory account of [herself]".

In the 1860s, in the wake of concern in official circles in Britain about the supposed connection between prostitutes, venereal disease and demoralization in the armed forces, Canada, following the British lead, introduced a regulatory regime which made it possible for prostitutes to be subjected to medical inspection and, if found to be diseased, detained for compulsory treatment in a certified hospital. However, in Canada the legislation was rarely enforced and was soon allowed to lapse.[2]

In all of this early legislation, with the partial exception of the bawdy house provisions, the emphasis of the law was on penalizing the prostitute. The philosophy seems to have been that the male population was entitled, without sanction, to seek the services of prostitutes, but insofar as the morality or health of the community might be compromised by such activity, the target of the law was properly the purveyors and not the customers of the business.

In the late 19th and early 20th century, the emergence of a more paternalistic concern on the part of the legislators with the protection of girls and young women from the ravages of vice, often associated with the alleged scourge of "white slavery", led to the addition of a series of provisions which had the protection of "virtuous womanhood" as their objective. These included a litany of offences proscribing procuring, and "living on the avails" of prostitutes. Together with the earlier streetwalker and bawdy house offences, they were included in the Canadian *Criminal Code*.[3]

Largely as a result of the efforts of women involved in the so-called "social purity movement", legislation designed both to rehabilitate prostitutes and to prevent children opting for that way of life was also enacted across the country at the provincial level. These regimes, which allowed for special detention orders for prostitutes and the removal of female adolescents from their own homes, were often as repressive in application as the streetwalking provisions.[4]

The dual elements in the thinking of lawmakers of the prostitute as both moral and legal outcast, and the need to protect respectable women from the wiles of perverse males, has continued to influence the law and its enforcement through the 20th century. The bawdy house provisions, with their uniquely Canadian focus on keeper, prostitute and customer, remain in the *Criminal Code* in sections 193 and 194. The purely status offence of streetwalking was retained in the *Code* until 1972 when it was replaced by the present soliciting provision, section 195.1.[5] The list of procuring offences continues to exist in section 195(1) of the *Code*, subject to recent changes which extend their application to both males and females.[6] Although the special regulatory regimes designed to deal with the public health or morals problems caused by prostitution are now historic memories, more general legislation on public health and child welfare exists which provides the possibility of regulatory control over prostitution and its side effects.

In analyzing Canadian criminal law as it relates to prostitution, it is important to recognize that prostitution itself is not an offence. With the repeal of the old streetwalker section in 1972 (commonly known as the "Vagrancy" or "Vag. C" provision), being a prostitute on the street ceased to be an offence. Section 193 still contemplates an inmate of a bawdy house being charged. However, nowhere is the act of prostitution, or engaging in sexual services for reward, in and of itself proscribed. It is, of course, possible that acts of prostitution will be caught under other sections of the *Code*, for example, as gross indecency under section 157. However, it will normally be the act of indecency which is the focus of the prosecution in that instance, rather than the fact that it also involves prostitution.

The *Criminal Code* concerns itself with some of the circumstances in which prostitution takes place and is encouraged, and several of its side effects. More specifically it addresses three types of problems, namely:

the institutionalization and commercialization of prostitution: the bawdy house offences;

the general promotion of prostitution and the control and manipulation of prostitutes: procuring and living on the avails;

the public nuisance effects of street prostitution: street soliciting.

Furthermore, insofar as prostitution and its practice have criminal law consequences, the latter are no longer confined in their application to the female prostitute.[7]

2. The Bawdy House Offences

The bawdy house provisions are found in sections 193, 194, 179, 180 and 181 of the *Code*.

193. (1) Every one who keeps a common bawdy-house is guilty of an indictable offence and is liable to imprisonment for two years.

(2) Every one who

    (a) is an inmate of a common bawdy-house,

    (b) is found, without lawful excuse, in a common bawdy-house, or

    (c) as owner, landlord, lessor, tenant, occupier, agent or otherwise having charge or control of any place, knowingly permits the place or any part thereof to be let or used for the purposes of a common bawdy-house,

is guilty of an offence punishable on summary conviction.

(3) Where a person is convicted of an offence under subsection (1), the court shall cause a notice of the conviction to be served upon the owner, landlord or lessor of the place in respect of which the person is convicted or his agent, and the notice shall contain a statement to the effect that it is being served pursuant to this section.

(4) Where a person upon whom a notice is served under subsection (3) fails forthwith to exercise any right he may have to determine the tenancy or right of occupation of the person so convicted, and thereafter any person is convicted of an offence under subsection (1) in respect of the same premises, the person upon whom the notice was served shall be deemed to have committed an offence under subsection (1) unless he proves that he has taken all reasonable steps to prevent the recurrence of the offence.

194. Every one who knowingly takes, transports, directs, or offers to take, transport, or direct any other person to a common bawdy-house is guilty of an offence punishable on summary conviction.

179. (1)
"common bawdy-house" means a place that is

    (a) kept or occupied, or

    (b) resorted to by one or more persons

for the purpose of prostitution or the practice of acts of indecency;

"disorderly house" means a common bawdy-house, a common betting house or a common gaming house;

"keeper" includes a person who

    (a) is an owner or occupier of a place,

    (b) assists or acts on behalf of an owner or occupier of a place,

    (c) appears to be, or to assist or act on behalf of an owner or occupier of a place,

    (d) has the care or management of a place, or

    (e) uses a place permanently or temporarily, with or without the consent of the owner or occupier;

"place" includes any place, whether or not

    (a) it is covered or enclosed,

    (b) it is used permanently or temporarily, or

    (c) any person has an exclusive right of user with respect to it.

"prostitute" means a person of either sex who engages in prostitution;

"public place" includes any place to which the public have access as of right or by invitation, express or implied.

180. (1) In proceedings under this Part,

(a) evidence that a peace officer who was authorized to enter a place was wilfully prevented from entering or was wilfully obstructed or delayed in entering is, in the absence of any evidence to the contrary, proof that the place is a disorderly house;

(d) evidence that a person was convicted of keeping a disorderly house is, for the purpose of proceedings against any one who is alleged to have been an inmate or to have been found in that house at the time the person committed the offence of which he was convicted, in the absence of any evidence to the contrary, proof that the house was, at that time, a disorderly house.

181. (1) A justice who receives from a peace officer a report in writing that he has reasonable ground to believe and does believe that an offence under section 185, 186, 187, 189, 190 or 193 is being committed at any place within the jurisdiction of the justice may issue a warrant under his hand authorizing a peace officer to enter and search the place by day or night and seize anything found therein that may be evidence that an offence under section 185, 186, 187, 189, 190 or 193, as the case may be, is being committed at that place, and to take into custody all persons who are found in or at that place and requiring those persons and things to be brought before him or before another justice having jurisdiction, to be dealt with according to law.

(3) Except where otherwise expressly provided by-law, a court, judge, justice or magistrate before whom anything that is seized under this section is brought may declare that the thing is forfeited, in which case it shall be disposed of or dealt with as the Attorney General may direct if no person shows sufficient cause why it should not be forfeited.

(4) No declaration or direction shall be made pursuant to subsection (3) in respect of anything seized under this section until

(a) it is no longer required as evidence in any proceedings that are instituted pursuant to the seizure, or

(b) the expiration of thirty days from the time of seizure where it is not required as evidence in any proceedings.

(5) The Attorney General may, for the purpose of converting anything forfeited under this section into money, deal with it in all respects as if he were the owner thereof.

(6) Nothing in this section or in section 445 authorizes the seizure, forfeiture or destruction of telephone, telegraph or other communication facilities or equipment that may be evidence of or that may have been used in the commission of an offence under section 185, 186, 187, 189, 190 or 193 and that is owned by a person engaged in providing telephone, telegraph or other communication service to the public or forming part of the telephone, telegraph or other communication service or system of such a person.

2.1 Keeping a Bawdy House, Being an Inmate or Found in

Section 193(1) makes it an indictable offence for anyone to keep a common bawdy house, with a maximum of two years imprisonment. Section 193(2) creates three different summary conviction offences:

(a) being "an inmate of a common bawdy house" (s.193)(2)(a);

(b) being "found without lawful excuse, in a common bawdy house" (s. 193(2)(b));

(c) "as owner, landlord, lessor, tenant, occupier, agent or otherwise having charge or control of any place knowingly "permitting" the place or any part thereof to be let or used for the purposes of a common bawdy house" (s. 193(2)(c)).

Section 193(3) requires that notice of a conviction under section 193(1) (the "keeping" offence) be served on "the owner, landlord, or lessor of the place in respect of which the person is convicted or his agent". The owner, landlord or lessor may fail to exercise any right which he has to end the tenancy or right of occupation of the person whose conviction prompted the notice. By virtue of section 193(4), such failure will result in the owner, landlord or lessor being "deemed to have committed an offence under subsection (1) the "keeping" offence, if a subsequent conviction takes place under that subsection concerning the same premises. The owner, landlord or lessor will only avoid this result if he can prove "that he has taken all reasonable steps to prevent the recurrence of the offence".

The term "common bawdy house" is defined in section 179(1) of the *Code* to mean "a place that is (a) kept or occupied, or (b) resorted to by one or more persons, for the purpose of prostitution or the practice of acts of indecency". The word "place" in turn is defined to include "any place, whether or not (a) it is covered or enclosed, (b) it is used permanently or temporarily, or (c) any person has an exclusive right of use with respect to it". This is a very extensive definition which covers a far greater range of establishments than the traditional brothel, embracing even very transitory locales, such as parking garages or lots.[8]

There are also three ancillary provisions in sections 180 and 181 which relate to the bawdy house offences. Section 180(1) provides that "evidence that a peace officer who was authorized to enter a place was wilfully obstructed or delayed in entering it, in the absence of any evidence to the contrary, is proof that the place is a disorderly house". The latter term includes a "common bawdy house" (s.179(1)). Section 180(1)(d) creates a further presumption by stipulating that, in any proceedings against any person under section 193(2)(a) (being an inmate) and section 193(2)(b) (being a found in), evidence that a person was convicted under section 193(1) (keeping a common bawdy house) in respect of the same premises is, "in the absence of any evidence to the contrary", proof that the premises were a common bawdy house. It is a requirement that both charges arose out of the same set of events.

Finally, section 181 makes provision for the seizure of evidence from, and the arrest of people found in, premises being used as a bawdy house or that police believe are being used as such. Section 182 and 183 which empowered the police to enter and search a common bawdy house for a female suspected of being therein and to question both her and her keeper under oath were repealed in 1982.[8]

In order to secure convictions under section 193, it is first necessary for the Crown to establish that the premises in question were a common bawdy house. Judicial interpretation of the definition in section 179(1) has produced the following results:

(a) premises used by only one person for the purposes of prostitution or the practice of acts of indecency can constitute a common bawdy house.[9] This means that the single prostitute operating out of her own residence is open to prosecution under section 193(1);

(b) where premises contain several rooms, it is not essential that every one be used for purposes of prostitution or acts of indecency for the establishment to be characterized as a common bawdy house. Nor does a particular room have to be used exclusively for the offending purposes to qualify;[10]

(c) the premises must have been used habitually for the purpose of prostitution or the practice of acts of indecency.[11] Consequently, proof of a single act or even a small number of acts on a single evening would not be sufficient to warrant a finding that the premises were a bawdy house;

(d) "prostitution" is the offering by a person of his or her body for lewdness for payment in return.[12] Sexual intercourse is not required. Thus the masturbation of men by women working at massage parlours has been held to constitute prostitution;[13]

(e) "practice of acts of indecency" embraces a similarly wide range of sexual practices. In recent lower court decisions, the tendency has been to apply a "community standard of tolerance". Thus in an Ontario decision, the activities of a heterosexual group sex club were found not to offend that standard.[14] The average reasonable person, it was concluded, would be ready to tolerate such activity, at least where no attempt is made to proselytize and the owner is careful about the ages and sensibilities of those invited to participate. By contrast, much to the concern of the gay community, successful prosecutions have been brought against the owners, operators and employees of gay bars, health spas and steambaths at which sexual acts take place.[15]

Section 158(1) of the *Code* creates a defence to charges of buggery and gross indecency under section 155 and 157 respectively in the case of "any act committed in private" between "a husband and his wife" or "any two partners each of whom is twenty-one years or more of age, both of whom consent to the commission of the act". This defence does not extend to "acts of indecency" under section 193 even though those acts take place in private.[16]

In determining whether the Crown has satisfied the onus of proving that the place in question was a common bawdy house, the court will look at such factors as: the view of the accused; the reputation of the establishment in the community; the character, appearance and conduct of those frequenting it; hours and frequency of visits, and whether agreements were made between inmates and visitors. Proof that sexual conduct took place on the premises is not essential, although it obviously helps.[17]

Under section 193(1) the Crown not only has to prove that the establishment was a common bawdy house, but also that the accused was "keeping" it as such. The latter term is not defined in the *Code*, although the noun "keeper" is. According to section 179(1) that term includes: the owner or occupier; one assisting or acting on behalf of the owner or occupier; or, one actually acting or appearing to act on behalf of the owner or occupier. The courts have rejected the argument that the definition in section 179 applies to the term "keeping" on the ground that reference to temporary use in section 179 overlaps with two of the offences in section 179(2), i.e. being an inmate or found in. To apply the broader term would, therefore, make these clauses superfluous. The essence of "keeping" is that a person provides accommodation.[18] It is also clear that the accused must be aware that the place "kept" was being used for prostitution or acts of indecency.[19] If he is aware that the premises are being "kept" by someone else, for example a tenant, for these purposes, the lesser offence in section 193(2)(c) is available.

In the case of the operator of a hotel or motel, the fact that a sole prostitute resorts to it for the purpose of prostitution does not convert the whole establishment into a bawdy house. However, if the operator is aware that prostitution is taking place in the establishment and the use is habitual, the establishment or part of it may be so characterized. The prostitute may also be charged with "keeping", but only if there is evidence of frequent use of a particular room.[20]

The three summary conviction offences in section 193(2) have given rise to few reported cases. No cases deal with the matter of being a found in (s. 193(2)(b)). The only reported case on being an inmate (s. 193(1)(a)) establishes that "inmate" means "inmate for the purposes of prostitution", meaning someone actively involved in prostitution.[21] The offence in section 193(2)(c) of being "owner, landlord, lessor, tenant, occupier, agent or otherwise having charge or control of the place" and "knowingly [permitting] the place or any part thereof to be let or used for the purposes of a common bawdy house" has also received little attention. It is, however, the view of the courts that merely being an owner of such premises is not enough. He must also have "charge or control" of them. The person caught is the one:

> who has the right to intervene forthwith and prevent the continued use of the premises as a common bawdy house and whose failure to do so can be considered as the granting of permission to make use of the premises as and from the time he gained knowledge [of the activities].[22]

The courts have demonstrated considerable caution in applying the presumptions contained in sections 193 and 180. In *R. v. Jacobs*[23] the British Columbia Court of Appeal refused to apply the presumption in section 193(4) where an agent of a landlord gave the tenant, whose conviction under section

193(1) had been registered, notice to quit but failed to follow it up. In dealing with the presumption in section 180(1)(a), the wilful obstruction or delay of a peace officer must be firmly established by the prosecution.[24] Even then it seems that the accused merely has to raise a reasonable doubt as to whether the premises in question were a common bawdy house. This would also be true in the case of the presumption against the alleged inmate or found in contained in section 180(1)(d).[25]

2.2 Transporting to a Bawdy House

Section 194 makes it an offence, punishable on summary conviction, for any person to knowingly take, transport, direct, or offer to take, transport or direct any other person to a bawdy house. This section has not been the subject of any reported cases. It seems to have been designed to deal with taxi drivers servicing the "trade", although its terms are broad enough that it could be applied to rather more innocent and random behaviour, such as directing someone to a bawdy house on request.

2.3 Problems of Application and Enforcement and Criticisms of the Present Law

The crime statistics put out annually by Statistics Canada reveal that between 1974 and 1982 (the last year for which statistics are available), the bawdy house offences which were the subject of charges by the police fluctuated between a high of 1,143 in 1975 and a low of 269 in 1982. The figures for the individual jurisdictions produce the interesting fact that enforcement varied in intensity across the country. (See Figure 1) Few, if any, charges were laid under the bawdy house provisions of the *Code* in the Maritime provinces. Despite similar population figures for Ontario and Québec, the figure for charges was consistently from five to ten times higher in the former than in the latter. In the West, the majority of the charges were laid in British Columbia and Alberta, but were proportionally much lower than in Ontario. As with the Maritimes, there was very little activity in the northern Territories.

In the absence of a detailed study of enforcement patterns, and, in particular, of the application of both resources and enthusiasm by certain police forces across the country, it is difficult, if not impossible, to explain these annual and regional variations. All that can be offered are speculative comments. The regional studies on prostitution, commissioned by the Department of Justice for the Committee, do reveal differences in police attitudes towards bawdy houses. The reports relate typically to massage and body rub parlours, which seem to be the most common form of institutional bawdy house these days. In the Maritimes, the attitude of the police is that they will not intervene unless they receive complaints from the public, suspect that other forms of criminal activity are taking place on the premises, or are inspired by the desire of Revenue Canada to tax "the wages of sin". As the researcher in the Maritimes reported, apart from the exceptional situations noted "this form of prostitution is tolerated by formal control agencies in the Atlantic provinces".[26] By contrast, although the police interviewed in Ontario claimed that the massage and body rub business had declined significantly in that province since 1970, where they do operate there is concern that they are often fronts for sinister interests, such as the Mafia, and thus need to be charged and put out of business.[27]

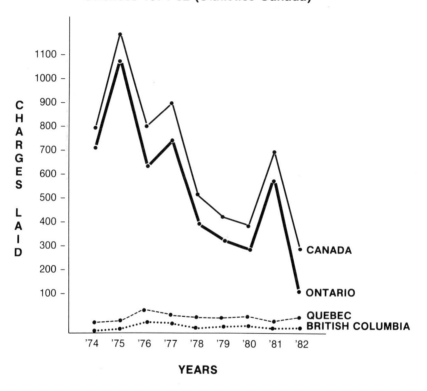

Figure 1 — Charges for Bawdy House Offences 1974-82 (Statistics Canada)

A further possible explanation for the variation in the statistics may be differences in the policies of particular communities towards these establishments. In certain cities, Montréal and Calgary for example, they are effectively outlawed by local by-laws, while elsewhere they may operate with little interference. Whatever the reasons, the statistics provide evidence of variations in police and prosecutorial practice, which raises questions about the resolve of enforcement authorities in this area of the criminal law, and whether the running and inhabiting of bawdy houses is clearly seen as a "national problem".

It is agreed by the police that the enforcement of the law on bawdy houses is a time consuming and expensive process. Typically, to sustain a charge the police will have to "stake out" the establishment over a period of time to establish a pattern of use, and then use undercover techniques to implicate the operator or user of the premises. The complicated character of these operations can be seen in the research study done for the Committee in Québec:

> In order for a place to be considered a common bawdy-house there must be evidence of constant comings and goings (the number of people who arrive and depart and the duration of their visits) and proof that these comings and goings are frequent (several prostitutes and clients daily and the same prostitute on many occasions during the whole observation period, with a three-day minimum), and that sexual services are offered there for remuneration.
>
> Such evidence is gathered mainly by observation (notes on arrivals and departures) and/or by "tailing" suspects. Generally, photographs are taken of the prostitutes and, particularly, of the clients who come and go. Clients' licence plates make it possible to obtain their names and addresses. Once the raid has been conducted, the clients are contacted as witnesses: their photographs, taken in front of the common bawdy-house, encourage the most reluctant clients to admit having had sexual relations with a particular person, for a particular fee, on the date and at the time in question.
>
> Sometimes the clients may be driving service vehicles or company cars. Since the same vehicles might be used by several people, and since the client cannot be identified from the licence plates, a more direct form of identification is required. If the raid is planned within a short period and if there is no risk of the police presence being divulged, the client is intercepted coming out of the common bawdy-house. Otherwise, the client's vehicle is identified to highway-patrol officers in marked cars who intercept it on the grounds of a possible traffic violation which permits them to obtain the driver's identity.
>
> Additional evidence about how establishments are run and about the identity of the main keepers is obtained through infiltration. One or more police-officer couples (male and female officers) are assigned as a client and prostitute to obtain inside information. In general, a contract with a police officer is sufficient evidence. An officer acts as a client with an actual prostitute. He hands over marked bills in payment for her services. Once the money has been handed over, and before the sexual relations takes place, his colleagues — stationed outside — carry out the raid as planned.[28]

This process can be further complicated by the guile of the suspect. Those who operate institutional bawdy houses often try to insulate themselves from attack by charging a fee for legitimate services, ostensibly leaving it to the operative and customer to agree on "ancillary services". Moreover, as revealed by police interviewed by the reseacher into prostitution in the Prairies, the problems of gaining the necessary evidence against prostitutes using premises are aggravated by their tactics in switching keys with each other and thereby avoiding the use of the same room more than once or twice a night.[29] The Edmonton police, in a letter to the Committee, noted that their problems were enhanced because the courts had rejected the element of habitual use in the case where a date rents a hotel room and then turns the key over to a prostitute to use for the rest of the day. The Québec research report on prostitution points out that

> owners or managers of common bawdy houses will go as far as refusing to rent a prostitute a room more than once daily. This way they can claim they did not know the person was a prostitute, that they believed he or she was a regular, but ordinary, customer.[30]

412

In addition to the problems of variable enforcement and the difficulties in constructing a firm case for the prosecution, there are several problems of principle with the provisions. In light of the fact that neither prostitution nor being a prostitute is a crime, it may be questioned why, in Canadian law it is still an offence to be an inmate of or a customer found in a bawdy house. The retention of these offences seems to contradict the distinct tendency of the criminal law in modern times not to penalize sexual conduct, even when paid for, which takes place in private. The same argument may also be made in relation to the prostitute operating out of her own residence. Whatever the possible objections to commercialization of prostitution, they have no obvious reference to the conduct of the individuals engaged in acts of prostitution.

A second claim relates to the legislative presumptions, or "reverse onus" clauses applied in bawdy house cases. In the first place, it is questionable whether section 180(1)(a) will survive challenge under the *Charter*, in particular under section 11(d), which reads: "Any person charged with an offence has the right...to be presumed innocent until proven guilty according to law in a fair and public hearing by an independent and impartial tribunal". In challenges to reverse onus clauses so far, the courts have made it clear that a clause will be struck down unless the presumed fact can be rationally linked to the proven fact or facts.[31]

It is difficult to see how the character of a disorderly house can be presumed from the failure to grant entrance to a peace officer. The provision in section 180(1)(d) which presumes that the accused is an inmate or found in of a disorderly house when another has been convicted of "keeping" that establishment, is also suspect. While it does not offend the above principle, it does contradict another basic notion, that proof of fact in one proceeding is not proof of it in another. Accordingly, it may well contravene section 11(d) of the *Charter*, the presumption of innocence provision, or section 7 which contains the right not to be deprived of life, liberty or property except in accordance with the principles of fundamental justice.

3. The Procuring and Pimping Offences

3.1 Procuring

Section 195(1) of the *Criminal Code* enumerates nine different offences relating to procuring. The subsection reads:

Everyone who

    (a) procures, attempts to procure or solicits a person to have illicit sexual intercourse with another person, whether in or out of Canada,

    (b) inveigles or entices a person who is not a prostitute or a person of known immoral character to a common bawdy house or house of assignation for the purposes of illicit sexual intercourse or prostitution;

    (c) knowingly conceals a person in a common bawdy house or house of assignation;

(d) procures or attempts to procure a person to become, whether in or out of Canada, a prostitute,

(e) procures or attempts to procure a person to leave the usual place of abode of that person in Canada, if that place is not a common bawdy house, with intent that the person may become an inmate or frequenter of a common bawdy house, whether in or out of Canada,

(f) on the arrival of a person in Canada, directs or causes that person to be directed or takes or causes that person to be taken, to a common bawdy house or house of assignation,

(g) procures a person to enter or leave Canada, for purposes of prostitution,

(h) for the purposes of gain, exercises control, direction or influence over the movements of a person in such manner as to show that he is aiding, abetting or compelling that person to engage in or carry on prostitution with any person or generally,

(i) applies or administers to a person or causes that person to take any drug, intoxicating liquor, matter or thing with intent to stupify or overpower that person in order thereby to enable any person to have illicit sexual intercourse with that person,...

is guilty of an indictable offence and is liable to imprisonment for ten years.

The offences listed in section 195(1) can be committed by either males or females. Proceedings in respect of them must, by virtue of section 195(4), be commenced within one year of the time when the offence is alleged to have been committed. Moreover section 195(3) provides that in the case of each of these offences "no person shall be convicted... upon the evidence of only one witness unless the evidence of that witness is corroborated in a material particular by evidence that implicates the accused." Although, as the penalty provision suggests, these are considered to be serious offences, the original framers of the provision seem to have harboured doubts about the veracity or trustworthiness of some of those who might be expected to come forward and complain that they had been victims of this sort of conduct.

Several, but by no means all of the provisions on procuring have been subject to judicial interpretation in reported cases with the following results:

(a) the word "procures" in section 195(1)(a) requires that the accused has taken an active part in bringing the two people together. Thus a taxi driver who merely drove one party to meet another was found not guilty of procuring.[32] Just how active a part is uncertain, as shown in conflicting decisions over whether taxi drivers who actually arrange liaisons are caught by the provision;[33]

(b) "illicit" in section 195(1)(a) has been given a broad interpretation by appeal courts in both British Columbia and Ontario.[34] As the British Columbia court said, the term is used in the sense of "not being sanctioned or permitted by-law and not necessarily in the sense of constituting a criminal offence";

(c) it is necessary to prove under section 195(1)(a) that "illicit sexual intercourse" actually took place, but this requirement may be circumvented by laying the alternative charge of attempting to procure;[35]

(d) the separate offence of attempting to inveigle or entice may be read into section 195(1)(b).[36] Presumably the same argument could be made in relation to clauses (c), (f), (g), (h) and (i);

(e) to secure a conviction under section 195(1)(d), procuring or attempting to procure a person to become a prostitute, it is essential to establish that the accused intended to convert an "innocent" person to prostitution. Thus the Alberta Court of Appeal in *R*. v. *Cline* [37] acquitted a man on a charge under this clause when it was shown that the woman in question was an undercover police woman posing as a prostitute from another city. The court held that the accused lacked the necessary intent.

Clauses (c), (e), (f), (g) and (h) have not been the subject of interpretation in reported cases. With the exception of clause (h), exercising control, direction or influence, there is no evidence that charges are laid under the other categories.[38]

3.2 Living on the Avails

195. (1) Everyone who...

(j) lives wholly or in part on the avails of prostitution of another person,
is guilty of an indictable offence and is liable to imprisonment for ten years.

Section 195(1)(j) "living on the avails" (normally described as "pimping") is, by comparison with some of the procuring offences, utilized frequently. Moreover, it has given rise to a number of reported decisions which have attempted to clarify its purpose.

The term "living on" has been construed to mean "living parasitically on". As the British Columbia Court of Appeal commented in *R*. v. *Celebrity Enterprises Ltd.*[39] which involved a charge of conspiring to live on the avails against a night club which collected an admission fee from every prostitute using its facilities for meeting clients:

in order that a male may live on the avails of prostitution of another person who is a female the male must at least receive either in kind all or part of the female's proceeds from prostituting herself or have those proceeds applied in some way to support his living. It is her avails he must live on, indirect benefits resulting to him from her practising prostitution are not avails of her prostitution.[40]

The evidence in that case did not warrant such a conclusion and the charge was dismissed. By the same token, anyone providing commercial or professional services, for example, a tradesman, doctor or lawyer, to a prostitute, cannot be characterized as living on the avails.

Less clear is whether a single payment is suffcient to found a conviction. While decisions in Saskatchewan and British Columbia seem to conflict on this point, the conflict may be more apparent than real because in the B.C. case, in which a conviction was sustained, there was evidence that the accused lived or consorted with prostitutes.[41]

Although the Québec Court of Appeal in R. v. Fisette [42] concluded that proof of the actual use of the avails for living is crucial to a finding of guilt, the decisions of other courts are inconsistent with this.[43]

The application of the presumption in section 195(2) raised by evidence of the accused living with or being habitually in the company of prostitutes, has also commanded attention from the courts. Indeed, there is disagreement between the Courts of Appeal in British Columbia and Ontario over whether the accused has to adduce evidence to counter the evidence of consorting led by the Crown. The Ontario view, which denies that this is a requirement, seems more in tune with general judicial caution towards presumptions of this kind. It is quite possible that the Crown's evidence will itself contain weaknesses which leave a reasonable doubt in the mind of the court.[44]

Despite the fact that the subsection refers to the company of "prostitutes", which has led some counsel and one court to suggest that the presumption does not apply where the evidence is that the accused lived or consorted with a single prostitute, the weight of authority seems to run in the opposite direction.[45] The word "habitually" in the presumption provision has been interpreted to mean that the accused was in the company of a prostitute or prostitutes "for the most part".[46] As long as the period of contact is significant there is no requirement of continuous liaison. This interpretation obviously facilitates the use by the Crown of the presumption.

Unlike the procuring offences subsections (3) and (4) of section 195 do not apply to "living on the avails".[47]

3.3 Problems of Application and Enforcement and Criticisms of the Present Law

Procuring, despite its elaborate treatment in the Criminal Code, is not an offence under which a significant number of charges are laid in Canada. (See Figure 2) The crime statistics of Statistics Canada show that the figure for the whole of Canada between 1974 and 1982 fluctuated between 100 and 200 charges per annum. As in the case of the prosecution of bawdy house offences, Ontario accounts for the majority of the charges laid. The offence is an unattractive one to the police and prosecutors for a variety of reasons. In the first place, a number of the clauses of section 195(1) seem to have little relationship to the realities of prostitution in the late twentieth century. Secondly, even where the offence and the facts fit, the requirement of corroboration is often a difficult one to satisfy. The result is that, if the facts are favourable, the alternative charge of living on the avails will also be laid and pursued with more vigour. Thirdly, the one year limitation ʹperiod on prosecution of procuring offences may present a bar to prosecution even if the other difficulties can be surmounted.

**Figure 2 — Charges for Procuring 1974-82
(Statistics Canada)**

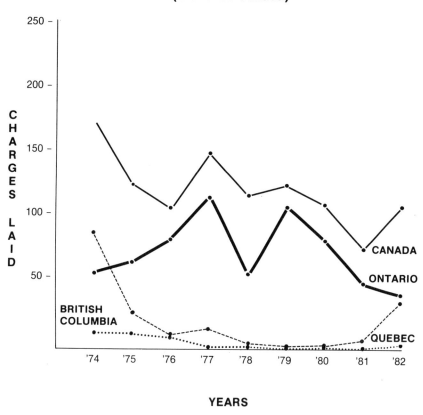

The crime statistics are singularly unhelpful when it comes to forming a picture of the legal reaction to pimping. For some reason the figures for "living on the avails" are lumped in with those for soliciting without any attempt to distinguish them. As the global figure for charges related to "other prostitution" has dropped from 2,217 per annum in 1974 to 220 in 1982, (See Figure 3) a period during which there has been a dramatic decline in the prosecutions for street soliciting, it is perhaps safe to assume that the figures for "living on the avails" have fallen somewhere between those for procuring and for the bawdy house offences, and perhaps closer to the former.

Although the successful prosecution of this offence does not require corroboration, police authorities are agreed that enforcement is difficult; the activities of pimps are sufficiently clandestine in most instances that it is only when a complaint is lodged by a prostitute who has been badly mistreated and

417

is willing to testify, that there is any chance of securing a conviction. Even when, as sometimes occurs, the police use surveillance methods to develop an adequate evidential basis to lay a charge, they are often frustrated in the result. As a police officer interviewed by the researcher on prostitution in the Prairie region put it:

> Charging pimps is a time consuming and expensive task. With one guy, it took me eight months of fairly constant surveillance to obtain one successful charge against a pimp. Another one, ****, was recently given two and one-half years for living off [sic] the avails. It took fourteen months of surveillance to get him. Add to that the time spent for the police keeping track of victims that are going to testify. We had one recent case where we were ready to take the case to trial, and the key witness ended up in a psychiatric ward.[48]

The reality, then, is that it is normally only in the case of an ongoing saga of violence and its threat that conditions are created in which the police are likely to act.

At the level of institutional prostitution, the charge of living on the avails is sometimes brought against escort and dating services. Unlike the massage parlour or body rub establishment, which occupies premises which the customer visits, these services go to the clients. Accordingly, it is not possible to utilize the bawdy house provisions. The same difficulties noted in the case of bawdy house prosecutions exist in these cases. The cost of getting the necessary evidence is high, and often is not justified by the outcome.

In the study of prostitution undertaken in Ontario, the researchers concluded, on the basis of their discussions with police representatives, that "[t]his type of operation often requires many extra man-hours and the additional use of wire taps and other forms of electronic surveillance. It is not uncommon for a $250,000 operation to warrant ten thousand dollars in fines".[49] Furthermore, as the equivalent study done in British Columbia points out, convictions are often difficult to secure at all because the operator will argue, often with success, that all he or she does is to introduce the parties, an arrangement which has no sexual connotations. It is only after the parties have met that the sex-for-money bargain is made, allegedly without the proprietor's knowledge.[50]

The overall difficulties of enforcement in these cases are summed up most graphically in the Québec report on prostitution:

> Obtaining evidence on dating, escort, hostess and modelling agencies, and photo studios or networks of "call-girls" or "call-boys", is much more complicated. Unless electronic bugging is used, telephone calls are not very revealing because the operators of such businesses are often very experienced and very careful about what they say over the telephone. Clients must come to the agency where, generally, no prostitution takes place. The staff there act ''itators for prostitutes who are "members" of the agency. The client is contact with the prostitute by telephone or by bell-boy, and a meeting is arranged, but always at a differet location.

Unless there is actually prostitution at the agency, or unless one or more prostitutes regularly provide their services at the same location, it is impossible to establish evidence of common bawdy-house against the prostitutes. Efforts are mainly made to arrest the facilitator people for procuring. Electronic bugging generally makes it possible to prove that the agency staff have some degree of control over what is going on. What is difficult to prove is that these facilitators receive a share of the proceeds.[51]

At the level of principle, it is likely that similar to its counterparts in the bawdy house provisions, the reverse onus clause in section 195(2) will be subject to challenge under the *Charter*. This subsection presumes the fact of living on the avails from the accused residing with or being habitually in the company of prostitutes. Although there may be a rational link between the presumed fact and living with prostitutes, it is doubtful whether the same can be said of the supposed connection produced by being habitually in their company. As in the case of the reverse onus clause in section 180(1)(a), this provision would offend "the right to be presumed innocent" in section 11(d) of the *Charter*.

4. The Street Prostitution Offence

4.1 Soliciting

195.1 Every person who solicits any person in a public place for the purpose of prostitution is guilty of an offence punishable on summary conviction.

179.(1) "public place" includes any place to which the public have access as of right or by invitation, express or implied.

Section 195.1 which replaced the previous street walker or "Vag. C" provision makes "every person who solicits any person in a public place for the purpose of prostitution" guilty of a summary conviction offence. The main reason for the change in the law in 1972 was that increasing opposition had been voiced over the maintenance of a status offence which discriminated against women.[52] The substitution of an offence which emphasized the element of soliciting was an attempt, it seems, to characterize the public manifestations of prostitution as a form of nuisance.

The provision is typically vague in substance, and it has been left to the courts to give it meaning. The primary issue presented to the courts was the meaning to be ascribed to the term "solicits". The Supreme Court of Canada addressed the matter in *R. v. Hutt* in 1978.[53] In that case, an undercover police officer operating from a car stopped the vehicle close to the accused. After the two smiled at each other, the accused got into the car with the agreement of the officer and inquired whether he wanted a girl. He agreed and proceeded to drive the car to a nearby hotel parking lot where the accused was arrested. The court decided that Ms. Hutt had not been guilty of soliciting. The majority determined that the word "solicits" involves a necessary element of "importuning" which means "to solicit pressingly or persistently". Here there had been nothing "pressing or persistent" about the accused's conduct. In speaking for the majority, Justice Spence indicated that it had been the intent of Parliament in changing the law on street prostitution to concentrate on acts which contribute to the public inconvenience.[54]

Exactly what amounts to "pressing or persistent conduct" is still uncertain. The subsequent Supreme Court decisions in *Whitter* and *Galjot*[55] have shed some light insofar as it was made clear that it is not "pressing or persistent" if a prostitute approaches a number of individuals in sequence with a single entreaty to each. In other words, there has to be evidence of a pattern of annoyance directed at one individual. This further refinement still leaves doubt as to the type and intensity of conduct which is required. Although Justice Spence was of the opinion that it was not necessary to prove that the accused in the *Hutt* case engaged in conduct which was "troublesome, worrying, pestering or annoying", law enforcement authorities have been inclined to assume that such conduct is essential.

In addition to construing the word "solicits" in *R. v. Hutt*, Justice Spence, although it was not germane to the decision in that case, indicated that in his opinion the undercover officer's car could not be characterized as a "public place", as required by section 195.1.[56] This opinion has added to the general uncertainty surrounding the scope of the provision and of the definition in section 179(1), and is in conflict with the interpretation given by other courts to the same term in section 138 which applies to Part IV of the *Code*.[57]

The omnibus bill (Bill C-19) introduced early in 1984 by the then Minister of Justice, The Honourable Mark MacGuigan, attempted to cure this problem by making it clear that the term "public place" embraces a motor vehicle in a public place. The present wording of the definition and its reference to places to which the public have access by invitation, express or implied, means that it embraces a wide range of off street premises, such as bars, restaurants and hotel lobbies.

Another controversy over the meaning of the section has been whether a customer as well as a prostitute can be charged with soliciting. While the British Columbia Court of Appeal has concluded that the wording "solicits...for the purpose of prostitution" cannot have been intended to catch the customer,[58] its counterpart in Ontario has reached the opposite conclusion by pointing to the use of the phrase "every one who solicits" rather than "every prostitute who solicits" in the section.[59] As neither of these decisions was appealed to the Supreme Court, the issue has yet to be resolved definitively. The omnibus bill introduced by the federal government in 1984 sought to put the matter beyond debate by making it clear that customers are open to prosecution under the section.

A recent amendment to Section 179(1) of the *Criminal Code* has put it beyond question that section 195.1 applies to both male and female prostitutes.[60]

4.2 Problems of Application and Enforcement and Criticisms of the Present Law

The crime statistics relating to street soliciting suffer from the same lack of precision as those for living on the avails. As the figures for the two offences are grouped together, it is impossible to establish the exact figures for each offence. What is clear is that the overall figures for charges laid by the police under this imprecise category have declined more or less steadily since 1974. (See Figure 3) The figure for that year was 2,217. It had dropped to 1,684 by 1977, and to 674 by 1979. After increasing to 843 in 1980, it fell back to 702 in 1981. In 1982 the figure declined dramatically to 220. Given the traditional difficulties with detecting and prosecuting the offence of living on the avails, and assuming that, in the absence of any change in the interpretation of the living on the avails section, the figures for that offence have remained relatively constant, the decisive downward trend in the statistics shows that soliciting has been translated from by far the more dominant element in the figures 10 year ago, to minor significance today.

As in the case of the statistics relating to the bawdy house and procuring offences, Ontario accounts for the largest proportion of cases reported or known. Interestingly, however, there was much less disparity with other of the more populous jurisdictions between 1974 and 1977, than there has been since. (See Figure 3) For example, in 1974, out of 2,217 cases in which charges were laid, Ontario accounted for 1,051, British Columbia 632, and Québec 421. The equivalent figures for 1977, out of 1,684, were 804, 312, and 372. By contrast, in 1980, out of a total of 843 cases in which charges were laid, Ontario accounted for 753, British Columbia for 11 and Québec for 54. The equivalent figures for 1981, out of a total of 702, were Ontario 676, British Columbia 0, and Québec 6. In 1982, although the overall figures had declined dramatically to 220, Ontario still represented 191 of those cases, with B.C. at 5 and Québec at 13. While the Prairie statistics show the same, but less dramatic, pattern of shrinkage as in B.C. and Quebec, the figures for the Maritime provinces and the northern Territories have remained constant, with figures below 5 per annum.

What do the statistics reveal about the fate of section 195.1 of the *Code* as an instrument for dealing with street soliciting? The first point to notice, as the research report on prostitution in Vancouver makes clear,[61] is that the decline in both cases reported or known and prosecutions begins not in 1978, as is popularly believed, but in 1974-75. The national figures for offences cleared by charge for the years 1974 to 1977 are 2,217, 2,002, 1,807, and 1,684 respectively. This suggests that even before the decision in *R. v. Hutt*[62], the police were finding the new street soliciting provision less satisfactory and viable than its predecessor, (the "Vag, C" section) as a response to street prostitution.

Clearly the figures dropped significantly after 1977. The figures for offences cleared by charge for the period 1978 to 1981 were 1,058, 644, 843, and 702 respectively. This decline has been associated with the pronouncement

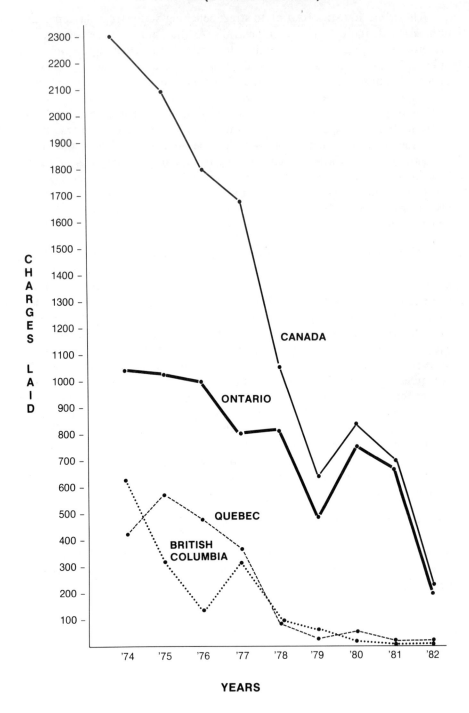

Figure 3 — Charges for other Prostitution Offences
(Incl. street soliciting and living on the avails)
1974-82 (Statistics Canada)

CHARGES LAID

CANADA

ONTARIO

QUEBEC

BRITISH
COLUMBIA

YEARS

of the decision of the Supreme Court of Canada in *Hutt* which introduced the requirement of "pressing or persistent" conduct to the offence in section 195.1 and raised doubt over whether the term "public place" includes a motor vehicle in a public place. There is no doubt that this decision and its presumed impact on lower courts had a profound effect on police and prosecutorial attitudes, being viewed by them as a substantial roadblock to successful prosecution. The statistics, however, do not show clearly that this conclusion was inevitable.

As the figures for charges set out earlier in this paragraph demonstrate, the slide between 1978 and 1981 was fitful. More instructive, however, is the fact that the figures for charges in Ontario, after dropping to 480 in 1979 from 811 in 1978, increased to 753 in 1980, and decreased to 676 in 1981. These compare with figures which hovered around the 1,000 mark between 1974-76. The statistics show that the pattern of decline was by no means constant, being much more significant in Québec and British Columbia than in Ontario.[63]

Even under the unfavourable conditions flowing from the *Hutt* decision, reactions from law enforcement authorities varied across the country. As evidence presented to and research carried out for the Committee confirms, some police forces showed greater resolution in using section 195.1, even in its revised form, than did others. On the one hand, for example, representatives of the City of Toronto indicated to the Committee that the Toronto police continued using section 195.1 regularly after 1978, and that it was only with the *Whitter* and *Galjot* decisions in 1981,[64] which ruled out conviction of a prostitute who approached a number of people in turn, that they decided that section 195.1 had become a "broken reed".[65] On the other hand, as the research study on prostitution in British Columbia shows, during the same period the Vancouver police force was prosecuting substantially reduced numbers of cases of soliciting under the street soliciting provision.[66] This variable pattern suggests that the decline in charges for soliciting, at least until 1981, had as much, if not more, to do with the dissatisfaction of some police forces with the liberal impulses of the Supreme Court of Canada than with any inherent weakness in the law.[67] Only with the decision of that Court in *Whitter* and *Galjot* were conditions attached to the operation of section 195.1 which clearly limited its effect.

The figures for 1982 require explanation. The dramatic decline which took place that year is not attributable to the lack of activity by the police against street prostitution. In fact, they were more active than they had been since 1977 and their efforts were more successful. This spate of activity was not due to any change of heart over the value of the *Code* provision. It is explained by the fact that during 1982 a number of major cities were utilizing anti-street prostitution by-laws which focused on loitering or the offer to sell or purchase sexual services rather than on soliciting. This proved to be a far more effective way of securing convictions than was section 195.1.[68] As a consequence, the latter provision was largely ignored. Despite the reversal by the Supreme Court of Canada in 1983 in *R. v. Westendorp*[69] of this attempt by municipalities to proscribe or control street prostitution, there is little evidence that the use of section 195.1 is being revived.

There is no doubt that in the cities affected by street prostitution, the view of the police is that they are powerless to control it by formal legal mechanisms, especially by the invocation of the *Criminal Code*. The police view put simply is that the Supreme Court through *Hutt,* Whitter and *Galjot* has made it impossible to use the *Code* effectively to stem or at least control street prostitution, and consequently, has created the conditions in which it has been able to thrive and expand. In the minds of the police, unless a street prostitute puts "a half nelson" on, or unmercifully pesters an individual citizen, there is little or no chance of a successful prosecution. The frustration of the police with the courts is evident in the anecdote related to the Québec researchers:

> A plainclothes police officer was seated in a club featuring female dancers. He was playing the role of the rich customer, displaying a large wad of bills. A dancer approached him and asked if she could "dance" for him, specifying that there were four different types of "dance" she could do. At his request she explained that for ten dollars she would dance on his chair, for twenty she would allow him to fondle her while she danced on his knees, for forty dollars she would perform fellatio under the tablecloth, and for fifty she would agree to sexual relations in the washroom. The police officer replied that he would think about her proposals. During the next few minutes the dancer approached him twice more, encouraging him to decide quickly. The judge who heard the case found that there was no harassment and that, consequently, no solicitation had taken place according to Section 195.1.[70]

The perceived evidential difficulties of the police are summed up most pungently in an observation by a police officer to the Prairie researcher on prostitution:

> The evidence needed for prostitution right now is staggering. You need a persistent female that directly says she wants to sell herself. You need to see the money transaction. You just about need to see the sexual act. What are you going to do - pull out your badge half way through the act?[71]

The view of the police authorities of the adverse effects of prostitution activity on the urban environment and its impact on the community is seen in the brief to the Committee from the Calgary Police Commission:

> Since [Hutt], Calgary like many Canadian cities has experienced an inability to deal effectively with the ever growing numbers of street prostitutes or to control their visibility or blatant and intense activities. One only has to drive one's vehicle along 3rd or 4th Avenues in the City of Calgary between 1st and 5th Streets West during any afternoon or evening to appreciate the extent of the problem. This growing street activity by prostitutes has resulted and continues to result in interference with the normal business activities in these areas as well as with pedestrians and has resulted in an increase in violence among pimps and prostitutes. It has created and continues to create a danger to the public particularly young women who have the misfortune to find themselves in these areas when there is a heavy concentration of prostitutes.[72]

The police have felt particularly frustrated with their apparent inability to use the law effectively in communities such as Vancouver and Halifax where street prostitution is conducted in residential areas. In these cities, in addition to the complaints of business people, they have also been faced with a growing chorus of outrage from both individuals and groups with members who live in the affected areas.[73] The communities are distressed at the actual and perceived danger and annoyance caused to them by the activities of prostitutes, customers, pimps and general onlookers, and damage to their property. The police response is typically that they have been left powerless by the courts to invoke the criminal law to deal directly with the problems, and that, apart from employing their slender resources to investigate other crime which may be associated with prostitution, and using informal policing methods to control the situation perfunctorily, there is nothing they can do to resolve the situation on a long term basis.

In some instances the frustration with the law has an international dimension to it. In Niagara Falls, Ontario, because it abuts Niagara Falls, New York and is so close to the City of Buffalo, the police and the community at large view the increase in the incidence of street soliciting as stemming directly from the comparatively benign state of Canadian law and the difficulties with its enforcement. This, together with tougher laws on prostitution in the state of New York and more resolute enforcement in the City of Buffalo, has caused an influx of prostitutes and their managers with which the Canadian city is unable to cope.[74]

While there may well have been a gap between the perceived ineffectiveness of the law in section 195.1 and its actual potential, even after 1978, it is now clear that the section is of minimal value in addressing the problems associated with street prostitution. The combination of restrictive judicial interpretation of and police restraint in appealing to it have produced a hiatus which has had the effect of implanting in the minds of the public the view that the section is entirely inadequate, even if it has not been proved to be entirely ineffective in reality. With judges who appear to be reticent about convicting under it, law enforcement authorities who are unwilling to use it, and a public who have been persuaded that it is useless, it is difficult to see how it can be infused with new life in its present form.

A further criticism of section 195.1 is that the provision itself does not make it apparent whether the customer as well as the prostitute can be charged and convicted. As was pointed out in an earlier section, there is conflicting appellate authority from Ontario and British Columbia on this issue.[75] Representatives of women's and civil liberties groups, in particular, in their presentations before the Committee, pointed to the unsatisfactory state of the law with this element of uncertainty in it. Moreover, they pointed out that, insofar as one jurisdiction has rejected the notion that the customer can be charged under section 195.1, Canadian law maintains a long standing and insidious double standard which treats the prostitute alone as the criminal. There is, they believe, no justification for such discrimination.

In principle, the criticism is accurate. Moreover, at a pragmatic level, until the matter is resolved in accordance with the notion of equal treatment, it is possible that the section will be challenged successfully under the *Charter*. Because the *Code* provision itself is vague, a challenge might be sustained under section 7 of the *Charter* which affords the right not to be deprived of life, liberty, and security of the person except in accordance with the principles of fundamental justice.[76] Furthermore, although American jurisprudence is not particularly encouraging in this regard, a prostitute might succeed in challenging the provision under section 15 of the *Charter* which recognizes the equality of every individual before and under the law, and grants equal protection and benefit of the law without discrimination.[77] Given the relatively benign attitude of Canadian appellate courts towards prostitutes in prosecutions under section 195.1, it is not entirely fanciful to suggest that such an argument would strike a responsive chord with some judges.

Footnotes

[1] C. Backhouse, "Canadian Prostitution Law 1839 to 1972" in Canadian Advisory Council on the Status of Women, *Prostitution in Canada* (1984), at 7-8.

[2] *Ibid.*, at 8-9. For the British situation see J. Walkowitz, *Prostitution and Victorian Society: Women, Class and the State* (Cambridge: Cambridge University Press, 1980).

[3] *Ibid.*, at 11-12. *The Canadian Criminal Code*, 55 & 56 Vict. (1892), c. 29 (Canada) contained provisions on procuring (see s. 185). The 'living on the avails' provision was added in 1913 (3 & 4 Geo v (1913), c. 13, s. 9 (Canada)).

[4] Backhouse, "Canadian Prostitution Law 1839 to 1972" at 15-6.

[5] *The Criminal Code Amendment Act* 1972, S.C., c.13, ss.12, 15.

[6] *The Criminal Code Amendment Act* 1980-2, S.C., c.125, s.13.

[7] See *The Criminal Code*, s. 179(1) for definition of "prostitution".

[8] See *R. v. Pierce* (1982), 66 C.C.C. (2d) 388 (Ont.C.A.). On the Canadian law on bawdy houses in general see J. Russell, "The Offence of Keeping a Common Bawdy-House in Canadian Criminal Law", (1982) 14 *Ottawa L. Rev.* 270.

[9] *R. v. Cohen* (1939), 71 C.C.C. 142 (S.C.C.); *R. v. Worthington* (1972), 22 C.R.N.S. 34 (Ont. C.A.).

[10] *R. v. McLellan* (1980), 55 C.C.C. (2d) 543 (B.C.C.A.); but see *R. v. Broccolo* (1976), 30 C.C.C. (2d) 540 (N.B.Prov.Ct.).

[11] *R. v. Patterson* (1968), 3 C.R.N.S. 23 (S.C.C.); *R. v. King* (1965) 2 C.C.C. 324 (Ont.C.A.); *R. v. Evans* (1973), 22 C.R.N.S. 32 (Ont.C.A.).

[12] *R. v. Lantay* (1965), 3 C.C.C. 170 (Ont.Prov.Ct.), relying on *R. v. De Munck*, [1918] 1 K.B. 635. A much broader definition which would catch all sexual relations between unmarried men and women, was used in the two earlier decisions: *Dubé* v. *R.* (1948), 94 C.C.C. 164 (Que.C.A.) and *R. v. Turkiewich* (1962), 38 C.R. 220 (Man.C.A.). It seems unlikely, however, that this broader definition would garner much support today. In this regard, it is to be noted that the *Lantay* definition has been used in interpreting "prostitution" in section 179 of the *Criminal Code*.

[13] *R. v. Lantay* (1965).

[14] *R. v. Mason* (1981), 59 C.C.C. (2d) (Ont.Prov.Ct.). See *R. v. Stewart* (1965), 47 C.R. 75 (Alta.Prov.Ct.); masseuses masturbating male customers in massage parlours.

[15] See *R. v. Pisces Health Spa* (1981), 63 C.C.C. (2d) (Alta. S.C., App.D). See also the unreported cases discussed in Russell, "The Offence of Keeping a Common Bawdy-House in Canadian Criminal Law" at 298-304.

[16] *R. v. Laliberté* (1973), 12 C.C.C. (2d) 109 (Que.C.A.).

[17] *R. v. Roberts* (1921), 36 C.C.C. 381 (Alta.S.C., App.D.); *Dubé* v. *R.* (1948); *R. v. Blais* (1946), 1 C.R. 190 (Ont.C.A.); *R. v. Leroy* (1951), 14 C.R. 299 (Que.C.A.); *R. v. Sorko* (1969), 4 C.C.C. 241 (B.C.C.A); See also *Theirlynck* v. *R.* (1931), 56 C.C.C. 156 (S.C.C.).

[18] *R. v. McLellan* (1980), 55 C.C.C. (2d) 543 (B.C.C.A.); *R. v. Evans* (1973), 22 C.R.N.S. (Ont.C.A.); See also *R. v. Kerim* [1963] S.C.R. 124.

[19] *R. v. Baskind* (1975), 23 C.C.C. (2d) 368 (Que.C.A.); *R. v. Durand* (1951), 12 C.R. 293 (Que.C.A.).

[20] *R. v. Broccolo* (1976).

[21] *R. v. Knowles* (1913), 21 C.C.C. 321 (Alta.S.C.).

[22] *R. v. Wong* (1977), 33 C.C.C. (2d) 6 (Alta.S.C., App.D.).

23 *R. v. Jacobs* (1941), 75 C.C.C. 337 (B.C.C.A.).

24 *R. v. Jung Lee* (1913), 22 C.C.C. 63 (Ont.H.C.); *R. v. McEwan* (1932) 59 C.C.C. 75 (Alta.S.C., App.D.); but see *R. v. Theirlynck* (1931).

25 *R. v. Hellenic Colonization Assoc.* (1943), 80 C.C.C. 22 (Alta.S.C., App.D.); *R. v. Mack* (1960), 128 C.C.C. 285 (B.C.C.A).

26 N. Crook, *Prostitution in the Atlantic Provinces* WPPP#12 at 95.

27 J. Fleischman, *Prostitution in Ontario:* An Overview WPPP#10 at 64-5.

28 R. Gemme, A. Murphy, M. Bourque, N. Nemeh, N. Payment, *Prostitution in Québec* WPPP#11 at 45-6.

29 Lautt, *Prostitution in the Prairies* WPPP#9 at 16.

30 R. Gemme et al, *Prostitution in Québec* WPPP#1 at 49.

31 See *R. v. Oakes* (1983), 2 C.C.C. (3d) 339 (Ont.C.A.).

32 *R. v. Quinn* (1918), 30 C.C.C. 372 (Ont.C.A.).

33 *R. v. Quinn* (1918); *R. v. Simpson* (1959), 30 C.R. 367 (B.C.Co.Ct.).

34 *R. v. Turner* (1972), 8 C.C.C. (2d) 76 (B.C.C.A.); *R. v. Robinson* (1948), 6 C.R. 343 (Ont.C.A.); *R. v. Deutsch* (1983), 5 C.C.C. (3d) 41 (Ont. C.A.).

35 *R. v. Gruba* (1969), 2 C.C.C. 365 (B.C.C.A.); *R. v Deutsch* (1983), at 34.

36 *R. v. Wing* (1913), 22 C.C.C. 426 (Ont.C.A.).

37 *R. v. Cline* (1982), 65 C.C.C. (2d) 214 (Alta.S.C., App.Div.).

38 See Crook, *Prostitution in the Atlantic Provinces* WPPP#12, Appendix 2.

39 *R. v. Celebrity Enterprises Ltd.*, [1978] 2 W.W.R. 562 (B.C.C.A.).

40 *Ibid.*, at 580.

41 *R. v. Nyshimura*, [1920] 2 W.W.R. 994 (Sask.C.A.); *R. v. Cavanaugh* (1941), 77 C.C.C. 79 (B.C.C.A.).

42 *R. v. Fisette* (1960), 32 C.R. 281 (Qué.C.A.).

43 *R. v. Nobulsi* (1965), 48 C.R. 344 (Qué. C.A.); *R. v. Novasad* (1939), 72 C.C.C. 21 (Sask.C.A.).

44 *R. v. Johnson* (1940), 74 C.C.C. 324 (B.C.C.A.); *R. v. Vitale* (1969), 7 C.R.N.S. 78 (Ont.C.A.).

45 *R. v. Sheeley* (1972), 26 C.R.N.S. 309 (Ont.Co.Ct.); *R. v. Nobulsi* (1965), 48 C.R. 344 (Qué.C.A.) The contrary view is expressed in *R. v. Fisette* (1960) at 42.

46 *R. v. Johnson* (1940).

47 There is some authority to the effect that the evidence of a prostitute on a living on the avails charge is the evidence of an accomplice and therefore requires a corroboration warning - see *R. v. Fleming* (1960), 129 C.C.C. 432 (Ont.C.A.). However, this view was rejected in *R. v. Clemens* (1980), 52 C.C.C. (2d) 259 (B.C.C.A) and its correctness may be doubted.

48 Lautt, *Prostitution in the Prairies* WPPP#9 at 13.

49 Fleischman, *Prostitution in Ontario* WPPP#10 at 43.

50 Lowman, *The Vancouver Field Study on Prostitution* WPPP#4 at 46-7.

51 Gemme et al, *Prostitution in Québec* WPPP#8 at 10.

52 The change in the law followed in the wake of specific criticism of the vagrancy provision in *The Report of the Royal Commission on the Status of Women in Canada, (1970).* See also Parl. Deb. H.C. Vol. II, 1970, at 1699-1700, 1704-5, 1708, 1721, 1724, 1775.

53 *R. v. Hutt*, [1978] 2 S.C.R. 476.

54 *Ibid.*, 484.

55 *R. v. Whitter*; R. v. *Galjot*, [1981] 2 S.C.R. 606.

56 *R. v. Hutt* (1978).

57 See *R. v. Figluizzi* (1981), 59 C.C.C. (2d) 144 (Alta. Q.B.); *R. v. Wise* (1982), 67 C.C.C. (2d) 231 (B.C.Co.Ct.); *R. v. McEwen*, [1980] 4 W.W.R. 85 (Sask. Prov. Ct.).

58 *R. v. Dudak* (1978), 41 C.C.C. (2d) 31 (B.C.C.A.).

59 *R. v. Di Paola* (1978), 4 C.R. (3d) 121 (Ont.C.A.).

60 *The Criminal Law Amendment Act*, S.C., 1980-2, c.125, s.11.

[61] Lowman, *Vancouver Field Study on Prostitution* WPPP#8 at 2-3.

[62] *R. v. Hutt* (1978).

[63] It should be pointed out that the Québec figures were undoubtedly affected from 1980 by the introduction of By-Law 5464 by the City of Montréal in May, 1980. This by-law proscribed loitering, soliciting and offering to purchase social services. See Gemme et al, *Prostitution in Québec* WPPP#4 at 36.

[64] *Supra*, note 55.

[65] See House of Commons, Minutes of Proceedings and Evidence of Standing Committee on Justice and Legal Affairs, Issue No. 96, June 10, 1982, 5-12 (material submitted to Special Committee on Pornography and Prostitution).

[66] Lowman, *Vancouver Field Study on Prostitution* WPPP#8, II, fig. 51.

[67] The point here is not that the law after *Hutt* was satisfactory. It was not, in the sense that the Supreme Court had failed to suggest what might now constitute the "soliciting" in the context of the gloss made by it to section 195.1. What is apparent is that some police forces decided that no further assistance could be expected from the courts and that rather than seek further clarification, a preferable strategy was to downplay section 195.1 and press for legislative changes. See D.L. Winterton, "The Dilemma of Our Prostitution Laws" (1980) 9 *Can. Police Chief* 5.

[68] See Gemme et al, *Prostitution in Québec* WPPP#11 at 67, 69. While there were no cases completed under section 195.7 of the *Criminal Code* in 1982, and no arrests in 1983 in the Montréal Urban Community, there were 401 completed cases under by-law 5464 in 1982 and 339 arrests under a series of by-laws aimed at street prostitution in 1983.

[69] *R. v. Westendorp* (1983), 2 C.C.C. (3d) 330, (S.C.C.).

[70] Gemme et al, *Prostitution in Québec* WPPP#11 at 48-9.

[71] Lautt, *Prostitution in the Prairies* WPPP#9 at 12.

[72] Calgary Police Commission, *Street Prostitution* (Brief to Special Committee on Pornography and Prostitution) January 1984, at 2-3.

[73] A number of well organized and articulate community groups to combat street prostitution have developed, including C.R.O.W.E. (Concerned Residents of the West End) in Vancouver, T.R.O.S.S. (Toronto Residents on Street Solicting); and the Halifax Downtown Residents Association.

[74] Fleischman, *Prostitution in Ontario: An Overview* WPPP#10 at 70-2.

[75] *R. v. Dudak* (1978) and *R. v. Di Paola* (1978).

[76] Neither Canadian nor United States authority has evinced any great enthusiasm for striking down criminal law provisions as opposed to municipal by-laws, see Part II, Chap. 4.

[77] See Chap. 32.

Chapter 30

General Criminal Law Provisions and their Impact on Prostitution

1. Introduction

As has already been mentioned, it is possible that other provisions in the *Criminal Code* which deal with broader forms of criminal conduct and include the criminal contexts or side effects of prostitution, may be used as the basis for prosecuting prostitution-related conduct. Indeed, it was suggested to the Committee by a number of women's groups that these more general provisions should provide a satisfactory basis for prosecution, without the need to resort to special offences related to prostitution. This suggestion was related, in particular, to advocacy of the repeal of section 195.1 of the *Criminal Code* (street soliciting).

2. The More General Offences

2.1 Gross Indecency

157. Every one who commits an act of gross indecency with another person is guilty of an indictable offence and is liable to imprisonment for five years.

158. (1) Sections 155 and 157 do not apply to any act committed in private between

   (a) a husband and his wife, or

   (b) any two persons, each of whom is twenty-one years or more of age,

both of whom consent to the commission of the act.

(2) For the purposes of subsection (1),

   (a) an act shall be deemed not to have been committed in private if it is committed in a public place, or if more than two persons take part or are present; and

   (b) a person shall be deemed not to consent to the commission of an act

(i) if the consent is extorted by force, threats or fear of bodily harm or is obtained by false and fraudulent misrepresentations as to the nature and quality of the act, or

(viii) if that person is, and the other party to the commission of the act knows or has good reason to believe that that person is feeble-minded, insane, or an idiot or an imbecile.

138. In this Part

"public place" includes any place to which the public have access as of right or by invitation, express or implied;

There are apparently no reported cases in which section 157 has been utilized against either a prostitute or customer relating to the sexual conduct in which they have been engaged.[1] However, the Committee has been informed by representatives of police forces in Winnipeg, Calgary, Ottawa and Toronto that section 157 either has been or is being successfully invoked in some cases in which prostitution is involved. This is so with street prostitution, where the sexual acts will often have been committed in public, for example, in a public park or parking lot. However, its use is attended with some difficulty. Despite the public location it is still necessary for the Crown to prove that an act of gross indecency took place. This has been interpreted by the Ontario Court of Appeal to mean "a very marked departure from the decent conduct expected by the average Canadian in the circumstances that....existed".[2] Accordingly, only if prostitutes and their customers choose to conduct their sexual liaisons in an open and brazen way in public are they subject to successful prosecution under this head.

A second problem may lie with the characterization of this offence as indictable with a prison term of up to five years. The Winnipeg Police Force informed the Committee that in their experience, some judges had proved reticent about convicting under this section, with the result that the policy adopted in that city has been to lay the lesser charge of "indecent act" under section 169.

3. The Public Nuisance Offences

3.1 Indecent Acts

169. Every one who wilfully does an indecent act

(a) in a public place in the presence of one or more persons, or

(b) in any place, with intent thereby to insult or offend any person, is guilty of an offence punishable on summary conviction.

Whether or not a prostitute and customer can be successfully prosecuted under this section for sexual conduct in public or a prostitute for advertising services in a public place, depends on whether the act is classified as "indecent". The case law suggests that a community standard test is taking hold and is being applied in such a way that the conduct in question has to be particularly offensive, for example, a couple making a sexual spectacle of themselves.[3]

432

Assuming, as several lower courts have done, that the definition of a "public place" in section 138 covers a motor vehicle in a public place, offensive sexual activity in a car would be covered.[4] However, it is a further requirement that the offending conduct occur in the presence of one or more third parties. Accordingly, if the pair follow the usual practice of finding a secluded spot to carry through the terms of their agreement, it is unlikely that they could be prosecuted successfully, unless their judgment about their privacy proves to be wrong.[5]

Given these problems, it is unlikely that this section will avail the Crown in cases of prostitution, except where prostitute, customer or both act recklessly.

Information which the Committee has gleaned from police forces in major Canadian cities underlines the difficulties mentioned above. With the exception of the Toronto and Winnipeg Police Forces, both of which seem to have had some success with prosecutions under this section, most forces do not invoke it in street prostitution cases. The Vancouver police pointed to the difficulty in its use created by case law which had determined that the requirement of exposure to another person or persons in s. 169(2) is not satisfied by exposure to a police officer.[6]

3.2 Nudity

170. (1) Every one who, without lawful excuse,

    (a) is nude in a public place, or

    (b) is nude and exposed to public view while on private property, whether or not the property is his own,
is guilty of an offence punishable on summary conviction.

    (2) For the purposes of this section a person is nude who is so clad as to offend against public decency or order.

    (3) No proceedings shall be commenced under this section, without the consent of the Attorney General.

Although both subsection (2) and the case law suggest that complete nudity is not required by this section, it is clear that an advanced state of undress or exposure of the body is necessary.[7] Unless the conduct of the accused prostitute or customer is particularly blatant and potentially subversive of public order, the use of the section is academic in the case of street prostitution.

3.3 Causing a Disturbance

171. (1) Everyone who

    (a) not being in a dwelling-house causes a disturbance in or near a public place,
        (i) by fighting, screaming, shouting, swearing, signing or using insulting or obscene language,

> (ii) by being drunk, or
>
> (iii) by impeding or molesting other persons...
>
> is guilty of an offence punishable on summary conviction.

"Causing a disturbance" is one of four offences set out in section 171. Clearly the terms of section 171(1)(a)(i) could cover situations involving conflict between prostitutes and their customers, between prostitutes and pimps and between prostitutes themselves which adversely affect members of the public, including police officers.

Despite earlier reticence on the part of the courts, they now seem willing to accept evidence of emotional disturbance to an individual caused by the objectional forms of conduct mentioned as disturbance.[8] The Committee heard from the Calgary Police Force that this clause has been successfully invoked in such circumstances. Less clear is whether section 171(1)(a)(iii) which might be thought to provide a way of attacking the more aggressive forms of soliciting, is viable as a means of curbing street prostitution. Both police and Crown prosecutors report that the attitude of provincial court judges seems to be that this provision is not available to circumvent the restriction imported by *R. v. Hutt* into section 195.1.[9] In short, they tend to use a "pressing or persistent" gloss in construing the words "impeding or molesting".

3.4 Loitering and Obstructing

> 171. (1) Every one who
>
> (c) loiters in a public place and in any way obstructs persons who are there...
>
> is guilty of an offence punishable on summary conviction.

Unlike section 171(1)(a)(iii) there is no requirement in section 171(1)(c) to establish that the accused's conduct amounted to a disturbance. The ostensible attractions in this clause as a means of curbing street soliciting have not been realized. Although the Toronto police report some success in using this clause prior to 1983, the experience of other Forces has been uniformly bad when they have tried to invoke it. The Ontario Court of Appeal in *R. v. Munroe*[10] recently made it clear that the provision has a very limited application. The court, mindful of the demise of the old "Vag. C." offence of loitering, determined that loitering in this context means loitering without a purpose. As prostitutes and their customers can be said to have a purpose, they do not fall within the terms of the proscription. Obviously the courts are also unwilling to use this provision to compensate for the restrictive interpretation given by the Supreme Court to section 195.1.

3.5 Disturbing the Peace

> 171. (1) Every one who
>
> (d) disturbs the peace and quiet of the occupants of a dwelling-house by discharging firearms or by other disorderly conduct in

a public place or who, not being an occupant of a dwelling-house comprised in a particular building or structure, disturbs the peace and quiet of the occupants of a dwelling-house comprised in the building or structure by discharging firearms or by other disorderly conduct in any part of a building or structure to which, at the time of such conduct, the occupants of two or more dwelling houses comprised in the building or structure have access as of right or by invitation, express or implied,
is guilty of an offence punishable on summary conviction.

Section 171(1)(d) creates the offence of disturbing the peace and quiet of the occupants of dwelling houses by disorderly conduct in a public place or in a common area of a residential building. On the surface this might be thought to provide potential solace to the residents of areas adversely affected by street prostitution. To date there are no reported cases, and the police in the cities adversely affected by prostitution in residential areas doubt its efficacy in street prostitution cases. The problem is that there is uncertainty as to what amounts to "disorderly conduct" in the context of this provision. It seems unlikely that random instances of disturbance would be caught.[11] Accordingly, it is safe to assume that a pattern of disturbing the peace and quiet of local residents would be required before a prosecution would succeed.

3.6 Trespassing at Night

173. Every one who, without lawful excuse, the proof of which lies upon him, loiters or prowls at night upon the property of another person near a dwelling-house situated on that property is guilty of an offence punishable on summary conviction.

This section is likely to be of use only in the case of a prostitute or customer "loitering" on premises close to a public place. In that event the Crown has to establish that the conduct of the accused amounted to "hanging around".[12] The police in several major cities suggest that the provision has the "peeping tom" in contemplation rather than the prostitute or customer.

3.7 Common Nuisance

176.(1) Every one who commits a common nuisance and thereby

(a) endangers the lives, safety or health of the public, or

(b) causes physical injury to any person,
is guilty of an indictable offence and is liable to imprisonment for two years.

(2) For the purposes of this section, every one commits a common nuisance who does an unlawful act or fails to discharge a legal duty and thereby

(a) endangers the lives, safety, health, property or comfort of the public, or

(b) obstructs the public in the exercise or enjoyment of any right that is common to all the subjects of Her Majesty in Canada.

Strangely enough in the *Code* section on common nuisance, the definition of the offence punishable under the *Code* (section 176(1)) and the definition of "common nuisance" as a term of legal art (section 176(2)), diverge. A *Code* prosecution is possible only if the Crown can prove danger to the lives, safety or health of the public, or actual physical injury. So framed, there are few, if any, street prostitution situations which would qualify. The definition of "common nuisance", however, extends to danger to the property or comfort of the public, as well as their obstruction, and thus formulated could well be employed in street soliciting cases.

The dichotomy in the section is explained by the fact that, while the *Code* establishes the offence as having a narrow ambit for purposes of punishment under its regime, it recognizes that for other purposes the notion of "common nuisance" may have a broader meaning.[13]

The implications of this for street soliciting may be seen in *Attorney General of British Columbia* v. *Couillard*.[14] In that case the Attorney General of British Columbia sought an interim injunction against certain named alleged prostitutes to enjoin them from operating in Vancouver's West End. The basis for the action was that their activities and those of others like them constituted a public nuisance. Chief Justice McEachern of the province's Supreme Court granted the injunction. He was satisfied on the basis of evidence produced before him that the defendants were prostitutes active in the area in question.

Concern has been voiced about whether merely being a prostitute in a public place should be characterized as a nuisance, which is the effect of this judgment. Moreover, it is questionable that the judge was correct in hinting as he did, that this was a case in which the Attorney General was entitled to invoke his power to call the civil process into play in support of the criminal law. It was nowhere established that a *Criminal Code* offence which required restraining was committed or threatened. However, the Chief Justice was undoubtedly correct in suggesting that there is a species of public offence, common nuisance, which is remediable in appropriate cases by the civil remedy of the injunction.

The upshot of this decision is that what is essentially a civil action for a civil remedy may be brought against street prostitutes, and presumably their customers, invoking the broader definition of common or public nuisance accepted by the common law of crimes. In short, what the *Code* cannot achieve directly may be achieved indirectly by this route. What remains uncertain as a result of this decision is how far the Attorney General has to go in establishing his case against the individual defendants.

4. Communicating Venereal Disease

253. (1) Every one who, having venereal disease in a communicable form, communicates it to another person is guilty of an offence punishable on summary conviction.

(2) No person shall be convicted of an offence under this section where he proves that he had reasonable grounds to believe and did believe that he did not have venereal disease in a communicable form at the time the offence is alleged to have been communicated.

(3) No person shall be convicted of an offence under this section upon the evidence of only one witness, unless the evidence of that witness is corroborated in a material particular by evidence that implicates the accused.

(4) For the purposes of this section "venereal disease" means syphilis, gonorrhea or soft chancre.

This provision of the *Code* is so encumbered with limitations that even if, as is unlikely, the victim of the disease who contracts it in the course of prostitution-related activities complains of it, and has one of the limited list of maladies mentioned, it is unlikely to provide a viable basis for prosecution in prostitution cases. In particular, given the clandestine character of most relationships between prostitutes and customers, the corroboration requirement seems insurmountable. Section 58 of Bill C-19 introduced by Minister of Justice MacGuigan in 1984 sought to repeal section 253 of the *Code* on the grounds that disease of this sort are a public health matter, and that no use is made of the section in practice.

5. Intimidation

381. (1) Every one who, wrongfully and without lawful authority, for the purpose of compelling another person to abstain from doing anything that he has a lawful right to do, or to do anything that he has a lawful right to abstain from doing,

   (a) uses violence or threats of violence to that person or his spouse or children, or injures his property,

   (b) intimidates or attempts to intimidate that person or a relative of that person by threats that, in Canada or elsewhere, violence or other injury will be done to or punishment inflicted upon him or a relative of his, or that the property of any of them will be damaged,

   (c) persistently follows that person about from place to place,

   (d) hides any tools, clothes or other property owned or used by that person, or deprives him of them or hinders him in the use of them,

   (e) with one or more other persons follows that person, in a disorderly manner, on a highway,

   (f) besets or watches the dwelling-house or place where that person resides, works, carries on business or happens to be, or

   (g) blocks or obstructs a highway,
is guilty of an offence punishable on summary conviction.

(2) A person who attends at or near or approaches a dwelling-house or place, for the purpose only of obtaining or communicating information, does not watch or beset within the meaning of this section.

Although there are, in theory, situations involving street prostitution which would fit within the ambit of this section of the *Code*, it is likely that the courts, in tune with their cautious attitude to other more general offences, would convict only in the clearest cases of harassment. None of the major city police forces consulted by the Committee utilize this section in prostitution cases. Although at least one provincial Court of Appeal has said that this section is not confined in its application to industrial disputes and trade union activity, law enforcement authorities seem to work on the assumption that it is.[15]

6. Taxation Legislation

The application of taxation legislation and the operations of Revenue Canada in relation to prostitution activities is shrouded in a certain amount of mystery.

Prostitution, in common with any other economic activity, is subject to taxation. The problem from the point of view of the prostitutes and the operator of a prostitution business is that there are certain dangers inherent in declaring income for tax purposes, not the least of which is that the police will secure the information and use it as a basis for a charge of living on the avails. The effect of these risks is probably to induce most individuals engaged in prostitution activities not to file. However, the latter decision may well result in criminal charges under the *Income Tax Act*, if it is discovered that the individual has been working and not declaring the resulting income. Research done on prostitution in the Maritimes makes it clear that a number of madams operating escort and dating services have been caught in this bind. In at least one such case, the delinquency of the operator in not declaring prostitution income was used as a bargaining point by the prosecution authorities, who agreed to drop *Criminal Code* charges if the madam undertook to pay back taxes.[16]

In one noteworthy case, *Minister of National Revenue* v. *Eldridge,*[17] a prostitute (a call girl) who had filed tax returns, appealed the Department's assessment of her net income on the ground that it failed to take adequate account of business expenses. She also appealed a penalty for tax evasion. The judge, while accepting a variety of business expenses associated with her trade, including rental expenses, telephone inspection, protection fees to the police, liquor payment fees, payment of bail bonds for arrested 'girls' and payments to casual employees for which vouchers were submitted, rejected argument that she could claim deductions for expenses where she had suppressed or destroyed the records. In his mind, this was a voluntary act on her part. The case was remitted to the Minister for reassessment in accordance with the judge's findings, and the penalty was confirmed.

The decision illustrates the dilemma faced by prostitutes, who in some instances are quite ready to accept their civic obligations. Although the situation is not clear, the Committee has the impression that taxation legislation and the sanctions which attend non-compliance are normally invoked only where the delinquent tax payer is notoriously involved in a

438

prostitution business. For the rest, especially the street prostitutes, it is presumably not worth the time and effort of taxation authorities to investigate and lay charges.

7. The Utility of these Provisions

An analysis of these more general *Code* provisions and their application demonstrates that they are of limited value in combatting prostitution, especially street prostitution. In a number of instances, the provisions are so limited, for example, sections 173, 176 and 253, that their use is entirely academic. In other cases, the interpretation given to the provisions by the courts either limits their substantive ambit directly, for example, section 381, or requires such an aggravated degree of conduct, for example, sections 169 and 171(1)(c), that the same result is achieved indirectly. It is clear that the courts, especially at the provincial court level, are resistant to the idea that these provisions should be used to compensate for the limitations in section 195.1. Crown prosecutors and police sense this and tend not to proceed. Even in communities where more vigorous attempts have been made to invoke some of these provisions, rebuffs by the courts have blunted the enthusiasm of law enforcement authorities for using them.

It should be pointed out that even if the provisions were more viable, there is some doubt as to whether they would be widely used. Both the studies commissioned by the Department of Justice and submissions from police forces indicate that the police feel considerably aggrieved that in dealing with street prostitution, they are reduced to making their way through a maze of *Code* provisions to find a section which might avail them. The view of the police seems to be that if they are expected to deal resolutely with street prostitution, they require the tools to counter it effectively. For them, that means stiff and precise sections relating specifically to street soliciting. As Superintendent McNeney of the Investigation Division of the Vancouver Police stated in a letter to the Committee on behalf of Chief Stewart:

> In general, the socially harmful conduct referred to [i.e. that flowing from prostitution] is an effect of prostitution on our streets. The prostitutes and their customers are the cause. It is impossible to effectively deal with harmful conduct, without enforceable statutes governing the open soliciting by prostitutes. The nine *Criminal Code* provisions listed above [i.e. dealt with in this section] have very simply proven not to be the answer.

8. Other Forms of Criminal Conduct Associated with Prostitution

Evidence from police forces in the major Canadian cities indicates that other forms of crime are associated with prostitution. In their brief to the Committee, the Calgary Police Commission provided statistics on the level of street prostitution-related crime in that city between June 17, 1981 and December 9, 1983. During that period there were 115 such crimes.[18] These included:

Theft over $200.00 - 24(20.9%)
Assault - 14(12.2%)
Wounding - 11(9.6%)
Robbery with Violence - 7(6.0%)
Indecent Assault - 7(6.0%)
Assault occasioning Bodily Harm - 6(5.2%)
Rape - 5(4.3%)

Living on the avails and procuring counted for 12(10.4%)and 4(3.5%) respectively. "Others" amounted to 25(21.7%). The contexts of the reported crimes varied, but typically involved offences by prostitute on customer or vice-versa, by prostitute against bystander, pimp against prostitute, or prostitute against prostitute.

It has been suggested to the Committee by some women's groups that if street soliciting were to be decriminalized, the focus of the law would then become what it appropriately should be, namely the prosecution of conduct which is palpably criminal. Law enforcement authorities counter this argument by asserting that if the public manifestations of prostitution are not effectively controlled by the criminal law, other forms of criminal conduct associated with it can be expected to proliferate. In short, they argue that, prostitution, especially street prostitution, is a notorious cause of or contributor to other forms of crime and that any figures related to prostitution will represent but a small proportion of the criminal activity which actually takes place.

These claims and counterclaims are difficult to deal with, because there is in Canada an absence of serious research which can demonstrate clearly that prostitution, especially street prostitution, is a significant cause of or patently attracts more general criminal activity. It would appear that some crime is caused or attracted, and that it is generated by the activities of relatively few people. However, it is not clear whether an area in which street prostitution occurs is necessarily less law abiding than a similar area in which it does not exist. An American study in Boston concluded that the latter was not proven.[19]

It is clear that individual Canadian police officers have doubts about official claims linking prostitution to widespread criminality. The Prairie researcher on prostitution reports that

[p]olice respondents are fully aware of the richness of the street culture, and several police made it clear that in their minds at least, all the other aspects of other illegal activities within that culture would occur whether prostitution were present or not. Only one policeman [of the 46 respondents] assumed that if street prostitution were stopped, that all illegal activities would be substantially decreased.[20]

In the view of the Committee the debate is, in the absence of more extensive data, likely to be inconclusive and, therefore, unhelpful. The important question is whether the public manifestations of prostitution generally produce the sort of harms and the degree of harm which the criminal law should specifically address.

A further issue is the relationship between the sort of violent and coercive conduct which is often involved in procuring and pimping, and other generic offences involving violence. Although there was substantial agreement among those who appeared before the Committee that both these forms of conduct warrant harsh sanction by the criminal law, particularly when associated with violence or its threat, the Committee has thought it important to consider that the offences of both procuring and pimping overlap with offences which deal with the actuality and threat of physical or psychological violence. As a consequence, a question arises as to whether special provisions are required to deal with prostitution-related conduct of this sort.

The offences in the *Code* which are often exemplified in the conduct of pimps and procurers are: (i) assault and sexual assault (sections 244-246); (ii) kidnapping (section 247); and (iii) extortion (section 305).

244. (1) A person commits an assault when

    (a) without the consent of another person, he applies force intentionally to that other person, directly or indirectly;

    (b) he attempts or threatens, by an act or gesture, to apply force to another person, if he has, or causes that other person to believe upon reasonable grounds that he has, present ability to effect his purpose; or

    (c) while openly wearing or carrying a weapon or an imitation thereof, he accosts or impedes another person or begs.

(2) This section applies to all forms of assault, including sexual assault, sexual assault with a weapon, threats to a third party or causing bodily harm and aggravated sexual assault.

245. Every one who commits an assault is guilty of

    (a) an indictable offence and is liable to imprisonment for five years; or

    (b) an offence punishable on summary conviction.

245.1 (1) Every one who, in committing an assault,

    (a) carries, uses or threatens to use a weapon or an imitation thereof, or

    (b) causes bodily harm to the complainant,

is guilty of an indictable offence and is liable to imprisonment for ten years.

(2) For the purposes of this section and sections 245.3 and 246.2, "bodily harm" means any hurt or injury to the complainant that interferes with his or her health or comfort and that is more than merely transient or trifling in nature.

245.2 (1) Every one commits an aggravated assault who wounds, maims, disfigures or endangers the life of the complainant.

(2) Every one who commits an aggravated assault is guilty of an indictable offence and is liable to imprisonment for fourteen years.

245.3 Every one who unlawfully causes bodily harm to any person is guilty of an indictable offence and is liable to imprisonment for ten years.

246.1 (1) Every one who commits a sexual assault is guilty of

    (a) an indictable offence and is liable to imprisonment for ten years; or

(b) an offence punishable on summary conviction.

246.2 Every one who, in committing a sexual assault,

(a) carries, uses or threatens to use a weapon or an imitation thereof,

(b) threatens to cause bodily harm to a person other than the complainant,

(c) causes bodily harm to the complainant, or

(d) is a party to the offence with any other person,

is guilty of an indictable offence and is liable to imprisonment for fourteen years.

246.3 (1) Every one commits an aggravated sexual assault who, in committing a sexual assault, wounds, maims, disfigures or endangers the life of the complainant.

(2) Every one who commits an aggravated sexual assault is guilty of an indictable offence and is liable to imprisonment for life.

246.4 Where an accused is charged with an offence under section 150 (incest), 157 (gross indecency), 246.1 (sexual assault, 246.2 (sexual assault with a weapon, threats to a third party or causing bodily harm) or 246.3 (aggravated sexual assault), no corroboration is required for a conviction and the judge shall not instruct the jury that it is unsafe to find the accused guilty in the absence of corroboration.

247.1 (1) Every one who kidnaps a person with intent

(a) to cause him to be confined or imprisoned against his will,

(b) to cause him to be unlawfully sent or transported out of Canada against his will, or

(c) to hold him for ransom or to service against his will, is guilty of an indictable offence and is liable to imprisonment for life.

(2) Every one who, without lawful authority, confines, imprisons or forcibly seizes another person is guilty of an indictable offence and is liable to imprisonment for five years.

(3) In proceedings under this section the fact that the person in relation to whom the offence is alleged to have been committed did not resist is not a defence unless the accused proves that the failure to resist was not caused by threats, duress, force or exhibition of force.

305. (1) Every one who, without reasonable justification or excuse and with intent to extort or gain anything, by threats, accusations, menaces or violence induces or attempts to induce any person, whether or not he is the person threatened, accused or menaced or to whom the violence is shown, to do anything or cause anything to be done, is guilty of an indictable offence and is liable to imprisonment for fourteen years.

(2) A threat to institute civil proceedings is not a threat for the purposes of this section.

It is quite possible to lay these charges for these offences against procurers and pimps, and in some instances they have been, either as independent counts or alternative charges to procuring or living on the avails. In the former instance, it may not have been possible for the Crown to adduce sufficient evidence to move for a conviction on one or other of the two special offences. In the latter instance, the more general offence may have been invoked as a fall back position (if living on the avails fails, the court might still convict on assault), or because of the aggravated circumstances attending the case (the victim was kidnapped and forced to engage in acts of prostitution, or was subjected to aggravated assault because she did not please her pimp), the accused should be convicted on more than one count and sentenced accordingly.

In the present *Code*, the special and the more general offences coexist because there are aspects of procuring and pimping which do not fall neatly within the purview of violence or its threat. Both procuring and pimping may be established without proving actual or anticipated force. The emphasis in both offences is certainly on an odious form of exploitation but that can be established without proving violence or threat of force on the part of the procurer or pimp. The second reason seems to be that procuring and living on the avails are relational offences, that is, they take place normally within the context of an ongoing exploitative relationship. The latter, if anything, is the primary objective of the law's concern, rather than the single incident which may have triggered the charge. The more general offences, by contrast, are geared to dealing with single instances without any obvious concern, except in relation to sentencing, with the presence of a pre-existing power relationship between the accused and the victim. A third and complementary reason for the coexistence of the various provisions is that in some instances, it allows the Crown to seek a more severe penalty. This could happen where the Crown has come upon the existence of a procuring or pimping relationship as the result of a complaint alleging less serious criminal conduct, for example, a simple assault.

As long as the law continues to attack procuring and pimping on the basis of a broad rationale of exploitation, however exerted, it is difficult to see how offences like assault, kidnapping or extortion can satisfactorily accommodate fully that type of conduct. Perhaps there would be less argument in favour of the special offences if they were confined to contexts in which force is applied or threatened. However, it may be argued that there will be situations in which it is important to preserve offences which stress the relational factor.

In particular, the other offences, especially kidnapping and extortion, may not fit the facts, and the penalty for assault may not fully reflect the exploitative nature of the conduct. It may be cold comfort to a prostitute who is constrained to remain in prostitution by constant threats of force against her that, unless the Crown can establish that she was kidnapped or the victim of extortion, the best she can hope for is that the procurer or pimp be found guilty of simple assault and imprisoned for up to five years. In other words, unless the more general provisions can be precisely framed to reflect the relational element, there is a rational argument for the retention of procuring and living on the avails as separate offences.

Footnotes

[1] There is a hint in *R. v. J.* (1957), 21 W.W.R. 248 (Alta.Prov.Ct.) that if the fellatio involved in that case (on a young male by his fiancée) had been provided by a stranger for money there would have been a conviction.

[2] *R. v. Quesnel* (1980), 51 C.C.C. (2d) 270 (Ont.C.A.).

[3] See *R. v. Hecker* (1980), 58 C.C.C. (2d) 66 (Yukon Terr.Ct.) (accused acquitted for briefly exposing buttocks in an attempt to be humorous).

[4] *R. v. Figluizzi* (1981), 59 C.C.C. (2d) 144 (Alta.Q.B.); *R. v. Wise* (1982), 67 C.C.C. (2d) 231 (B.C.Co.Ct.).

[5] In *R. v. Miteli* (1977), 36 C.C.C. (2d) 321 (Ont.Prov.Ct.Cr.D.) it was held that it is no defence to a charge under this section that the accused was unaware that he was being observed.

[6] *R. v. Hastings*, [1947] 4 D.L.R. 748 (N.B.S.C. App.D.).

[7] See *R. v. Verrette* (1978), 40 C.C.C. (2d) 273 (S.C.C.).

[8] See *R. v. Swinimer* (1978), 40 C.C.C. (2d) 432 (N.S.S.C., App.D.); *R. v. Berry* (1980), 56 C.C.C. (2d) 99 (Ont. C.A.); *Whitehouse v. Reimer (No. 2)* (1981), 61 C.C.C. (2d) 134 (Alta.Q.B.); *R. v. Peters* (1982), 65 C.C.C. (2d) 83 (B.C.C.A.).

[9] The Committee understands that this has been the case in Vancouver where it is believed by the police and prosecutors that provincial court judges would react unfavourably to any attempt to use section 171(1)(a)(iii) ("impeding or molesting") to get around *Hutt*.

[10] *R. v. Munroe* (1983), 5 C.C.C. (3d) 217 (Ont.C.A.). See also *R. v. Gauvin* (1984), 11 W.C.B. 441 (Ont. C.A.).

[11] An intrusive pattern of conduct would be required, such as continuing noise from a parked car, or shouting between prostitutes.

[12] *R. v. Andsten* (1960), 33 C.R. 213 (B.C.C.A.).

[13] See *Martin's Criminal Code*, 1955, (Toronto: Cartwright & Sons, 1955) at 282-96 for the history and rationale of this provision.

[14] *Attorney General of British Columbia v. Couillard* (1984), 14 C.C.C. (3d) 169 (B.C.S.C.). Compare *Attorney General of Nova Scotia v. Beaver*, Dec. 19, 1984 (unreported) N.S.S.C.Tr.Div. in which MacIntosh J. rejected an application for an interim injunction against street prostitutes in Halifax on the ground that this action represented an attempt to usurp the federal parliament's criminal law power by civil means. The judge seems to have accepted that the injunction was being sought to support the criminal law in this case.

[15] See *Re Regina and Basaraba* (1975), 24 C.C.C. (2d) 296 (Man. C.A.).

[16] Crook, *Prostitution in the Atlantic Provinces*, Working Papers on Pornography and Prostitution (W.P.P.P.) Report #12, Department of Justice, Ottawa, 1984 at 56.

[17] *Minister of National Revenue v. Eldridge*, [1964] C.T.C. 545 (Exch. Ct.).

[18] Calgary Police Commission, *Street Prostitution* (Brief to Special Committee on Pornography and Prostitution, January 1984), Appendix V.

[19] B. Milman, "New Rules for the Oldest Profession: Should we Change our Prostitution Laws?" (1980) 3 Harvard Womens L.J. at 1.

[20] M. Lautt, *Prostitution in the Prairies* W.P.P.P.#9, at 27.

Chapter 31

Control and Regulation of Prostitution by Provincial and Municipal Law

1. The Relative Powers to Limit Prostitution

As indicated in Part I, Section II, Chapter 3, the ability of the provinces and municipalities to develop legal strategies to deal with prostitution depends upon the division of powers between the federal parliament and the provincial legislatures within the Canadian Constitution.

The extent of the powers of the federal Parliament and the provincial legislatures to limit prostitution-related activity was untested until recently. However, in the wake of the perceived weaknesses of section 195.1 of the *Criminal Code*, several of the municipalities most affected by street prostitution passed by-laws to curb street soliciting. This movement on the part of municipalities was challenged and the courts had the opportunity to clarify the relative domains of federal and provincial jurisdiction.

The by-laws enacted in Calgary, Montréal, Vancouver and Niagara Falls were ostensibly grounded in the powers granted to those municipalities by special or general provincial legislation. They made it an offence either to loiter for the purposes of prostitution or to offer to sell or purchase sexual services in a public place. The by-laws provided for fines on conviction and for imprisonment in the case of default. Sentencing judges were also empowered to award costs against the convicted person.[1]

Statistics received by the Committee from these cities indicate that the by-laws were vigorously enforced by the local constabularies. The brief from the Calgary Police Commission, for example, reveals that 530 charges were laid under that city's by-law between June 25, 1981 and the end of 1982.[2] This compares with Statistics Canada's report of 75 charges under section 195 (for procuring, living on the avails and street soliciting) for the whole of Alberta in 1979, and 12 charges in 1980.

The Calgary by-law was challenged in *R. v. Westendorp*,[3] a case which ultimately reached the Supreme Court of Canada in 1983. The by-law made it an offence to be or remain on the street for the purpose of prostitution. "Prostitution" was defined as "the sale or offering for sale of sexual services and includes the purchase or offering to purchase of sexual services". The Supreme Court determined that the by-law was outside the powers assigned to the province as it amounted to an attempt to enact criminal law, thus invading federal legislative authority. The power to legislate criminal law, said the court, resides exclusively with the federal Parliament.

The demise of the Calgary by-law was sufficient to persuade the other municipalities with similar provisions that they should no longer attempt to enforce them. The decision in *Westendorp* clearly rules out attempts by municipalities to proscribe prostitution related activities. The municipalities have no power to make "criminal law" on prostitution. Moreover, given the exclusive nature of the federal Parliament's jurisdiction over prostitution-related activities as crimes, the bar to provincial or municipal legislation would exist, even in the absence of federal legislation.

2. The Power to Regulate Prostitution

There is nothing in the judgment of the Supreme Court in *Westendorp* which prevents a municipality from exercising the power given to it by provincial legislation to regulate or license business activities within its territory. It is, of course, essential that regulation or licensing is the genuine objective of the by-law. If it is proscription in the garb of regulation, then it is likely to be struck down as an attempt to enact criminal law.

Since *Westendorp*, three municipalities have introduced or are seriously considering by-laws which attempt to limit street prostitution by invoking the regulatory power to grant or withhold business licences. Montréal, in a by-law which involves a wide variety of street businesses or services, makes it an offence to engage in such activity on the street or on the exterior part of adjacent private property, unless authorized by by-law.[4] A Niagara Falls by-law enacted in 1984 is similar to that in Montreal, although it refers simply to the offer to sell or purchase "services" upon the street.[5] Vancouver has drafted and is considering a by-law which seeks to prohibit the conducting of specified businesses in public places. "Conduct of business" includes the act of negotiating the sale or purchase of a service or commodity. To date only one business is listed in the proposed schedule of prohibited business, to wit "sexual services".[6]

In principle, provisions of this type have a better chance of surviving challenge because it can be argued that they represent an attempt to control street business in general. If, however, they are seen to be in substance (as Vancouver's proposed by-law in its present form may be) directed solely towards the eradication of street prostitution, then a court may well determine that they represent a "backdoor" attempt to legislate criminal law.[7]

Apart altogether from possible constitutional complications, those who enforce the by-laws see pragmatic difficulties with their application. Police authorities in Montréal report that the street business by-law is assisting in controlling street prostitution in that community. However, the application of the by-law does not appear to be causing a reduction in the overall dimensions of the problem.

Chief André De Luca of the Montréal Police informed the Committee that during 1983, under both the original by-law (that relating specifically to street prostitution) and the new business control by-law, there were 339 charges relating to soliciting for the purpose of prostitution.[8] For the first 6 months of 1984 no less than 323 charges were laid under the new by-law. Chief De Luca sees this as evidence that the by-law is not serving to reduce the incidence of street prostitution in that city. He attributes that problem directly to the lack of power of arrest and detention under municipal by-laws in Montréal. There is thus no guarantee that those charged will appear in court. Moreover, the inclination of many who are charged is to immediately return to the streets. Where convictions are secured, the police doubt that the fines handed down have any significant deterrent value.

The power which municipalities typically possess to license businesses has also been used to attempt to regulate other forms of prostitution activity, for example, escort services and massage parlours. It is well established and was confirmed by the Supreme Court of Canada in *City of Prince George* v. *Payne*[9] that a municipality cannot use this licensing power to make it unlawful to carry out a legal business activity. However, this restrictive view may be tempered by the possibility of municipalities using their "zoning power" to prevent the location of such establishments and businesses within their jurisdiction. Such a move by Vancouver was upheld recently in *Red Hot Video* v. *City of Vancouver*.[10] Apart from a dubious dictum from the Divisional Court of Ontario[11], the case law does support the proposition that municipalities may regulate as opposed to banning such establishments and businesses through the enactment of by-laws.[12]

Escort services and massage parlours are typically required to secure business licences like any other commercial operations. Some municipalities have gone the further step of enacting special by-laws relating to these particular businesses. These are normally so drafted as to make it expensive to operate such an establishment, and at least try to limit the type and volume of sexual services provided.

An instructive example in the case of escort services is the City of Saskatoon's "Dating and Escort Service By-law".[13] The by-law establishes an annual licence fee of $2,000 for the business, and in addition requires that each "dater" or "escort" possess a licence, the annual rate for which is $500. The latter type of licence cannot be held by a person not in the employ of a licensed service, and the applicant for a licence must submit "a written recommendation signed by or on behalf of the Chief of Police". A list must be kept by the operator of the 'escorts' or 'dates', and their vital statistics. The list must be furnished on demand to any peace officer or to the Chief Licence Inspector. The operator of a service is required to maintain a record of each transaction, including the name, address and phone number of the client, the name of the escort, the time and date of her arrival, the type of service provided and her fee. The business is limited to the hours between 7:00 a.m. and 12:30 p.m. and advertisements involving sexual suggestion are prohibited. Infractions incur a fine ranging between $200 and $500.

The Saskatoon by-law was challenged in 1983 on the ground that it represented an attempt to enact "criminal law".[14] It survived that challenge, the judge determining that it was a valid exercise of the City's power to regulate local businesses. In a more recent decision of the Court of Queen's Bench in Manitoba, an escort services by-law was upheld notwithstanding that it imposed a higher fee for such establishments.[15] The court went on to say that it was proper for city council to act on moral grounds in enacting such legislation and that such a by-law was not in violation of section 7 of the *Charter*.

Massage parlour by-laws have also been enacted by some Canadian municipalities.[16] A provision which is common to most of these enactments is that which prohibits any licensee from permitting an attendant to administer a massage unless the attendant is wearing clean, washable, non-transparent outer garments covering the body from neck to knee.[17]

Whether or not this type of provision achieves its apparent purpose of discouraging sexual arousal and encounter, the by-laws themselves have proved resistant to constitutional challenge. The courts in these cases have been careful to distinguish criminality on the one hand and morality on the other. Their view is that provinces, and through them, municipalities, have a legitimate concern with morality and can legislate on it providing the legislation comes within one of the recognized areas of provincial jurisdiction. In these cases, the legislation was characterized as regulation of a local business and, therefore, within the "property" and "civil rights" class of subjects within section 92(13) of the *British North America Act*.[18]

The message from the courts is that with regulatory regimes designed in whole or in part to control prostitution, validity will depend upon whether the primary thrust of the enactment is regulation rather than proscription. Relevant to that question will be the generality of the regulation (Does it apply to a range of businesses or activities or exclusively to prostitution?), and, if it is specific, whether, on balance, its purpose seems to be to permit the activity within limits or to proscribe it.

Far less contentious constitutionally are the municipal by-laws which reflect the power granted to municipalities to control noise, littering, vehicular traffic, parking and obstruction of sidewalks and other public areas. In theory, these provide a means of controlling some of the problems associated with street soliciting. However, difficulties with obtaining adequate evidence, especially from members of the public, the absence of a power of arrest and the modesty of fines seem to have persuaded most police forces and prosecutors that the results which can be expected do not justify the effort. Where these by-laws are used, they are seen as temporary expedients to show the public that the police are active, or to show prostitutes that the police still have a residuum of control of the streets.

3. The Impact of Other Provincial Laws

There are other elements of provincial law with prohibitive control and regulatory features. Although they do not address prostitution in particular, they can be invoked to deal with some of its side effects. It is unlikely that any of these legal expedients, at least as they presently operate, would be open to constitutional challenge under the division-of-powers doctrine.

3.1 Landlord and Tenant Law

It is customary to find in rental agreements for accommodation provisions that prevent the tenant from conducting himself or herself in a manner that disrupts or inconveniences other tenants in the same building. Typically, rental agreements regarding residential premises also contain provisions prohibiting the tenant from carrying on business out of his or her premises. At common law, breach of provisions such as these allow the landlord to commence proceedings to have the tenancy terminated and the tenant ejected.[19]

In most provinces, legislation has been enacted which either expressly or implicitly protects the landlord's rights in these particulars. Legislation relating to residential tenancies in Alberta, Saskatchewan and Ontario, for example, contains statutory covenants or conditions upon the tenant which oblige him or her not to interfere unreasonably with the enjoyment of the landlord and other tenants of other households, and to refrain from carrying on or allowing illegal businesses or activities on the leased premises.[20]

In each province, in the event of a breach of the covenant or condition, that landlord may apply to a court, rentalsman or rental tenancies commission for a remedy, including termination of the tenancy.[21] Therefore, prostitutes who use their apartments for purposes of prostitution may run the risk of having their tenancies concluded (in addition, of course, to being prosecuted for keeping a common bawdy house).

At a more general level in the landlord and tenant legislation of several provinces, in particular Manitoba, New Brunswick, Ontario and Prince Edward Island, express provision is made for the landlord's right of re-entry where the tenant or other person has been found guilty under the *Criminal Code* of keeping a "disorderly house".[22]

As the definition of "disorderly house" under s. 179(1) of the *Code* includes a common bawdy house, this legislation lends specific sanction to the termination of any lease, including a commercial lease, whenever the premises are being used for the purposes of prostitution or the practice of acts of indecency. As a result, the clandestine social operations of some massage and body rub parlours will be under risk of closure under provincial law as well as prosection under the *Code*.[23]

3.2 Highway Traffic Legislation

Highway traffic acts, or their equivalents in each of the provinces, proscribe the operation of motor vehicles in a way which constitutes a danger or annoyance to other members of the public. More particularly, they contain provisions which prohibit the use of vehicles in such a way as to cause obstructions or unnecessary noise. Such provisions are available to the police in the case of vehicular traffic which is attracted by street prostitution activity. In fact, it appears that these provisions are rarely invoked. The reason most often given by police is the difficulty of acquiring adequate evidence, although, given the notoriety of prostitution in certain urban locations, it is difficult to see why the gathering of proof is such an insurmountable problem.

One police force, that in Calgary, was unsuccessful in its attempt to invoke the "stunting" section of the *Alberta Highway Traffic Act* to convict a street prostitute.[24] Section 125(1) of the *Act* makes it an offence to "perform or engage in any stunt or other activity on a highway that is likely to distract, startle or interfere with other users of the highway." However, that rebuff related more to the Alberta Court of Appeal's feeling that the behaviour of the accused did not fall within the proscribed form of activity, rather than any inadequacy in the evidence. It seems that the general disenchantment of police forces with the overall state of the law relating to street prostitution lies at the root of the reticence to use this type of provincial legislation.

3.3 Nuisance Law

As the judgment of Chief Justice McEachern in *Attorney General of British Columbia* v. *Couillard*[25] demonstrates, it is possible to invoke the notion of public nuisance as a basis for restraining those who engage in street prostitution. The full implications of this judgment have yet to be determined. As has already been pointed out earlier in the Report, there is no doubt that there is solid authority supporting the Attorney General's right to intervene to seek a civil injunction to restrain a public nuisance. Indeed, as Madame Justice McLachlin pointed out in a subsequent attempt by a private citizen to secure an extension of the geographic area of the earlier injunction, in the absence of any proof of peculiar damage to an individual citizen, the Attorney General is the only one who can act in such circumstances.[26] What is left unclear by the *Couillard* decision is how far the Attorney General must go in establishing an actual or anticipated nuisance on the part of the accused. The principles of nuisance law would suggest that he has to prove that the accused has engaged in such conduct before, and can be expected to do so again.[27]

A private individual may bring an action in private nuisance for an injunction and/or damages to restrain or to compensate for the harm done by prostitution. The availability of the action is limited to the occupiers of premises, and is designed to protect their interest in the peaceful and quiet enjoyment of their property. In the absence of tangible harm to the occupier or his property, the degree of interference must be such that no reasonable person should have to suffer it. Actions of this nature against neighbourhood brothels have succeeded in both Canada and England.[28] However, as with most civil litigation, the cost factor often works against enthusiastic pursuit of this option and may be exacerbated by the fact that what the plaintiff may be seeking is an end to the interference or inconvenience rather than compensation.

3.4 Petty Trespass Legislation

Some provinces have petty trespass or protection of property legislation which makes it an offence, punishable by a fine, to trespass on property without the consent of the owner. In some statutes, conviction depends upon explicit notice having been given,[29] whereas in others, breaches may also occur where the trespass is on land which by its character may be seen to belong to someone, for example, a garden.[30]

This legislation has been used from time to time to charge prostitutes who have ventured onto private property.[31] Its viability, of course, depends upon proof of trespass and an intrusion onto land of the type and in the circumstances contemplated by the legislation. Therefore, its applicability is limited.

3.5 Public Health Legislation

Although there are no longer public health provisions addressed specifically to prostitutes, there are sections in contemporary *Public Health Acts* which are general enough to be used against any person or group considered to be a carrier of sexually transmitted diseases (STD's).

Under provincial public health legislation, where a public health official has reasonable grounds to believe that a person is infected with venereal disease, he or she may serve a notice on the individual to undergo medical examination.[32] Furthermore, if the person is found to be suffering from venereal disease, then the official has the power to take the additional step of seeking ministerial or judicial approval to have the carrier confined for treatment until the official is satisfied that the individual is free of infection.[33] Power is also granted to medical health officers or the physicians of jails and correctional institutions to examine persons suspected of being infected with venereal disease within such institutions, and to order their treatment if they are found to be infected.[34]

In Ontario, Newfoundland and Saskatchewan, provisions exist which allow forcible entry to premises by public health officials.[35] In Ontario, legislation permits compulsory examination of the inhabitants on the premises, and in Saskatchewan, there is provision for the closure of dance halls, restaurants and hotels. None of these actions require the authorities concerned to secure a warrant. Generally, under public health legislation, fines are leviable for those who disobey orders made under the legislation, or who are obstructionist or deceitful in their dealings with public health officials.[36]

This legislation is draconian in the sense that it grants to public health authorities the power to detain people without the safeguards provided by the criminal law. As two Canadian legal experts have observed:

> In a criminal trial the onus is on the Crown prosecutor to prove the accusation, not simply to the satisfaction of the judge and jury, but beyond a reasonable doubt.[37]

The same writers have also pointed to the troubling absence of the normal process demanded by the *Criminal Code*, i.e. the issue of a warrant, as a prelude to forcible entry.[38] All of this raises questions about the validity of such provisions in light of the *Charter*.

The tenor of the legislation obviously reflects governmental concern to respond quickly to control possible spreaders of infection. Some public health experts doubt the value of this approach, believing that voluntary and consensual strategies are far more likely to allow them to get to the source of an infection in the community and to deal effectively with it.[39]

Despite the significant powers accorded to public health authorities to direct and detain, there is no evidence from the regional studies conducted for the Committee that these powers are used against prostitutes as individuals or as a group.

The reality seems to be that most adult prostitutes are well aware of the risk of contracting STD's. Accordingly, they take preventative measures to minimize their infection, and tend to have regular check-ups either at public health clinics or by their own physicians. The Committee was advised of one case in which two Calgary males who had had sexual liaisons with prostitutes in Thailand, were found to be infected with an exotic strain of STD. There was concern about its local spread among Calgary prostitutes, and the public health authorities apparently dealt with the matter in a low profile, consensual way.[40]

4. The Utility of these Provisions

In the same way in which the police and prosecutorial authorities demonstrate reticence in utilizing the more general provisions of the *Criminal Code* to combat the side effects of prostitution, so do they in the case of provincial and municipal legislation. The main reason for the reticence is the same: the feeling on the part of the law enforcers that these are, at best, limited and transitory expedients, and that they should not be required to navigate this complex of provisions when the federal Parliament could easily provide an effective means of dealing directly with the problem.

For a short period it did look as if the street prostitution by-laws presented a viable substitute which they were prepared to enforce vigorously. However, the Supreme Court of Canada has closed off that option.[41]

Footnotes

1 See e.g. Montréal Urban Community By-law 5469, 26 May, 1980; City of Calgary By-laws 25 M 81 and 27 M 81, June 25, 1981.

2 See Calgary Police Commission, *Street Prostitution* (Brief to Special Committee on Pornography and Prostitution, January 1984).

3 *R. v. Westendorp* (1983), 2 C.C.C. (3d) 330 (S.C.C.).

4 Montréal Urban Community By-law 333, 3a (in force 1 Nov. 1983).

5 City of Niagara Falls By-law 84-173, 1984.

6 To date the by-law has not been passed.

7 Montréal By-law 333, 3a survived constitutional challenge in *Clermont* v. *The Queen*, April 1984.

8 For table of charges, see R. Gemme et al, W.P.P.P.#11 at 67.

9 *City of Prince George* v. *Payne* (1977), 75 D.L.R. (3d) 1 (S.C.C.).

10 *Red Hot Video* v. *City of Vancouver* (1984), 5 D.L.R. (4th) 61 (B.C.S.C.).

11 *Information Retailers Association of Metropolitan Toronto Inc.* v. *Municipality of Metropolitan Toronto* 15 Oct. 1984, unreported (Ont. Div. Ct.).

12 See e.g. *Sharmark Hotels Ltd.* v. *Municipality of Metro Toronto* (1981), 121 D.L.R. (3d) 415 (Ont. Div. Ct.); *Koumoudouros* v. *Municipality of Metropolitan Toronto* (1984) 6 D.L.R. (4th) 523 (Ont. Div. Ct.). Contrast: *Nordee Investments Ltd.* v. *Corp. of Burlington* 25 July 1984, unreported (Ont. C. A.), in which a by-law which attempted to regulate nudity in eating establishments was struck down as an attempt to prohibit any form of activity, including dancing, where there was exposure of breast or buttock. For other examples of cases supporting the proposition in the text, see notes 15 and 18.

13 City of Saskatoon, By-law 6098, 23 Aug. 1982.

14 *R. v. Dunits* 23 Aug. 1983, unreported (Sask. Prov. Ct.).

15 *Canada (Eve Studio)* v. *City of Winnipeg*, [1984] 4 W.W.R. 507 (Man. Q. B.).

16 See e.g. City of Edmonton By-law 4844, 10 Nov. 1976; City of Saskatoon By-law 6066; City of Ottawa By-law L-6; Metro Toronto By-law 107-73.

17 The by-laws also control the hours of operation; the standards of cleanliness; record keeping; and the location of massage (cubicles or rooms must not be locked). "Massage" typically includes "kneading, manipulating, rubbing, massaging, touching or stimulating, by any means of a person's body or part thereof". Some but not all require that masseuses and masseures have professional qualifications.

18 *Cal Investments* v. *City of Winnipeg* (1978), 83 D.L.R. (3d) 699 (Man. C. A.); *Re Try-San International Ltd.* v. *City of Vancouver* (1978), 83 D.L.R. (3d) 236 (B.C.C.A.); *Re Moffat and City of Edmonton* (1979), 99 D.L.R. (3d) 101 (Alta. S. C. App. D.). In *R. v. Nault* 1983, unreported (Sask. Prov. Ct.), By-law 6855 of the City of Regina was struck down because it allowed only members of the Saskatchewan Association of Masseurs to operate massage parlours in the City. This was invalid, said the court, as the City had no authority to award monopoly business rights.

19 Williams, Rhodes, *Canadian Law of Landlord and Tenant* (5th Ed. by F. Rhodes, Vol. II, Toronto: Carswell Co., 1983) at 12-43 to 12-48. A right of entry for breach of covenant only arises if given by the lease. In its absence the lessor may have an action for damages.

20 *Landlord and Tenant Act*, R.S.A. 1980, c. L-6, s. 16; *Residential Tenancies Act*, R.S.S. 1978, c. R-22, s. 20(1), stat. cond. 7(1); *Residential Tenancies Act*, R.S.O. 1980, c. 452, s. 38.

21 *Ibid.*, Alta, s. 20; Sask., s. 20(1); Ont., s. 41.

[22] *Landlord and Tenant Act*, R.S.M. 1970, c. L70, s. 17(2); *Landlord and Tenant Act*, R.S.N.B. 1973, c. L-1, s. 9; *Landlord and Tenant Act*, R.S.O 1980, c. 232, s. 18(2); *Landlord and Tenant Act*, R.S.P.E.I. 1974, c. L-7, s. 10. In Ontario the landlord has the same right of re-entry if the premises are used as a body-rub or adult entertainment parlour, except where the establishment is operated under a license granted under the *Municipal Act*.

[23] See *R*. v. *Ramberran*, [1978] 1 W.W.R. 19 (Man. Prov. Ct.).

[24] *R*. v. *Jones*, [1983] 4 W.W.R. 144 (Alta.S.C.App.D.).

[25] *Attorney General of British Columbia* v. *Couillard* (1984), 14 C.C.C. (3d) 169 (B.C.S.C.).

[26] *Stein* v. *Gonzalez*, [1984] 6 W.W.R. 428 (B.C.S.C.).

[27] In *Attorney General of Nova Scotia* v. *Beaver*, 19 Dec. 1984, unreported (N.S.S.C.), in which like the *Couillard* case the Attorney General of Nova Scotia sought an interim injunction to prevent prostitutes from plying their trade in certain areas of Halifax, MacIntosh, J. sidestepped the issue of whether a nuisance had actually been proven. He found against the Attorney General on the ground that this was an attempt by the province by civil action to usurp the criminal law power of the federal parliament and thus *ultra vires*.

[28] See *Poirier* v. *Turkewich* (1964), 42 D.L.R. (2d) 259 (Man. Q. B.); *Thompson - Shwab* v. *Costaki*, [1956] 1 All E. R. 652 (C.A.).

[29] See *Petty Trespass Act*, R.S.A. 1980, c. P-6, s. 1.

[30] See *Trespass to Property Act*, R.S.A. 1980, c. 511, s. 2, 3; *An Act to Protect Property*, S.N.S. 1982, c. 13, s. 3.

[31] See Lautt, *Project T.A.P. Towards an Awareness of Prostitution: An Empirical Study of Street Prostitution in the Prairie Region* W.P.P.P.#9 at 17.

[32] See e.g. *Venereal Diseases Prevention Act*, R.S.A. 1980, c. V-2, s. 8(1); *Venereal Diseases Prevention Act*, R.S.O. 1980, c. 521, s. 4(1), (2).

[33] *Ibid.*, Alta. s. 9; Ont. s. 4(3), 5, 6.

[34] *Ibid.*, Alta. s. 13, 14; Ont. s. 8, 9.

[35] R.S.O. 1980, c. 521, s. 27; R.S.N. 1970, c. 38, s. 22; R.S.S. 1978, c. V-4, s. 17.

[36] See R.S.A. 1980, c. V-2, s. 27; R.S.O. 1980, c. 521, s. 12(1). In both instances imprisonment is provided for in default of payment.

[37] Rozovsky, *Legal Sex* (Toronto: Doubleday Canada Ltd., 1982) at 71.

[38] Rozovsky and Rozovsky, "Sexually Transmitted Diseases and the Law" (1973) 74 *Can. J. Pub. Health* at 135.

[39] Haug and Cini, *The Ladies (and Gentlemen) of the Night and the Spread of Sexually Transmitted Diseases* W.P.P.P.#7 at 15-21.

[40] Interview with Dr. G. Bonham, Chief Medical Officer of Health, City of Calgary, February 1984.

[41] *R*. v. *Westendorp*, note 3.

Chapter 32

Prostitution and the Charter of Rights and Freedoms

The advent of the *Charter of Rights and Freedoms* raises a series of specific questions about the validity of proscriptive or regulatory law relating to prostitution. This is so whether the present law or proposals for amendment are being considered.

Guarantee of Rights and Freedoms

1. The *Canadian Charter of Rights and Freedoms* guarantees the rights and freedoms set out in it subject only to such reasonable limits prescribed by law as can be demonstrably justified in a free and democratic society.

Fundamental Freedoms

2. Everyone has the following fundamental freedoms:

(a) freedom of conscience and religion;

(b) freedom of thought, belief, opinion and expression, including freedom of the press and other media of communication;

(c) freedom of peaceful assembly; and

(d) freedom of association.

Mobility Rights

6. (1) Every citizen of Canada has the right to enter, remain in and leave Canada.

(2) Every citizen of Canada and every person who has the status of a permanent resident of Canada has the right

(a) to move to and take up residence in any province; and

(b) to pursue the gaining of a livelihood in any province.

Legal Rights

7. Everyone has the right to life, liberty and security of the person and the right not to be deprived thereof except in accordance with the principles of fundamental justice.

11. Any person charged with an offence has the right

(d) to be presumed innocent until proven guilty according to law in a fair and public hearing by an independent and impartial tribunal;

Equality Rights

15. (1) Every individual is equal before and under the law and has the right to the equal protection and equal benefit of the law without discrimination and, in particular, without discrimination based on race, national or ethnic origin, colour, religion, sex, age or mental or physical disability.

(2) Subsection (1) does not preclude any law, program or activity that has as its object the amelioration of conditions of disadvantaged individuals or groups including those that are disadvantaged because of race, national or ethnic origin, colour, religion, sex, age or mental or physical disability.

The three *Charter* decisions in which challenges have been made to the present law on prostitution are basically unhelpful. In one, the issue was dropped; in a second, the decision of the trial judge finding an infringement of the right to livelihood provision of Section 6, was nullified by a subsequent decision of the Supreme Court of Canada in another case; in the third, the judge rejected the argument on infringement without significant elaboration of his reasons.[1] Despite this unpromising start, by considering both the American experience and trends in Canadian judicial thinking in other contexts, it is possible to venture opinions.

Arguments based on freedom of expression in Section 2 by those engaged in prostitution are unlikely to succeed. Our courts may be reluctant to characterize "expression" as including the communications of those who procure or solicit sexual services. Even if they are not, the need to preserve the prostitute from those who would exploit him or her, and to protect the public from harassment and street crime, are likely to be considered more important social objectives than protecting communications of this type.[2] Accordingly, criminal law provisions which appear to conflict with this right may be justified by the invocation of Section 1.

Also doubtful is the success of the argument used before some courts in the United States that laws prohibiting prostitution or soliciting amount to an interference with the right of freedom of association. The latter right is guaranteed by the *Charter* in Section 2. The view of the American courts is that a distinction has to be made between casual associations, such as those engaged in by prostitutes and customers, which are clearly not protected, and serious attempts to form groups dedicated to the political, economic or cultural goals of its members, which are protected.[3] This is an approach which seems likely to appeal to Canadian judges.

It is doubtful, too, whether the argument based on freedom of association would have any more success in the case of the relationship between pimp and prostitute. Although this relationship has some of the attributes of more permanent association, it often involves coercion. Even if the right to association was seen to be applicable in these types of relationships, it would not be difficult for the Crown to make a persuasive argument that the social values in conflict with this exercise of rights are entitled to protection.

458

The right to gain a livelihood, recognized in section 6 of the *Charter*, received brief recognition as a viable basis for challenging the criminality of being the inmate of a "bawdy house" in *R. v. Friesen*.[4] However, that line of argument was effectively closed by the Supreme Court's decision in *Law Society of Upper Canada v. Skapinker*.[5] It stated that the right to a livelihood cannot be divorced from the element of inter-provincial mobility, which is referred to in the same section.

The American courts, showing a significant degree of inventiveness, have developed the right to privacy as a constitutionally protected right. The right, which seems to reflect the view that personal autonomy is important in the modern state, has been used to strike down legislation directed at private sexual conduct, for example, the use of contraceptives by married persons, their sale to unmarried persons, and the termination of a pregnancy.[6] However, the courts in the United States have concluded that prostitution, because it is by its very nature commercialized, has thereby a public character which removes from it the protection afforded by the right to privacy.[7]

Although the Supreme Court in *Southam Inc. v. Hunter*[8] recognized an element of protected privacy in section 8 of the *Charter*, "the right to be secure against unreasonable search or seizure", it is most unlikely that a right to privacy will be readily conceded by the Canadian courts. The *Charter* does not expressly recognize such a general right, and it is unlikely that, at least in the short term, Canadian judges will wish to be as inventive as their American counterparts. If Canadian judges were to recognize such a right, it would, on the basis of the American experience, provide no protection in the case of the public conduct associated with prostitution, for example, soliciting. There may be greater success in appealing to the right in the case of private sexual conduct for a fee, for example, in a bawdy house, although here again, the element of commercialization might prevent recognition of the right. Assuming that a complainant were to leap the infringement hurdle, a court could no doubt find a more important social purpose underlying the proscription, for instance, the need to protect others from exploitation, which would justify the invocation of section 1.

The equality rights in section 15, if subject to broad interpretation by the courts, might afford protection in some prostitution situations. Clearly the provisions in the Canadian *Criminal Code* which proscribe soliciting, the running of bawdy houses and "living on the avails" could all be characterized as discriminatory. Moreover, the patterns of enforcement of the soliciting provision which effectively victimize the prostitute while ignoring the customer, are unequal in their impact.

It is doubtful whether this section will, in fact, provide much solace to the various interests mentioned. The courts are unlikely to apply this section in a vacuum, and can be expected to make qualitative distinctions between both the claimants seeking its protection and the interests at stake. Bawdy house operators and pimps are not likely to rank very high in the scheme of things, and, therefore, have little chance of invoking the section successfully.

Prostitutes may, however, fare better. They have been subject to a long history of discrimination, and their personal liberty is infringed with greater regularity than that of most citizens. Although American jurisprudence has shown little understanding of the social and legal disabilities of prostitutes, the record of Canadian judges, particularly at an appellate level in dealing with the soliciting provisions in the *Code*, suggests a rather more benign attitude.[9]

The viability of section 15 for challenging the unequal enforcement of the law is not at all clear. In the United States this argument has received little or no sympathy. There the courts have imposed a high standard of proof on the challenger to bring in evidence of discriminatory practices, and have added the requirement that the practice be shown to be deliberate. Even then the courts have been prone to accepting the arguments made by police forces favouring this discriminatory type of enforcement.[10] The Canadian courts have not yet had cause to address this issue.

The availability of section 7 as a basis for challenging the law proscribing prostitution-related activities depends, in part, upon whether the courts see it as having purely procedural significance or possessing substantive qualities. If its effect is merely procedural, then it will only avail challengers in situations in which vagueness is alleged. The American experience, as well as a decision of the Ontario Court of Appeal under the Bill of Rights, suggests that the courts are willing to allow the legislatures a fair degree of leeway in the framing of criminal law provisions.[11] Should section 7 be seen as having substantive content, then it could be used to invalidate the abridgment of the right, rather than the process. The latter is an unlikely development in Canada, as the framers of the *Charter* chose their wording to try and obviate that type of intervention by the court, which has been common in the United States, referring to "principles of fundamental justice" rather than "due process". Furthermore, the Canadian courts have a record of caution when it comes to reading fundamental substantive justice into what appear to them to be procedural protections.

The other legal right which may provide a basis for challenge is that contained in section 11(d) of the *Charter* on the presumption of innocence. It is possible that this could be successfully invoked in the case of the operation of the legislative presumptions (reverse onus clauses) in the *Criminal Code*, including several relating to prostitution offences. Canadian courts have already dealt with reverse onus clauses under the *Charter*, in particular in the context of narcotics control legislation.[12] The message is clear: that unless the presumed fact can be rationally linked to the proven fact or facts, the clause may be struck down. Consequently, clauses such as those which presume the character of a disorderly house from a refusal to grant entrance to a peace officer, and living on the avails from being habitually in the company of prostitutes, may well not survive challenge.

This admittedly speculative survey does not leave the members of the Committee entirely confident about the ability of the courts to use the *Charter* to any significant extent in dealing with the human rights problems surrounding prostitution, except in relation to vagueness under section 7 and reverse onus clauses under section 11(d). A more extensive, positive, judicial response to rights arguments in this field will depend largely on the interpretation given to the equality rights in section 15. All that can be said at this stage is that Canadian judges seem inclined to require a strong reason, such as involvement in other forms of criminal activity or the creation of a discernable public nuisance, for convicting prostitutes of criminal offences. Whether this will translate into acceptance of the argument that prostitutes are, or can be, discriminated against as a group, remains to be seen.

Despite this uncertainty, the Committee has made the assumption, in considering the present law and in fashioning recommendations on prostitution, that possible challenges on the ground of offence to the presumption of innocence and infringement of the equality rights of prostitutes, will receive sympathetic consideration by the courts.

Footnotes

1 *R.* v. *Westendorp* (1983), 2 C.C.C. (3d) 330 (S.C.C.); *R.* v. *Friesen* 27 April 1984, unreported (Ont.Prov.Ct.), overruled in *Law Society of Upper Canada* v. *Skapinker* (1984), 11 C.C.C. (3d) (S.C.C.); *Attorney General for B.C.* v. *Couillard* (1984), 14 C.C.C. 169 (B.C.S.C.).

2 See *People of Illinois* v. *Johnson*, 376 N.E. 2d 381 (Ill. C.A., 1978).

3 *Ibid.*

4 *Supra*, note 1.

5 *Law Society of Upper Canada* v. *Skapinker*, *supra*, note 1.

6 *Griswold* v. *Connecticut* 38 U.S. 479 (Sup. Ct., 1965); *Eisenstadt* v. *Baird* 405 U.S. 438 (Sup. Ct., 1972); *People* v. *Onofre* 424 N.Y.S. 2d 566 (Sup.Ct. App.Div., 1980).

7 *In re Dora P.*, 418 N.Y.S. 2d 597 (App.Div., 1979).

8 *Southam Inc.* v. *Hunter* (1984), 11 D.L.R. (4th) 641 (S.C.C.).

9 See *R.* v. *Hutt*, [1978] 2 S.C.R. 476 418; *R.* v. *Whitter and Galjot* (1981), 64 C.C.C. (2d) 1 (S.C.C.).

10 See *People* v. *Superior Court of Almeda County* (1977), 562 P. 2d 1315 (Cal. S.C., 1977).

11 See *R.* v. *Hislop* (1980), 5 W.C.B. 124 (Ont. C. A.).

12 See *R.* v. *Oakes* (1983), 2 C.C.C. (3d) 339 (Ont. C.A.) (reverse onus provision in *Narcotics Control Act* struck down). For reverse onus clauses related to prostitution in Criminal Code see s. 180(1)(a) and 195(2).

Chapter 33

International Conventions and Agreements Relating to Prostitution

The international community has from time to time directed its attention to prostitution. As a result there are international conventions and agreements which either directly or indirectly address the problems of prostitution.

1. The International Conventions on Prostitution

Prior to 1951, the international agreements pertaining to the active sexual exploitation of women were largely focused on the international traffic in women and children, starting with the "white slave trade" and later broadening into female slavery in general as an appreciation of the global dimensions of the "trade" in women and children emerged. Canada is a party to most of these early accords. Remarkably, however, it is not party to the first Convention which addressed and condemned prostitution per se, the *United Nations Convention for the Suppression of the Traffic in Persons and the Exploitation of the Prostitution of Others*, adopted in 1951.[1]

This agreement, which was the first to recognize male as well as female prostitution, focused upon the exploitation of prostitutes as the dominant problem, calling upon states to adopt laws proscribing procuring, pimping and the operation of brothels.[2] At the same time, states agreed not to take repressive measures against prostitutes, and in particular, not to subject them to special registration regimes.[3] The *Convention* also embodies agreement to use social, educational and health services to combat prostitution and to provide for the rehabilitation and adjustment of its victims.[4]

The 1951 *Convention* is the most recent Convention dealing with prostitution, although its importance and the desirability of further states signing it has been underlined from time to time in subsequent reports and resolutions. In 1959, for example, a report prepared for the Economic and Social Council, among other things, rejected the criminalizing of prostitution as a solution to the problem, although it was ready to countenance provisions penalizing its public nuisance aspects.[5] Until recently, however, the 1951

Convention has been largely ignored. Many countries failed to ratify it, or continued to enforce laws contrary to its provisions. It was not until the 1974 Mexico World Conference on the International Year of Women that governments were pressured to ratify the *Convention* and the U.N. was asked to undertake further study of the issue.

In 1982, a report was commissioned by the Secretary-General to examine implementation of the 1951 *Convention*. The report of the Special Rapporteur, M. Fernand-Laurent, issued in 1983, adopted a feminist/human rights approach to the subject of prostitution, emphasizing the unacceptability of discriminatory practices against prostitutes; the link between pornography and the demand for prostitution; the dangers in procuring, especially where children are involved; and the need to develop programs to demonstrate the personal and social dangers in taking up prostitution.[6] The Report also cautioned against requiring prostitutes to denounce their procurers or pimps, until programs are implemented to train and reabsorb them into society. It further recommended that governments consult with and financially support competent non-governmental groups, including prostitutes' groups, to aid in rehabilitation, as long as the groups do not advocate the recognition of prostitution as a profession.

In the wake of the Report, the Economic and Social Council passed a resolution recommending a series of steps by states: to stop discrimination of prostitutes; to curb the pornography industry; to punish all forms of procuring, especially those involving minors; to develop preventative educational programs, and to train and reabsorb into society those leaving prostitution.[7] A resolution was subsequently introduced and passed in the General Assembly in February, 1984 which, after pointing to United Nations initiatives to protect women and the economic and social conditions responsible for prostitution, called upon states to use humane measures, including legislation, to combat prostitution and to provide protection to the victims of prostitution by education, social guarantees and employment opportunities for them.[8]

2. Canada's Position

Canada's failure to become a party to the 1951 *Convention*, seems to flow from its innate fear of accommodating it in the Canadian federal system and especially the need for provincial agreement on educational, social and public health initiatives. This is more plausible than the lame rationalizations that the *Convention* merely consolidated earlier Conventions which Canada had ratified (the *Convention* in fact contained several novel elements). The country's failure to ratify does not necessarily signify a lack of sympathy with its substance. Canada is a party to the *International Bill of Human Rights* and its constituent documents which, in broad terms, seek to end the exploitation of other human beings.[9] It is also a party to the 1979 *Convention on the Elimination of all Forms of Discrimination against Women*.[10] The latter affirms the equality of men and women in all spheres of life and invites parties to "repeal all national penal provisions which constitute discrimination against women".[11] In addition, article 6 states that "States Parties shall take all appropriate measures, including legislation, to suppress all forms of traffic in women and exploitation of prostitution of women".

Canada abstained from supporting the General Assembly Resolution of February, 1984 which sought to implement the Fernand-Laurent Report on the grounds that the resolution inappropriately proposed to "combat prostitution" and was basically sexist in nature; that rather than advancing equality for women, it implied that women needed to be protected; and that it did not address the issue of child prostitution. The Canadian delegation, it seems, was not impressed with the rationale of the Special Rapporteur for the absence of reference to male prostitution, which was that the victims of procurement are largely female and that further study is needed on male prostitution. The fact that child prostitution was addressed in the Report appears to have been ignored.

Apart altogether from Canada's record in relation to formal acceptance or rejection of these agreements and resolutions, the Canadian law on prostitution has at least a formal similarity with the legal regime contemplated by the 1951 *Convention*. The identification is not complete because the law in Canada still penalizes prostitutes who are inmates of "bawdy houses". Moreover, Canadian law enforcement authorities and social welfare agencies are not entirely sensitive to the rights of prostitutes to equal treatment by the law and to dignity. In the area of educational, social, and public health strategies of the type anticipated by the *Convention*, Canada is still at a very primitive stage in its policy.

Footnotes

[1] U.N. Treaty Series, No. 1342, 1951. Generally on this topic see D. Sansfaçon, *United Nations Conventions, Agreements and Resolutions on Prostitution and Pornography*, Department of Justice, Ottawa 1984 WPPP # 3.

[2] *Ibid.*, Arts. 1 and 2.

[3] *Ibid.*, Art. 6.

[4] *Ibid.*, Art. 16.

[5] United Nation, *Study on Traffic in Persons and Prostitution*, Department of Economic and Social Affairs, 1959, New York, 12.

[6] Economic and Social Council, Activities for the Advancement of Women: Equality, Development and Peace, *Report of Mr. Jean Fernand-Laurent, Special Rapporteur on the Suppression of the Traffic in Persons and the Exploitation of the Prostitution of Others*, E/1983/17.

[7] U.N. Economic and Social Council Resolution 1983/30.

[8] General Assembly Resolution (A/RES/38/107).

[9] United Nations, Resolution 217 (III). International Bill of Human Rights; A Declaration of Human Rights in D. J. Djonovich, *United Nations Resolutions, Series I - Resolutions Adopted by the General Assembly*, Vol. II, 1948-49, New York, 1973, 135-43.

[10] United Nations, Resolution 34/180. Adopted by the General Assembly, Dec. 18, 1979.

[11] *Ibid.*, Art. 2(g).

Chapter 34

Legislative Proposals for Changes in the Law Relating to Prostitution

1. Introduction

Attempts have been made in recent years to initiate or introduce legislative amendments to the *Criminal Code* provisions on prostitution. With the exception of amendments to section 195(1) to allow for the prosecution of females, as well as males, for procuring and living on the avails, and the extension of the definition of prostitution in section 179 to include both males and females, these attempts have been unsuccessful.[1]

The Standing Committee on Justice and Legal Affairs of the House of Commons undertook a study of street soliciting in 1982, which resulted in a report the following year. In it, a series of recommendations for amendments to section 195.1. were made. While several of these recommendations were embodied in legislation proposed by the Minister of Justice, the Honourable Mark MacGuigan, during 1984, others were not. Specifically, Bill C-19 introduced by the Minister was designed to extend the application of section 195.1 to customers as well as prostitutes and to define "public place" as it applied to that section, so that a motor vehicle in a public place would be covered.[2] The Bill died on the Order Paper with the subsequent proroguing of Parliament.

2. The Report of Justice and Legal Affairs Committee

After extensively canvassing the views of a wide variety of groups, including police, municipalities, residents' associations, women's organizations, social action societies and legal experts, the Standing Committee on Justice and Legal Affairs of the House of Commons issued a report on street soliciting in 1983.[3] On the basis of its study and of the representations made to it, the majority of the Committee concluded that the state of the law on street soliciting under section 195.1, had not been satisfactory since the decision of the Supreme Court of Canada in *R.* v. *Hutt*.[4] As a result, the police in several Canadian cities had been rendered largely powerless to control street prostitution and its perceptible spread to certain residential areas. A minority of members were not satisfied that the present law had been proved to be inadequate. The Standing Committee, as a whole, concluded that in light of the Supreme Court's decision in *R. v. Westendorp,*[5] any criminal law initiative lay exclusively in the hands of the federal Parliament. The option of consigning the problem of street prostitution to the provinces and municipalities to curb it by licensing strategies, was considered neither practical nor desirable.

The Standing Committee was unanimous in concluding that some clarification of section 195.1 was necessary to ensure that customers as well as prostitutes could be charged under the section. Beyond that, there was a divergence of opinion. The majority of the Standing Committee determined that the way to respond to the unsatisfactory situation was to stiffen the impact of the section. Firstly, they recommended that the definition of "public place" in section 179, which applies to section 195, be amended to read:

> Public place includes any place to which the public have access as of right or by invitation, express or implied; or any vehicle situated in a public place, and further includes any private place that is open to public view.

They further recommended the following changes to section 195.1 itself:

> 195.1 (1) Every person who solicits any person in a public place for the purpose of prostitution is guilty of an offence punishable on summary conviction.
>
> (2) For the purposes of subsection (1), "person" shall be deemed to include the person soliciting the services of a prostitute.

This subsection retained the present summary conviction offence of soliciting and put it beyond doubt that a customer, as well as a prostitute, can be charged with and convicted of it. In addition a new offence was included:

> 195.2 (1) Every person who offers, or accepts an offer, in a public place, to engage in prostitution is guilty of an offence punishable by a fine of not more than $500.00, or in default of payment, by no more than fifteen days imprisonment.
>
> (2) For the purposes of subsection (1), "person" shall be deemed to include the person engaging or seeking to engage the services of a prostitute.

This offence would, as the report puts it, "[lower] the standard of prohibited conduct from soliciting to sexual dealing in a public place, while still requiring an overt act".[6] At the same time, the penalty would be less severe than that for soliciting. In the minds of the majority of the Standing Committee, this offence would make it much easier for the police to enforce the law. What is left unsaid is that to secure prosecutions under the new provision, the police would have to use undercover techniques to induce the prostitute or customer to make or accept an offer. The Committee rejected an alternative formulation suggested by one of its members which would have made an "offer to purchase" the offending act, and thus limit prosecutions to customers.[7]

All the members of the Standing Committee were able to agree on the need for a new offence for the punishment of those who seek to purchase or accept sexual services from juveniles:

> 195.3 Everyone who offers or accepts an offer to engage in prostitution with a person under the age of 18 years, whether or not he believes the person is 18 years or more, is guilty
>> (i) of an indictable offence and is liable to imprisonment for two years,
>
> or
>> (ii) of an offence punishable on summary conviction.

In making this recommendation, the Standing Committee was mindful of the far more comprehensive study of child prostitution undertaken by the Badgley Committee. However, they felt that the problem warranted an immediate response from Parliament. The Committee was unable to achieve unanimous agreement on the question of whether or not a mistake by the accused as to the proper age of the young person, should be considered relevant. The majority felt that it should not be a defence, preferring to rely on the summary conviction option and prosecutorial discretion to relieve any perceived harshness.

Because of the substantial changes involved in these recommendations, and an admitted lack of thoroughness in the evidence presented to the Standing Committee, the majority recommended a mandatory review clause:

> 195.4 The operation of sections 195.1 to 195.3 shall be reviewed by such committee of the House of Commons as may be designated or established by Parliament for that purpose within three years after the coming into force of these provisions, and the committee shall within a year after the review is undertaken or within such further time as the House of Commons may authorize, submit a report to Parliament thereon including a statement of any changes the committee would recommend.

Although the recommendations of the Standing Committee relating to the inclusion of customers within the term of section 195.1, and the extended definition of a public place, were accepted by the government and included in the Bill, the other recommendations were suspended pending further study and report by our Committee.

Footnotes

1 *The Criminal Code Amendment Act* S.C. 1980-2, c. 125, s. 11.

2 *The Criminal Law Reform Act*, 1984, Bill C. 19, c. 48.

3 Report of Justice & Legal Affairs Committee in Minutes of Proceedings of the Justice and Legal Affairs Committee, issue No. 126 (1983).

4 *R. v. Hutt* [1978] 2 S.C.R. 476.

5 *R. v. Westendorp* (1983), 2 C.C.C. (3d) 330 (S.C.C.).

6 Report of Justice & Legal Affairs Committee in Minutes of Proceedings of the Justice and Legal Affairs Committee, issue No. 126 (1983) at 5.

7 *Ibid.*

Section III

Legal and Social Reactions to Prostitution in Other Countries

Summary

In accordance with its mandate, the Committee undertook or had research commissioned into legal approaches and social attitudes to prostitution in a number of other countries. Not surprisingly, the most valuable and instructive information came from countries with social systems and cultural roots similar to those of Canada. In particular, we found the experiences of the United States, England and Wales, Australia, New Zealand and continental European countries helpful in focusing and developing our own views. An examination of the law and social reactions to prostitution in the United States is contained in Chapter 35; that of England and Wales, Australia and New Zealand in Chapter 36; and that of five continental European countries in Chapter 37. Finally, we propose some conclusions in Chapter 38.

Chapter 35

The United States

The United States, with 50 different jurisdictions, and constitutional authority for criminal law reposed largely in the states, exhibits a far more complex pattern of legal proscription and regulation than that in either Canada or Britain. However, there are common elements in the law of a number of states which make it possible to set out at least the general features of the law.[1]

Overall, the law relating to prostitution in the United States is more draconian in substance than its counterparts in Canada or Britain. During the first two decades of the century (the "Progressive Era"), stiff legislation was passed at both the federal and state level to deal with prostitution.[2] This was largely as a result of concern related to a supposed dramatic increase in venereal disease, the "scandal" of white slavery, and the great influx of immigrants who were assumed to be ignorant of American values. Although this legislation has been challenged on constitutional grounds on many occasions, it has emerged largely unscathed from those challenges.

The power of the U.S. Congress to pass criminal law provisions is limited with respect to prostitution. Federal legislation has been limited to the protection of the armed services from prostitution; the denial of entry to aliens for purposes of prostitution; and the interstate transportation of prostitutes or operation of prostitution businesses. The most significant piece of legislation in practice has been the *Mann Act* which was adopted in 1910 to stop the so-called "white slavery" trade.[3]

The major provision in the *Act* proscribes the tranportation of women in interstate or foreign commerce for purposes of prostitution, debauchery or other immoral ends.[4] In practice it has been applied not only to procuring and pimping, but to less evocative situations such as taking a mistress, a potential wife and a secretary over a state line.[5] It is irrelevant that the woman knew and consented as long as the accused had the requisite immoral intent.[6] Special sections are included to deal with the transportation of persons under 21 years of age, and the keeping of an alien woman for prostitution or other immoral purposes.[7]

In recent years, prosecutions under the *Mann Act* appear to have declined, reflecting the existence of more important federal law enforcement priorities as well as the rather dated character of the legislation.

With the exception of certain counties in the State of Nevada in which legalized brothels are countenanced, prostitution or its contexts and side effects are proscribed in every state. The act of prostitution itself is proscribed in 46 states. This means, in theory at least, that there is no immunity for such acts which take place in private. Typically, prostitution is defined as the engaging or the offer to engage with another in sexual conduct for a fee. Soliciting is an offence in 45 states, and loitering in 9. With soliciting there is often the requirement of some overt conduct on the part of the prostitute. Under section 240.37 of the *New York Penal Code*, for example, repeated interference with citizens by stopping them or their cars is required. It is these primarily public offences which are most often used by the police in enforcement.

All states have provisions relating to "pandering" (arranging for or inducing a person to become a prostitute), and to pimping. As well, the vast majority proscribe the keeping of a brothel or "house of assignation". *Red Light Abatement Acts* allow civil actions to be brought against premises used for prostitution, and city ordinances prohibit the operation of massage parlours. With pandering and pimping police enforcement is effectively limited to situations in which a prostitute registers a complaint. In the case of brothels and other sexual service establishments, enforcement again tends to be selective, depending upon citizens' complaints.

Some 20 states have "patronizing" provisions which allow prosecution of customers. Section 232.02 of the *New York Penal Code* provides an example of a definition of patronizing: a person patronizes a prostitute when he pays a fee to engage in sexual conduct, or when he solicits for the purposes of engaging in sexual conduct for a fee. In most states the provisions relating to the practice of prostitution and soliciting and loitering for purposes of prostitution, apply to both male and female prostitutes.

It is still an offence in many states for two adults to engage in "consensual sodomy", whether homosexual or heterosexual, and in the appropriate circumstances, prostitutes and their customers have been charged with that offence. In a minority of states related laws proscribing vagrancy, fornication and adultery have been used to prosecute prostitutes.

As one would expect in a country with such vast demographic divergences, the forms of prostitution and enforcement vary. Despite the seemingly harsh state of the law in almost every jurisdiction, overt prostitution exists and often flourishes in major urban centres such as New York and Los Angeles. In much smaller centres and rural areas there is usually no visible problem, although prostitution often occurs behind closed doors. In large cities, apart from occasional "clamp downs", the police can do little more than "chase" the problem. In an area like Manhattan, for instance, despite the best efforts of the

Public Morals Division, and arrest figures which have climbed from 11,000 in 1979 to 15,000 in 1983, street prostitution thrives.

Prostitution in other forms is dealt with on an admittedly selective basis, in response to citizen complaints and the perception that the local community is suffering. By contrast, given the necessary will on the part of the police, effective enforcement against street prostitution, in particular, is feasible in smaller centres and is no doubt assisted by more general social pressures. Except in those states in which there are loitering provisions, the normal method of enforcement is the use of decoys. They are typically male and the prostitute is usually the victim of the exercise. However, some forces do periodically use female officers as decoys and arrest customers.

The notorious exceptions to the nationwide pattern of law and enforcement in the United States are the counties in Nevada which have legalized brothels.[8] That state has seven counties in which prostitution is legal. In five others, the legalization of prostitution is provided for by local option.

The typical county ordinance contains a preamble which relates the ordinance to the objectives of reducing the incidence of venereal disease and the crime rate. It then goes on to establish a board comprising the county commissioners, the sheriff and the district attorney to authorize brothel licences and to regulate their operations. The ordinance contains details of the licensing procedure, provisions for the registration of each prostitute and a requirement of weekly health examinations for all brothel prostitutes.

Each prostitute must carry a valid police card which is issued only after fingerprinting and a check for any previous police record, excluding prostitution offences. Details of licence fees for the establishments also appear in the ordinance. Some of the ordinances also specify the number and location of the brothels. Municipal codes in the communities which contain brothels are much briefer, merely stating that various forms of prostitution-related activities are illegal, except the operation of a brothel in a specified location or area.

In addition to these official requirements, each community has customs governing the operation of the brothels or "ranches" and the conduct of the prostitutes. These are characteristically very limiting, and in some instances, repressive. In Winnemuca, for instance, prostitutes must leave town on their time off; their families cannot live in the community; their cars must be registered with the police and their use is very limited. Men are not allowed to operate brothels and men other than customers can go to the premises only if on legitimate repair errands. Finally, no non-resident female can visit a brothel or drive through the area, apparently to deter "angry wives" from pursuing their spouses "across the line". If a prostitute breaches one of these regulations her card is confiscated and she has 24 hours to leave town.

There has been increasing criticism of these "customs", the impingement on civil liberties involved and the fact that they lack legislative form or sanction. The authorities are reported to be less than enthusiastic about a move in the latter direction lest it open a debate on the whole issue of legalization.[9]

In recent years, the issue of prostitution has become a matter of vigorous debate in the United States. Civil liberties and feminist groups, as well as prostitutes themselves, have been at the forefront of advocating the decriminalization of prostitution and associated offences such as soliciting and loitering. Their recommendations are based on what they argue is an interference with the prostitute's right to privacy. They also emphasize the constant harassment and abuse to which prostitutes are subjected, and the abject failure of repressive laws to deal with the root causes of prostitution, let alone its annoying features. The Nevada "model" of legalization and regulation is considered, if anything, worse than the status quo, because it approaches a form of legalized servitude.

Legislatures have generally been slow to move. Although more and more states are repealing antiquated provisions penalizing sexual activities in private, there seems to be no action to overhaul the law relating to prostitution. Most courts have taken a conservative approach, rejecting a series of arguments that the prostitution offences contravene the Constitution. Accordingly, criminal and regulatory-law has remained largely intact.

Footnotes

[1] See D. Sansfaçon, *Pornography and Prostitution in the United States* W.P.P.P.#2 at 27-41.

[2] M. Conolly, *The Response to Prostitution in the Progressive Era*, Chapel Hill: University of North Carolina Press, 1980.

[3] The official title was the *White Slave Traffic Act*, U.S. Statutes at Large, 1910, Vol. 36, at 825-7.

[4] *Ibid.*, s. 2421.

[5] *Caminetti* v. *United States*, 242 U.S. 470 (1917); *Rockwell* v. *United States*, 111 F. 2d 452 (1940, Circ.C.A., 9th Circ.); *Simon* v. *United States*, 145 F. 2d 345 (1944, Circ.C.A., 9th Circ.); *White* v. *United States*, 261 F. 2d 907 (1959, Circ.C.A., 6th Circ.); *Cleveland* v. *United States*, 329 U.S. 14 (1946); *Burgers* v. *United States*, 294 F. 2d 236 (Circ.C.A., 9th Circ.), Cert. denied 274 U.S. 747 (1927).

[6] *Qualls* v. *United States*, 149 F. 2d 894 (1945; *Hart* v. *United States*, 11 F. 2d 499 (1926, Circ.C.A., 9th Circ.); *Hattaway* v. *United States*, 399 F. 2d 431 (1968); *United States* v. *Pelton*, 578 F. 2d 701 (1978, Circ.C.A., 8th Circ.).

[7] *White Slave Traffic Act*, U.S. Statutes at Large, 1910, ss 2422-2424.

[8] E. Pillard, "Legal Prostitution: Is it Just?" 2 *Nevada Public Affairs Review* 1982, at 43.

[9] Recent press reports from Nevada suggest that investigation is underway of the conduct of the police in the town Winnemuca in regulating prostitution and the local "ranch".

Chapter 36

Commonwealth Countries

1. England and Wales

The social realities of and legal reactions to prostitution in England and Wales parallel very closely those in Canada. As in Canada, prostitution itself has never been considered a legitimate focus for criminal law proscription, at least as far as females are concerned. Male prostitution, which falls within the designation of indecency between men, is proscribed without the exceptions recognized by section 158 of the Canadian *Criminal Code* (i.e. consensual and private liaisons between two adults of 21 years or older).[1] As in Canada, it is the contexts and side effects of prostitution which normally draw sanctions.

The offences of keeping or permitting the use of premises as a brothel are similar to the equivalent bawdy house provisions in the *Criminal Code*.[2] However, the English law does not penalize the inmates or those found in a brothel. Furthermore, by judicial interpretation, it is not an offence for a single prostitute to use her place of residence for purposes of prostitution.[3]

The *Sexual Offences Act* distinguished between the procuring of a woman and that of a girl under 21 years of age. The former is related to prostitution, the latter to "unlawful sexual intercourse".[4] Unlike their Canadian counterparts, these provisions are brief and to the point. The offence of living on the earnings of prostitution is similar to the Canadian offence of "living on the avails", and is similarly reinforced by a presumption.[5] However, the presumption is wider than that in section 195 of the *Criminal Code,* which includes both living with and being habitually in the company of prostitutes, and the exercise of control, direction or influence over a prostitute's movements.

In the case of street soliciting a distinction is made between the activities of male and female solicitors. Under section 32 of the *Sexual Offences Act* it is an offence for a man "persistently to solicit or importune in a public place for immoral purposes". Therefore, an intention to prostitute is not required. By contrast, section 1(1) of the *Street Offences Act* requires that for a "common prostitute" (i.e. a known female prostitute) to be guilty of an offence she must "loiter or solicit in a street or public place for the purpose of prostitution".

Unlike section 195.1 of the Canadian *Criminal Code*, the Crown has to establish that the woman was a "common prostitute", but has the option of alleging either loitering or soliciting. In practice, the loitering route is used more frequently by the police, because it does not require evidence of importuning or harassment. Furthermore, it can be enforced without resort to undercover stratagems. "Cautioning", an interesting procedure which originated in Scotland, has been grafted onto the law in this area.

Where the police have observed the activities of one who is loitering or soliciting and who has not been previously convicted, they will caution her about her conduct and the implications of continuing to work the streets. If she is found loitering or soliciting a second time, a second caution is issued. A third incident brings a formal charge. This device, which was designed to provide a means whereby novice prostitutes might be persuaded of the error of their ways and directed towards helping agencies, has been a failure in practice, because the "message" is rarely taken.[6]

As evidence that the English law has been less sensitive than its Canadian counterpart to the traditional double standard in culpability, there is no provision under which the customer of a street prostitute can be charged for his part in initiating or carrying through the liaison.

As in other countries, law reformers in England and Wales continue to struggle with the issue of how best to control the less desirable consequences of prostitution. The Criminal Law Revision Committee has been particularly active in this regard, and has canvassed a broad spectrum of opinion in formulating its positions.[7] However, there does not seem to have been the same concern, at a national level at least, to investigate and address the social roots of the problem of prostitution.[8] To date, at least, the assumption seems to be that prostitution is a social fact, and that all that can reasonably be done, apart from haphazard application of social service strategies, is to fashion the law to contain as far as possible the problems of exploitation and public nuisance associated with prostitution.

Despite the fact that the *Street Offences Act 1959* strengthened the law against street prostitution, the law has not been successful in ridding the streets of prostitutes. Indeed, the evidence is that in certain cities and locations they frequent the streets in increasing numbers. The frequency and intensity of enforcement varies between cities and within them, depending upon police priorities and philosophy, the sufficiency of human and financial resources and the level and focus of complaints from the public. Selective enforcement also seems to obtain in relation to the other prostitution-related offences, i.e. running common bawdy houses, procuring and pimping, and the police do not appear to be any more successful in using the law to get at the pimps and procurers than they have been in Canada.

The depth of the public's concern fluctuates depending on whether as individuals or as a group, they feel threatened by prostitution. As in North America, some neighbourhoods tolerate it while others object strenuously.

480

Several recommendations or suggestions have been made in recent years by the Criminal Law Revision Committee for improvements in the law. The Committee has recommended that the present provisions on "brothels" replace that word with a reference to premises used for purposes of prostitution. Moreover, it is suggested that the immunity from prosecution under the law given to a single prostitute working out of her residence should be extended to two prostitutes sharing a residence.

The rationale for this is that such a move would give more security to prostitutes, allowing them to share living facilities and child care responsibilities, and to provide each other with emotional support and companionship. It might also lead to a reduction in street prostitution.

The Committee is not willing to extend the number beyond two, lest what it describes as "nests of prostitutes" are encouraged. Moreover, it is not in favour of prostitutes, even in small numbers, setting up commercial "trick pads" away from home, as this would inevitably lead to the commercial exploitation of prostitution, as well as to unreasonable interference with the use and enjoyment of adjacent premises by neighbours.[9]

The Committee has also considered procuring and living on the earnings.[10] On procuring it has suggested that the present provisions be replaced by more detailed and extensive sections covering the organization of prostitution generally; advertising the services of prostitutes; the arranging or facilitating of the making of contracts for prostitution; and living on the earnings. Such a provision, which would encompass much more than the present law, seems to reflect a strong opinion that the commercialization of prostitution should be hit hard by the law. Included would be the touts, transporters, escort service and massage parlour operators and anyone else advancing prostitution.

On pimping, the Committee sees the direction or control of the prostitute as more disturbing than merely living on the earnings and would make that the focus of the law, elevating it from the position of a mere presumption.

With street prostitution, the Committee has recommended the dropping of the term "common" as pejorative, but insists on retaining the condition that the accused be a prostitute. Obviously sensitive to criticisms that the present law embodies an unjustifiable double standard, they have further recommended the addition of an accosting offence which would cover the use of a motor vehicle for the purpose of soliciting a woman for prostitution; the soliciting of a woman persistently for purposes of prostitution, and the soliciting of a woman for "sexual purposes" in a way likely to cause her fear. The double standard is retained, but in a far less extreme form. The Committee wishes to retain the current distinction in the law between male and female soliciting, but suggests that soliciting for "sexual purposes" be substituted for the present reference to "immoral purposes".[11]

The recommendations and suggestions of the Committee are based on the view of the Wolfenden Committee that the function of the criminal law is:

> To preserve public order and decency, to protect the citizen from what is offensive or injurious, and to provide sufficient safeguards against exploitation and corruption of others, particularly those who are specially vulnerable because they are weak in body or mind, inexperienced or in a state of special physical, official or economic dependence.[12]

The Committee also shares the Wolfenden view that it is not the function of law to intrude into the private lives of citizens or to enforce particular patterns of behaviour, other than to carry out the legitimate functions of the criminal law. The law, especially if subjected to the fine tuning suggested by the Committee, will, they feel, strike a reasonable balance between the two objectives of the protection of the public and the immunity of private liaisons. Furthermore, the Committee believes this is an accurate reflection of public opinion.

In short, the Committee seeks to preserve what it sees as a pattern of sound values underlying the evolution of the English law relating to prostitution, and rejects any radical departure from the pattern, either in the direction of regulation or decriminalization, although both were recommended by certain interest groups to the Committee. The report gives little consideration to problems of enforcement, apart from recognizing that they exist, and the impression is left that the Committee sees the role of the law as that of selective pro-active or reactive control.

2. Australia

Unlike the *Canadian Constitution* the Australian Constitution gives jurisdiction over criminal law to the states. There are eight Australian criminal law jurisdictions: the states of New South Wales, Victoria, South Australia, Western Australia, Queensland and Tasmania and the Northern and Australian Capital Territories. This analysis of Australian law on prostitution focuses on five states (excluding Tasmania, the smallest).[13]

Australian criminal law is largely derived from the common law of England. In New South Wales, Victoria and South Australia, significant bodies of statutory-law have been enacted which coexist with the common law except insofar as the legislation has not replaced or amended the common law. In both Queensland and Western Australia, wholesale restatement of the criminal law in codified form has occurred.

The law relating to prostitution varies considerably across the five states. In Queensland and Western Australia it represents an intriguing blend of English law as it was at the turn of the century and several indigenous provisions related to the perceived problems of a frontier society. South Australia retains the traditional core of English law but over the years has instituted modest amendments to remove anacronisms and address special problems. In New South Wales and Victoria the law embodies an amalgam of some traditional provisions and extensive reworking of the law to reflect more modern thinking and realities. In New South Wales this latter movement has involved a degree of decriminalization of prostitution-related activity; in Victoria recent steps have been taken to move from a proscriptive to a regulatory regime for some types of prostitution establishments.

The codified systems in force in Queensland and Western Australia adopt a draconian attitude to sexual offences in general, and prostitution-related activity in particular. Homosexual activity between consenting males remains an indictable offence in both jurisdictions,[14] which means that the prostitution law relates exclusively to female prostitution. Street prostitution is still dealt with as a form of vagrancy, in which merely loitering in a public place for purposes of prostitution is culpable,[15] paralleling the state of Canadian law prior to 1972. As in England, homosexual soliciting in public is related to "immoral purposes" rather than to "prostitution",[16] reflecting the harsher approach to homosexual activity in both jurisdictions.

Like street prostitution, "living on the earnings of prostitution" is considered a vagrancy offence. In Queensland the offence is complemented by a presumption similar to that in section 195(3) of the Canadian *Criminal Code*, i.e., living with or being habitually in the company of prostitutes, but with the alternative factor of "no visible" or "insufficient" means of support.[17] This presumption is absent in the equivalent Western Australian provisions. The latter dubs a person convicted of the offence a "rogue and vagabond".[18]

Both states have offences relating to the keeping of brothels[19] included in vagrancy legislation as well as in their *Criminal Codes*, although it appears that vagrancy legislation is more regularly invoked. The vagrancy provisions apply to the operations of an individual prostitute, as well as to commercial establishments. The law in Queensland includes a subsection which specifically empowers the owner of an establishment which he has reasonable grounds to suspect is being used as a brothel to serve the occupier with a notice to quit.[20] The statute also contains a bizarre provision which requires the occupier of premises suspected of being a brothel by "any two respectable citizens" to provide the Police Commissioner with information on the inmates of the premises on peril of a fine or imprisonment if he fails to do so.[21]

In 1971, public concern at the growth of the massage parlour industry in Queensland led to the inclusion in the vagrancy legislation of a proscription against "using" such establishments for purposes of prostitution.[22] The effect of this provision is to make prostitution per se illegal in such establishments when more than an isolated liaison is involved.

Under the criminal codes of both states, exploitation and procuring is addressed in a series of sections which cumulatively read like section 195(1) of the Canadian *Criminal Code*.[23] A clue to the vintage of these provisions is given by a common subsection which absolves the inmate of a brothel of any legal responsibility for taking and using clothing which is not her own in order to enable her to leave the establishment.[24]

In Queensland, prostitution tends to take place off the streets in massage parlours or through escort services. The police evince some frustration at the present law which is very strict in the case of prostitution establishments such as massage parlours, but makes no special provision for the prosecution of escort services. Although no reforms, other than the 1971 amendments on massage parlours, have been made in recent decades, the authorities are monitoring developments elsewhere and reform is anticipated in the future. In Western Australia official police policy is one of "conditional toleration and containment", with activity directed towards maintaining an acceptable standard of conduct by participants and keeping the trade as free as possible of criminality, public annoyance and the exploitation of juveniles.

The law in South Australia has some similarities with that in the former jurisdictions. However, it seems to reflect a less draconian and dated attitude towards prostitution-related activity, as well as containing one or two unique provisions. The street prostitution provisions follow the pattern of proscribing both soliciting and loitering discussed earlier, but apply equally to both male and female prostitutes.[25] A unique provision allows a police officer to enter any place of public entertainment whenever he thinks proper and order any "common prostitute" to leave it, with penalties attached to refusal to comply, or to returning to the establishment.[26] The provision, which was introduced in 1936, is designed to control prostitution activity in night clubs and bars.

The offence of living on the earnings is similar in substance to that in Queensland, but has a more demanding presumption which requires proof of "living with", being "habitually in the company of" *and* having "no visible means of support".[27] A second unique provision makes it a specific offence to receive "any money paid in a brothel in respect of prostitution".[28] The section makes subject to sanction not only the financial rewards of brothel owners and managers, but also prostitution itself when it occurs in a brothel.

The keeping of a brothel is an offence in South Australia, although prosecution is contingent upon the written consent of a senior police officer.[29] Moreover, not only is there a provision penalizing landlords who permit their premises to be operated as brothels, but also the landlord of leased premises which have been so used can order an assignment of the lease.[30] The Supreme Court of South Australia has recently determined that the common law offence of "keeping a common bawdy house" still obtains in the state with a penalty which is much more severe than that in the *Police Offences Act*.[31] The offences of exploitation and procuring are also recognized, but are stated more simply than their counterparts in Queensland and Western Australia.[32]

In an interesting example of guilt by association, the *Police Offences Act* makes it an offence to consort with or, as an occupier of premises, to "harbour" prostitutes.[33]

Street prostitution in South Australia is minimal and the police report that as a result of greater vice squad attention, the number of brothels has decreased. In contrast, escort services have proliferated because they are not specifically proscribed by existing legislation.

A 1980 report by a legislative committee in South Australia made a number of recommendations for reform of the law relating to prostitution.[34] The most significant recommendation was that certain elements of prostitution-related activity be decriminalized, in particular non-violent procuring and living on the earnings of adult prostitutes, and consorting with reputed prostitutes. The suggested amendments narrowing the definitions of procuring and pimping reflected the committee's view that the law should not intrude into consensual, non-violent relationships between adults. Regarding brothels, the report seems to have accepted the presence of massage parlours in industrial or commercial areas, but stated strongly that the law should be used to prevent their spread to residential areas. The report advocated the retention of anti-soliciting provisions in the criminal law, but recommended their application to both prostitutes and customers. To date, no action has been taken on these recommendations.

New South Wales, the most populous and urbanized state in Australia, instituted major reforms of the law relating to prostitution in 1979 as part of a general policy of decriminalizing "victimless crime".

The offence of street soliciting was repealed in 1979, although under the *Offences in Public Places Act* of that year a more general offence of conduct close to a public place or school causing reasonable people to be "seriously alarmed" or "affronted" was enacted.[35] This provision was utilized to charge homosexuals who were soliciting prior to 1984 when homosexual conduct between consenting adults ceased to be a crime in the state.

Because decriminalization resulted in a dramatic increase in a residential suburb of Sydney, the *Prostitution Act* of 1979 was amended in 1983 to proscribe soliciting near a dwelling, school, church or hospital for purposes of prostitution (as well as the same activity in a school, church or hospital).[36] The effect of this is to prohibit soliciting in residential areas whether by males or females. The provision in the *Offences in Public Places Act* was also amended to refer clearly to persons of either sex engaging in offensive conduct.[37] The effect has been to reduce significantly the level of soliciting in the residential suburb which had been adversely affected.

The *Prostitution Act* of 1979 retained proscriptions against the more repugnant aspects of prostitution. Thus under section 5, living wholly or in part on the earnings of prostitution is an offence which is tied to a presumption similar to that in South Australia.

The present state of the law in New South Wales regarding brothels is confused. Although the repeal of the *Summary Convictions Offences Act* in 1970 abolished brothel-keeping offences, section 6 of the *Prostitution Act* of 1979 made an offence out of using or keeping a massage parlour, bath house, etc. for purposes of prostitution, on the apparent ground that this amounted to false advertising; in other words, a brothel should be called a brothel. However, the *Act* also makes it an offence for an operator to advertise that he is running a brothel.[38] So although it is legal to run a brothel, it is illegal to advertise that fact.

The situation has been further complicated by a decision of the Supreme Court of New South Wales that the *Disorderly Houses Act* of 1943 is still in force, on the ground that the *Prostitution Act* is not a complete code of the law in this area.[39] The 1943 *Act* allows a judge, on application citing reasonable grounds for suspicion, to declare any premises a disorderly house, with penalties for continuing to operate it as such, as well as for those who frequent it. The police have full powers of search and seizure in the case of premises declared a disorderly house.[40] As in Canada, a "disorderly house" includes a brothel or common bawdy house.

On exploitation and procuring, New South Wales has adopted a simple provision making it an offence:

(a) to procure, entice or lead away a person, not being a prostitute, for purposes of prostitution;

(b) by fraud, violence, threat or abuse of authority, or by use of a drug or alcohol to procure, entice or lead away *any person* for purposes of prostitution.[41]

Prostitution has been a problematic and controversial subject in New South Wales in recent years, and a parliamentary sub-committee was established in 1984 to inquire into all aspects of the activity in the state. The Committee will be making recommendations in due course.

Like New South Wales, Victoria has a body of criminal law which is an amalgam of the common law and statute. Street soliciting and even loitering for the purpose of prostitution are still offences, although unlike Queensland, Western Australia and South Australia the provision is drawn so that customers can be charged.[42] Police women posing as prostitutes are used for this purpose. Police practice is to proceed against prostitutes under the loitering option. While the soliciting and loitering provision apply to both male and female prostitutes, it is still possible to charge homosexuals with soliciting for "immoral sexual purposes".[43]

Living on the earnings of prostitution is an offence under the *Vagrancy Act* with a presumption which extends not only to living with or being habitually in the company of, but also to proof of control over action, or influence over the movements of a prostitute.[44] Interestingly, too, a justice may, in response to an "information on oath" that there is reason to suspect that a house is being used for prostitution and that residing within is someone living on the earnings of the prostitute, issue a warrant to the police to enter and search and to arrest the former and bring that person to court to answer a charge.[45]

The law in Victoria in relation to brothels has undergone significant change recently. The purpose of the *Planning (Brothels) Act* of 1984[46] is to legalize and regulate licensed brothels, while providing harsher penalties for prostitution-related activities taking place in unlicensed brothels.

486

The *Act* is a response to the proliferation of massage parlours in the state and flows from the report of a working party set up by the state legislature, which advocated controlling the problem by means of zoning mechanisms.[47] The *Act* deals with;

(a) control of the location of brothels;

(b) control of the ownership of and access to brothels; and

(c) the abolition of offences for prostitution-related activities in brothels.

The 1984 legislation amounts to an amendment of the *Town and Country Planning Act* of 1961.[48] That *Act* sets out a detailed regulatory process for general and specific urban and rural planning in Victoria. By section 9, local authorities are empowered to approve "planning schemes" for those areas which *may* include certain matters, for example, provisions prescribing, prohibiting or regulating the use of land or buildings for specific purposes; on the power of entry and inspection and on enforcement. Under section 27, an authority which has developed a "planning scheme" may issue a permit containing any conditions required by its scheme, subject to various notice and appeal requirements under the *Act*. Rejected permit applicants have a right of appeal to the Minister of Planning and Environment.

The 1984 *Act* does not regulate the location of brothels themselves. Rather it establishes them as a use of land for which a permit may be issued under the *Town and Country Planning Act*. "Brothel" is defined in the *Act* as "Land to which people of both sexes, or of either sex, resort for purposes of prostitution."[49]

Although the definition has been incorporated as a form of land use in the Melbourne Metropolitan Planning Scheme, other municipal authorities have rejected it or have the power to reject it.

The Ministry of Planning and Environment has produced guidelines to assist planning authorities in making brothel location decisions, and to provide a rational and consistent basis upon which to determine permit applications.[50] The guidelines include:

(1) Stipulations on the zones in which brothels may be permitted (office, business, industrial, "public purpose" and special use zones) and prohibited zones (residential, rural, farming, conservation and landscape interest);

(2) Methods of protecting residential property in non-residential zones and retail premises in commercial zones;

(3) Prescribed distances from schools and other institutions to which children resort;

(4) Desirable distances from churches, hospitals and other community facilities;

(5) Requirements for neighbourhood lighting and the clear identification of brothels in multi-use buildings;

(6) Provisions to prevent clustering of such establishments;

(7) Prescriptions on relevant zoning classifications relating to the size of brothels.

The guidelines also specify the procedures to be followed in an application for a brothel permit. All applications are to be considered on their merits in zones in which the use is not expressly forbidden. All applications must be advertized, and outline fully the plans for and detailed operation of the facility. Permits may be issued for a limited time to allow the planning authority to monitor its effect on the neighbourhood.

The 1984 *Act* contains effective measures to ensure that its provisions are not being contravened:

Under section 49A(1A):

(1) A police officer can enter such an establishment at any reasonable time when he has reasonable grounds for believing that an establishment is being used as a brothel, to determine whether contraventions of the planning legislation or scheme are taking place;

(2) By virtue of section 49, the penalties for failing to comply with planning controls have been increased to ($6,000.00 (Aust) maximum for a first offence and $9,000.00 (Aust) for a second, with $600.00 (Aust) maximum for each day of a continuing infraction);

(3) A court may declare that one who contravenes the planning law, scheme or conditions of the permit in operating a brothel is not eligible to hold a permit to run a brothel for up to 10 years according to section 49(1B);

(4) The Supreme Court may declare that an establishment is a proscribed brothel where satisfied that an establishment is being run without a permit, or that certain specified offences are taking place within it, the declaration being publicized in the Government Gazette; the police in turn are empowered to publicize the declaration within the community (section 49F and G);

(5) It is an offence:

(a) to enter or leave a proscribed brothel, unless the accused can prove he was on a lawful purpose, or ignorant of the declaration;

(b) to have a serious criminal record and be found in a proscribed brothel;

(c) to run a business, trade, profession or calling from such an establishment;

(d) for the owner of the premises to allow the establishment to be run as a brothel, unless he took all reasonable steps to evict the occupier; and for an occupier to permit it, unless he can prove that he took reasonable steps to prevent such use (sections 49(I) and 49(M));

(6) The police are given sweeping power to enter the premises forcibly at any time under section 49(N).

Under section 49(E), brothels which are granted permits are subject to prescribed health requirements for the protection of both prostitutes and customers. A permit may not be granted to anyone who has been convicted within the previous five years of a drug related or indictable offence punishable for one year or more, nor to any person where the owner or occupier of the land has been so convicted (section 27A). By the same section, if a permit is granted and it is later found that the grantee is ineligible because of a conviction it may be revoked within 35 days. Furthermore, it is an offence for a permit holder to allow a person under the age of eighteen to enter or remain in a brothel by virtue of Section 49D.

To prevent the concentration of brothels in the hands of one person or company, the law prohibits a person holding an interest in more than one permit; interest is defined in terms of a grant to him personally, to his company, to a business associate, contractual partner or spouse (section 49C).

Although the criminal law which proscribes the operation of brothels and certain activities within them remains,[51] the relevant legislation has been amended by the *Planning (Brothels) Act* of 1984 to abolish penalties for prostitution activities in brothels with a planning permit. Thus it is no longer possible for the operator of a licensed brothel to be convicted of living on the earnings of prostitution, operating, using or leasing premises as a brothel, or keeping a "disorderly house".[52] Moreover, an amendment to the *Summary Offences Act* reduces the possibility that a person can be charged with soliciting in a licensed brothel.[53] The 1984 *Act* has not, however, affected the application of procuring offences.

The major provisions of the *Planning (Brothels) Act* came into operation on July 2, 1984. Certain provisions were not proclaimed immediately to allow an amnesty period for existing illegal massage parlours to obtain planning consent.

Under the *Crimes Act* of Victoria, it is an indictable offence to detain persons against their will in premises for purposes of illicit sex, or in brothels.[54] The *Act* also contains two general and simple procuring provisions which make it an offence to procure or attempt to procure (a) "a person to become a prostitute in any part of the world", and (b) "a person who is not an inmate of a brothel to become an inmate of [one] in any part of the world"[55].

By judicial interpretation, the essence of procuring is that the accused took some action, whether in the form of pressure, persuasion, inducement, proposal or otherwise, which influenced the mind of the other person to engage in sexual conduct, and that the accused intended that result.[56]

The bold steps taken by the state of Victoria in allowing the establishment and maintenance of brothels, subject to those regulations, has not exhausted discussion and debate on prostitution in that state. An "Inquiry into Prostitution" was established by the government in September, 1984 to enquire into and report upon the social, economic, legal and health aspects of prostitution in all its forms insofar as those matters are relevant to the powers and functions of the Victorian Parliament and Government.[57]

The Inquiry must present its report by September 1, 1985 and include recommendations on further reform and amendment of the law.

Communication with the individual in Victoria conducting the Inquiry suggests that it is too early to gauge the impact of the *Planning (Brothels) Act*, although some potential problems are perceived with it. Although it seems to have been accepted with equanimity in urban areas, there has been hostility in rural areas with the result that some rural municipalities are endeavouring to zone out brothels. This has raised questions over whether local government is the proper place to repose jurisdiction. A second concern is that the provisions for enforcement will prove difficult to apply, because of uncertainty over the identity of the real owner. This has lead to a suggestion that it should be the manager who is licensed and takes legal responsibility. Moreover, it seems as though land in zones where brothels may be approved is rising in value. This may mean that only the wealthiest entrepreneurs can afford to operate such establishments. Until more time has passed, it remains to be seen how this combination of decriminalization and planning law will work.

3. New Zealand

The law in New Zealand on prostitution-related activities is contained in three statutes and is similar to that in England and Wales, with one notable exception.

As in Canada, England and Australia, prostitution itself is not a crime. A revised street soliciting provision was introduced in 1981 which makes it an offence subject to a maximum fine for a person to offer "his or her body or any other person's body, for the purpose of prostitution".[58] This provision, which is similar to that proposed by the Canadian House of Commons Justice and Legal Affairs Committee in 1983,[59] is broader than the section it replaced which required both the elements of "loitering" and "importuning".

Living on the avails of prostitution is an offence which is similar in substance to that defined in section 30(1) of the United Kingdom *Sexual Offences Act* of 1956,[60] except that it applies to both male and female perpetrators and contains no presumption.[61]

In New Zealand the procuring provision in the *Crimes Act* states quite simply:

Everyone is liable to imprisonment for a term not exceeding five years who, for gain or reward, procures or agrees to procure any women or girls to have sexual intercourse with any male who is not her husband.[62]

The provisions on keeping, managing or being the lessor or landlord of premises being used as a brothel are modelled on the *Criminal Law Amend-*

ment Act 1885 (U.K.).[63] However, the statutory definition of brothels in New Zealand makes it clear that in contrast with the English situation, the term includes one woman working out of a residence.[64] As in Canada "prostitution" has been interpreted broadly to extend to any indecent sexual act for payment.[65] In recent years the *Crimes Act* has been amended to include a parallel provision relating to homosexual brothels. Interestingly, the maximum penalty for conviction is twice that for the female offence.[66]

The unique feature of the New Zealand law on prostitution-related activities is embodied in the *Massage Parlours Act* of 1978.[67] This statute was passed in response to concern over increasing evidence of prostitution services being provided by massage parlours. However, unlike the state of Victoria in Australia where the reaction has been to allow and regulate the provision of such services by massage parlours, in New Zealand the approach has been to try and stamp it out. The purpose of the legislation then is to control the operation of such establishments with a view to ensuring that they are not used as brothels.

After defining "massage" to include "rubbing, kneading, or manipulating the human body or any part of it, whether for the purpose of relaxing muscle tension, stimulating circulation, increasing suppleness or otherwise" the *Act* proceeds to deal with licensing, and the consequences of running an unlicensed massage parlour.

Section 5(1) of the *Act* requires operators to be licensed, and attaches a $10,000 (N.Z.) fine or three months imprisonment to those who are not. Moreover, under section 6(2)(a) any one who has been convicted of a prostitution-related offence (brothel keeping, living on the earnings, procuring or soliciting), a drug offence, or who has had a licence revoked within the preceding five years, may not apply for a licence.

Under section 8, qualification for a licence must be made to Magistrate's Court; section 11 provides that the Magistrate must satisfy himself that the applicator "is a proper person to carry on the business of operating a massage parlour". No guidelines have been issued to assist this screening process.

For a massage parlour to operate within the law, it must be in the effective control of an approved licensee; masseurs and masseuses must be 18 years of age or more, and not convicted of any of the offences mentioned in section 6(2)(a). A complaint against a licensee can be filed by the police or any other person. Under section 27 a court has power to cancel or suspend the licence, impose a fine or order termination of employment or dismiss the complaint, if improper.

The grounds for cancellation of a licence include: (a) conviction of the licensee or his manager of an offence under section 6(2)(a); (b) a second conviction under the *Massage Parlours Act*; (c) conviction of any offence leading to a conclusion that the licensee is not a proper person to run such an establishment; (d) failure of adequate supervision of masseurs and masseuses resulting in their conviction of a prostitution-related offence or performing acts of prostitution. The court may order the dismissal of an operative who performs acts of prostitution during the course of his or her employment, or who by reason of conviction for any offence is deemed not to be a proper person for such employment (section 32).

Appeal provisions are set out in section 33, which provides a right of appeal against adverse decisions on licences and continued employment to the Supreme Court. Sections 34-39 outline the powers and duties of the police under the *Act*. They are authorized to enter and inspect the licensed premises at any time.

Footnotes

[1] *Sexual Offences Act* 4.5 Eliz. II, 1956, c. 69, ss. 13, 32.

[2] *Ibid.*, ss. 33-35. Furthermore by s. 36 it is an offence "for the tenant or occupier of any premises to be used for the purposes of habitual prostitution".

[3] Home Office, Criminal Law Revision Committee, Working Paper on Offences relating to Prostitution and Allied Offences, H.M.S.O. London, 1982, at 20.

[4] *Sexual Offences Act*, ss. 22, 23.

[5] *Ibid.*, s. 30.

[6] Working Paper on Offences relating to Prostitution, at 30-3 and see Criminal Law Revision Committee, 16th Report, *Prostitution in the Streets*, 1984 Cmnd. 9329, H.M.S.O. London, at 8-9.

[7] *Ibid.*

[8] There is, however, some evidence of concern at the local level, see London Borough of Camden Policy and Resources (Police Sub-Committee), Report on Research Regarding the Establishment of a Specialist Unit to Co-ordinate Services to Prostitute Women, May 31, 1984.

[9] For the recommendation on brothels, see Working Paper on Offences relating to Prostitution at 19-25.

[10] *Ibid.*, at 9-17.

[11] For the recommendation on street prostitution, see Working Paper on Offences relating to Prostitution, and *Prostitution in the Streets*.

[12] *Report of the Committee on Homosexual Offences and Prostitution*, 1957, Cmnd. 247, H.M.S.O., London.

[13] The structure and substance of the Tasmanian *Criminal Code* is similar to that in Queensland and Western Australia. The Australia Capital Territory (Canberra) is governed largely by the law of New South Wales and the criminal law of the Northern Territory is modelled on that of South Australia.

[14] *Criminal Code*, Stat. Queensland 1899, 63 Vic. No. 9, s. 211; *Criminal Code*, Stat. W.A. 1902, No. 14, s. 184.

[15] *Vagrants, Gaming and Other Offences Act*, Stat. Queensland 1931-78, s. 5(1); *Police Act*, Stat. W.A. 1892, No. 27, s. 59.

[16] *Vagrants, Gaming and Other Offences Act*, *Ibid.*, s. 5(1)(b); *Police Act*, *Ibid.*, s. 59.

[17] *Vagrants, Gaming and Other Offences Act*, *Ibid.*, s. 5(1)(c), 55(iv).

[18] *Police Act*, Stat. W.A. 1892, ss. 769(1), 66.

[19] *Vagrants, Gaming and Other Offences Act*, Stat. Queensland 1931-78, s. 8(1)(a); *Police Act*, Stat. W.A. 1892, s. 76 F.

[20] *Vagrants, Gaming and Other Offences Act*, *Ibid.*, s. 8(3).

[21] *Ibid.*, s. 10.

[22] *Vagrants, Gaming and Other Offences Act*, Stat. Queensland 1971, No. 69, s. 8 A.

[23] *The Criminal Code* (Queensland), s. 231, 235; *The Criminal Code* (W.A.), s. 191.

[24] *The Criminal Code* (Queensland), s. 231; *The Criminal Code* (W.A.), s. 194(3).

[25] *The Police Offences Act*, Stat. S.A., 1953, No. 55, s. 25.

[26] *Ibid.*, s. 73.

[27] *Ibid.*, s. 26.

[28] *Ibid.*, s. 28.

[29] *Ibid.*, ss. 27, 28, 30.

[30] *Ibid.*, ss. 29, 31.

[31] *Radak* v. *Daire* (1982) 30 S.A.S.R. 60 (S.C.).

[32] *Criminal Law Consolidation Act*, 1935-75, s. 64.

[33] *The Police Offences Act*, Stat. S.A., 1953, s. 13, 21.

[34] *Report of the Select Committee of Inquiry into Prostitution,* South Australia, 1980.

[35] *The Offences in Public Places Act*, Stat. N.S.W. 1979, No. 63, s. 5.

[36] *The Prostitution Act*, Stat. N.S.W., 1979, No. 71, as amended 1983, No. 12, s. 8 A.

[37] *The Offences in Public Place (Amendment) Act*, Stat. N.S.W., 1983, s. 5(2).

[38] *The Prostitution Act*, Stat. N.S.W., 1979, s. 8.

[39] See *In re Applications of Shepherd*, [1983] 1 N.S.W.L.R. 96 (S.C.).

[40] *The Disorderly Houses Act*, Stat. N.S.W. 1943, No. 39, s. 10.

[41] *The Crimes Act*, Stat. N.S.W. 1900, s. 91.

[42] *The Summary Offences Act*, Stat. Vict. 1966, No. 7405, as amended by the *Crimes (Social Offences) Act*, Stat. Vict. 1980, No. 9509, s. 18.

[43] *Ibid.*, s. 18(b).

[44] *The Vagrancy Act*, Stat. Vict. 1966, No. 7393, s. 10.

[45] *Ibid.*

[46] *The Planning (Brothels) Act*, Stat. Vict. 1984, No. 10094.

[47] See Report by Working Party to the Minister of Planning of Environment on Location of Massage Parlours, Oct. 1983, Melbourne, Victoria.

[48] *The Town and Country Planning Act*, Stat. Vict. 1961, No. 6849.

[49] *The Planning (Brothels) Act*, Stat. Vict. 1984, s. 3.

[50] Guidelines on the Location of Brothels, May, 1984, Ministry for Planning and the Environment, Melbourne, Victoria.

[51] See *The Vagrancy Act*, Stat. Vict. 1966, s. 11. See also s. 12.

[52] See amendments to the *Vagrancy Act*, *Ibid.*, s. 10.

[53] *The Summary Offences Act*, Stat. Vict. 1966, s. 18, 18A.

[54] *The Crimes Act*, Stat. Vict. 1958, No. 6231, s. 61.

[55] *Ibid.*, s. 59.

[56] *R.* v. *Pikos*, [1967] V.R. 89 (S.C.).

[57] Terms of Reference, "Inquiry into Prostitution", Melbourne, Victoria, September, 1984.

[58] *Summary Offences Act* 1981, Stat. N.Z. 113, s. 26.

[59] See Part III, Section II, Chapter 34.

[60] *Sexual Offence Act* 4 & 5 Eliz. II, 1956, c. 69.

[61] *The Crimes Act* 1961 Stat. N.Z. 43, s. 148.

[62] *Ibid.* s. 149.

[63] 48 & 49 Vict., c. 69.

[64] *The Crimes Act* 1961, Stat. N.Z. 43, s. 147(2).

[65] See *R.* v. *Robinson*, [1978] 1 N.Z.L.R. 709.

[66] *The Crimes Act*, 1961 Stat. N.Z., s. 146.

[67] *The Massage Parlours Act* 1978, Stat. N.Z. 13.

Chapter 37

Continental European Countries

The five countries which were researched for the Committee, France, West Germany, Denmark, The Netherlands and Sweden, present a wide range of legal responses to prostitution. At one end of the spectrum is France which has a series of criminal provisions which would be familiar to a Canadian lawyer. At the other is Denmark which, despite a small number of residual criminal provisions, in reality practises decriminalization. Between those poles are Sweden, which until recently at least, had similarities with Denmark but has now moved towards wider proscription, and Germany and The Netherlands which employ a mixture of criminal law and regulation. With the possible exception of France where there seems to be a gap between public opinion and government policy on the legal control of prostitution, the current law is a fairly faithful reflection of public sentiment in each country.[1]

1. France

Until 1946, legalized prostitution existed in France in the sense that brothels ("maisons de la tolérance") were permitted and both they and their inmates subject to regulation. With the abolition of that regime, the substance of the law has developed in a way which approximates the current state of Canadian law.[2]

The *Penal Code* contains a separate offence of "running" or permitting the use of premises which are accessible to or used by the public, for purposes of prostitution. In the case of a conviction for "running", the judge has the power to order closure, revoke the licence or confiscate the assets of the establishment. Furthermore, if a landlord refuses to take action against a tenant convicted of running such an establishment, a judge has the power to terminate the lease.[3]

The *Code* in section 334 also sets out a list of offences relating to procuring and pimping. In addition to those offences which would be familiar to us, the French include: (a) knowingly cohabiting with an habitual prostitute; (b) maintaining a personal relationship with one or more prostitutes and a lifestyle which is out of proportion to personal income; (c) interfering by threats, pressure, ruses etc. with associations working for the reform of prostitutes and the prevention of prostitution. By section 334(1) a series of special circumstances, including the youth of the partner, the use of violence or threats, the carrying of a weapon, a familiar relationship with the partner, and the offender's public position, are considered to be aggravating factors. In the cases of running a brothel, procuring or pimping, the judge also has the power to curtail temporarily the convicted person's civil liberties, for example, the individual's right to vote, as well as to confiscate the profits from prostitution.[4]

It is an offence punishable by a fine for a person to solicit "by means of gestures, words, texts, or by any other means" in a public place in France. By judicial interpretation this has been construed as meaning merely loitering and repeatedly "looking at" passersby.[5]

The *Penal Code* provisions are considered exclusive, in the sense that municipalities may not impose proscriptions on prostitution.

After complaints in 1975 that law enforcement in the area of prostitution was lax, law enforcement authorities stepped up their efforts. Predictably the greatest increase in prosecutions has been for soliciting, a fact which led to a dramatic protest by prostitutes in Paris that same year. Notwithstanding that outburst of sentiment, enforcement in the area of street soliciting remains vigorous. Legislative machinery for the establishment of homes for former prostitutes does exist. However, only a small number of *départements* (counties) have set up such establishments. Since 1975, societies for the aid of prostitutes have been allowed to act as civil claimants in criminal trials for procuring, to demand compensation for the outlay required to assist former prostitutes. Apparently such compensation has been paid, but does not cumulatively cover the expenses actually incurred by the societies.

A public opinion poll conducted in 1978 in France showed that 71% of the population was opposed to the prohibition of prostitution; 50% were in favour of decriminalizing brothels, and 59% considered prostitution a social necessity. Despite this significant degree of doubt about the desirability of the present legal regime, successive governments have chosen to sustain it. The present French government has, however, committed itself to improving the capacity of the police to pursue procurers more effectively.

Recently an inter-departmental committee of the French government reported in favour of decriminalizing the activities of prostitutes, as far as possible, specifically suggesting review of the law on soliciting and living with an habitual prostitute. The committee also favours special education programs for former prostitutes to facilitate their social reintegration.

In 1983, a number of prostitutes organized to secure recognition of prostitution as a normal form of labour, with the same entitlements as other jobs. This organization has not found a sympathetic ear in government, although it is clear that the policies of the tax collector towards prostitutes has mellowed somewhat in the intervening period.

2. West Germany

The West German law on prostitution combines both criminal law proscription, which applies at the federal level and is aimed at the exploitative and commercial elements of prostitution, and by-laws which are enacted under the authority of the states. The by-laws combine both regulatory and proscriptive elements and are directed at its nuisance effects.[6]

The current German *Penal Code* dates from 1973. In introducing the *Code*, the government of the day indicated that the prostitution provisions were not directed to moral harm done by the encouragement of extra-marital relationships but designed to protect the young and the prostitutes themselves. In fact, the provisions reflect this policy choice.

Section 180 of the *Penal Code* makes it an offence to procure for purposes of prostitution a person under the age of 18 years. The section further prohibits the inducing of a person under 21 years to engage in or continue in prostitution. Both offences carry with them the penalty of imprisonment.

Under section 180(a) a person who runs an establishment in which others prostitute themselves is liable to imprisonment for "procuring" if:

(a) the prostitutes are kept in a position of economic or personal dependency;

(b) prostitution is furthered by anything more than the simple provision of rooms;

(c) the prostitutes are provided with lodgings, urged to prostitute or are exploited financially for that purpose;

(d) prostitutes are actively recruited; or

(e) prostitutes under 18 are provided with any sort of facilities.

As the mere provision of rooms to prostitutes is not caught by this section it has been possible for local authorities to authorize or set up so-called "eros centres", (usually apartment blocks with rooms which are rented to prostitutes for reception of customers). The courts have held that the owners or managers of these centres do not fall afoul of the law as long as they provide only basic facilities. Those who run "call girl" agencies, on the other hand, have been convicted under this section.

Pimping is also subject to the federal law. Section 181(a) of the *Code* prescribes imprisonment for anyone who engages in "exploitative pimping". This latter term embraces the elements of exploitation; supervision for financial gain; inducing continuation of a prostitute in the profession; and, arranging contact with clients. The operators of prostitution establishments have been convicted under this section for making introductions. The regular receipt of money, even in large sums, does not by itself constitute "exploitative pimping". There must have been some element of "undue influence" by the accused.

497

Furthermore, merely providing protection to a prostitute does not amount to "supervision" under this section, unless there is also control of payments to the prostitute.

Section 181 of the *Code* also makes it an offence liable to imprisonment to traffic in human persons. This includes the use of force, threat or ruse to induce someone to be a prostitute, and recruiting or abducting someone from a foreign country to perform sexual acts by exploiting that person's vulnerability.

The *Code* penalizes the conduct of prostitutes themselves in only two instances: for repeated violation of local by-laws prohibiting soliciting and for soliciting for clients in the vicinity of schools or other places frequented by young people.

The states have the power under the *Code* to pass by-laws prohibiting prostitution in parts of towns and between certain hours in order to protect the young and public decency. If a by-law is enacted, at least one area must be exempted.

All states, with the exception of West Berlin, have such by-laws designed to control street prostitution. In the state of Hamburg, for instance, the by-law for the City of Hamburg limits public solicitation in the "prostitution areas" to certain hours, except for one area in which it is allowed all day. In the latter, the streets are blocked off and young people and non-prostitute females are not allowed in that area.

Tied in with the by-laws is the power which the states are given under the federal *Law on the Repression of Venereal Diseases*, to demand that prostitutes register themselves and appear for regular medical check-ups. All the states have such regimes. In Hamburg, for instance, all prostitutes are required to register themselves at the office of the central health inspector and to visit the office for a weekly medical examination.

As in the other countries examined, prostitution in West Germany manifests itself in a variety of forms and settings, the street, bars, windows, sex clubs and private premises. The police in the City of Hamburg report that most prostitutes, especially the younger ones, have a relationship with a pimp. The main distinguishing feature in the German situation is the existence of state-approved centres for prostitution. The rental cost in these centres is such that only those with numerous clients can afford them. Advertising in local papers by prostitutes using their apartments or hotels is widely employed. According to police reports, juvenile prostitution is on the increase and there has been a growth in the number of sex clubs outside the official "red light areas". It is also the case that unregistered prostitutes tend to outnumber those who are registered.

Enforcement under the dual regime of criminal law and regulation presents problems as it does in other countries. Enforcement is particularly vigorous and reasonably effective in the approved prostitution areas, and in the neighbourhood of "eros centres". However, as street prostitution usually transcends geographic boundaries, the police do not claim to have entirely contained that particular problem. Investigation of procuring and pimping offences is extremely difficult because prostitutes rarely agree to testify. Even when they do file complaints, prosecution may fail for lack of adequate evidence. It is hoped that newly established police details specializing in organized crime and undercover work will improve enforcement possibilities in this area.

Penalties for prostitution-related offences appear somewhat lenient by Canadian standards. In particular, for the offences which draw imprisonment, i.e., trafficking or exploitative pimping, the average term is one year.

Debate on the law relating to prostitution has been engendered by the women's movement which rejects all repressive measures against prostitutes. In their opinion, the latter result in the victimization of prostitutes without dealing with the root causes of the problem. In the state of Hamburg, the Bureau for the Emancipation of Women established by the state Senate, has urged the repeal of all by-laws prohibiting street soliciting. Moreover the Bureau has criticized the state approval of "red light" areas, because this makes it easier for pimps and landlords to exploit the prostitutes, and has objected to the discriminatory regulations concerning medical examinations. There are signs that this feature of the regulatory system will be dropped in the near future.

3. Denmark

The law relating to prostitution in Denmark, like the law relating to sexual offences in general, has been significantly relaxed in recent decades. This has occurred exclusively through changes in enforcement practice.[7]

The law on prostitution combines both criminal proscription through the *Penal Code* and local police regulation. Two *Penal Code* provisions which were formerly used to penalize prostitutes and their sponsors, the offence of leading "a life of idleness", i.e. not pursuing a lawful occupation, (section 199), and encouraging or inviting indecency or displaying an immoral mode of living, (section 233), are no longer utilized.

Promoting and commercially exploiting prostitution are specifically addressed in the *Code*. By virtue of sections 228 and 229 a wide variety of offences relating to pimping, procuring, keeping a brothel, etc., are punishable. Pimping embraces both actively controlling and passively "living on the avails." Moreover, the provisions are broad enough to catch the man sharing an apartment with a prostitute and the hotel owner or landlord who rents facilities to prostitutes at excessive rents. Apart from those offences which assume a heterosexual relationship, homosexual prostitution is governed by the same provisions.

At the local level, the *Code* provisions are complemented by police regulations which proscribe offensive modes of soliciting. Street prostitution exists in Denmark and is most evident in Copenhagen and other major cities. Window soliciting and large-scale brothels are practically unknown. Private activity seems to revolve around small-scale massage parlours, escort services and call girl operations. Visible sex clubs and saunas are rare. An increase in the number of drug-addicted girls operating as street prostitutes has been noted in the past 15 years, although the Copenhagen police feel the problem is now contained.

As indicated above, sections 199 and 233 are not now enforced. The demise of the former is associated with an increase in unemployment and the fact that social aid is considered a legal source of income. Street soliciting rarely attracts police action, except where it is practised in unusual places. By tradition, street soliciting in Denmark is confined to very small and well defined areas of the cities and towns and there is rarely cause for interference. The police do, of course, intervene when other forms of criminal activity occur.

Enforcement against those involved in the commercialization and exploitation of prostitution has declined considerably since the early 1970s. The average annual figure for convictions for all such offences is 25. The low figure is explained in part by the abolition of the Copenhagan police vice squad in 1971, and by a perceptible decrease in the incidence of exploitative pimping. Although pimping was very prevalent in Denmark in the 1950s and 1960s, prostitutes have become more independent in recent decades. The suggestion is made that decreasing criminality in practice has reduced the need for pimps. Where there is a relationship between a prostitute and a man who is sustained by her, it is, in most cases, voluntary. It is thought that the majority of Danish prostitutes are economically independent, even though they may live with and sustain a husband or "fiancée". It is also perceived that prostitution in Denmark is becoming increasingly "deprofessionalized" in the sense that more and more individuals are working part time.

Prostitution by minors is treated with greater concern, especially where the young person is under 15 or the practice is related to drug dependency. Street level guidance clinics exist in affected neighbourhoods, and both public and private agencies offer assistance. Notwithstanding these strategies, the problem continues to exist and drug dependent juvenile prostitutes remain the most miserable and visible reminder that more needs to be done.

At the level of public opinion, the women's movement in Denmark, as in other countries, has opened up debate on prostitution. However, unlike the debate in Sweden and Norway in which most feminists seem to be in agreement, there is a division of opinion in Denmark. Those who deplore prostitution by and large do not favour more repressive laws even for exploiters or customers (the latter being seen as the victims of closed sexual attitudes), but advocate vigorous social strategies and educational programs to combat prostitution.

Ranged against them is a more radical group, including prostitutes, who see prostitution as a legitimate occupation and entitled to legal and social approval and protection like any other. The latter have organized pro-prostitution groups to further the interests of prostitutes and to challenge the view of anti-prostitution feminists. Despite two reports advocating the liberalization of the prostitution laws, successive Danish governments have eschewed amending or repealing the laws, preferring to minimize their impact in practice.

4. The Netherlands

As in West Germany, there is a dual regime of criminal law proscription and local regulation, although in Holland, it seems there has been significant pressure for prostitution to be dealt with exclusively at the local level.[8]

Since 1911, the Dutch *Penal Code* has contained provisions which penalize the procuring of minors (section 250), habitual or occupational procuration (section 250(2)) and trafficking in women or minors of either sex (section 250(3)). Recently the Dutch Minister of Justice announced his intention to repeal section 250(2). There is also a provision which proscribes "living on the avails" (section 423.2). The Minister of Justice has proposed amending this section of the *Code*, narrowing it to catch only those pimps who by force or threat of it induce prostitutes to share the profits of the business with them.

Municipalities in Holland have the power to and do regulate commercialized prostitution by zoning and licensing regulations. Moreover they use so-called "police regulations" to prohibit the owners and tenants of premises from allowing their property to be used for the purpose of prostitution. Interestingly, in light of the Canadian experience with attempts to control prostitution at the local level, these regulations have been upheld by the High Court, because they have as their purpose the preservation of public order, an objective which is not encompassed by the national criminal law.

Police regulations are also employed to prohibit loitering, standing or sitting in or at a public place, and in some cities have been framed to penalize customers as well. In many cities, however, certain streets or areas are expressly exempted from the operation of the soliciting by-laws. In Amsterdam, the Mayor has the power to issue a list of exempt streets. The High Court has also upheld the constitutionality of the soliciting regulations.

In the area of health regulation, some local authorities provide special clinics for prostitutes, but prostitutes are not obliged to use them.

Prostitution is reported to be fairly widespread in cities and towns in Holland, although the Mayors indicate that the sex industry has not grown in recent years. Male prostitution is most noticeable in the larger cities. It has been noted by authoritative sources that pimping is less prevalent than it used to be. However, increases are reported in the number of prostitutes employed by sex clubs and in the incidence of drug addiction.

On the enforcement side it seems that the authorities have effectively given up prosecuting under the *Penal Code*, except in the case of the procuring of minors. Enforcement is pressed more vigorously at the local level, although on an admittedly selective basis. The objective is, apparently, the stringent enforcement of bawdy house and street or window soliciting regulations outside the exempted areas. Within the exempted areas, the police do not intrude even in commercialized establishments, unless there is evidence of under-age prostitution, prostitution by foreigners, other criminal activity, blatant exhibitionism or expansionism. There is evidence, too, of co-operation between some city governments and the owners of sex clubs to improve the physical condition of exempted areas.

Although prostitution has not been the subject of public opinion sampling in Holland, the community seems to accept the current permissive policy of selective control. There are, as one would expect, complaints from particular communities of the adverse nuisance effects, especially from street and window prostitution. However, municipalities are often willing to respond to complaints by stiffening regulations or their enforcement, and even by offering financial support to disturbed residents who wish to relocate. Rotterdam has been attempting, to date without success, to relocate its "red light" area.

Women's rights groups have also been active in Holland in recent years. They have argued that high priority be given to the prevention of exploitative and coercive forms of prostitution, and that prostitutes enjoy the same legal and social protections afforded to other workers. Some feminist writers have advocated the establishment of commercial sex businesses operated by collectives of prostitutes. They, along with the Mayors of both Rotterdam and Amsterdam, have pressed for the repeal of the adult procuring provision in the *Penal Code* to allow for more local initiative. As indicated above, the government seems to have taken up these proposals.

5. Sweden

Sweden handles prostitution as a matter of law exclusively through its *Penal Code*. However, its ambit is confined to the exploitative elements of prostitution. Sweden is, moreover, one of the few countries which have attempted to deal with prostitution by other social mechanisms, in particular by educational strategies.[9]

The criminal law in Sweden confines its attention in the area of prostitution to procuring, living on the avails and the operation of bawdy houses. Under chapter 6, section 7 of the *Penal Code* it is an offence habitually for personal gain to encourage or exploit another's immoral mode of life, or to induce one under 21 years into such a life. The gravity of the crime and thus the penalty (imprisonment) are increased if the exploitation is widespread or ruthless. "Immoral mode of life" typically embraces more or less occupational female and male prostitution. The encouragement can take place in a variety of contexts, including the operation of a brothel or supplying the prostitutes with the names of clients. Exploitation covers the activities of pimps but also of the landlords who charge exorbitant rents to prostitutes. A lesser penalty is exacted under the same provision for encouraging temporary sexual relations between others.

By virtue of chapter 16, section 8 of the *Code*, a person who obtains or attempts to obtain sexual services from an individual under 18 years is guilty of the seduction of a youth.

The *Real Property Code*, chapter 12 section 42, provides that rent is forfeited and the landlord is entitled to cancel the lease where rented premises are being used for criminal activities. The drafters apparently considered that this extended to premises used for prostitution.

There are no provisions either in the *Code* or at the local level which proscribe soliciting. According to the Committee on Prostitution set up by the Swedish Parliament (Riksdag) which reported in 1981, prostitution has been decreasing in Sweden in recent years, both on the streets and behind closed doors. It is suggested that this decline reflects a general heightening of the social conscience and debate on prostitution, and the more regular intervention of social welfare authorities.

Despite this trend, prostitution is still a major social problem and a visible one in the largest cities. A very small percentage of prostitutes in Sweden are under 18 and homosexual prostitution is a relatively minor problem. At an institutional level, massage parlours and sex clubs providing sexual services exist in some of the major cities. However, with the enactment of a new and restrictive law on live shows in 1982, the number of sex clubs has declined significantly. It is reported that the majority of female prostitutes come from difficult social backgrounds; for example, about 50% of street prostitutes have criminal records. The proportion of drug users seems to vary greatly from locality to locality.

The police enforce the law as effectively as they can, although the absence of a soliciting offence may make the figures appear modest. For the period 1974-1982 convictions for procuring were approximately 30 per year.

At the level of social policy, steps have been taken, especially in Stockholm and Malmo, by both public authorities and social workers to reduce prostitution. After an extensive study by the Committee on Prostitution of Parliament, the Swedish Government introduced legislation in 1981 which included various measures to prevent prostitution.

A central principle of the legislation is that prostitution should not be accepted as a social given and that efforts in many fields are needed to counteract it. More particularly, the society should be able to offer the necessary social and economic security to people to obviate the need to take up prostitution. Furthermore, it is considered essential to provide open and objective education about sexual matters both in school and later in life. It is apparent, therefore, that the statute commits various authorities and organizations to attempt to reduce the causes of and the need for prostitution.

The legislation which became effective in 1982 obliges the Swedish government to fund research on methods of preventing prostitution, and on ways and means of increasing the awareness of both potential customers and young girls of the undesirability of encouraging or engaging in prostitution.[10]

An even more recent statute has been introduced which attempts to reform the law relating to prostitution.[11] The legislation takes up the recommendations of the Committee on Sexual Offences, a parliamentary committee on which the Swedish women's movement is strongly represented. In reviewing the penal provisions relating to prostitution, the committee took as an underlying principle that the purpose of the law should be to penalize all those who are involved in the commercialization of prostitution and the exploitation of prostitutes.

The committee did not, however, advocate stricter laws against customers on the basis that this would tend to drive prostitution underground, thus hampering attempts to help those practising prostitution. The committee did recommend extending liability for those promoting or exploiting another person's prostitution, by removing the requirement of habitual conduct, by adding the offence of financial exploitation, and by penalizing enticing anyone, of whatever age, into prostitution. The committee further recommended that a landlord should be criminally liable for procuring if he allows another to practise prostitution on premises which he owns. This is designed to allow for the prosecution of the owners of brothels and sex clubs, in particular.

Footnotes

[1] This chapter draws upon a study commissioned for the Committee by the Department of Justice. See J. Kiedrowski and J. van Dijk, *Pornography and Prostitution in Denmark, France, West Germany, the Netherlands and Sweden* W.P.P.P.#1.

[2] *Ibid.*, 39-51.

[3] *Code Pénal*, 1982-3, Paris: Dalloz, s. 335(6)

[4] *Ibid.*, s. 335(1)(3)

[5] Cour de Cassation, Crim. 28, Nov. 1962.

[6] Kiedrowski and van Dijk, *Pornography and Prostitution in Denmark, France, West Germany, The Netherlands and Sweden* W.P.P.P.#1, at 63-74.

[7] *Ibid.*, at 17-27.

[8] *Ibid.*, 86-96.

[9] *Ibid.*, 107-119.

[10] Government Bill concerning *Certain Measures Against Prostitution*, 1981-82.

[11] Government Bill concerning *Amendments in the Penal Code (Sex Offences)*, 1983-84.

Chapter 38

Conclusions

The drawing of any firm conclusions from this comparative survey has to be approached with caution. The data are not drawn from the work of a single researcher or research group, so there are differences in methodology which may belie too many assertions about what seems to work and what does not. Moreover, it is also important to be sensitive to the social and cultural differences between countries reflected in different approaches to prostitution, which may make generalizations difficult.

That having been said, some tentative conclusions may be hazarded. In the first place, it seems clear that law by itself enjoys no special claim to be a solution to prostitution within society. Indeed, it seems that those countries, the majority, which have ignored the importance of non-legal, social responses to prostitution have experienced less success in controlling prostitution than those, such as Sweden, Denmark and Holland, which have recognized the value of social strategies in changing attitudes and responding to the human problems associated with prostitution. There is at least the impression that while those countries who use legal mechanisms, especially the criminal law, to deal with prostitution merely chase an ever elusive and growing problem, the states in which at least tentative steps have been taken to try to understand and deal with the causes of prostitution as a social phenomenom, are making some headway. At least they appear to be containing it. In the case of Sweden there is evidence that the employment of social and educational strategies is actually reducing the incidence of prostitution.

Secondly, the survey suggests that there is no necessary correlation between the existence of harsh criminal law provisions and effective control of prostitution. It may be a truism that a legal regime is no better than the level of will and ability to enforce it, but it is a truism which escapes many people including some law enforcement authorities.

The United States which has overall the most draconian provisions on prostitution, with the possible exception of Queensland and Western Australia, has a very uneven record when it comes to effective control of prostitution through the criminal law. In the larger cities on the one hand, the application of the criminal law in most instances is a "will o'the wisp" enterprise which achieves little more than harassment of the prostitutes. On the other hand, in smaller centres, vigorous enforcement and thus effectiveness of the law seems to have had its effect of ridding communities of at least the public manifestations of prostitution. This process is no doubt also assisted in the smaller communities by other factors such as lack of anonymity, and non-legal social pressures.

This variable pattern of enforcement and thus effectiveness of the law seems to be replicated in France, England and Wales, Canada, New Zealand and Australia all of which have emphasized criminal law proscriptions in addressing prostitution.

Thirdly, there is little evidence that decriminalization necessarily results in an increase in prostitution and related criminality. Although the informal Canadian and legislated New South Wales experiences with street prostitution point in that direction, it is not supported by the evidence from The Netherlands and Denmark where the figures for prostitution seem to be stable.

This difference in experience has to be put into context. Comparing the rather piecemeal approach in Canada and New South Wales with the more integrated and extensive decriminalization in the European countries suggests that the impact of decriminalization depends on whether it is a random or planned process. In particular it seems to make a considerable difference in terms of results whether a move to decriminalization is balanced by the replacement of the criminal law with some form of regulation. Despite the romantic notion entertained in some quarters that all will be well with the world of prostitution if only the criminal law is removed, the practical truth, it seems, is that it will not. All of the opportunities for damage, abuse and exploitation remain.

The study suggests that if prostitution is removed from the reach of the criminal law, it will have to some extent to be regulated as any other business, indeed as a particularly risky business, if there is any hope of neutralising the inherent risks to the participant, and of obviating the concern, and indeed harm, it causes to members of the public.

The survey suggests that in what is an imperfect world the most satisfactory short term solution to the problem of prostitution has been achieved in those countries in which, like Denmark, prostitution is operated as a regulated business, or which like The Netherlands, mix selective application of the criminal law with regulation of the trade in defined geographic locations. Of particular note is the fact that in both countries there are reports that with the removal of the threat of criminal prosecution from the prostitutes and acceptance of the regulation of prostitution as a business, the influence of pimps, at least of the odious, exploitative variety has decreased. The reason: prostitutes have found it possible to operate individually without the need of a "protector" and in some instances to organize themselves on a small business basis free from commercial exploitation by others.

508

Although, with the notorious exception of Nevada, the regulatory approach has not attracted significant attention or support in common law jurisdictions, it is worth noting that one Australian state, after considerable discussion, has decided to permit the establishment of regulated brothels, in a way which utilizes existing regulatory structures for land use and which is designed to suit its demographic realities.

The survey, it must be said, does reveal that decriminalization and regulation can present special problems which are as troubling as those which obtain in criminal law regimes. Nothing in the research survey suggests that either the West German or the Nevada regulatory approaches to prostitution merit emulation. In the former, the combination of state approved prostitution apartment blocks and the regimented registration of prostitutes for public health purposes is unappealing. In Nevada there is ample evidence that the "regulation" applied to the running of prostitution ranches at worst borders on bondage and at best involves serious infringements of the civil liberties of those working there. Furthermore, control is reposed at the local level, where the opportunities for venality may be greatest.

The material in the survey suggests that any system of regulation which might replace or coexist with criminal proscription requires both considerable study and careful development. A move in this direction is only likely to be both legitimate and successful if it reflects a genuine attempt to balance all of the interests involved: that of the community in protecting itself from offensive or intrusive conduct; that of the prostitutes and customers in having a safe and healthy environment in which to conduct their liaisons; and that of the state in preserving legality and public order.

Finally, it is clear from the survey that it is crucial to any planned and reasoned approach to prostitution that both the political will and resources be applied which will allow a combination of long term social engineering and short term legal control mechanisms to work. So far, the only country of those surveyed which has given formal recognition to this reality and developed a national commitment is Sweden.

Section IV

Recommendations on Prostitution

Summary

Section IV contains the Committee's recommendations on prostitution. In Chapter 39, an analysis is made of the results of a National Population Study on Pornography and Prostitution conducted for the Committee, as well as of the various options suggested to the Committee in briefs and oral representations. Chapter 40 sets out the specific recommendations and the rationales of the Committee.

Chapter 39

The Range and Character of Suggested Options

During its hearings and through briefs and representations made to it, the Committee heard and considered a wide range of views as to what should be done about the phenomenon of prostitution in Canadian society. We think that it is important to set out the various suggestions that were put to us and the strengths and weaknesses of each as a prelude to elaborating our own recommendations and the rationales for them.

1. The Lack of Consensus

It should be made clear at the outset that there is little evidence of a broad social consensus in Canada on prostitution and what should be done about it. Whatever may have been the situation in the past, when a consensus may have existed, in today's pluralist climate opinion on the matter reflects the diversity of social values and moral perception which we observe and hear around us.

The existence of a significant divergence of opinion is seen quite clearly in the National Population Study on Pornography and Prostitution conducted for the Committee during 1984 which involved a canvass of 2,018 Canadian men and women over the age of 18.[1] The results of the survey are questionable to some extent in that respondents were required to answer multiple questions without necessarily reflecting carefully on the consistency of their answers to them. However, the figures do at least give the impression that opinion is close to evenly divided on what, if anything, should be done about prostitution.

The figures from the survey show that Canadians by a two to one majority (62% against 35%), consider the exchange of sexual services for money unacceptable. Moreover, wide ratios are evident in relation to the perceived harms flowing from prostitution: organized crime (60% to 11%); violence (59% to 16%); venereal disease (69% to 20%); adverse effects on property values (62% to 16%). The ratio diminishes, however, to 53% compared with 42% where the sexual exchange is for something other than money. Moreover, when asked whether they were offended by soliciting by a prostitute and by men looking for a prostitute, a more modest majority (52% to 42% and 56% to 36% respectively) agreed that they found such conduct offensive.

When the figures relating to the acceptability of certain types of prostitution activities and suggestions as to what role the state should play in dealing with prostitution are considered, the lack of a consensus is accentuated. Although only 11% as opposed to 84% found street prostitution acceptable, and 28% as opposed to 67% considered designated "red light" areas acceptable, the ratio shrank to 38% to 55% in the case of brothels, to 45% to 52% in the case of "prostitution in private", and 43% to 52% in the case of escort and call girl services.

The figures relating to strategies reveal that 62% as compared with 29% of the respondents favour toughening the law against prostitutes, and 71% to 6% giving increased power to the police to control prostitution. However, as many as 40% as opposed to 47% said that they favoured decriminalization of prostitution-related activities, and significant numbers favoured the use of various regulatory expedients to control prostitution, for example zoning (61%), and licensing prostitutes (63%). A majority felt that the government should increase social service funding (59% to 33%), and improve social services initiatives in this field (57% to 36%). Despite general support for the adoption of social and one or more legal strategies, a large majority of Canadians evince pessimism over the likelihood of any expedients making a difference. Indeed 92% as compared with 5% felt that prostitution will always exist, no matter what is done to combat it.

These figures suggest that Canadians, by a large margin, consider prostitution to be an unfortunate and undesirable social fact. Moreover, a sizeable majority see it as socially harmful. However, they see it as a social given, and are not sanguine that any expedient to remove it will be successful. Perhaps not surprisingly they are seriously divided and confused when it comes to devising legal strategies to deal with it. Somewhat less doubt is evinced in relation to the desirability of developing social strategies to respond to it.

2. The Briefs and Representations

The briefs and representations which we received fall basically into four categories. First of all, there are those who feel that the way to deal with prostitution is to increase the rigour of the criminal law. The second view, which represents the opposite end of the spectrum, is that prostitution-related activities should, as far as possible, be decriminalized; that is, removed from the embrace of the criminal law, unless they involve other forms of criminal conduct. The third view is that the social reality of prostitution should be recognized and that it should be legalized and subjected to a regulatory form of control. As might be anticipated, there were variations within each of these groupings. Furthermore, there was in some instances overlapping at the edges. In one instance, there was a conscious blending of the criminalization and decriminalization options which represents an additional category.

2.1 Further Criminalization

The view that the criminal law should be stiffened to deal with prostitution varied in both extent and intensity. The most extreme position which was espoused by a very small proportion of those making submissions, mainly representatives of fundamentalist Protestant churches, was that both the act of prostitution and the status of a person as a prostitute should be attacked by the criminal law. This line of thinking depends upon the conviction that the criminal law is a direct and necessary reflection of Christian, or more correctly, Christian Old Testament morality, and that the criminal law must be used as an instrument for restoration of traditional and timeless religious and moral values. The acts of prostitution and being a prostitute are sins against God and therefore crimes against the society.

Although in theory this view has the advantage of removing the present uncertainties in the law and substituting clear and unyielding precepts, it represents a narrow and unforgiving view of both society and human nature. There is no place within it for differences in social and moral opinion and practice which clearly exist in our society, nor for compassion, unless it is tied to a conscious decision on the part of the sinner and wrongdoer to repent. It clearly disregards the right of every individual in Canadian society to be treated with concern for his or her human dignity. Effective enforcement would require the establishment of an extensive and intrusive apparatus of morals police, and thus constant infringements of civil liberties. The failure to set up such an enforcement apparatus would reduce the law to purely symbolic status. While such a statement enshrined in law might provide some solace to those of stern faith who have this rigid view of the world, it would have no relationship to mainstream opinion in the country, and be of no practical value whatever.

Rather more pragmatic reasons exist for the argument, which emanated from a number of sources, that the existing law should be stiffened to make it possible for the police to control street prostitution more effectively and to allow them to secure convictions more easily. This view proceeds from a stated position that, however irksome prostitution in general may be, there is no reason for the law to intrude unless it becomes publicly offensive and harms other citizens. Accordingly, the concern with the law is not what takes place in private, but the public manifestations of prostitution.

This view had two variants. In the first place there were a small number of individuals who live in residential areas affected by street prostitution, especially Vancouver, who felt that the only satisfactory solution to the problem was a return to the "Vag. C." provision of the *Criminal Code* repealed in 1972. This, it will be remembered, allowed the police to arrest and charge women as streetwalkers unable to give a good account of themselves. Although this view was openly espoused by very few presenters, the Committee had at least the impression from some of the comments made by police authorities, and a certain nostalgia for the "good old days", that a return to "Vag. C", or the introduction of a special loitering offence, would meet with the approval of certain segments of the law enforcement community. This view reflects the concern that they should have the least complicated and most effective means of responding to street prostitution.

The second strain of opinion which was widely espoused by the police (representing the official position of the Association of Chiefs of Police), the Mayors and Councils, community and commercial groups and individuals in Vancouver, Toronto, Montréal, Halifax, Niagara Falls and other major cities with residential or commercial areas adversely affected by street prostitution, favoured the adoption of the series of recommendations made by the House of Commons Standing Committee on Justice and Legal Affairs in its 1983 report on street prostitution.[2] Particular emphasis was placed, in these representations, on the addition of a new offence of offering or accepting an offer to engage in prostitution, the application of the law to both prostitute and customer, and the redefinition of "public place" to embrace a motor vehicle in a public place. These changes are seen as necessary to repair the damage done by the Supreme Court of Canada in interpreting section 195.1 as requiring pressing and persistent conduct on the part of the prostitute.

An interesting variant of this approach was that proposed by the brief submitted by the Canadian Advisory Council on the Status of Women which recommended that the new offence recommended by the Standing Committee on Justice and Legal Affairs apply to all solicitations in public places for whatever purpose, rather than being confined to those for prostitution.

There is little doubt that the espousal of either of these two expedients would improve the record of the police in controlling the street prostitution situation. A "Vag. C" or loitering provision would enable them to "clean up" any area where their own priorities or complaints from the public demand it. However, the price to be paid would be reversion to a status offence, in that mere suspicion of being a prostitute in a public place would be sufficient to warrant both charge and conviction. There is nothing to suggest that this would be any more acceptable in our society today than it was in 1972 when the former provision was repealed.[3] Unless there is a move to criminalize prostitution itself, it is difficult to see how it is possible to justify criminalizing the mere fact or suspicion of someone being a prostitute. Moreover, this type of provision is open to the objection that it is quite possible that perfectly innocent parties, for example individuals waiting for their friends in public places, will be caught by it.

The second suggestion is less objectionable in the sense that it requires some evidence of an attempt to enter an agreement to provide or be provided with prostitution services. Moreover, in theory it removes the double standard which has been inherent in the traditional substance of the law. There are, however, difficulties with it. In the first place, its success will depend upon the use by the police of undercover techniques, as they have to have evidence of at least an offer made or accepted, something which it may be difficult and costly to divine by listening devices. There are objections in principle to a system which encourages self-incrimination, especially in an area of activity which is by and large relatively insignificant in its criminality. Secondly, there is the associated reality that the manpower imbalance in police forces between male and female officers is such that it is generally much easier, not to mention more acceptable, for the police to use male, i.e., customer, than female, i.e., prostitute, decoys. Accordingly, while the substance of the law would make no distinction between prostitute and client, there would be a distinct differential in terms of enforcement impact. Thirdly, both this and the previous view fail to recognize the general realities of enforcement of this type of morals provision. The fact that typically police forces are not provided with the resources to enforce prostitution-related offences on other than a random basis and have more important ongoing priorities, suggests that the only consequence of the inclusion of tougher offences in the *Criminal Code* would be to shift the location of the problem rather than to cure it. There is little evidence to suggest that in the days when Vag. C held sway it did any more than to confine street prostitution to those areas where no one would object, or if they did, the objections were not taken seriously. Nothing which the Committee heard or has read suggests that with tougher law of the type recommended, the street prostitution problem will be solved. The most that can be claimed is that it might be better controlled by these strategies.

Although the recommendation of the Canadian Advisory Council on the Status of Women represents a valiant attempt to give the new offence less of a discriminatory flavour, it is unlikely that it would be used in practice for anything else than street prostitution. If that is a correct assumption, the type of provision recommended would be open to all the objections which can be levelled against the narrower formulation.

2.2 Decriminalization

The view that, as far as possible, prostitution-related activities should be removed from the reach of the criminal law, was espoused by a majority of womens' group which took a position on prostitution. They included individual prostitutes, gay rights organizations, groups of and individual social workers, some mainline church groups, civil liberties organizations and a minority of municipal politicians, the most notable being the Mayor of Ottawa, Her Honour Marion Dewar.

Although there were some differences in detail, the representations by these interests advocated the removal of street soliciting from the *Criminal Code*; the repeal of the common bawdy house provisions, or at least their loosening to allow small numbers of prostitutes to work out of their residences; and the use of other *Criminal Code* provisions supplemented by provincial legislation and municipal by-laws, to deal with the nuisances surrounding and associated with street prostitution. In some briefs, too, it was made clear that pimps and procurers should be pursued by-law enforcement authorities with greater purpose.

This view proceeds from the strongly held position that prostitutes are essentially victims of a sexist society who live in a legal twilight zone in which their status is at best uncertain, who are subject to violence from those who use their services or otherwise prey on them, and who are harassed by law enforcement authorities. The observation is made that the law in its present state has not solved the prostitution problem, but rather exacerbated it. Although not condoning prostitution as a way of life, proponents of this view consider that for those adult prostitutes who wish to pursue this lifestyle, they should be able to do so in a way which is consonant with their right to dignity and freedom from exploitation. Moreover, they feel that the removal of legal impediments would provide an opportunity to address the far more important objective of removing the causes of prostitution and providing support systems for both active and reformed prostitutes.

It is difficult to disagree with the critique by those who espouse this view of both the substance and application of the present law and the abject failure of Canadian society to deal imaginatively and humanely with prostitution. There may, however, be problems with the notion that, by sweeping away the provisions in the *Code* specifically relating to prostitution and applying other law, both federal and provincial, adequate control mechanisms will continue to exist. Given the record of both law enforcement authorities and the courts on the applicability of more general *Criminal Code* provisions to prostitution-related problems, there is not too much room for optimism that this complex of provisions will be any more effective than the present law. This would be cold comfort to those who live and work in areas which are adversely affected by street prostitution. The relevant sections could, of course, be amended to focus more clearly on the special context of prostitution activity, but that would hardly amount to a purging of prostitution-related offences from the *Code*. We would merely be substituting one set of prostitution-related offences for another. Similar concerns exist in the case of provincial legislation and municipal by-laws, with the additional complication that the courts, especially the Supreme Court of Canada, have made it clear that any attempt by the provinces or municipalities to enact "criminal law" in this area will be struck down.[4]

There may also be problems with the contention that all that needs to be done is to decriminalize without any concern for the further issue of whether other legal strategies might be needed to control or regulate it. While legitimate concern can be evoked for the lot of prostitutes, it does not necessarily follow that they should enjoy some special immunity from the law which applies to the rest of the population. Although the proponents of this view have great concerns about substituting regulation for proscription, it is difficult to see how some degree of regulation could be avoided, especially where the result of decriminalization would be the creation of possibilities for commercialization of prostitution. There are strong arguments to be made for not only the application of existing legislation and regulations to such establishments, for example labour standards, public health, business licensing and zoning requirements, but also for special provisions which address the special risks inherent in the activity of prostitution.

518

2.3 Legalization (or Regulation)

The third option put before us was that prostitution should be recognized as a social fact, and that, rather than blinding ourselves to this reality and utilizing totally discredited mechanisms of the criminal law to deal with it, we should legalize and regulate it. This line of thinking which was espoused by and large by individual presenters including a minority of municipal politicians, and one residents' group from Vancouver, was not attended by any common view as to how legalization and regulation might best be achieved. The various suggestions included government licensed brothels; the establishment, by zoning, of "red light" districts; the more indirect expedient of the dispersed location of both street prostitution and common bawdy houses by zoning; the licensing of prostitutes, including those working the streets, and the compulsory medical examination of prostitutes.

Among the advantages seen in this approach were the relative ease of enforcement; the acceptance of prostitution as a business and an improved self image of prostitutes operating such enterprises; an attendant reduction of reliance on pimps and other exploiters; the better maintenance of public health, and increased revenue to municipal government from licence fees.

As should already be apparent from the discussion of provincial and municipal control and regulation of prostitution in Part III, Section II, Chapter 31, certain elements of prostitution as a business are already subject to regulation in some parts of Canada, although this is typically not admitted. All of the suggestions received by the Committee advocating legalization favour the extension of the regulatory approach with more openess as to its purpose. Although the approach has some attractions at an intellectual level, there are both moral and practical difficulties with it. The first objection is that this view assumes that prostitution will always exist. For those who see it as a manifestation of a sexist society, that is definitely not an acceptable option, particularly when it results in the establishment of a legal regime which will reinforce sexist values.

Secondly, there is strong sentiment in some quarters that either government-run or even government-licensed prostitution establishments puts the state into the role of endorser of the activity or even that of pimp. While it may be questioned how far the state commits itself to active approval of an activity by merely licensing it in order to control it, the sentiment mentioned will not be easily quieted without a well developed argument as to why this approach is especially desirable. A third concern flows from the record of the one developed system of licensed prostitution in North America, that in Nevada.[5] The evidence suggests that the prostitution ranches in that State operate with little concern for the civil liberties of the prostitutes, and that venality exists in the administration of the system. Unless Canada was to erect a national system of regulation similar to that relating to gun control and gambling, regulation would be in the hands of the provinces and municipalities. Doubt is voiced in particular over whether municipalities will be able or willing to operate regulatory regimes with the necessary degree of commitment, the requisite resources and an adequate blend of humaneness and propriety. Concern is also expressed about the ability and resolve of municipal government to keep out undesirable elements from control of the business. There is the further worry that, if regulation were to be left to the municipalities, an uneven pattern of control and license would emerge, which could turn some communities into veritable "sex havens". Given interest and commitment at the provincial level and necessary resolve to make regulation work, these problems would not necessarily be insurmountable. However, in a decentralized system of government such as ours they need to be carefully weighed.

The legitimate concern about potential infringement of the civil liberties of prostitutes is accentuated in the case of the suggestion that compulsory medical examination should be applied to prostitutes as part of a system of regulation. There is certainly evidence from jurisdictions in which such regimes have operated that prostitutes have been and certainly feel victimized. Moreover, the suggestion is based on the questionable assumption that prostitutes are a high risk group in terms of communicating sexually transmitted diseases.

2.4 A Combination of Further Criminalization and Decriminalization

Finally, the Committee heard and considered an interesting fourth option which blended the toughening of the criminal law and the decriminalization option. In its most developed form, as articulated by Professor Connie Backhouse and a group of women law students at the University of Western Ontario, the argument is that prostitution should not be treated as a social given in Canada and that the law should address its root cause, the apparent need on the part of men to satisfy their particular sexual urges and proclivities through the availability of a special class of women ready to respond for money. It is this male behaviour which creates the need for prostitutes and furnishes the conditions in which other males are able to exploit them, in particular the procurers and pimps. The proponents of this view went on to suggest that we should not, as a society, continue to countenance such exploitative demand and behaviour, and the law should be invoked to penalize firmly and consistently both the consumers of and traders in women's sexual services. In concrete terms this means making it an offence to purchase or offer to purchase the services of a street prostitute, to stiffen the penalties for operating a bawdy house, and living on the avails, and to remove the corroboration and time limitation requirements from the procuring offences. At the same time, the victims of the aberrational behaviour of males, the prostitutes, should be recognized as such and the proscriptions against them removed from the *Code*.

The underlying motivation of this approach is one with which we can empathize. However, there is a fundamental question which may be raised, and this is whether the law is likely to provide the instrument for social change which the advocates of this view desire. It may be argued that it is social strategies such as education and other forms of non-coercive socialization which are the most likely to succeed, and that law can at best play an ancillary role in changing attitudes and behaviour. This approach also depends on acceptance of the thesis that prostitutes really have no desire to engage in this sort of life, and that, even if they do, they should be protected from their own rash choices. It is at least arguable that the presumption should be that an adult person has the responsiblity for making decisions about lifestyle and career and should not be shielded from that responsibility and its consequences unless he or she is being grossly exploited.

In the detailed form in which the proposal is put, there are some inconsistencies of purpose. If the law is to be used as a major strategy for rooting out this form of sexism, it is strange that the legal responsibility of customers should be limited to those who choose to use the services of street prostitutes. There is, indeed, every reason, in principle, why it should also run to those who use the services of prostitutes in private. The problem here is, of course, the one raised above, that society would need a repressive form of morals police to enforce such a broadly based proscription. However, without it the notion that the law has a significant role to play in reducing the demand for prostitution loses a good deal of credibility. It was suggested to the Committee in reply to a question along these lines that by using the law to move prostitution off the streets the securing of such services would be made that much more expensive, which would provide a disincentive to potential male customers. To what extent the "sins of the flesh" are amenable to such reasonable cost/benefit analysis is difficult to determine without the sort of research which would relate the model to the demand for and provision of sexual services with Canada.[6]

It is not beyond the bounds of possibility, too, that a *Criminal Code* provision which distinguished between the buyers and sellers of sexual services would be open to *Charter* challenge under the equality provisions in section 15. To counter the challenge a very convincing argument would have to be made that the relationship between customer and prostitute is so unequal and the prostitute so generally disadvantaged that special protection is warranted.

The Committee has weighed each of these suggested options carefully. Moreover, it has found opinions in most of them with which it can identify. In fashioning its own recommendations, it has been influenced in some respects by the specific suggestions of groups and individuals, in others by the process and substance of the reasoning contained therein, and in yet others, by both.

2.5 Social Strategies

In addition to the range of legal options set before us, a number of groups and individual presenters were very helpful in suggesting various social strategies which should be adopted to deal with prostitution. Indeed, in some cases, the point was made that we should be looking to non-legal strategies and mechanisms to deal with the problem, rather than the blunt instrument of the law. The briefs and presentations which dwelt on these issues came from individuals and groups of social workers; women's groups and individual women; male organizations against the exploitation of women; some mainline church organizations, and several politicians.

The suggestions which were seen as complementary included:

1. Raising public awareness of the incidence of social abuse of and incest with children in Canadian society.

2. Improving not only the enforcement of the law against but also the treatment opportunities for those engaging in sexual abuse and incest.

3. Introducing or improving programs of social and sex education, with emphasis on responsible approaches to sexuality.

4. Applying greater funds and energy to institutions and programs for runaway youths engaged in prostitution, in particular drop-in-centres, hostels, work and recreation programs and the employment of greater numbers of street workers.

5. Dedicating funding to the development of havens and halfway houses for adult prostitutes and their assimilation back into the community.

6. Conducting more extensive research into prostitution as a social phenomenon.

These recommendations reflect a deep and well placed concern to view prostitution as a problem which can only be addressed satisfactorily as one which typically has its roots in childhood sexual and socialization experiences. The report of the Committee on Sexual Offences against Children and Youths (Badgley Committee), the studies commissioned by the Department of Justice for the Committee and presentations by social workers and agencies all suggest that for many prostitutes, the introduction of the trade came during the teenage years. The message is clear that any set of strategies which are directed solely at adult prostitutes will fail.

The Committee has found all of these suggestions useful in formulating its own view of prostitution as a social problem, and in developing its recommendations.

Footnotes

1 Peat, Marwick & Partners, *A National Population Study of Prostitution and Pornography* W.P.P.P.#6.

2 See Part III, Section II, Chap. 34.

3 *The Criminal Code Amendment Act*, S.C. 1972, c. 13, s. 12.

4 *R.* v. *Westendorp* (1983) 2 C.C.C. (3d) 330 (S.C.C.).

5 See Part III, Section II, Chap. 32.

6 For an article which suggests that the use of the law to increase the costs of doing prostitution business does result in a decrease in demand, see M. Fish, "Deterring Sex Sales to International Tourists: A Case Study of Thailand, South Korea, and the Philippines", (1984) 8 *Int. Journ. Comp. and Applied Crim. Justice* 175. There may be difficulties, however, in extrapolating from the specific context of tourist demand to the broader range of domestic demand for prostitutes.

Chapter 40

The Committee's Recommendations on Prostitution

1. Introduction

As a result of its hearings, the research commissioned by the Department of Justice for the Committee and our own research, the Committee has concluded that an overall strategy to deal with prostitution should emphasize both legal and social reform.

The reasons for the existence of prostitution and its continuation are clearly complex and difficult to determine. Further, the reasons which might account for the phenomenon in one society do not necessarily account for its presence in another. Nor is prostitution viewed with the same mix of inevitability, dislike and acceptance that is characteristic of the Canadian response to the situation.

Within Canadian society, prostitution is seen not just as a social phenomenon but as a social problem. That is, it is an issue to which we should direct our attention and resources in order to effect some change in the current situation. As a society we view prostitution from this perspective because of our religious and philosophical beliefs about human nature and sexual relations in particular, and because our legal, economic and social systems have resulted in prostitution being carried out in a certain way.

While religious and philosophical consideration lead to a questioning of whether prostitution should or must disappear from our society, or whether we should and must assume that the selling of sexual services will always be with us, it is evident that the current ways in which prostitution is carried out are problematic from virtually everyone's point of view. We need, therefore, to look at our society to determine whether we can bring about changes which would at least eliminate the most harmful aspects of the current situation.

The analysis of the legal system and its effect on prostitution practises has been the focus of our attention, but we know that prostitution cannot be addressed solely through the law. It is apparent from all the information we have considered that the current practise of prostitution in Canada is also related to three interdependent factors: (a) the pervasiveness of sexism in Canadian society; (b) our partial recognition of the complexities of sexuality and sexual preference; and (c) the failure to develop educational and social programs to assist young Canadians in dealing with problems of sexism, sexuality and sexual identity in a responsible, confident way. These are conditions which are much more likely to be susceptible to long range social planning than to transitory legal expedients.

2. The Economic and Social Responses to Prostitution

Conscious attempts have been made by the federal, provincial and territorial governments to work towards economic and social equality between the sexes, and some of these efforts have borne results. Still, however, the right of women to equal participation and treatment, in all aspects of our society, has yet to be fully realized.

While, as we have suggested earlier, the causes of female prostitution are complex, it is true that economic disadvantage is one of the elements, whether it be in the home and family background of the individual prostitute, in her own living experience or in both. It seems to us that until Canadian society comes to terms with the causes of economic disparity between men and women, then the likelihood that a proportion of women will seek to support themselves and their families through prostitution will continue to exist.

Although economic factors are perhaps more significant in producing female prostitution, they also play a role in male prostitution. Here the economic roots of prostitution are related in part to the problems which disaffected youth may have in surviving in a highly competitive labour market, and in part to the discrimination in employment that some gays, and gay males in particular appear to encounter. The latter problem is accentuated in the case of transsexual individuals who may find themselves virtually unemployable.

Eradicating economic disparity and discrimination in employment will, we realize, take a long time. Nonetheless, we are confident in asserting that one of the reasons, and perhaps the major reason, that women and young people prostitute themselves is economic. To the extent that women have equal opportunity to participate in the economic system then the decision to become a prostitute will not be made because that seems to be the only possible option. Equality in employment cannot and will not be achieved in isolation from other advancements in women's status. Similarly it is our belief that improvements in women's status will signal an acceptance of a greater commitment to equality in our society, that will affect all minority groups and will assist in their full participation in Canadian society, again decreasing the likelihood of prostitution being seen as the only viable career.

526

Recommendation 50

The government of Canada in conjunction with the governments of the provinces and territories should strengthen both their moral and financial commitment to removing the economic and social inequalities between men and women and discrimination on the basis of sexual preference.

The Committee also believes that adequate social programs must be available to support and assist women and young people in need. The present economic climate is conducive to cuts in social services and programs. To the extent that such cuts are made, we believe that more women and young people will see their only means of livelihood being in prostitution. Equally, if social programs are cut the opportunities for prostitutes to move out of the business will be lessened.

Recommendation 51

The government of Canada in conjunction with the governments of the provinces and territories should ensure that there are adequate social programs to assist women and young people in need.

Typically, sex and sexuality in our society have been considered matters outside the legitimate focus of social discourse. It seems to have been assumed that, by a process of osmosis, male and female will develop an understanding of their sexual roles, be able to cope with their sexual feelings and understand how to interact sexually. Not surprisingly, sexual information and self-perception have often come through a variety of extrafamilial and non-professional sources, and in particular, through the strange brew of fact and fiction served up by peers. Accordingly, the deep-seated views that males are naturally aggressive and need to have their sexual appetites satisfied, while females are passive, dutiful and sexually submissive, tend to be projected from one generation to another. We may have hoped that the so-called "sexual revolution" of the 1960's was going to change all of this, and it may be that for some women it has produced release from the sexual subservience of the past. However, in retrospect, it appears as if one of the major consequences of this movement towards sexual liberation may just have been to cause some men to insist on publicizing and glorifying their stereotyped dominance in sexual matters. The liberation of women, in this context, is all too frequently the freedom to be a Playboy bunny or other sex object.

The corollary to the dominance of men, of course, is the subordination of women. The acceptance that women are subordinate and unequal has a lot to do with prostitution: its acceptance as an enduring social phenomenon rests on our acceptance of the notion that women exist, in part, to answer men's sexual needs. Until Canadian society recognizes the seriousness of these wrong perceptions, and the immense personal and social harm which they cause, any chance of creating a social atmosphere which does not, in effect, promote prostitution is slight.

Recently another aspect of our awkwardness with sexuality has manifested itself. We do not seem to have dealt confidently or generously with persons who find that they are homosexual in their orientation. It is hardly surprising that we find an increasing number of males particularly juvenile males, prostituting themselves as a means of exploring and confirming their sexual identity.

Any discussion of the roots of prostitution in the distorted notions of sexuality which exist in our society would be incomplete without mention of the sexual background and experiences of those males who use the services of prostitutes or who exploit them financially and emotionally. As we stated earlier, the Department of Justice research studies reveal precious little about the motivations of customers, procurers and pimps. Nor is there very extensive research literature at all on these players in the game. What research there is suggests that some of these people at least have themselves been victims of sexual abuse or repression which has manifested itself in aberrant and abusive behaviour to women. Others do not appear to have had such experiences but use the services of prostitutes for expedient reasons, which include the desire to have sexual relations which are impersonal and carry no responsibility.

Significant changes in sexual attitudes and practices within a society depend upon both education and other forms of socialization. Clearly, the dividends of such programs are not immediately realized and will take time to have perceptible beneficial impact. However, the Committee feels very strongly that we should make a start now. Our hearings revealed a need for educational programs in Canada specially geared to deal with sexuality in a responsible and sensitive way. We understand that this vacuum is not always attributable to educators. The parents in a community must be responsive to the idea of such programs if they are to be successful, and some parents have serious reservations about the programs in general or a particular program.

It is our belief that governments, federal, provincial and territorial have to take the lead in this area, by funding a significant national program of research into sex and sexuality, and education about these issues which would attract leading experts from both Canada and abroad, and specific pilot projects for use and testing across the country. In particular, it is important, as the Badgley Committee Report points out, that particular attention be directed towards educational programs on sexual abuse and the risks inherent in prostitution. We believe that with the necessary commitment at the governmental level, supplemented by private support, especially from foundations, we can make great progress towards engendering more responsible and mutually caring attitudes towards sex and sexuality among young Canadians.[1] We think it particularly suggestive that the Swedish Government and Parliament have committed that nation in recent years to an ambitious program of this sort.[2]

Recommendation 52

> **The government of Canada, in co-operation with the provinces and territories, should provide financial support for both research into and the implementation of sensitive and relevant educational programs on human sexuality for use in the country's schools; in particular the governments should jointly fund a National Centre and Program in Sexuality and Life Education to bring together the leading scholars and clinicians in the field to conduct research and formulate program and pedagogical models.**

Although the Committee is convinced that long term strategies of the type outlined above are absolutely necessary if, as a nation, we are to begin to remove the causes of prostitution, we also think it highly unlikely that significant results are going to be achieved overnight. Progress will be slow and will demand great patience. In the meantime, prostitution will continue. This means that society will be faced with the question of what to do about those who for one reason or another have been drawn into this life and remain in it, as well as those who have tried it but have decided to leave it. We are also inclined to believe that even with new and more mutually respectful attitudes towards sexuality, there will be some for whom sex will continue to be an impersonal experience for one reason or another, and who will want to purchase or sell it.

Given the likely continuance of prostitution as a social phenomenon, it is vitally important that consideration be directed to the welfare of those who are or have been involved in this life. The research done for the Committee on prostitution in Canada indicates that: (a) there are all too few social agencies and programs which meet the special needs of active or reformed prostitutes; and, (b) even where they do exist, they are viewed with some suspicion by the prostitutes. That the latter is not a necessary concomitant of such initiatives is shown by the relative success of the support provided to male homosexual prostitutes by gay groups, and of some programs for reformed prostitutes.

There is no doubt that there are serious difficulties in developing bonds with active prostitutes. They may be closely controlled by pimps who do not want to have third parties intrude, or, they may want to steer clear of any group or individual who they feel will be judgmental. In the light of these problems, it is important that programs which are developed are voluntary and staffed by people sensitive to the realities of the street scene and who will respond to need, rather than intruding. We hope that former prostitutes will be invited to help in such programs in order to play a very useful role in counselling clients and advising fellow agency workers. We are inclined to believe that, because there is need for flexibility in approach, there is room for initiatives by both public and private agencies, and that public funding should be directed to both. With the necessary incentives and adherence to standards, there are likely to be positive consequences which flow from private community initiative for and committment to programs of this type. Apart from the obvious benefits of community involvement in local problem solving, it is entirely possible that private organizations will be particularly imaginative in programing. Moreover, if they can establish both a good service reputation and a firm funding base in the private sector, they may find it easier to avoid the vagaries of government fiscal policies. It is, however, important that, whatever the agency, the approach be supportive without being judgmental, avoiding at all costs the view that their major objective is reform or (worse still) repentance. This is a field in which misplaced moral fervour or even unthinking condescension can be extremely counterproductive.

Recommendation 53

> **The government of Canada in conjunction with the governments of the provinces and territories should undertake the direct funding or indirect**

financial support of community groups involved in the care and welfare of both practising and reformed prostitutes, so that adequate social, health, employment, educational and counselling services are available to them.

As we have indicated earlier in this report, given the time frame and resources with which we were working, it was not possible for us to commission and sustain the sort of research which would allow a complete picture of prostitution as a social phenomenon. We think that we have discovered enough about it to make the recommendations above, and a series of recommendations for reform of the law. We feel strongly that governments at the federal, provincial and territorial level need to collaborate closely in commissioning further research on prostitution, as a means of progressively informing attempts to remove the economic and social conditions which contribute to prostitution, and to deal with its adverse impact on those who are engaged in it. In particular we think that further research needs to be done on the character and motivations of customers, pimps and other male parties to prostitution; on the careers of prostitutes, including their introduction to the trade and tenure in it; on the working conditions of the complete range of prostitutes, including street prostitutes, call-girls, and operatives in escort services and massage parlours; and on the more pervasive problem of sexual abuse.

Recommendation 54

The government of Canada in co-operation with the governments of the provinces and territories should commission further research on prostitution as a means of informing attempts to address it as a social phenomenon, and to deal effectively with its adverse impact on those who are or who have been involved in .

3. Legal Responses to Prostitution

Although the Committee is convinced that the conditions in which prostitution thrives can only be satisfactorily addressed in the long run by well conceived and well-executed social strategies, it is also of the view that law has a role to play in dealing with it. There is no reason, in our opinion, for insulating the activity of prostitution from the law. To do so would be to attach a special immunity to it which would have no justification whatever, and in particular, would ignore the very real harms, conflicts and opportunities for exploitation which are associated with it.

The assertion that the law should have reference to prostitution does not dispose of the question of how the law should relate to this form of conduct. In our legal tradition it has been the criminal law which has been the dominant vehicle for dealing with it. It is only incidentally that prostitution has fallen within the ambit of administrative regulation. We have thought it important to set out our views about the ways in which the law should apply to prostitution, prior to articulating our specific recommendations.

We believe very strongly that the present law relating to prostitution is unsatisfactory for a number of reasons, some of which relate to philosophy and others to more pragmatic considerations. As so often happens with the development of criminal law, the present *Criminal Code* provisions reflect a number of underlying policies introduced at different times which do not sit well with each other. Moreover, it is clear that there has been a significant divergence between the potential of a particular provision for affecting behaviour and promoting effective enforcement and its record in practice.

We pointed to the two rather incongruous motivations for the criminal law relating to prostitution in Chapter 29: on the one hand, the view that prostitution as a social problem is the product of loose morals amongst women, and on the other, that women must be protected from immoral and devious males. In practical terms, this has resulted in prostitutes taking special legal responsibility for the adverse social consequences of the liaisons they form, and women in general being considered incapable of protecting themselves from "the blandishment of cads and rogues" with secret sexual agendas. As a consequence, women are treated as "whores" or "madonnas" depending on male assessments of their relative worth, without any recognition of their views or feelings, let alone of the problems which give rise to prostitution. Apart altogether from whether this part of the criminal law has any rhyme or reason to it, it reflects a sexist view of women.

The view that women are the more culpable parties in the relationship with customers dies hard. Although, as we have pointed out in the analysis of the present law, the repeal of the "Vag. C" provision from the *Code* removed the most glaring aspect of the double standard, vestiges of it remain. Mention has been made in Chapter 29 of the uncertainty which prevails as to whether section 195.1 extends to both customers and prostitutes, as a result of conflicting appeal decisions in Ontario and British Columbia.[3] Leaving that issue aside, it is clear that enforcement practices, whether in relation to prosecutions under the *Code* provision or municipal by-laws, have invariably focused on the prostitute. From the point of view of the police, this makes operational sense. It is the prostitute who is visible, known, and less likely to be subject to embarrassment if charged. Police forces are still predominantly male in composition, and this feature accentuates such enforcement practices.

While prostitutes still tend to be on the receiving end of the law vis-à-vis customers, they are afforded little effective protection by the law when it comes to exploitation by those who profit from their activities. As we have pointed out in our analysis of the law and its enforcement, it is both difficult and costly to secure convictions for running common bawdy houses, procuring, and living on the avails. Typically, the police have to resort to expensive surveillance and undercover ploys which take both time and money, often without any certainty that a conviction will be secured. Accordingly, the police tend to respond only when complaints are registered by citizens or by prostitutes who have been victimized. Thus the ability of the criminal law to deal with exploiters is much more apparent than real.

Although female prostitutes and their activities have been the focus of the criminal law traditionally, male prostitutes have been almost totally ignored until recently. True, homosexual activity, even in private, was the subject of criminal sanctions and often harsh and intrusive enforcement for many years. However, the application of the law seems only infrequently to have been related to prostitution. Given the draconian quality of the law on homosexuality, there was little chance that those offering homosexual services would do so in public. In private, their conduct was no different from those engaging in sexual activity without payment. The relaxation of the law relating to homosexuality has changed this. Those with a homosexual orientation who wish to offer sex for money, typically teenagers, are no longer reticent about seeking customers in public.

Although the living circumstances of male prostitutes are different in some ways from those of their female counterparts, especially in the absence of pimps, they too are subject to discriminatory treatment. The male street prostitute tends to be viewed with considerable distaste and suspicion by some police officers who find it difficult to identify in any way with someone of a different sexual orientation. Thus, while police officers are often well disposed or at least paternalistic towards female prostitutes, they often despise male prostitutes. The result is that they tend to be rougher and more peremptory in their treatment of the latter, and less likely to assist when he is the victim of criminal conduct, for example, assault or theft. Furthermore, the police record on raiding male prostitution establishments, especially bath houses, has tended to be much more vigorous and aggressive than that on massage or body rub parlors involving heterosexual sex.

Because of the haphazard and inconsistent way in which the law of prostitution has developed, it ignores the tensile quality of prostitution and the linkages between the various forms of prostitution. More particularly, the law, in both its substance and enforcement, fails to recognize the reality that if pressure by the law is exerted in one context or location, it will produce a shift of the activity to another setting or location. This is seen in street prostitution where police charges or harassment in one location will produce a migration or dispersal of prostitutes to other areas which appear to be less subject to police scrutiny and public concern. It is also manifest in the examples of prostitution moving on or off the streets in correlation to vigorous enforcement against street soliciting, soliciting in bars or bawdy house activity.

In the absence of widespread and coordinated campaigns of enforcement, to which neither the police nor the public seem committed, the result is that the law enforcement authorities merely spend their time chasing the problem rather than resolving it. Although it might be objected that this is, to a large extent, the product of the sad fate of section 195.1 at the hands of the courts, it is our impression that it is a problem which afflicts any jurisdiction with criminal law provisions relating to prostitution, even those in which prostitution itself, in all its manifestations, is criminal, such as most jurisdictions in the United States. The enactment of draconian provisions against prostitution simply does not ensure its demise.

The final general criticism to be made relates to the moral and practical ambiguity of the present law. On many occasions at our hearings, we were told by those who favoured the introduction of stiffer provisions relating to street prostitution that they were not concerned with the morality of prostitution, merely the public distress and harm which it causes. It seemed to be implicit in this view that somehow soliciting and prostitution were beyond the reach of law if conducted in private. This is, of course, not the case.

Although, as we have pointed out, the law on prostitution is only enforced in a perfunctory way, it is nevertheless enforced from time to time, even in relation to activities in private. The result is that there is just enough in the way of uncertainty about the prostitute's legal status whether on the street, using a private residence, or while employed by an escort service or massage parlour, that the individual concerned has the sense of being a legal outcast. Needless to say, the greater facility one has for operating in complete privacy and confidence, a facility which is typically a reflection of relative wealth, the easier it is to escape scrutiny. Accordingly, the law in its operation favours those who have the resources to be discreet, while victimizing those who are not so blessed. In the result, while we talk of prostitution being free of legal sanction, we in reality use the law indirectly and capriciously to condemn or harass it, providing no safe context for its operation except that which can be bought by the prostitute of means, or, as is more likely, the well-heeled sponsor or sponsors.

The law on prostitution, as presently constituted, has not achieved what is presumably its theoretical object, that of reducing prostitution (or even of controlling it within manageable limits). Moreover, it operates in a way which victimizes and dehumanizes the prostitute. Change in the law is, in our opinion, clearly needed.

We see no virtue in replacing the present system with a more repressive regime. There is no evidence in the history of this country, or in those countries like the United States which retain a draconian system, that the results of such an approach would justify it. Indeed, we are inclined to think that a move in that direction would subvert any attempt to treat prostitution sensitively as a major social problem. Unlike some of those who appeared before us, who seem to see criminal law as some magic solution to social problems, we are only too aware of its shortcomings. Criminal law can, of course, affect people's behaviour in beneficial ways, and provides a vehicle for society to make its corporate displeasure known when someone has breached its rules. We doubt its validity, however, when it fails to change behaviour, and can only be indifferently enforced. Not even the transcendant symbolic function of criminal law, which is also important, can compensate for these weaknesses.

The approach which the Committee takes stems from its concern to underline the elements of equality, responsibility, individual liberty, human dignity and appreciation of sexuality which we have emphasized in Chapter 2. It is our belief that as long as prostitutes continue to be open to prosecution as, for example, the inmates of bawdy houses or for soliciting on the streets, our concern with prostitution will continue to be misdirected and the law will get in the way of more beneficial social strategies. Although we do not in any way favour people pursuing prostitution as a career, we also believe that adults who determine that they want to pursue that lifestyle and do so without engaging in incidental criminal activity should be able to do so with dignity and without harassment. Accordingly, we are of the opinion that the prostitution-related activities of prostitutes should be decriminalized as far as possible.

We have more sympathy for the prostitute than for the customers whose sexual demands generate the business in prostitution, who do not have to suffer the general hazards and indignities of the prostitute's life and who find it easier to remain anonymous. Yet we find no justifiable basis for singling out customers for special treatment by the criminal law. The suggestion that the criminal law should punish and deter only the male players in prostitution, including the customers, could not, we think, work without the vigorous and extensive enforcement which we have rejected above. Moreover, it again attaches too much significance to legal expedients as the effective instrumentalities of social change. Accordingly, we favour the decriminalization of the prostitution-related activities of customers as far as possible.

We are aware that prostitution-related activities do cause harm and interference to third parties. The activities may be tied in with non-prostitution-related conduct which contravenes other sections of the *Criminal Code*. Moreover, the activities may be conducted in such a way that they cause unreasonable interference with others. In our minds, there is no justification for shielding prostitutes or customers from legal responsibility for criminal acts or for creating definable nuisances. The argument that the prostitutes are victims and, therefore, not accountable for their acts, which was made before us on occasion at the hearings, is, in our opinion, no more compelling than it is in the case of disadvantaged individuals in general. The law, necessarily we believe, is of the view that all adults, with the exception of those who are mentally incompetent, take full legal responsibility for their actions.

Recommendation 55

> **The prostitution related activities of both prostitutes and customers should be removed from the Criminal Code, except insofar as they contravene non-prostitution related Code provisions, and do not create a definable nuisance or nuisances.**

It is not enough, in our opinion, merely to advocate the decriminalization of the activities of prostitutes and customers, subject to the exceptions mentioned. Attention must be directed also to those *Code* provisions which address the commercial and exploitative characteristics of prostitution. This, we believe, must be done in the light of concern for the welfare of prostitutes and for the effect of their activities on others. If prostitution is an inevitable part of life, at least in the short run, then it should operate in the least offensive setting.

To its credit, the law has traditionally sought to deprecate and punish the commercialization and exploitation associated with prostitution. We are inclined to believe, however, that the concern has been too broad. We are of the opinion that prostitution-related activities should not take place in public places because of the offence involved and the proven dangers to prostitutes which the street life produces. The question thus arises whether some leeway should be provided to it off the street. We believe that it should. However, if some allowance is made for its legal operation in private, it should operate in a way which will minimize the chances of harm to third parties and the community at large, reduce the opportunities for commercial crime, and ensure the health and welfare of the prostitutes. The question is how far to go in removing or limiting the present *Criminal Code* provisions in order to achieve these objectives.

With the exception of one member of the Committee, Ms. Ruffo, we have rejected the possibility of removing from the *Criminal Code* all the provisions which deal with the context and side effects of adult prostitution. These sections deal with bawdy houses, procuring and living on the avails, and soliciting. Repealing them completely would mean that the exploitation and coercion of prostitutes could only be dealt with by the general provisions of the *Code*.

Ms. Ruffo is of the opinion that persons engaged in the business of prostitution should be treated like any other person engaged in business. She feels that the maintenance of special regulations in this domain contributes to the continuation of the exploitative schemes already denounced in this part of the Report.

The evidence gathered during public hearings held across Canada supports, in Ms. Ruffo's opinion, her view that persons engaged in the business of prostitution are full members of society, responsible in all respects, liable for their actions and enjoying the same liberty, dignity and equality as any other person. Consequently, Ms. Ruffo objects to supporting the attitude of a paternalistic society which, on the one hand, would create special regulations for persons conducting the business of prostitution, for example, by allowing them to receive their clients in their residence on the condition that they be no more than two, and which, on the other hand, will turn these persons into criminals if they do not obey that regulation. She observes that, on the one hand, we protect these people as if they were incompetents, while on the other hand, if they break certain rules, which moreover are completely discriminatory, they will be penalized as criminals.

How can the Committee, she asks, in such an inconsistent manner, and at the risk of losing its credibility, talk about equality, dignity and liberty?

Ms. Ruffo notes that persons engaged in other businesses, for example, shoemakers and hairdressers, cannot work in their home unless they have a permit to do so; they are governed by-laws and rules. Besides, they do not find themselves in criminal court if they contravene the provincial laws or municipal regulations concerning their commercial activities. In contrast with persons engaged in the business of prostitution, their commercial activities are not regulated in any special way.

Ms. Ruffo is convinced that Canadian society has been given a rare opportunity to seriously reconsider the problems of inequality and of the exploitation of people for the benefit of others. Obviously, the present situation is not the happiest one, the point is not to perpetuate it unnecessarily.

It is the view of Ms. Ruffo that, in this type of activity as in several others, people are the prisoners of degrading occupations; society must increase its efforts to make it possible for each of them to have access to more gratifying and humane work.

Finally she questions why we should retain special provisions in the *Criminal Code* if we sincerely believe that persons engaged in the business of prostitution have the same right to equality, dignity and liberty as do others. The law she points out, applies to them in the same way as it does to other people and they should be protected by the law in the same way.

The other members of the Committee, while sympathetic to the objectives of this total decriminalization approach, are not satisfied that the more general *Criminal Code* provisions are adequate to take account of the relational exploitation which is apparent in prostitution. Offences such as assault, kidnapping and extortion tend to concentrate upon single incident criminality. Moreover, we worry lest removing from the *Code* all mention of the exploitation of prostitutes by bawdy house operators, pimps and procurers simply appears to endorse the activities of these potential exploiters. Thus, we think that the criminal law should continue to concern itself with prostitution establishments (bawdy houses), procuring, and living on the avails. However, we think that the constraints on these activities should be narrowed in ambit.

Over and above these concerns with the criminal law, we are not at all sure that in the absence of greater discussion and debate between the various levels of government, the result of a total devolution now of legal responsibility to the provinces and municipalities would produce the anticipated result. Indeed, we incline to the view that there would be significant resistance by provincial and municipal authorities to devising regulatory regimes to replace the present complex of criminal law provisions.

We think that the procuring and living on the avails sections of the *Code* should be retained, but the emphasis in them should be on the use or threat of violence, rather than exploitation in general. We take the point that, unless there is a very clear reason for doing so, the criminal law should be used sparingly if at all to protect responsible adults from personal relationships, which although not ideal, are not characterized by the actuality or threat of physical harm. Moreover, we are of the view that including non-coercive relationships in the *Code* achieves nothing in practical terms, because typically they do not give rise to prosecutions. Although we recognize the difficulties in devising more effective methods of enforcing the law against violent and abusive procurers and pimps, we are of the view that any change in the law along the lines suggested should be complemented by the development and funding of special units in police forces to investigate and neutralize their activities. We are aware that certain police forces in the United States which have developed special details to work humanely and sensitively with prostitutes have had some success in pursuing the pimps exploiting these people.

Application of this narrower concept of criminal behaviour would result in individuals, and also some businesses, falling outside the ambit of the criminal law. This would be true, for instance, of escort and dating services which take the business to the client rather than the reverse. From the research reports which were conducted in the Department's research program, we have the impression that these businesses are often run in a business-like fashion, are safe for the prostitutes and are usually much less exploitative than are parasitic pimps. If no force or coercion is used in their operations then they would not be caught by the prohibition. They would, however, be subject to municipal regulation. Municipalities have shown that they have the will, capacity and ingenuity to establish and enforce regulatory regimes, which, while demanding, are by no means impossible for escort or dating services to comply with.

Recommendation 56

> **In the Criminal Code provisions dealing with exploitative conduct other than running a prostitution establishment, the concern of the criminal law should be confined to conduct which is violent or which threatens force; special police details or units should be established, and adequately funded, where required, to investigate and prosecute violent and abusive procurers and pimps; any prostitution business which operates without contravening the Criminal Code should be subject to municipal regulation.**

The present bawdy house provisions proscribe all prostitution establishments, even a single prostitute operating out of a residence. The majority of the Committee favour a relaxation of that requirement. Originally considering an exemption for only one prostitute operating out of her residence (which is the present law in the United Kingdom) we were persuaded in the course of our deliberations to recommend that the exemption extend to two prostitutes working out of their residence. This option may well provide a desirable alternative to working the streets, because we expect it would be free of the exploitative elements normally associated with bawdy houses. By restricting the exemption to those working out of their own residences, we hope we have minimized the chance that entrepreneurs would promote clustering of prostitutes together into some *de facto* commercial premises. Two prostitutes together might well help each other, with rent, child care, and emotional support, instead of exploiting each other. Where two are together, they could do for each other the things which a pimp is sometimes said to do, i.e., provide support or resources in a crisis.

However desirable this small-scale alternative to street activity may be, we are concerned that under the residential exemption which we propose, uncertainty as to the legal status of prostitutes working out of their own homes may remain. Municipalities have the power to zone and license businesses.

Even a *bona fide* exercise of such power by a municipality may reduce opportunities to utilize the one- or two-person exemption. Other problems with the exemption involve disparities between the prostitute carrying on this business and other providers of service: we hesitate to put in place a regime that in fact gives an advantage to the prostitute over other businesses in terms of where they can operate. Problems of avoiding nuisances to neighbours will also have to be contended with. Because the one, or two, person exemption is not, in fact, an ideal solution, we have proceeded beyond it to explore the idea of permitting prostitution activities in small-scale non-residential prostitution establishments. These may well provide a way of avoiding some of the lingering difficulties of an *ad* hoc type of exemption. We are aware, however, that this option itself presents some negative as well as some positive features.

We recognize that this suggestion will be a controversial one and did not reach it lightly. However, given what we consider to be the desirable aim of moving prostitution off the streets, and the questionable status of residential prostitution, it is an option which, we feel, should be considered.

It is our belief that given the opportunities for exploitation and public nuisance in commercialized sex, such an exemption can only be justified where strong and effective regulatory mechanisms are in effect. Moreover, we wish to make it clear that such establishments, if established, should be non-residential and small in scale. They should under no circumstances permit the employment of those under 18. Given the division of powers in Canada, we are convinced that any moves to relax the law on prostitution establishments beyond a one, or two, person exemption of the type suggested must be the responsibility of the provinces.

Recommendation 57

> **The criminal law relating to prostitution establishments should be drawn so as not to thwart the attempts of small numbers of prostitutes to organize their activities out of a place of residence, and so as not to prevent provinces from permitting and regulating small scale, non-residential commercial prostitution establishments employing adult prostitutes.**

4. Amendments to the Criminal Code

4.1 Street Prostitution

Recommendation 58

1. **Repeal section 195.1 of the Criminal Code.**

2. **Amend section 171 of the Criminal Code as follows:**

   SECTION 171(1):   DISORDERLY CONDUCT, INDECENT EXHIBITION, LOITERING, SOLICITING, ETC.

   (1) Everyone who
   (a) not being in a dwelling house causes a disturbance in or near a public place,

538

(i) by fighting, screaming, shouting, swearing or using insulting or obscene language,

(ii) by using sexually offensive remarks or suggestions,

(iii) by being drunk, or

(iv) by impeding or molesting other persons,

(b) openly exposes or exhibits an indecent exhibition in a public place,

(c) loiters in a public place and in any way obstructs persons who are there,

(d) stands, stops, wanders about in or drives through a public place for purposes of offering to engage in prostitution or of employing the services of a prostitute or prostitutes and on more than one occasion.

(i) beckons to, stops or attempts to stop pedestrians or attempts to engage them in conversation,

(ii) stops or attempts to stop motor vehicles,

(iii) impedes the free flow of pedestrian or vehicular traffic, or of ingress or egress from premises adjacent to a public place

(e) disturbs the peace and quiet of the occupants of a dwelling house by discharging firearms, by any of the forms of conduct in paragraphs (a), (b), (c) or (d) of this subsection, or by other disorderly conduct in a public place,

(f) not being an occupant of a dwelling house comprised in a particular building or structure, disturbs the peace and quiet of the occupants of a dwelling house comprised in the building or structure by discharging firearms or by other disorderly conduct in any part of the building or structure to which at the time of such conduct, the occupants of two or more dwelling houses comprised in the building or structure have access as of right or by invitation, express or implied,

is guilty of an offence punishable on summary conviction subject to a maximum fine of $1,000.00.

(2) In the absence of other evidence, or by way of corroboration of other evidence, a summary conviction court may infer from the evidence of a peace officer relating to the conduct of a person or persons, whether ascertained or not, that a disturbance described in paragraph (1)(a), (d), (e) or (f) was caused or occurred.

3. Remove definition of "public place" from section 179(1) of the Criminal Code, and revise the definition of "public place" in section 138 of the Code to read

'public place' includes any place to which the public have access as of right or by invitation, express or implied, doorways and hallways of buildings adjacent to public places and to vehicles situated in public places.

COMMENTARY

Although the partial decriminalization approach adopted by the Committee and evident in its proposals on bawdy houses, procuring and living on the avails detailed below, can be expected to make the provision of prostitution services in private more attractive, it would be naive to suppose that these changes will spell the complete demise of street soliciting. Economic and social realities, especially the relative ease and speed of providing the services required and the desire of the customer for anonymity, the demands of pimps, as well as personal preference, will lead some prostitutes to take to the streets. Furthermore, it is clear that as long as street prostitution exists, annoyance and interference will accrue to others, whether members of the public using the streets or other public places, or residents or occupants of adjacent properties. The Committee is of the view that those who are adversely affected by street prostitution are entitled both to consideration by the law, but more than that, to forms of legal protection which can be effectively enforced. There is to our minds no justification for ignoring the disturbance and interference with the peace and quiet of citizens which is associated with street prostitution. Few, if any, of those who are not currently affected by the nuisance caused by street prostitution would be ready to ignore its negative impact on them, if suddenly and consistently confronted by it. Although doubts were expressed to us in the course of our study about the necessity and merit of using the criminal law to deal with this problem, we have concluded that it must continue to have application. The analysis by the Committee of constitutional problems associated with the enactment of proscriptive law by the provinces and municipalities; the difficulties associated with developing any satisfactory regulatory regime for street prostitutes and the risks and uncertainties of civil litigation, have persuaded us that the *Criminal Code* must be used to deal with the adverse side effects of street soliciting.

Having said that the criminal law has a justifiable role to play here, it is important to state clearly what we think its focus should be. In the opinion of the Committee, it is the nuisance caused to citizens, whether by harassment or obstruction on the street, or by unreasonable interference with their use and enjoyment of property, which is the ill to be addressed. This means that some perceptible interference with members of the public or neighbouring occupiers must be proven. There is no justification, in the minds of Committee members, for reviving the old status offence of being a street walker unable to give a good account of herself. We also believe that it should not be sufficient basis for attaching criminal responsibility that a prostitute or a customer offer to engage in prostitution. Apart from the fact that it is difficult to characterize this as an intolerable interference, the methods which would be employed by the police to secure convictions are unacceptable. While undercover and decoy work may be necessary in certain cases to provide a basis for prosecution in the case of serious crime, we see no justification for its use in dealing with this relatively minor form of criminality. Accordingly, we do not agree with the Report of the Justice and Legal Affairs Committee of the House of Commons that a new offence of "offering to engage in prostitution" should be inserted in the *Code*.

The Committee is further of the view that the present soliciting section of the *Code* is unsatisfactory as a vehicle for proscribing the nuisance effects of street prostitution. Clearly its inclusion in the *Criminal Code* reflects a concern to give soliciting a nuisance characterization. Unfortunately, by interpretation the courts, especially the Supreme Court of Canada in *R. v. Hutt*[4] and *R. v. Galjot and Whitter*[5] have unduly narrowed its application. The notion of nuisance in criminal law extends beyond interference with the individual citizen to interference with the public at large, in effect to interference with the environment represented by streets, public places and neighbouring premises. Viewed in this light there is no reason why the nuisance effects of street prostitution should be confined to the ongoing harassment of one individual, and not extend to the overall interference caused to citizens in the vicinity by a pattern of entreaty to a succession of individuals. Whatever the doctrinal weaknesses in the case law, the Committee is convinced that both the caution with which the courts now treat section 195.1 and the conviction in the ranks of the law enforcers that it is worthless, have deprived it of any force, and that it should, therefore, be repealed.

What the Committee suggests in its place is the amendment of section 171 of the *Code*, a provision which already has a distinctive nuisance flavour to it, so that it will relate clearly to the nuisance problems associated with street prostitution and does so in a way which makes it clear what sort of conduct is unacceptable.

Section 171(1)(a) is revised by making it clear in clause (ii) that sexually offensive language in a public place directed at another person should not be tolerated. This represents a response to the feeling of anger and frustration which many women who live in or travel through areas affected by street prostitution feel at the verbal abuse to which they are subjected by prospective customers of prostitutes. A new paragraph (d) has been added to section 171(1) which deals explicitly with the nuisance impact of street soliciting. This express reference is first of all designed to ensure that the adverse effects of street soliciting are a species of general nuisance conduct, thus making it impossible for the courts to ignore or circumvent them, as they have done in prosecutions relating to prostitution under the section in its present form. Secondly, it seeks to explain, in some detail, just what the nature of the nuisance is. The latter lies not only in the repeated solicitation of one individual, but extends to sequential overtures to members of the public in the area. It is the adverse effect on the locale which is stressed rather than the impact on a particular person. Thus, more than one overture, whether it be in relation to a particular individual, or to two different individuals in sequence, is sufficient to establish a nuisance.

The wording of paragraph (d) also makes it clear that it is designed to apply to customers as well as to prostitutes. It contemplates conduct from a vehicle as well as that on the street, and refers to "offering to engage in prostitution or of employing the services of a prostitute or prostitutes". This formulation would embrace the potential customer on foot or who is curb crawling. Existing paragraph (d) of Section 171(1) has been split into two paragraphs (e) and (f) in the revised section. Paragraph (e) represents an attempt to define more clearly what is disorderly conduct which disturbs those occupying dwelling houses adjacent to public places. As presently worded the paragraph is vague in substance and ambit. The amended form would make it clear that prostitution-related activities of the type caught by the new paragraph (d) could also be proceeded against under new paragraph (e).

Section 171(2) has been retained and made applicable to paragraphs (a), (d), (e) and (f). The purpose of this subsection is to get round the difficulty that prosecution of conduct which disturbs, interferes, or annoys has traditionally depended upon citizen complaint and willingness to testify. Complaints, as the Committee heard during its hearings, are not often forthcoming because of the feared consequences and the trouble of going to court. Moreover, when they do occur they are sometimes suspect as involving unduly subjective judgment on the part of complainants. Subsection (2) allows the prosecution to proceed on the basis of police evidence or corroboration of the circumstances. Given the problems mentioned above, and the reality that in some of these situations it will only be the police officer observing the whole scene who can see its nuisance effects, the Committee believes the subsection should be retained as amended.

We have recommended a higher maximum fine than is the norm for a summary conviction offence ($1,000.00 rather than $500.00) to provide greater flexibility to the courts in the case of the repeat offenders.

With the repeal of section 195.1, the present definition of "public place" in section 179(1) would become redundant. However, there is an identical formulation of "public place" in section 138 which applies to the whole of Part IV of the *Code*, including section 171. It is the Committee's view that this definition should be revised along the lines suggested for two reasons. In the first place, although the definition of "public place" in section 138 has been interpreted by some courts to embrace a vehicle in a public place,[6] the dictum of Spence J. in *Hutt*,[7] which doubted this in the case of the section 179(1) definition, means that the matter needs to be put beyond debate. This is particularly important in the light of our formulation of clause (d) of section 171(1). We have also considered it desirable to make it clear that, for purposes of this section of the *Code*, the definition extends to doorways and hallways of adjacent premises which may not be covered by the wording "any place to which the public have access as of right or by invitation, express or implied".

What are the implications for law enforcement of these provisions, especially the recharacterization of the nuisance effects of street prostitution? First of all, the police will not be able to arrest and charge prostitutes or customers for merely being present in a public place. Nor will they be able to move against them for attempting to make contact with another individual, unless it is part of a sequence of intrusive conduct. Thirdly, they will not be able to proceed by setting up an individual prostitute or customer so that the individual makes an offer to sell or purchase sexual services. What the police will be able to do is to arrest and charge when they have sufficient evidence that the individual or individuals concerned have been guilty of more than one overture, or instance of obstruction whether to a particular member of the public or to the public in the area. This evidence can be obtained by visual surveillance, and/or by the use of unobjectionable plainclothes operations.

Given the option of visual surveillance it seems to the Committee that it would be difficult for the police to argue on operational grounds that it is easier for them to nab the prostitute than the customer. Furthermore, we are inclined to believe that the formulation which we have suggested would make it easier for the police to take proactive measures, such as warning off.

In making these recommendations on street prostitution and its adverse effects the Committee is not naive enough to believe it has found the perfect solution. There is no guarantee that the law will be systematically and evenly enforced. That will depend, as it does with any criminal law provision of this nature, on the commitment of the law enforcement authorities. We do think that the suggested amendments provide the police with an opportunity to assess the problem in a particular area, whether on their own initiative or as a result of a complaint, and to move in if it is out of hand, without resort to heavy or under-handed tactics. At the same time, it provides some leeway to both prostitutes and customers to establish their liaisons on the streets, as long as that is done discreetly. If handled sensitively, we see it as the most satisfactory vehicle for establishing a balance between the various conflicting interests.

4.2 Procuring

Recommendation 59

1. **Substitute for the existing section 195(1) the following:**

   Everyone who
   (a) **by force, threat of force or by other coercive or threatening behaviour induces a person of 18 years or older to engage in prostitution with another person or generally,**
   (b) **by force, threat of force or by other coercive or threatening behaviour compels a person of 18 years or older to continue engaging in prostitution with another person or generally is guilty of an indictable offence and liable to imprisonment for 14 years.**

2. **Repeal subsections (3) and (4) of section 195.**

COMMENTARY

The suggested formulation for section 195(1) flows from our General Recommendation 7 and our belief that conviction for procuring should be related to the use or threat of force by the procurer on his victim. As we have argued above we see no justification in affording the protection of the criminal law to adults who form relationships, which, while not considered in their best interests by others, nevertheless represent an apparently genuine choice on their part. The present law on procuring is so framed that merely persuading an adult person to become a prostitute or to engage in prostitution is an offence. It reflects the view which was dominant at the end of the 19th century that adult women were not capable of making their own decisions on career and lifestyle, and needed to be protected from the guile of licentious males.

Although we believe that women, and indeed men, still need to be protected from forcible or physically threatening conduct which is designed to have them prostitute or continue to prostitute themselves, there is no justification for any broader protection.

In recommending this much narrower provision, we are also mindful of the infrequency with which charges are laid under section 195(1). We are aware that both subsection (3), which adds the requirement of corroboration and (4), which sets out a one year limitation period for bringing proceedings, and which we believe should be repealed, partially explain this dearth of prosecutions. However, it seems to us that the occasions on which procuring comes to the attention of the police will be rare, and like living on the avails will usually only result from a person having been physically abused or threatened with such treatment.

It will be evident that the formulation which we have suggested is much shorter and simpler than the present litany of nine procuring offences. In our opinion section 195(1) in its present form represents a parade of horrors, which even at the times it was enacted and amended, were in part the product of fiction rather than fact. The detailed articulation of the various ploys of procurers in the section was a conscious response to the supposed existence of a widespread "white slavery" trade. Recent research suggests that, while individual cases of procuring and abduction did take place, the existence of a trade, let alone a conspiracy, was more a figment in the minds of crusaders than a reflection of reality.[8] We find it suggestive that clauses (c), (e), (f), (g) and (h) have not given rise to reported cases. That does not mean that prosecutions have not occurred under these clauses. However, contact with several police forces suggests the absence of reported cases is an accurate reflection of general inactivity in these areas. If there are cases of abduction of a person to induce them to engage or continue in prostitution which do not fall within the new formulation, we are inclined to believe that they will be caught by section 247.1 (kidnapping).

As we explain in the commentary on our recommendations on financial support from prostitution (see below) we recognize that the narrowed ambit of responsibility for both procuring and pimping will leave certain prostitution businesses, especially escort and dating services, free to practice their business without criminal law sanction, as long as they refrain from strong arm tactics. For the reasons set out below we accept that result, and believe that Canadian society has other legal mechanisms available to it to regulate effectively such activity.

We see no justification for retaining clauses (3) and (4) which relate to corroboration and limitation of prosecution respectively. Both seem to reflect that view that, despite the felt need to protect women from crafty and immoral males, the women themselves may not be entirely trustworthy. Rather than this fear being dealt with simply in terms of a court weighing the evidence, the Crown is required to go that further step of finding evidence, other than that of the victim, which supports the victim's story, and to do all of this within a set period of time. These requirements seem to us to be yet another unfortunate vestige of the schizophrenic male view of women as frail and helpless on the one hand, but unreliable, and even scheming on the other, which traditionally permeated the law on sex offences in Canada, and does no credit to the modern law. We therefore recommend the repeal of both those clauses.

The penalty for this offence has been increased from 10 to 14 years. This reflects the narrowed formulation and our belief that the use of violence, threat of force or coercion to induce a person into or keep them in a life of prostitution which may itself in turn be marked by violence make this a very serious offence. To our minds, it ranks in gravity with aggravated assault (section 245.2) and extortion (section 305) both of which have a maximum penalty of 14 years.

4.3 Financial Support from Prostitution

Recommendation 60

1. **Substitute for section 195(1)(j) (living on the avails) the following:**

   Everyone who by force, threat of force or other coercive or threatening behaviour induces a person of 18 years or older to support him financially in whole or in part by acts of prostitution is guilty of an indictable offence and liable to imprisonment for 14 years.

2. **Repeal subsection (2) of section 195(1).**

COMMENTARY

These specific recommendations again flow from Recommendation 7 that the criminal law's concern with the exploitative aspects of prostitution in the case of adults should be limited to conduct which is forcible or threatens force.

The present formulation of the living on the avails clause is, of course, much broader. Indeed, it embraces a set of relationships which include some at least which are not characterized by violence or its threat. The designation "pimp" is one which is clearly used in a very loose and imprecise fashion in Canada. It extends from the most deplorable professional and thoroughly violent individual who exploits in every way possible a single prostitute or a group of prostitutes, to husbands or lovers, who, while they benefit from the prostitution of their partners, do not subject them to force or threat thereof. In some instances, it is clear that the involvement in prostitution is a reflection of the economic hardship of a couple, and an agreement by the female partner to contribute to the family budget. The point here is not to deflect attention from the totally unacceptable nature of parasitic pimping, or even the undesirability of individuals resorting to prostitution for purely economic reasons. It is to suggest that the present provision is so broadly drawn that it embraces relationships which, it may be said, do not deserve the attention of the criminal law.

As in the case of the present procuring provision, the reality is that typically the only cases which are prosecuted with any regularity by the police are those in which a complaint is laid by a woman that she has been physically abused or threatened by a pimp. Given that fact, and the assumption, which we think is a tenable one, that other forms of relationships are consensual, we believe that the criminal law should be limited in its ambit to forcible, threatening or coercive conduct.

The adoption of a more circumscribed provision on financial support from prostitution, like that on procuring, will have the effect of removing from the attention of the criminal law a number of prostitution businesses, in particular escort and dating services, which do not provide sexual services on their premises. Normally, the services provided take place in accommodation supplied or paid for by the customer. Under the present law such operations are subject from time to time to prosecutions for living on the avails. Given our concern to see prostitution move from the streets to more discreet private settings, we think it desirable to allow some leeway to such services. We are, of course, conscious of the dangers seen in allowing any rein to commercialized prostitution. Moreover, we are aware that law enforcement authorities in some parts of the country have concerns about the involvement of "organized crime" in this business. However, any doubts which we have are resolved by the reflection that a number of municipalities in Canada have introduced extensive and demanding by-laws relating to such establishments, by-laws which have survived constitutional challenge. We believe that municipalities have demonstrated that they have the will and capacity to use licensing provisions to control such operations effectively, so that the adoption of our recommendation should not herald a period of uncontrolled, commercialized prostitution. We also note, in passing, from our survey of the yellow pages in a number of Canadian cities that, despite the present state of the criminal law, escort and dating services seem to abound. Moreover, in the event of any violence, threat of force or coercion, the criminal law can be invoked, as it can, to deal with criminal conduct which is incidental to the prostitution business, for example drug trafficking.

Because we have recommended that prosecution for being supported financially by prostitution depends upon the use or threat of force, the presumptions contained in section 195(2) are no longer relevant and therefore should be repealed.

Again, we have recommended an increase of penalty from 10 to 14 years. We believe this to be justified to take account of not only the violence, threat of force or coercion, but also the broader relationship of which it is a part. As with violent procuring, we see this offence as being on a par with aggravated assault (section 245.2) and extortion (section 305).

4.4 Prostitution Establishments

Recommendation 61

    1. Replace existing section 193 of the Criminal Code with the following provision:

546

(1) Everyone who operates or aids in the operation of any place which is used in whole or in part for purposes of prostitution is guilty of an indictable offence and is liable to imprisonment for two years.

(2) Everyone who as owner, landlord, lessor, tenant, occupier, or otherwise having charge or control of any place, knowingly permits it to be let or used for purposes of prostitution is guilty of an offence punishable on summary conviction, subject to a maximum fine of $5,000.00.

(3) This section does not apply to:

    (a) a place of residence in which two residents of 18 years or more of age of that place engage in acts of prostitution;

    (b) a prostitution establishment licensed and operated in accordance with a regulatory scheme established by the provincial or territorial legislature in that jurisdiction.

(4) Where a person is convicted of an offence under subsection (1) the court shall cause a notice of the conviction to be served on the owner, landlord, or lessor of the place in respect of which the person is convicted or his agent, and the notice shall contain a statement to the effect that it is being served pursuant to this section.

(5) Where a person upon whom a notice is served under subsection (4) fails forthwith to exercise any right he may have to determine the tenancy or right of occupation of the person so convicted, and thereafter any person is convicted of an offence under subsection (1) in respect of the place, the person on whom the notice was served shall be deemed to have committed an offence under subsection (1) unless he proves that he has taken all reasonable steps to prevent a recurrence of the offence.

(6) For purposes of this section "place" includes any place, whether or not

    (a) it is covered or enclosed,

    (b) it is used permanently or temporarily, or

    (c) any person has an exclusive right of user with respect to it.

2. Repeal definition of "common bawdy house" in section 179(1) of the Criminal Code.

3. Repeal clauses (a) and (d) of section 180(1) of the Criminal Code.

COMMENTARY

These recommendations embody the specifics of the general position taken by the Committee in recommendations 55 and 57. In particular, they reflect the position that the activities of prostitutes and customers should not be the concern of the criminal law, unless they involve some form of criminal conduct which is independent of the agreement to engage in prostitution or the act of prostitution itself. Secondly, they flow from the belief that prostitution cannot be dealt with by the law on a piecemeal basis, but only by carefully linking the provisions on each aspect of prostitution-related activity. Moreover, they follow from the Committee's view, that, if prostitution is a reality with which we have to deal for the foreseeable future, then it is preferable that it take place, as far as possible, in private, and without the opportunities for exploitation which have been traditionally associated with commercialized prostitution.

The new section, which would replace the present bawdy house provision in section 193, drops the reference to "common bawdy house" and replaces it with the term "prostitution establishments". We make this change, because, although "common bawdy house" is broadly defined in section 179(1), it still conjures up the settled and permanent residential brothel of years gone by. There seems little point in preserving quaint terminology, when a more straightforward formulation can be used. Instead of referring to a common bawdy house, in subsections (1), (2) and (4) we propose to talk of "any place which is used in whole or part for purposes of prostitution". "Place" is defined in subsection (6) in the same terms that are currently found in section 179(1), thus preserving the widest scope for the characterization of a location as a prostitution establishment. The result of these changes is, of course, that the definition of "common bawdy house" in section 179(1) becomes redundant.

In place of the reference in the current section to "one who keeps" which, as we have seen in Part III, Chapter 29 has given rise to interpretative problems, we have substituted "everyone who operates or aids or assists in the operation of". The latter wording connotes much more clearly the combination of control and management which is required. This should rule out criminal responsibility for an owner where a prostitute or prostitutes uses a facility without his or her knowledge.

With the repeal of the existing definition of "common bawdy house" and the terminology used in the new formulation of the section the focus will be exclusively on establishments in which prostitution is practised. We have dropped all reference to "the practice of acts of indecency". This terminology harkens back to days when all sorts of sexual practices which were not in the limited glossary of respectable society were considered immoral and indecent. As we have noted in our analysis of the present law in Part III, Section II, Chapter 29, it has been used by the police to harass various gay establishments in which sexual activities between adults take place without payment. This change accords with the recommendations of the Badgley Committee that section 155 of the *Criminal Code* (buggery) and our own recommendation on children that section 157 (acts of gross indecency) be amended to limit their effect to acts on persons under the age of 18, and that section 158 which allows a limited defence to charges under both sections 155 and 157 be repealed.[9] The effect would be to leave such acts or practices by consenting adults outside the reach of the criminal law.

We have recommended a maximum fine of $5,000.00 for the "permitting" offence in subsection (2). We think that this is justified to allow the courts to deal resolutely with the owner or landlords, etc. who wilfully turn a "blind eye" to extensive prostitution activity on their property.

Subsection (3) of our recommended section embodies our belief that some leeway should be allowed by the law to one or two prostitutes to use their shared residence for the purpose of providing prostitution services, and to

548

small-scale non-residential commercial prostitution establishments should the provinces and territories desire to establish a proper regulatory scheme to license such places.

The existing definition of "common bawdy house" is broad enough to include a single prostitute using a residence for prostitution. It is our belief that it is preferable for prostitution to take place in private than in public. Apart from commercial prostitution establishments, the only realistic settings in which private acts of prostitution can take place are the residence of the prostitute, or the residence or accommodation of the customer. The latter are typically not touched by the existing law. We do not see why the former should be, and readily conclude that the law should no longer penalize one adult prostitute operating out of that person's residence.

We have considered whether the exemption might extend further. The Criminal Law Revision Committee in England, in its 1982 report, raised the possibility of extending the present exemption from prosecution for one prostitute operating out of a residence to two.[10] This, that Committee felt, might make it more attractive for prostitutes to use private premises, because they would be able to provide each other and their families with mutual support and help. The result might be to induce some prostitutes to move off the streets. The English Committee was not willing to extend the number beyond three lest "nests of prostitutes" be encouraged. We agree with the reasoning used by the Criminal Law Revision Committee for allowing a two person exemption for residential premises. We agree as well with their concern about "nests of prostitutes". In particular, we wish to avoid a situation where an exception designed to benefit the individuals really just encourages commercial operators to collect people together in a *de facto* commercial establishment. For the same reason, we have limited the exception to a residence, more particularly to the prostitute's own residence.

We hope that, for some prostitutes this sort of arrangement may provide a way of operating without being beholden to pimps. In that context, we note that in countries such as Holland and Denmark where small groups of prostitutes have been allowed to operate together out of a residence, or even a small business establishment, the result has been a diminution in the influence of pimps. We recognize that there is the potential in this recommendation for friction between the prostitute and neighbours. We do not wish to underemphasize the neighbours' interest in quiet enjoyment of their premises. However, we think that the landlord and tenant law of the provinces rather than criminal law, is the more appropriate vehicle for dealing with conflict problems. Initially, we recognize, it may be necessary to monitor closely the provincial law to see that it is sufficiently responsive.

We are aware that once residential activities are taken out of the *Criminal Code* they may become amenable to regulation pursuant to provincial jurisdiction. Some municipalities will doubtless regulate entirely in good faith, acting from motives like a desire to deal evenhandedly with prostitutes and others who operate businesses in their residences. However, it is not fanciful to suggest that some municipalities will use by-laws, especially zoning by-laws, to prevent prostitutes from operating from a place of residence. Whether the municipality acts for good or bad motives, any move to require business licences of prostitutes may come very close to a registration system, and is of concern on that ground alone. Accordingly, we do have some doubts about whether the residential exemption will actually achieve the objectives we had hoped it would.

We are not, however, abandoning the one, or two, person exemption. In many cases and many places, it may work well. The concerns above have, rather, led us to explore what we think of as another method for achieving the goals of moving prostitution to a private location while minimizing exploitation of the prostitutes themselves. That method is the commercial prostitution establishment. As we have stated above, we believe that the criminal law should not foreclose the option for a province to embark on a scheme of licensing and regulating this sort of establishment.

There are a number of reasons for exploring this option. If we follow logically our concern to see prostitution move off the streets into private settings, then there is no reason why we should stop at protecting escort services and residential prostitution activities from the reach of the criminal law, as these activities certainly satisfy the private settings requirement. Moreover, if an effective system of regulation can be mounted and applied, there is reason to expect that such establishments can be run safely, with a concern for the welfare of both prostitutes and customers, and in locales in which disturbance to residential accommodation is precluded. The experience in Holland and Denmark is that within a regulated system it is possible for prostitutes themselves to run their own businesses. The localization of prostitution in known premises should also make it easier for the police to monitor and control the situation.

On the other hand, we are aware of the risks which would characterize any attempt to allow the commercialization of this sort of activity. The operation of a commercial prostitution establishment is not the sort of business venture which can be expected to attract respectable control or investment, at least not in North America. Cultural patterns here are different from those in the European countries where such establishments operate in apparent harmony with their surroundings. Even with the strictest of rules concerning ownership, there are always strategies whereby sinister interests can control such enterprises through "respectable" fronts. While in theory the exemption might open up the prospect of a "cottage industry" operated and controlled by the prostitutes themselves, in reality the business may well be controlled by those who have the resources to purchase and develop property and both an instinct and capacity for survival, the commercial exploiters. It is questionable, moreover, whether the existence of such establishments will reduce significantly the street prostitution population. There are some who because of habit, appearance, or inclination, will not want to work in commercial establishments, or be accepted there.

Even this summary of some of the arguments for and against the commercial establishment gives some idea of the complexity of the issue, and the considerable implications of any decision to embark on such a scheme. Because of this complexity, and the constitutional realities of Canada, we have avoided the option of using the *Criminal Code* to regulate prostitution establishments. We are aware that the *Criminal Code* contains extensive provisions which have the effect of regulating both gun use and gambling. However, we also realize that the reforms which led to the inclusion of these provisions were made only after achievement of a significant measure of agreement between the federal and provincial governments on how to control these activities. As far as we know there has not even been discussion, let alone agreement, on whether and how off-street prostitution premises might be regulated. For the federal government and Parliament to foist such a system on the country would be, to put it mildly, a disastrous political move.

Instead of recommending a federal initiative here, we have opted for a *Criminal Code* clause which allows an exemption from the general proscriptive provision on prostitution establishments if, and only if, the provincial legislature has approved a regulatory regime under which such establishments may operate subject to control. This, we feel, recognizes that under the Constitution it is the provinces which have the power to regulate business within their borders. Moreover, it allows each province to discuss and decide whether as a matter of social policy it feels comfortable with a regulated system of prostitution establishment within its domain. Thirdly, it establishes primary responsibility for both political decision making and legal control with the provincial authorities and legislature.

Having opened up the possibility of regulated prostitution establishments operating within the law, we think it worthwhile listing the type of conditions which would be necessary to any such system of regulation. These reflect in part the product of our own thinking, drawn from comments at the public hearings and the application to this situation of the principles enunciated at the outset of this Report. We have also benefitted from considering the scheme recently introduced in the State of Victoria, Australia.[11] While we recognize that the Australian constitutional system is easier to work with when it comes to blending criminal law and administrative regulation, as both matters lie within the jurisdiction of the individual states, we believe that the regime set up in the State of Victoria to regulate brothels has some features which could fit into a provincial scheme in Canada.

In our opinion any regulatory scheme for the operation of prostitution establishments would have to contain in the first place a provision forbidding employment in such establishments of persons 18 years and younger. We take the view that such establishments should be small-scale and non-residential. The large, residential Mustang Ranch in Nevada was often cited to us in the course of the public hearings as the epitome of exploitation, and we have no wish to recommend that Canadian authorities become involved in endorsing any such operation. We recall to mind in this connection that many of the apparently dated provisions of the present *Code*, related to procuring, originated because of the perceived danger that residential premises lead to exploitation. It would be inconsistent to repeal these while recommending the innovation of a residential establishment.

It will be important to prevent concentration of these facilities in one area; to limit their location to strictly industrial or commercial zones; and to distance them from churches, schools and hospitals. All of these factors, of course, relate to the concern for nuisance which has motivated our other recommendations about prostitution. As we are concerned that both prostitutes and customers are protected while using the establishments, the full range of provincial legislation relating to public health, labour standards, and workers' compensation should be extended to them. It will also be necessary to establish clearly the operating conditions under which such an establishment can be run, with provisions as to numbers, hours of operation, facilities required, records to be kept and so on.

A public approval process will have to be established which allows for a full examination of applications; vetting of applicants; and input by the public. Control of more than one establishment by a single individual or other interest should be prevented, and anyone convicted of an indictable offence or offences should be excluded from the operation or management of such establishments. The police should be provided with adequate legal means of seeking entry to such establishments and investigating the operations where reasonable grounds exist to believe that criminal activity is taking or has taken place, or that a breach of the conditions of operation is occurring or has occurred. Finally, stiff penalties need to be established for the breach of the conditions under which a prostitution establishment can be operated.

Having recommended that the issue be left to provincial initiative, we do not wish to give the impression that the federal government has no role to play here. In the first place, the provision we have recommended requires involvement of the criminal law when a prostitution establishment does not operate under or in accordance with a provincially approved regulatory regime. Secondly, we see this report as having an important function in raising the consciousness of all Canadians about prostitution, its incidence and causes, and desirable social and legal strategies to deal with it. In our minds, prostitution has been accentuated as a social problem because as a society we have chosen to "sweep it under the rug". We hope that one of the results of this report is that it will stimulate greater discussion and debate on prostitution. Both the federal and provincial governments have, we feel, a key role to play in this process of engendering frank and full debate, and we hope that the question of the desirability and feasibility of allowing regulated prostitution establishments within the provinces will be seriously discussed by the federal Minister of Justice and his counterparts within the provinces.

We appreciate that what we have recommended in the way of an amendment to the *Criminal Code* by no means ensures that Canada will move in the direction of a system of regulated prostitution establishments. We are aware that, for many Canadians, regulated prostitution establishments are an anathema. However, we feel that, for the reasons adduced, this option should be put into the policy review process with the other means we have outlined above for removing prostitution from the street to a safe, non-exploitative environment. We hope that readers will sit back and reflect a little on whether what we suggest *may*, along with our other recommendations, achieve somewhat more in terms of positive social results than the present ill-tuned and ineffective system. In particular, as we have stated earlier, we hope that the recommendation will stimulate full, frank and reasoned discussion between the federal and provincial governments.

Subsections (4) and (5) of our proposal are retained from the existing section 193, and are, we believe, necessary to underline the responsibility of owners, landlords, lessors, tenants or occupiers to take the necessary remedial action when they find that their premises have been used for purposes of prostitution. In the absence of such action, and the continuation of the activity we see no difficulty in the law "deeming" the owner, landlord etc. to operate or assist in the operation of the establishment. Given the clear notice requirement this does not seem to us to offend the *Charter* in any respect.

It will be noted that no reference is made in the formulation of the new section to inmates of such establishments or those "found in" them. The omission means that being an inmate or "found in" will no longer be an offence. The change reflects our belief that the prostitution-related activities of both prostitutes and customers should be decriminalized.

The removal of inmates and "found ins" from the concern of the criminal law makes the presumption now used in paragraph 180(1)(d) of the *Code* redundant. That clause presumes that a person is an inmate or "found in" of an establishment where the keeper has been found guilty of running a common bawdy house. Paragraph 180(1)(a) of the present *Code*, which presumes the character of a disorderly house from the fact that an authorized peace officer is wilfully prevented from entering is, in our opinion, offensive to paragraph 11(d) of the *Charter*, the presumption of innocence provision. As we have pointed out in Chapter 32, Canadian courts have already made it clear that "reverse onus" clauses such as this will be struck down under the *Charter* if there is no rational connection between the actual and presumed fact. This particular clause clearly makes an association between an actual and presumed fact which has no rational basis.

We have recommended the repeal of section 194 (transporting a person to a bawdy house) for two reasons. In the first place it is so broad in its ambit that it embraces casual conduct which is by any standards unexceptional, for example, randomly directing a passerby to a bawdy house. Secondly, there is no evidence that it is used on anything other than a very infrequent basis. The reasons for this lack of use is probably the absence of any consistent pattern of conduct which could be described as touting. Undoubtedly, there are taxi companies, taxi drivers, desk clerks, barmen and others who benefit to some extent from the trade, and who might be said to encourage it indirectly. It is doubtful, however, that this type of activity generates a significant portion of their income, and it cannot be said that they are involved in the same way as the operator of the prostitution establishment, the pimp or procurer.

5. Miscellaneous Recommendations

There are several miscellaneous recommendations we wish to make which either flow from or tie in with those set out above. Three of these represent recommendations for repeal or specific examination of other sections of the *Criminal Code* and one addresses Canada's performance on prostitution at an international level.

We agree with the recommendation of the Badgley Committee that section 155 of the *Criminal Code* (buggery) should be amended so that it is limited to such conduct with a person of less than 18 years of age.[12] An offence would accordingly not exist in the case of such conduct taking place between adults. Furthermore, we favour amendment of section 157 (gross indecency) so that it will apply only to conduct with a person of less than 18 years and the repeal of 158 (the exception to 155 and 157 for consensual acts in private between husband and wife, and any 2 persons of 21 years of age and over). The effect of these changes would be to remove from the reach of the criminal law consensual sexual conduct between adults in private, whatever the number of participants.

While we are aware that these sections have not been utilized in the case of adult prostitution, they clearly could be so used. Section 155, insofar as it applies to adults in consensual settings outside the scope of section 158, and 157 both offend the notion that adult sexual activity in private should not in and of itself be the concern of the criminal law. Moreover, unless the changes suggested are made, there will be an obvious inconsistency with what we have recommended in relation to prostitution establishments, i.e. the dropping of the current reference to "the practice of acts of indecency".[13] The presence of this inconsistency would raise the spectre of section 155 and 157 being used to do what a new section on prostitution establishments could not do.

Recommendation 62

1. **Amend sections 155 and 157 of the Code, so that they no longer extend to consensual acts between those of 18 years or older.**

2. **Repeal section 158 of the Criminal Code.**

We are also of the view that the meaning and scope of section 176 of the *Criminal Code* needs to be clarified. As we have indicated in our discussion of the common nuisance section in section II, chapter 30, we believe that the present wording reflects the reality that not only is there a *Criminal Code* offence of common nuisance, but also a broader residual notion of common nuisance, which, insofar as it does not overlap with the *Code* offence, can be pursued by the Attorney General of Canada, or of a province, seeking a civil injunction. This view accords with that voiced in the commentary on section 176 (then 165) by J. C. Martin in the 1955 edition of *Martin's Criminal Code*.[14] Mr. Martin was research counsel to the *Royal Commission to Revise the Criminal Code* which reported in 1952. This commentary relates the earlier more detailed statement of common nuisance in the *Code* to its truncated form in the 1953-54 revisions to the *Code*. The commentator concludes that the criminal process for dealing with common nuisance is limited to acts "endangering the lives, safety, or health of the public, or causing physical injury to any person" by section 176(1), but implicitly recognizes the right of the Attorney General of Canada or the provinces, as is appropriate, to use the civil injunction to restrain other forms of common nuisance, for instance, interferences with "the property or comfort of the public" or "the obstruction of the public in the exercise or enjoyment of a right that is common to all subjects", which are the additional and residual forms of nuisance mentioned in section 176(2).

Although we are confident of our ground here, it is only because we had the advantage of reviewing the historical analysis mentioned above. The section itself would not necessarily lead to this conclusion. Indeed, we note that in the two recent cases in which the issue of the "right" of a provincial Attorney General to seek an injunction to restrain the activities of prostitutes as a common nuisance, no analysis was made of the meaning and scope of section 176.

More troubling is the fact that the judges reached opposite conclusions on the question of whether, or at least to what extent, the Attorney General of a province has the power claimed. Chief Justice McEachern in *Attorney General for British Columbia* v. *Couillard*[15] seems to have evinced no doubts about it, while MacIntosh J. in *Attorney General for Nova Scotia* v. *Beaver*[16] concluded that the attempt to exercise such a "right" in that case constituted a usurpation of the federal criminal power. It may be that both judges have a point. As we have said, there is every reason for contending that the provincial Attorney General has the power to seek a civil injunction to restrain one of the species of common nuisance which falls outside its criminal, i.e. section 176(1), definition. Although the effect of this may be to exact a penalty from the defendant for contempt if he fails to comply, the process does not seem in and of itself to infringe upon the federal jurisdiction over criminal law. However, it seems that Parliament has added specific common nuisance offences which go beyond the limits set out in section 176(1). It is arguable, for instance, that section 195.1 (soliciting) is an example. So presumably would be section 171 (causing a disturbance), both in its present form and with the amendments which we have suggested. What is the effect of a provincial Attorney General seeking a civil injunction against conduct which is the subject of a provision like sections 195.1 or 171 in the *Criminal Code*? Is the Attorney General usurping the criminal law (as Mr. Justice MacIntosh suggests), or aiding it (as Chief Justice MacEachern suggests), or can he be seen as legitimately pursuing a civil remedy, which can co-exist with whatever criminal provisions there are which could be said to cover the same substantive ground?

As both judges seem to have agreed, there is little doubt in England about at least part of the answer. The English courts, including the House of Lords, have made it clear that in pressing circumstances, the Attorney General can invoke the power to seek a civil injunction to aid the criminal law.[17] An obvious example would be where convictions for breaches of the criminal law by, and the penalties applied to, an individual or group of individuals, have no effect in stopping the criminal conduct in question. The answer is not so clear cut in

Canada because of the division of powers. If the provincial Attorney General wearing a civil hat enters where the provincial Attorney General wearing a criminal hat fears (or is unwilling) to tread, is that individual usurping the criminal law power? We are not sure we know the answer. What we do know is that discussion needs to take place between the federal Minister of Justice and his provincial counterparts on this issue. In the absence of a natural appeal in either of the two cases mentioned, it may be that the issue can be resolved by a reference to the Supreme Court of Canada. Alternatively, the two levels of government may wish to seek some sort of legislative accommodation. We think that the uncertainty here needs to be resolved.

Recommendation 63

> **In view of the uncertainty which surrounds the meaning and purpose of section 176 of the Criminal Code, and the confusion over the relationship between the nuisance provisions in the Code and the power of an Attorney General of a province to seek a civil injunction to restrain a common nuisance, the federal Minister of Justice and his provincial counterparts should, if necessary, make a reference of this issue to the Supreme Court of Canada, or seek a legislative solution to the problem.**

Although section 253 of the *Criminal Code* (communicating venereal disease) has a theoretical scope which is much broader than the context of prostitution, we believe that it should be repealed. As we have concluded in section II, chapter 30, it is hopelessly outdated in the etiological assumptions it makes; it clearly does not reflect modern knowledge on, or practice in relation to, sexually transmitted diseases (STDs). Secondly, the evidentiary requirements are so daunting that the section has almost never been used. We note that the Badgley Committee came to the same conclusion,[18] and that Bill C-19, introduced by Minister of Justice MacGuigan in 1984, would have removed it from the *Code*. We agree with the Badgley Committee that effective initiatives to combat and treat sexually transmitted diseases lie in the field of improved public health practice and administration.

Recommendation 64

> **Repeal section 253 of the Criminal Code.**

In considering Canada's record in the context of international initiatives to deal with prostitution, we were surprised to discover that this country had (a) not become a party to the 1951 *United Nations Convention for the Suppression of the Traffic in Persons and the Exploitation of the Prostitution of Others*; and (b) voted against the most recent attempt by the U.N. to stimulate action by states to combat prostitution. As we have hinted in the text in Chapter 33, we are not impressed with the official argument that the failure to ratify the 1951 *Convention* reflects the reality that the instrument was merely a consolidation of previous agreements to which Canada *is* a party. That argument is suspect because the 1951 *Convention* does include new elements; for example, the first reference to male prostitution in such a convention. We believe that the reason has more to do with the feared constitutional ramifications of ratifying an international agreement on matters which fall partly within provincial jurisdiction. The result, we understand, is that because the *Convention* is not ratified by Canada, no pressure is put on either the federal or provincial governments to explain how far their law and practice match the aspirations contained in the *Convention*. We find it ironic that this reticence should exist, when Canada took a leading role in the drafting and passage of related convention, that on the *Elimination of All Forms of Discrimination Against Women* of 1979. That agreement clearly overlaps with the 1951 *Convention* in that it calls for the repeal of laws discriminating against women by prostitution, and like the latter, has implications for both the federal and provincial levels of government in Canada. We have learned that in the case of the 1979 *Convention* both federal politicians and civil servants displayed considerable energy and enthusiasm in seeking federal inter-departmental and provincial agreement, thus allowing Canada to take a leadership role.

We do not understand the Canadian position on General Assembly Resolution 38/180 of February, 1984 which we described in Chapter 33. This resolution did no more than call for the use of humane efforts, including legislation, to combat prostitution, and to provide protection to the victims of prostitution by education, social guarantees and employment opportunities for them. While the preamble certainly emphasized the control of female prostitution, we do not think that the explanations given by the U.N. for the emphasis were unreasonable at that time.

We are of the opinion that Canada must engage in a serious review of its position vis-à-vis both the 1951 *Convention* and more recent initiatives by the United Nations. We are aware that certain of the recommendations we have made, if adopted, could be seen as contradicting the objectives of these international agreements and resolutions, more particularly those on procuring, pimping and the operation of prostitution establishments. We do not believe, however, that viewed in the broader context of a strategy which tries to blend long-term social and shorter term legal strategies, they are inconsistent with a humane approach to prostitution, which looks forward to a significant diminution in the incidence of this social phenomenon. However, whether or not Canada would feel welcome to ratify the 1951 *Convention*, any decision not to do so must be made and justified on grounds of principle, rather than expediency. Moreover, if the Canadian view is that the United Nations is taking too narrow or too facile a view of the problems of prostitution, then this country should, consistent with its performance on other initiatives of this type, be prepared to argue its case frankly in terms of the principles it considers appropriate and valid, rather than relying on arguments which give the impression of being specious.

Recommendation 65

Canada should review its position on its failure to become a party to the 1951 United Nations Convention for the Suppression of the Traffic in Persons and the Exploitation of the Prostitution of Others and its low profile international stance on prostitution and how to deal with it, in general; in particular, if it takes issue with some of the prescriptions of the Convention, or future resolutions of international bodies on prostitution, then it should be on grounds of principle rather than expediency.

Footnotes

[1] There are a number of examples already in this country. Inter-governmental initiatives in the research field, which are complemented by funding from private foundations and corporate sources, are a common means of encouraging new research endeavour.

[2] See Part III, Section III, Chapter 36.

[3] See *R* v. *Di Paola* (1978), 4 C.R. (3d) 121 (Ont. C.A.); *R* v. *Dudak* (1978), 41 C.C.C. (2d) 31 (B.C.C.A.).

[4] *R.* v. *Hutt*, [1978] 2 S.C.R. 476.

[5] *R* v. *Galjot and Whitter* (1981), 64 C.C.C. (2d) 1 (S.C.C.).

[6] *R.* v. *Wise* (1982), 67 C.C.C. (2d) 231 (B.C.Co.Ct.); *R* v. *Figliuzzi* (1981), 50 C.C.C. (2d) 144 (Alta Q.B.); *R.* v. *McEwen* (1980), 4 W.W.R. 85 (Sask. Prov. Ct.).

[7] *R.* v. *Hutt* (1978).

[8] See M. Conolly, *The Response to Prostitution in the Progressive Era* (Chapel Hill: University of North Carolina, 1980); J. Walkowitz, *Prostitution and Victorian Society: Women, Class and the State* (Cambridge: Cambridge University Press, 1980).

[9] The Badgley Report at 46-8 and 63.

[10] Criminal Law Revision Committee, *Working Paper on Offences Relating to Prostitution and Allied Offences* (1982), Home Office, London, H.M.S.O. at 19-22.

[11] See Part III, Section III, Chapter 35.

[12] Badgley Report at 54.

[13] *Ibid.*

[14] *Martin's Criminal Code*, 1955 (Toronto: Cartwright & Sons Ltd., 1955).

[15] *Attorney General for British Columbia* v. *Couillard* (1984), 14 C.C.C. (3d) 169 (B.C.S.C.).

[16] *Attorney General for Nova Scotia* v. *Beaver* 19 Dec. 1984, unreported (N.S.S.C.).

[17] *Gouriet* v. *Union of Post Office Workers*, [1977] 3 All. E.R. 70 (H.L.).

[18] Badgley Report at 63-4.

Part IV

Children

Chapter 41

Introduction

The mandate of this Committee includes a consideration of pornography and prostitution as they relate to children and young persons. In this part of our Report, we focus particularly on children and young people. A number of considerations have led us to this decision to gather our observations on children and young people into a single part of the Report, rather than dispersing them throughout the other chapters.

At the outset of the Report, we enunciated a number of principles which have guided us in formulating our recommendations, and which we believe should provide the foundation of legal action in these two areas. These principles are equality, responsibility, individual liberty, human dignity, and appreciation of sexuality. From the discussion in that chapter, it is apparent that many of these principles have applications to children and young people which differ from their applications to adults.

We do not, for example, consider that the principles of individual liberty and responsibility can be applied to children to the same extent as they can to adults. Children may well have valid claims to autonomy in wide ranges of conduct. However, the liberty to engage in behaviour which is regarded as harmful will be withheld from children with more frequency than it is withheld from adults. Various justifications may be offered for this. The child may be too young or inexperienced to appreciate the harmfulness of the behaviour, or its nature or extent. In addition, quite apart from the characteristics and maturity of the individual child, adult society may be protective of the state of childhood, which is seen as a time, firstly, for the enjoyment of innocence and, then, gradually, for development out of innocence. The exposure to certain kinds of influence or behaviour may be seen as a disruption of the valuable process of gradual maturation.

Of course, not all the reasons offered in support of restraining youthful autonomy or liberty are good ones. Nor are all the restraints imposed, even in the name of sound reasons, reasonable restraints. In the case of pornography and prostitution, however, we think that there is strong justification for treating children as vulnerable, and effecting some decrease in their liberty.

While viewing children and young people as vulnerable, we do not propose that it always be the state which serves as their protector. There is, to be sure, a clear role for the criminal law in deterring the most seriously offensive types of behaviour exploitative of young people, and for other legislation in regulating the impact of other kinds of behaviour. Social resources should, where appropriate, be deployed to assist young persons to cope with difficult situations. However, in our efforts to ensure that the state assumes its proper share of responsibility for the vulnerable, we do not intend to ignore the primary role which the family will play in guiding and assisting the young person. The family is, in fact, the child's first source of comfort, education and guidance.

Many of the recommendations which we make recognize the valuable role of the family and are intended to assist the family in performing that role. So, although we do see some diminution of the child's liberty of action as a necessary part of a proper regime to deal with pornography and prostitution, we do not contemplate that such diminution will always be a compulsory one, at the hands of the state. Nor do we wish to include in our plans any substantial diminution of parental responsibility toward their children and parental liberty to raise and educate them according to their own moral criteria. Our concern about state censorship of the media, for example, stems directly from our desire that families, rather than the state, be the principal influence on the child's developing tastes.

Although the principles of personal liberty and equality may have more restricted application to young people than to adults, we take the view that young people may often be as subject to the principle of responsibility as are the adults. In particular, youths who exploit other young people should be called to account for such conduct. There is little justification for allowing a theoretical concern with youthful vulnerability to assist in the creation of a new youthful type of predator. In this connection, we are very interested in the approach embodied in the *Young Offenders Act* [1].

The "Declaration of Principle" in that *Act* recognizes that although society has the responsibility to take reasonable measures to prevent criminal conduct by young persons, it must nevertheless be afforded the necessary protection from illegal behaviour. The Declaration also states that while young persons should not, in all instances, be held accountable in the same manner or suffer the same consequences for their behaviour as adults, young persons who commit offences should nonetheless bear responsibility for their contraventions. Also recognized with respect to the disposition of youthful offenders is the principle that young persons who commit offences require supervision, discipline and control, but because of their state of dependency and level of development and maturity, they have special needs and require guidance and assistance. [2]

The procedures provided in the *Young Offenders Act* to govern the trial and sentencing of youthful offenders, reflect this idea of responsibility tempered with accommodation to the special circumstances of the child.

562

Because of the availability of the *Young Offenders Act* to govern proceedings against young persons charged with offences, we are content that young people should take responsibility for their actions. However, we think that this responsibility should be the modified responsibility expressed in the *Young Offenders Act* principles.

We also believe that it is important for this Committee, and legislators, to focus more precisely not only on the differences between adults and young persons, but also on the similarities between them. For example, young people, like adults, have a need for recognition of their sexuality, and for ways in which to express and explore it without doing harm to themselves or others. They are, like adults, capable and desirous of artistic expression. Most importantly, they too are beings with dignity and integrity. All of these characteristics should, in our view, have a bearing on the response of the legal system to children and young people, just as the particular vulnerability of children should be recognized.

For purposes of our discussion, we consider all those under the age of 18 to be young people, and thus distinct from those we deem adults. There is still some variation in the "age of majority" across Canada, with ages other than 18 being the norm in some jurisdictions for purposes like consumption of alcoholic beverages, or driving. The age of leaving school is commonly less than 18, as is the age at which children are considered free to withdraw themselves from parental control. However, 18 is a significant age for many purposes related to majority in many jurisdictions. It is also, in our view, significant that the *Young Offenders Act* defines young person as a person under 18 years of age. There do not appear to be significant reasons for our recommendations to depart from the age of demarcation chosen for this recent and substantial reform of the juvenile justice system.

Footnotes

[1] S.C. 1980-81-82, c.110, proclaimed in force April 2, 1984.

[2] S.C. 1980-81-82, c.110, s.3(1)(b), 3(1)(a), and 3(1)(c).

Chapter 42

Pornography and Prostitution Involving Children

It was very evident at the public hearings that there were major and deeply felt concerns for children and young people in relation to pornography and prostitution. Important among them were concerns about the actual involvement of children in the production of pornography and as prostitutes, and the access and exposure of children to sexually explicit materials, which were considered to be inappropriate given the level of maturity of children and young people. It was impressed upon the Committee time and time again, that young people should be protected from the worst aspects of commercial sexuality and allowed the opportunity to reach adulthood without being subjected to corrupting or distorted views of human sexual relations. The Committee could not fail to be impressed by the sincerity with which groups and individuals made their arguments. There is no doubt in our minds that Canadians from coast to coast see the needs and rights of children and young people to be quite special and deserving of most particular attention.

While the Committee could not doubt the intensity and sincerity of the feelings and arguments made to it, it was apparent that much of the evidence put forward in support of these concerns was problematic. As we have indicated elsewhere in the Report, information on pornography and prostitution in Canada is sparse. This state of affairs certainly characterizes the information available with respect to children's involvement in these areas. Not suprisingly, therefore, those presenting briefs had to draw on research which is often less than satisfactorily carried out, which may report on experiences in other countries with different social and legal systems, or which speaks only to very particular instances of pornography or prostitution. Thus, while the Committee shares and supports the concern of those who urged us to protect children, we do not always find ourselves able to agree with the descriptions put forward as reflecting the current situation with respect to child pornography and prostitution in Canada.

1. Concerns Expressed at the Public Hearings

A number of very basic issues relating to children were identified in the course of submissions at the public hearings.

In the area of pornography, great concern was expressed at the perceived increase in the production and dissemination of child pornography. Where children were concerned, there was perceptibly less tolerance of certain kinds of material which might have been tolerated were the subject an adult. For example, some people appearing at the hearings considered unacceptable a photograph of a nude child, by himself or herself, even though the representation was not explicitly sexual. Mere nudity in photographs of adults was much more widely tolerated.

From the concern about child pornography stemmed recommendations for stiffer measures against those making, disseminating, or using this material.

Exposure of children to pornography, whether of the child or adult type, similarly attracted the concern of the public. There were many aspects to this concern. We were told of children being unwittingly and unwillingly exposed to offensive material, whether through the newsstands in a local variety store, an improperly or inadequately labelled videotape, or television broadcasts reaching the home receiver during family viewing hours. We were also told of young people seeking out material which their elders considered offensive or dangerous, either for amusement or, perhaps more troubling, as a way of trying to understand their own developing sexuality where less harmful methods were not readily available. The brief from the YWCA in Yellowknife summarizes very well the concerns which we heard, from groups in the south as well as the north:

> Children growing up in Yellowknife are fairly unsophisticated, by southern standards, in terms of their exposure to a variety of attitudes and lifestyles. In the last few years, Yellowknife has been inundated with material of a pornographic nature. It concerns the YWCA that the first introduction of young people to sexuality might very well be of a pornographic nature. As with parents everywhere, many Yellowknife parents do not for whatever reason, address the issue of sexuality with their children. We do not have sexual education classes in our schools in Yellowknife. For these reasons we at the YWCA are deeply concerned that our young people will be exposed to material which depicts sexuality in a degrading, violent and unhealthy manner, and that our young people will consider this to be an acceptable expression of sexuality.

> Repeated exposure to pornographic material, we fear, will have the effect of desensitizing children to the true nature of sadistic violence...

> The YWCA of Yellowknife is concerned that such desensitization of children will negatively affect the development of a healthy sexual self-image and attitudes of both boys and girls, and will negatively affect the development of healthy and satisfying sexual relationships of both young men and women.

> We are also concerned that the very presence of pornographic material suggests that the behaviour depicted in this material is condoned by our southern society. This may be interpreted as the norm and thus form the basis for standards of community acceptability, both by southern and other cultural groups in the north.
> *YWCA, Yellowknife*

With respect to prostitution, one of the major concerns of witnesses was how to prevent young people from taking up prostitution; similarly, finding ways of enabling or encouraging them to leave prostitution was a priority. Criminalizing the street prostitution activities of young persons was seen by some as a way of deterring prostitution or breaking the tie between the youngster and this way of life. There was, however, significant recognition that criminalizing these activities was at best a superficial solution, since the reasons why young people become prostitutes can be very complex. Without adequate support services for runaway youths, for victims of sexual or emotional abuse in the home, or for young people trying to leave prostitution, merely laying a criminal charge against the child would not be effective and could indeed be harmful. As the Centre de Services Sociaux Ville-Marie in Montréal pointed out:

> ...juvenile prostitutes are not a homogeneous group. Some are beginning their careers as prostitutes, some want to stay in prostitution, others want out. Some are involved in prostitution purely for economic reasons, some because the choices made available to them by others have been so unattractive that prostitution seems to be the best alternative. Still others are involved in prostitution because of their experiences of abuse and neglect. They are motivated by the ever present hope of having both their past, unmet psychological and material needs met.

The idea that such a diversity of problems can be addressed solely within the context of the criminal system did not find general support.

Special problems involving young people in the area of street prostitution were identified in the public hearings. Once young people have run away from home, they are faced with the problem of providing at least the basic necessities of life for themselves. Whether or not their original intention was to become a prostitute, they frequently find this their only option and move into the business. Too young to enter licensed premises or rent apartments, too young and often too ill-trained to get regular employment, young people are showing up in street prostitution in significant numbers. Thus, in those areas and districts where public impatience with prostitution is likely to be at its highest because of the public nuisance which is often involved, the juvenile prostitute population may be particularly vulnerable.

Throughout the submissions in both areas of our mandate, there emerged a strong recurring theme. This was the recognition that young people who engage in prostitution or use or see pornography are often merely the victims of adults. Certainly, the market for the services of the young prostitute, male or female, is largely an adult market, as is the market for child pornography. The merchants and entrepreneurs, whether they be the variety store owner, publisher, or pimp are for the most part adults. The briefs at the public hearings were very clearly in favour of bringing responsibility for children's involvement in these activities home to the adults who are the precipitating factor in it. This desire to focus on the adult market, or the adult actor in a transaction, took precedence over any inclination to penalize the child or young person. Measures aimed at eradicating what was clearly seen as exploitation were a high priority with those who made presentations to us.

Implementation of measures and programs for young people was a corollary to the desire for measures aimed at adult exploitation. The desirability of having positive sexual images and good erotic literature available to young people exploring their own sexuality was a recurring theme in the hearings. Sex education by parents and educators was often cited as crucial not only in diverting young people from becoming a market for offensive materials, but also in helping them to be a critical audience for what they do see in the mass media. Supportive programs for youngsters dealing with difficult home or street situations were described, and praised. Unfortunately, all too often, we heard of good programs which were falling victim to government austerity drives.

In addition to the many submissions we received concerning legislative reform and social and educational measures, there were comments about a disturbing cultural phenomenon underlying the overt manifestations of pornography and prostitution. It was pointed out many times that images in the media are increasingly depicting children as sexual objects in order to sell products. Ads showing young girls bare to the shoulder, made up and coiffed like courtesans to display perfume, and an ad for a man's shirt featuring a little girl bare to the waist level, were submitted to the Committee. These, and others using infantile sexuality to sell products, are subject to no control whatever, and form part of what many briefs described as an atmosphere of increasing tolerance of the sexual exploitation of children. As one brief argued:

> The message of "kiddie porn" is echoed everywhere... the image of eroticized childhood has permeated our culture—it pervades film, advertising, popular culture.
> *Women Against Pornography, Victoria*

2. Research Findings

Information with respect to children and pornography and prostitution in Canada comes from two major sources: the Report of the Committee on Sexual Offences Against Children and Youths (Badgley Report)[1] and the program of research completed for the Department of Justice in support of the work of this Committee.

The Badgley Committee on Sexual Offences was established with a specific mandate to investigate:

> ... the incidence and prevalence of sexual abuse against children and youths, and their exploitation for sexual purposes by way of prostitution and pornography. In addition, the Committee is asked to examine the question of access by children and youths to pornographic material.[2]

The Badgley Committee has, therefore, completed a wide-ranging review of all aspects of these issues as they relate to children. As part of its work, the Badgley Committee undertook an extensive program of research. This has provided us with a very up-to-date and comprehensive analysis of children and pornography and prostitution, and we have relied heavily on this committee's

568

research in developing our understanding of the issues. The research commissioned by the Department of Justice for this Committee was not focused specifically on children. Nevertheless, relevant information was obtained in many instances as the research projects proceeded.[3] In one project in particular, the National Population Study on Pornography and Prostitution,[4] the public's views were sought on what sort of material would be acceptable or unacceptable for the different media and different audiences. Here specific reference was made to material using child models and the availability or access of young people to sexually explicit depictions.

2.1 Pornography

The issue of children or young people and pornography in Canada really involves a question of their access to pornography rather than their involvement in its commercial production. All the evidence available to the Committee indicates that the commercial production of pornography using children as models does not occur in Canada. None of the briefs presented to the Committee, for instance, indicated that child pornography is being produced commercially in Canada. We are confident, therefore, that when we address the question of child pornography, we are dealing with questions of very small-scale, non-commercial production and accessibility to materials. Indeed, it is doubtful that any country which produces pornography condones the open and commercial use of children in its production.

The child pornography which is produced seems to be the work of amateurs. Men, and occasionally women, are involved in the photographing of children whom they know and in the exchange of photographs among people with the same sexual interests. It appears that after the material leaves the original photographer, sometimes after it has circulated for some time, the photographs may be used in a picture magazine produced by fly-by-night operators who again circulate the material, usually through the mails. Production of these magazines seems to take place in the United States, but the authorities have little success in tracking down the producers as the place, addresses and names of the magazines change frequently and continually. Indeed, many of these magazines contain no information as to where and by whom they are produced. As with virtually all the pornographic material available in Canada, it enters the country through direct mailing or the regular importation channels.

While we may feel somewhat reassured that the use of children in the production of pornography is not condoned and is infrequent, this aspect is, in fact, only one part of the issue. What is termed child pornography may take into account material other than that which depicts those under 18 in sexually explicit poses.

Child pornography epitomizes the difficulty we face in defining pornography and in deciding what action, if any, is appropriate. Whether or not someone considers a work pornographic depends on the subjective assessment of the viewer and is often a question of the intent of the user. What is labelled child pornography, therefore, is sometimes pictures of children in the nude or pictures of clothed children with their clothing slightly (and some would say provocatively) disarranged. Often there is nothing overtly sexual about the actual photograph and what people see as problematic is the assumed use to which the photograph will be put.

Equally difficult is the fact that although some photographs are obviously of young children, the age of other models is much more debatable. Indeed, in some instances it is explicitly stated that they are over 18. The issue then arises whether the concern is the potential harm to young people who are actually participating in the production, or whether it is the condoning of the message that sexual relations with children are acceptable, normal and perhaps even to be encouraged. Using models who look to be under 18 inculcates these ideas just as much as the use of those who are actually under 18.

If one extends the argument in this way, then written matter would be brought within the category of questionable material, even though this does not involve harm to participants. Thus, books and articles which condone or advocate sexual relations with children are arguably just as problematic as material which pictures such activities, since the message itself is being questioned and not just the way in which the message is delivered. These concerns consequently take the issue of child pornography in a different direction, to focus on the impact of the message on adults and children who have access to and use the material. It was this latter issue over which so many groups expressed concern at the public hearings.

As we have discussed in Part II, Section I, Chapter 6, pornography is more available in Canada today than it was five or ten years ago. This availability is related to the use of all forms of media, rather than just print or films, and to the selling or renting of pornography in a much wider variety of outlets than previously. There does not seem any doubt that pornography is widely available in all parts of the country, although there are regional differences, and that adult magazines in particular are available to children throughout the country. From the information presented to the Committee, it also seems highly probable that many young people have relatively easy access to pornographic videos, television shows and films. A major question, therefore, is whether we think it appropriate for children and young people to have easy access to such materials.

The research literature on the harms to individuals which can be associated with the use of pornography, deals exclusively with adults. As we have suggested elsewhere in the Report, there are insuperable ethical problems with exposing children to materials which might harm them. Based on the empirical research, therefore, it is impossible to demonstrate that exposure to pornography does have harmful consequences for children and young people. It should be clearly understood, however, that this lack of evidence does not mean that the contrary is true: that is, that pornography has no harmful effects on those exposed to it. The whole question is unresolved. People have suggested to the Committee, however, that even though the issue is unresolved, we should be very careful about the welfare of children, since they are seen as the most vulnerable group in society. Thus, while there may be no systematic evidence that pornography causes or does not cause changes in children's attitudes and behaviour, for the better or the worse, there are sufficient questions about the influence of the mass media in general, and about sexually explicit materials in particular, to suggest caution in making them easily and widely available to young people.

Furthermore, as we have argued elsewhere in the Report, we are concerned with depictions that can be seen to undermine the values which we believe are fundamental to our society. It is our view that material which uses and depicts children in a sexual way for the entertainment of adults, undermines the rights of children by diminishing the respect to which they are entitled. In particular, it interferes with their developing sexuality so as to distort it and to encourage the children so used to have aberrant views about human sexual relations.

We have already argued that some adult pornography is also unacceptable because of its distorted message and the resulting harm this causes to our values. It will be evident, given this view of some pornographic material, that we consider it essential to protect children from being exposed to it.

Given the mindless, degrading and sometimes violent depictions of human sexual relations common to some pornographic material, the argument that children should be protected from such distorting images is very powerful. We simply should not run the risk of encouraging young people to believe that the behaviour depicted in pornography is to be accepted or encouraged.

Concern about the possible effect of pornography increases to the extent that there may be no sources of countervailing information available to children and young people. Family life and sex education courses are not universally available in schools and it is not always apparent that parents deal effectively with these topics with their own children. Given these circumstances, we are particularly concerned that children may accept pornography because they do not have access to more accurate information.

It will be apparent that our argument rests on a belief that the harms which have to be demonstrated in order to justify intervention by the state are different for children in comparison with adults. Precisely because of their status as children, they are entitled to protection over a wider range of activities than are adults. That is, intervention by responsible people and authorities is justified before demonstrable physical or psychological harm occurs.

Confirmation of the concerns we heard at the public hearings to protect children from seeing sexually explicit material which is inappropriate for their age or under inappropriate circumstances, comes from the National Population Survey conducted for the Department of Justice in June and July, 1984. This survey involved a sample of 2,018 Canadians chosen so that they were representative of the over 18 year old population across the country, with the exception of the Yukon and Northwest Territories. The survey had several purposes, two of which were to determine:

> what the public considers to be offensive about prostitution and pornography, and perceptions about the harms (or benefits) of prostitution and pornography to themselves, their children and society in general

and

> the extent of public satisfaction with existing controls covering pornography and prostitution and preferences for various policy options.[5]

Out of all the issues investigated through the survey, the one on which there was overwhelming consensus was the use of children in sexually explicit material. Of the respondents, 94% agreed that sexually explicit material showing children is unacceptable in our society.

Canadians also believe that the harms associated with pornography are particularly evident in relation to children. Three-quarters of the respondents indicated that they thought that "exposure to pornography cannot help children develop healthy sexual attitudes" (76%) and that "availability of sex magazines in areas frequented by children is bad for them [children]" (78%).[6]

There are obviously very strong sentiments within Canada for ensuring that children are not used in the making of pornography, and that their access to such materials is more restricted than is currently the case.

As we have discussed in detail in the section on adults and pornography, there is no consensus among Canadians on how or if the material should be controlled when one is considering adults. Such a lack of consensus does not, however, carry over into the area of children.

For some people the issue of children's access to unacceptable material would be solved by the banning or censoring of all or much of the sexually explicit material now available through the entertainment media. If one takes those who expressed these views, together with those who would prefer to control children's access to the material rather than the material itself, it is evident that there is strong support for ensuring that children do not have access to pornographic material (See Table 4, Part II, Section I, Chapter 6).

2.2 Prostitution

Information from the research program undertaken by the Department of Justice, and from the Badgley Committee, confirms the information given at the public hearings that juvenile prostitution occurs across the country, in many mid-sized and all large cities.[7] Although the great majority of juvenile prostitutes work the streets, it is impossible to determine the size of the juvenile contingent. The problems of assessing the number of adults engaged in prostitution were discussed in Part III, Section I, Chapter 28, and these problems are compounded with respect to juveniles who do not want their age to be known by the various authorities. It also appears that more juvenile prostitutes work on an occasional or part-time basis, for example, just on weekends, so that the number of juvenile prostitutes fluctuates considerably during the week, as well as between seasons. As with adults, most of the prostitutes are female, although male juvenile prostitutes are more in evidence now than a few years ago. The ratio of female to male juvenile prostitutes, however, is unknown. With respect to male juvenile prostitutes, it is noteworthy that the majority, 75% according to the Badgley Committee's research, consider themselves to be homosexual.

Although very young people, for example, those 14 years or younger, are known to work the streets, most juvenile prostitutes appear to be 16 or older. This coincides with the age range at which some of the adult prostitutes said they began to work. Indeed, most adult prostitutes report starting in the business when they were juveniles although, clearly, this does not characterize all of them.

Just as the career of the adult prostitute is difficult to determine, so is the career of the juvenile. Juvenile prostitutes come from families at all economic levels and from families with a wide variety of social characteristics. Thus, it is difficult to find characteristics in the social backgrounds of these young people which one might argue would predispose them to choosing prostitution as a way to earn a living. Although it is by no means common to all the families of juvenile prostitutes, there is some indication that their families do experience difficulties and tensions in various ways. Divorce, or the absence of one parent, often the father, because of a family break-up or employment away from home, and the dependency on government financial programs appear to be characteristic of the families of many juvenile prostitutes. The majority of prostitutes interviewed by the Badgley Committee's researchers indicated that their home life was not a happy one and this was an important factor in their move to the streets.

The issue which currently receives considerable attention is that of the sexual abuse of children. It is thought that children whose normal sexual development is disturbed by incestuous or other abnormal sexual activities with adults, are likely to go into jobs where sexual precociousness is a prerequisite. Canadian research to date does not support this view.[8] Juvenile prostitutes are the victims of sexual abuse, but not to any significantly greater degree than other groups in society.

As was discussed in Part III, Section I, Chapter 28, however, our understanding of sexual abuse is at a very preliminary stage, and our conclusions about the level and severity of sexual abuse in the population as a whole, and among juvenile prostitutes in particular, are necessarily tentative. What can be stated at this time is that we do not know why some children who are sexually abused eventually turn to prostitution and others do not. Whether it is related to the severity of the abuse, or to the type and quality of the intervention following the incident, are questions to which we have no answers.

According to the Badgley Committee's data, however, the majority of juvenile prostitutes had had sexual experiences of one type or another by the time they were 13.

It also appears to be very characteristic of juvenile prostitutes that they dropped out of school before completing high school, most usually after grade 10. In addition, most of them have run away from home at least once and often several times, as a means of coping with problems with their families, but also as a way of dealing with school problems or of seeking adventure and new experiences. Typically the young people do not run away to become prostitutes, but their low levels of education and the need to support themselves make them particularly vulnerable to the lure of the streets. Economic reasons are indeed cited as the most common reasons for working as a prostitute. Knowledge about the profession typically comes from the media or from knowing someone who is already in the business, but there is little evidence to suggest that young people are actively coerced into prostitution. As the Badgley Report points out, however, there are all sorts of subtle inducements and pressures that may be exerted to encourage them to become part of the business.

One of the areas about which we have the least satisfactory information is in relation to the organization and control of juvenile prostitutes. Given the illegality of pimping, and moral disapproval of the pimping of juveniles, everyone engaged in the prostitution business is extremely reluctant to talk about the issue. Juvenile prostitutes run the risk of violence and physical abuse from their pimps if they talk about the relationship, because intimidation is a means of keeping the whole issue as quiet as possible. It appears that pimping is carried on only in relation to female prostitutes and only in a minority of cases. While 40% of the female juvenile prostitutes in the Badgley Committee's study indicated that they had been pimped at one time, only 10% indicated that they had a pimp at the time of the interview. In addition, adult prostitutes maintain that pimps avoid juveniles, if at all possible, because they are likely to bring them into increased conflict with the police. On this basis, the 10% figure might seem reasonable, but does not explain how such a high percentage of juvenile prostitutes come to have been pimped at some time, or how they now come to be independent operators. Just as the extent to which pimps are involved in the business remains a very debatable issue, so does the question of the prostitute's relationship to the pimp. Perhaps all that can be concluded at this time is that the relationships run from the totally exploitative and abusive to those which are freely chosen and mutually supportive. Which end of the continuum is most characteristic remains to be determined.

The services of juvenile prostitutes are usually bought by men aged between 30 and 50, who are married. Since customers are a very difficult group on which to collect information, researchers typically have to rely on the prostitutes' own assessments of their clients. There is, however, a remarkable degree of consistency in the descriptions of customers from one end of the country to another. The motivations of customers, and especially the motivations to seek out young prostitutes, are issues about which we can only speculate. We simply do not have any information which would lead to firm conclusions about this aspect of the business.

Juvenile prostitutes are most frequently requested to give oral sex or vaginal intercourse. Customers are likely to initiate contact with the prostitute and to indicate the services they are seeking. The sexual acts are usually performed in the customer's car, a hotel or motel room or an apartment belonging to the prostitute or someone else. The whole transaction is accomplished within half an hour.

Although some juvenile prostitutes indicate that they have regular customers, the sexual transaction is usually characterized by its anonymity and its speed. The prostitutes deliberately attempt to distance themselves emotionally from their customers and to provide the services for which they are paid as quickly as possible. This allows them to be back on the streets and be available to other customers and avoids any involvement with customers beyond the commercial transaction. While some of the juvenile prostitutes indicate that they enjoy their work, it appears that the majority of them find their situation to be anything but satisfactory.

The belief that the streets are a source of easy money continues to make the business attractive to young people. Estimates of income are difficult to obtain and even more difficult to substantiate. Juvenile prostitutes, like their adult counterparts, do not keep records of their transactions. Instead the level of earnings has to be reconstructed by calculating how many days a week and weeks a year a prostitute works, the average number of customers a week and typical prices for services. Much of this information depends on how accurately the juvenile prostitutes can remember their activities and the extent to which they wish to make known the full scope of their activities to people outside the business. The Badgley Committee reports that daily earnings average around $190 for the juvenile prostitutes in the national survey. This figure may be reflective of business on a good day in summer, and not be a very good indication of earnings throughout the year. Nevertheless, it is apparent that while some juvenile prostitutes earn very little, for example, under $50 a day, others are very much more successful in terms of their income. Female prostitutes tend to have higher earnings than males because they are not limited physiologically in the number of customers they can service in a day.

Despite the high level of earnings that at least some of the juvenile prostitutes attain, the young people typically have lifestyles that do not encourage planning or saving money. The money is earned and quickly spent, and any tentative plans the prostitutes may have to move out of the business are very difficult to attain. No money is accumulated to carry them out of prostitution and, indeed, the chances of them moving out would appear to rest on the consequences of intervention by various agencies and organizations, ranging from the family to the police.

It appears that most juvenile prostitutes have a criminal record. While the activities with which they are charged are not necessarily prostitution-related offences, it is apparent that the criminal activities are highly related to being a prostitute. Charges for soliciting are not very common because prostitutes are relatively circumspect in their behaviour, and rarely act in such a manner as to contravene the current interpretation of section 195.1 of the *Criminal Code*. Juvenile prostitutes are picked up for property offences such as shoplifting or theft, sexual offences, drug and alcohol offences, and assault. It would appear that most of the juvenile prostitutes acquire a criminal record after going on the streets and as a consequence of attempting to survive under very harsh conditions.

Drug and alcohol use may be one reaction to these conditions and one way of coping with the business. While some juvenile prostitutes indicated that they were heavy users of alcohol and drugs (about a third of the respondents in the Badgley Committee's research), it is apparent that most of them use such substances infrequently or not at all. Certainly, being on the streets appears to increase the opportunities for access to drugs, but this does not mean that juvenile prostitutes automatically become users. A further note of caution is also necessary on this issue, since we do not know whether the patterns of drug and alcohol use by juvenile prostitutes differ significantly from those of other young people. Thus, while it may seem reasonable to suppose that some of the young prostitutes seek to escape the worst aspects of the business through drugs and alcohol, we do not know whether this is a common response to life on the streets.

A further question related to health is the issue of sexually transmitted diseases (STD's). While adult prostitutes seem to be very aware of these problems, juveniles appear to be less well informed and to take fewer precautions. In some instances, the rates of infection are considerably higher than would be expected in the juvenile population, whereas in other cases, the rates are close to the normal level. Nevertheless, any rate of sexually transmitted diseases is a cause for concern and the fact that most juvenile prostitutes contract such a disease at some time is very serious. Many of the young people do seek routine medical check-ups, but some do not, and generally, juvenile prostitutes appear unconcerned about the possible long-term consequences for their health. STDs are just one more problem which is accepted as part of the life of being a prostitute.

The contacts of juvenile prostitutes with organizations attempting to dissuade them from working on the streets appear haphazard and frequently ineffectual. The police will pick up juvenile prostitutes on the streets and take them to child welfare agencies. Police officers typically see this action as being in the young person's own best interests, or as a way of lessening the number of prostitutes on the street and the associated disruptions. Social agencies are frequently not able to meet the needs of the juvenile prostitute. They lack the authority to hold juveniles for various assessments, they are under-funded and short of staff, and special programs to address the needs of this particular clientele are usually not in place. As the Committee heard time and time again, juvenile prostitutes can be back on the streets within a few hours of being picked up by the police.

On their own initiative, juvenile prostitutes use few social services. The ones they do use are usually those which assist with some immediate problem, for example, the need for medical attention, a room for the night or a meal. On the whole, juvenile prostitutes do not use social services designed to address issues with long-term consequences, such as training programs. Indeed, they appear to have a general contempt for social services and agencies and see themselves as being able to manage their own lives. Social services which have been most successful in assisting juvenile prostitutes are those which have been specially designed to meet their needs such as street worker programs or special hostels.

What happens to most juvenile prostitutes is unknown. Certainly some of them continue in the business as adults, but it is not clear that most of them simply graduate from being juvenile prostitutes to being adult prostitutes. Whether or not juvenile prostitutes move out of the business, and with what short and long term consequences for their lives, are issues which must be addressed in subsequent research.

Given the description of the concerns of those who appeared before the Committee, and the Committee's findings about the involvement in pornography and the nature of juvenile prostitution, let us now examine the present law, and how well it addresses those concerns.

Footnotes

[1] Badgley Report.

[2] *Ibid*, at 3.

[3] N. Boyd, *Sexuality and Violence, Imagery and Reality: Censorship and the Criminal Control of Obscenity*, Working Papers on Pornography and Prostitution (W.P.P.P.)#16; N. Crook, *A Report on Prostitution in the Atlantic Provinces* W.P.P.P.#12; M. El Komos, *Canadian Newspapers Coverage of Pornography and Prostitution, 1978-83* W.P.P.P. #5; J. Fleischman, *A Report on Prostitution in Ontario* W.P.P.P.#10; R. Gemme, A. Murphy, M. Bourque, M. A. Nemeh, and N. Payment, *A Report on Prostitution in Québec*, W.P.P.P.#11; M. Haug and M. Cini, *The Ladies (and Gentlemen) of the Night and the Spread of Sexually Transmitted Diseases* W.P.P.P.#7; C.H.S. Jayewardene, T.J. Juliani and C.K. Talbot, *Prostitution and Pornography in Selected Countries* W.P.P.P.#4; B. Kaite, *A Survey of Canadian Distributors of Pornographic Material* W.P.P.P.#17; John S. Kiedrowski, Jan, J.M. van Dijk, *Pornography and Prostitution in Denmark, France, West Germany, The Netherlands and Sweden* W.P.P.P.#1; M. Lautt, *A Report on Prostitution in the Prairies* W.P.P.P.#9; J. Lowman, *Vancouver Field Study of Prostitution, Research Notes* 2 vs., W.P.P.P.#8; H.B. McKay and D.J. Dolff, *The Impact of Pornography: an Analysis of Research and Summary of Findings* W.P.P.P.#13; T.S. Palys, *A Content Analysis of Sexually Explicit Videos in British Columbia* W.P.P.P.#15; Peat Marwick & Partners, *A National Population Study of Pornography and Prostitution* W.P.P.P.#6; D. Sansfaçon, *Agreements and Conventions of the United Nations with Respect to Pornography and Prostitution* W.P.P.P.#3; D. Sansfaçon, *Pornography and Prostitution in the United States* W.P.P.P.#2; Ian Taylor, *The Development of Law and Public Debate in the United Kingdom in Respect of Pornography and Obscenity* W.P.P.P.#14 Department of Justice, Ottawa, 1984.

[4] Peat Marwick & Partners, *A National Population Study of Pornography and Prostitution*, W.P.P.P.#6.

[5] *Ibid*., at 1.

[6] *Ibid*., at III-28 - III-39.

[7] Badgley Report.

[8] *Ibid*, Vol. I, Chap. 6.

Chapter 43

The Present Law

1. Pornography

There is no provision in the *Criminal Code* which addresses specifically the production, dissemination or use of child pornography.

There are, however, a number of substantive provisions in the *Code* which deal with obscenity or indecent materials generally. As these provisions have been analysed in detail in Part II, Section II, Chapter 7, only their main aspects and applicability to child pornography will be considered here. We shall also examine here the provisions of federal legislation other than the *Criminal Code*, which may affect child pornography.

1.1 Making, Possessing and Disseminating

Examining first the applicable provisions of the *Criminal Code*, we note that section 159 is the main section relating to obscenity. It prohibits, inter alia, the making, printing, publishing, distribution, circulating, selling, exposing to public view, or possession for any one of these purposes, of any obscene written matter, picture, model, phonograph record or other thing whatsoever. It also prohibits the public exhibition of a disgusting object or an indecent show.

Additional offences with respect to live shows are found in section 163. Subsection 163(1) makes it an offence for the lessee, manager, agent or person in charge of a theatre to present, give or allow to be presented or given an immoral, indecent or obscene performance, entertainment or representation. Subsection 163(2) makes it an offence to take part or appear as an actor, performer, or assistant in any capacity in an immoral, indecent or obscene performance, entertainment or representation in a theatre.

Section 164 of the *Code* creates the offence of making use of the mails for the purpose of transmitting or delivering anything that is obscene, indecent, immoral, or scurrilous. To reinforce this provision, prohibitory orders may be made under the *Canada Post Corporation Act*.[1] Subsection 41(1) of this *Act* allows the Minister to make an order prohibiting the delivery of mail addressed to or posted by any person that the Minister believes on reasonable grounds is committing or attempting to commit by mail an offence, or who is aiding, abetting, counselling or procuring any other person to commit such an offence. A prohibitory order may also be made against a person who, by means other than mail, is aiding, abetting, counselling or procuring any other person to commit an offence by means of mail.

One of the first questions arising in connection with these *Criminal Code* sections is whether what is popularly regarded as "child pornography" is within the scope of the words "obscene", "indecent" or "immoral" as used in those sections. Not only the meaning of those terms themselves, but also the impact of the so-called "community standards" test must be looked at to determine this question.

Section 159 contains a definition of obscene, but this statutory definition does not apply to the terms indecent and immoral used in sections 163 and 164. However, the common law definition of the terms, which does apply in connection with sections 163 and 164, also relies on the application of the community standards test which figures in the interpretation of section 158.[2]

Subsection 159(8) defines as obscene, "any publication a dominant characteristic of which is the undue exploitation of sex, or of sex and any one or more of the following subjects, namely crime, horror, cruelty and violence...". How this definition would apply to child pornography is a difficult question. The courts have convicted in cases where the material portrays incest[3] or juveniles engaged in sex.[4] Clearly, the more explicit the sexual conduct or the display of the child's sexual organs, the more likely the definition is to apply. However, nude still shots which show only the external sexual organs, particularly if the poses are not suggestive, may not be within the definition.

The application of the community standards test to determine whether something is obscene has important implications for juvenile pornography. In *Re Hawkshaw v. The Queen*[5] the Ontario Court of Appeal considered a charge under subsection 159(1) of the *Code*, arising from the making of an "obscene" picture. It held that the fact that the picture was intended solely for private viewing, and did not come into any hands other than those of the person who took the picture, are relevant in a consideration of what the Canadian community would tolerate. The implication, of course, is that there would be greater community tolerance if the material were designed only for private use, and a correspondingly greater difficulty in convicting under subsection 159(8).

Section 159 does not prohibit the possession of obscene material for private use. Private use has been generously defined by the courts. It may include showing obscene pictures to a friend or projecting an obscene film in one's own home.[6] It has also been held that showing obscene films in a community hall exclusively to invited friends and relatives is tantamount to a showing in a private gathering, and not prohibited by section 159.[7]

It may, however, be illegal under section 159 to make obscene material even for exclusively private use. Unfortunately, the law is not entirely clear on this point. In *Re Hawkshaw v. The Queen* the accused submitted to a developing laboratory a roll of film containing a picture of four persons, one of whom was performing fellatio on a seventeen year old boy. Although the Court accepted that the accused intended to use the photo only for private viewing, it nonetheless upheld his committal to stand trial for the offence of making or printing an obscene picture under section 159. Because the accused has appealed this decision to the Supreme Court of Canada, however, the issue raised by the case cannot be said to have been conclusively determined.

In addition to the *Criminal Code* provisions described above, section 14 and Schedule "C" of the *Customs Tariff* prohibit the importation into Canada of "books, printed paper, drawings, paintings, prints, photographs, or representations of any kind of an immoral or indecent character."[8] The contemporary Canadian community standard of tolerance has emerged as the decisive test in the Customs area as well as in connection with sections 159, 163 and 164 of the *Criminal Code* discussed above.[9]

Subsection 40(1) of the *Canada Post Corporation Act* requires that all mail from a country other than Canada containing or suspected to contain anything the importation of which is prohibited, shall be submitted to a Customs officer for examination. Customs officers are, in turn, required by subsection 40(3) of the *Act* to deal with all mail submitted to them under this section in accordance with the laws relating to the importation of goods. By means of the interrelationship between these subsections and the *Customs Tariff*, mail from outside Canada suspected of containing immoral or indecent material can be inspected.

These provisions with respect to mail and Customs regulations are significant to the issue of child pornography because the mails seem to be one of the frequently used ways of distributing and exchanging such material.

1.2 Involving Children in Pornography

There are a number of *Criminal Code* provisions which might apply in the case of someone securing the participation of a child or young person in the production of pornography. Subsection 168(1) of the *Code* penalizes anyone who, in the home of a child, participates in sexual immorality or indulges in any other form of vice, and thereby endangers the morals of the child or renders the home an unfit place for the child to be in. In *R. v. E. and F.*,[10] the mother of a child and the mother's common law husband were convicted where they had photographed the eleven year old child in sexually suggestive poses. One of the obvious difficulties in looking for widespread use of this section is the requirement that the acts take place in the home of the child. There is no other section which has a direct application to the activities of adults in procuring youngsters for pornography.

Where the child is photographed while engaging in sexual relations with other people, then a number of sections of the *Code* may be applicable to the conduct of the child's partner. These include the offences of a male having sexual intercourse with a female under 14 years of age, or between 14 and 16,[11] having illicit sexual intercourse with a step-daughter, foster daughter or female ward,[12] and committing buggery or bestiality[13] or an act of gross indecency.[14] The parent or guardian of a female person who procures her to have illicit sexual intercourse with a person other than the procurer, or orders, is party to, permits, or knowingly receives the avails of the defilement, seduction or prostitution of the female person, is guilty of an indictable offence.[15] There are comparable provisions relating to the owner, occupier, or manager of premises who permits a female under 18 to resort thereto for purposes of having sexual intercourse with a particular male person or persons.[16]

Persons involved in the preparation of child pornography might also be charged with counselling or procuring a person to be party to an offence,[17] with aiding or abetting a person to commit an offence,[18] with conspiracy to commit an indictable offence[19] or with conspiracy "to effect an unlawful purpose".[20]

With the repeal of the *Juvenile Delinquents Act,*[21] the general offence of contributing to the delinquency of a minor is no longer available to charge persons using young persons in pornography.[22] However, there may be recourse against child exploiters through provincial child welfare laws. For example, section 38 of the *Alberta Child Welfare Act* provides that a person who has the care, custody, control or charge of a child and who ill-treats, neglects, abandons or harmfully exposes a child or causes or procures such ill-treatment, is guilty of an offence.[23] The child welfare statutes of Prince Edward Island, Québec, Manitoba, Saskatchewan, the Yukon Territory and the Northwest Territories create similar offences.[24] Such provisions address the conduct of a parent or guardian who procures or participates in the exploitation of a child by involving him or her in the production of pornography. Because of the stipulation that the accused person have the "care, custody, control or charge" of a child, however, it may be doubtful whether provisions like section 38 of the *Alberta Act* can reach the conduct of third parties not in the child's family or household circle.

The *Alberta Child Welfare Act* also purports to regulate the employment of children over 12 years of age in entertainments; the structure of the *Act* indicates that children under 12 may not in any event be so employed. Before granting a licence for the employment of a child over 12, the Child Welfare Commission must be satisfied of the fitness of the child to take part in the proposed entertainment or series of entertainments without injury to his or her life, limbs, health, education or morals. The Commission must also be satisfied that proper provision has been made to secure the health and kind treatment of the child. It is made an offence for anyone to employ a child under 16 without a licence "for the purpose of singing, playing or performing for profit or of offering anything for sale in a public place or a place to which the public is admitted on payment."[25]

Although provisions of this nature aimed at employment may be useful in addressing some types of child sexual exploitation through pornography, they do not of course address the situation where a child is photographed or filmed without being "employed" - i.e. paid. It is, in our view, likely that many, if not most, of the situations which concern us do involve unpaid use.

One further observation is appropriate concerning provincial child welfare provisions. Again we will use the Alberta statute as an example. The child welfare authorities may detain a child who is neglected as that term is defined in the legislation. There are many aspects of the definition of "neglected child" which would allow the authorities to remove a child from parents who were involving him or her in pornography; for example, paragraph 6(e)(xii) defines as neglected any child "whose life, health or morals may be endangered by the conduct of the person in whose charge he is." There is even the possibility that the child could be apprehended not because of parental defect, but because of third party actions involving the child in pornography; a "neglected child" is defined in paragraph 6(a)(v) as one found associating with an unfit or improper person.

We have not, however, found any provincial child welfare provision which describes a child as "neglected" because of the child's involvement in pornography, whether as an actor or as an unwilling consumer. We note that the Report of the Committee on Sexual Offences Against Children and Youths commented upon the absence from child welfare legislation of any specific provision characterizing a child as neglected because of sexual abuse. The Committee recommended that provincial authorities undertake a full review of local legislation, addressing this terminology issue and other issues relating to the clear specification of the types of investigative responsibility for suspected cases of the physical and sexual abuse of children.[26]

We agree that provincial child welfare authorities should be encouraged to review the question of their response to child sexual abuse, and consider that the more limited issue of children's involvement in the production of pornography should be on the agenda of any such review. However, we caution that not every child who is involved in the production of pornography may necessarily be a "neglected child" within the philosophy of child welfare legislation. In our view, it is useful to bear in mind that a determination that a child is neglected can result in removal of the child from his or her home, either temporarily or, after a court hearing, for a longer period. It may involve intervention by state agencies in the family's life for periods of time and orders that a third party is not to associate with a child, like those discussed elsewhere in this chapter.

In some cases, it may well be desirable to involve youth authorities and precipitate outcomes like these. In other cases, it clearly would not. Very often, the family itself will be quite able to deal with the child's involvement in the production of pornography, once made aware that it is going on. It would be unfortunate if too focused a definition of neglected child were to precipitate state intervention in the family, as described above, each and every time a situation of exploitation, even by third parties, were discovered. This is not to say that the state should forbear from intervening in a proper case. The problem is to achieve a balance between respect for the autonomy and capacity of the family to deal with exploitation of its own children (especially but not always where such exploitation is by persons outside the family), and the provision of state assistance where that is needed.

Recommendation 66

> **Provincial child welfare authorities are encouraged to review their response to child sexual abuse, as recommended by the Committee on Sexual Offences on Children and Youths (at pp. 548-549). We recommend that the issue of children's involvement in the production of pornography should be on the agenda of any such review. However, we caution that not every child involved in the production of pornography may be a neglected child within the philosophy of child welfare legislation. Accordingly, we recommend that a balance be struck between recognizing the autonomy and capacity of the family to deal with exploitation of its own children and the provision of state assistance where that is needed.**

1.3 Overview

In our view, a number of serious deficiences exist in the present law relating to child pornography. Firstly, there is doubt as to whether the definition of obscene, or immoral, or indecent, would reach some types of material which arguably should be caught by the criminal sanction. Similarly, material prepared for only private use should not, in our view, escape criminalization. At present, it may do so, because of the application of what is, in effect, a more forgiving community standard for materials used privately. Our hearings and research have disclosed that private preparation and use of child pornography is a major mode of resorting to this material. We have also learned that contemporary Canadian community standards are running strongly against such private use.

We also note the absence of a really effective and direct sanction against persons who involve children in pornography. The sanctions against theatrical performances found in subsection 159(2)(b) ("indecent show") and section 163, do not really reach those whose use of children is private. Nor do the child welfare provisions aimed at regulating the use of children in "entertainments".

It must be recognized that much, if not most, exploitation of children occurs in situations which would be defined as private in our law. Existing criminal sanctions are not likely to reach much of the private exploitation of children. Even section 168 of the *Code* has application only where the offence takes place in the child's home, so that exploitation in someone else's home, or a hotel or studio, would not be reached. Section 166 criminalizes only the defilement of female children, and is addressed only to the parents or guardians of the child. Nor is it made clear in the section that securing the child's participation in the preparation of pornography would be criminal conduct.

The provisions of the *Code* criminalizing certain aspects of the production of child pornography have, in our view, obvious limitations and do not represent any serious alternative to a section dealing directly with the use of children in pornography. One of these limitations is that most of the sections listed apply only where the behaviour represented involves two or more persons; in some cases, one of the persons must be an adult for the section to apply. Thus, photographs of a child alone or of two children would not attract to the participants the sanctions described. Most particularly, the sections do not reach the conduct of the person who produces the pornography and benefits from it.

Although child welfare laws may be useful in many situations involving the use of children in pornography, they have several limitations. Not all the provinces have provisions which make it an offence to ill-treat or procure the ill-treatment of a child, and the sanctions attached to this offence in the jurisdictions where it does exist are, in any event, not large. Intervening in the family by way of the neglected child provisions of child welfare legislation is not always a good solution, particularly where the threat to the child has come from outside the family.

In our view, it is necessary to provide direct criminal sanctions which would deter the use of children in the production of pornography. Sanctions against possession of pornography involving children are also, in our opinion, important because they attack the market for such materials and arguably will thereby reduce the incentive to produce it.

Recommendation 67

We recommend the enactment of criminal sanctions for the production, dissemination, and possession of "child pornography".

In chapter 46 of this Part, we propose amendments to the *Criminal Code* to introduce criminal penalties for the production, dissemination and possession of child pornography. Before proceeding to describe those measures, however, we shall examine some of the unsuccessful legislative initiatives in this area.

1.4 Previous Reform Attempts

Since 1959, the year of the last reform of the *Criminal Code* sections dealing with pornography, a number of efforts have been made to introduce bills dealing specifically with child pornography. The thrust of such efforts has been twofold. Proponents of the bills have sought to have included in the *Code* a definition of "obscenity" which specifically mentions portrayal of children, and they have also sought to penalize persons for using children in pornographic materials.

Considering firstly those bills dealing with the definition of pornography, it is noteworthy that nine bills receiving first reading in the House of Commons on October 31, 1977 all proposed to add to the *Criminal Code* a section creating an offence for everyone who photographs, produces, publishes, imports, exports, distributes, sells, advertises or displays in a public place, anything that depicts a child performing a sexual act or assuming a sexually suggestive pose while in a state of undress. The bills all defined "child" as a person who is or appears to be under the age of 16 years. The bills defined "sexual act" as masturbation, any act of sado-masochism, and any act of anal, oral, or vaginal intercourse, whether alone or with or upon another person, animal, dead body or inanimate object. An attempted or simulated sexual act was included.[27] A tenth bill, also receiving first reading in October 31, 1977,[28] made it an offence knowingly to produce, publish, transmit, distribute, sell or receive for resale, a film or publication of any kind that depicts a child engaged in a sexually explict act. The definitions of "child" and "sexually explicit act" were the same as in the other nine bills.

All of these bills were referred to the Standing Committee on Justice and Legal Affairs. The Committee concluded that "so-called "kiddie-porn" is reprehensible and clearly unacceptable in contemporary Canadian society."[29] It recommended that the definition of obscenity in the *Criminal Code* be amended to include sexually explicit material involving children. The definition proposed by the Committee was that a matter or thing should be deemed to be obscene where it depicts or describes a child engaged or participating in an act or simulated act of masturbation, sexual intercourse, gross indecency, buggery or bestiality, or displaying any portion of its body in a sexually suggestive manner.[30] Child was defined as a person who is or appears to be under the age of 16 years.

Following the report of the Standing Committee, two attempts were made to have this definition or a similar one inserted into the *Code*. Bill C-434, a Private Member's bill introduced into the 1977-78 Session by Mr. Whiteway, sought to include the Standing Committee's definition in the *Criminal Code*. Bill C-21, proposed by the Minister of Justice, received first reading on November 21, 1978. This bill defined a matter or thing as obscene where it "unduly depicts a totally or partially nude child engaged or participating in an act or a simulated act of masturbation, sexual intercourse, gross indecency, buggery or bestiality, or unduly displaying any part of his or her body in a sexually suggestive manner."[31] Whereas Mr. Whiteway's bill tried explicitly to forbid reliance on evidence of community standards where child pornography was concerned,[32] the government bill used the term "unduly", which presumably would have provided the basis for the introduction of community standards evidence.

Neither of these bills was proceeded with. In 1981, however, Bill C-53 was introduced by the Minister of Justice. The bill created a number of offences relating to visual representations of a person under 16 years of age participating in sexually explicit conduct: inducing, coercing or agreeing to use a person under 16 to participate in such conduct for the purpose of making a visual representation; participating in the production of a visual representation; and making, printing, reproducing, publishing, distributing, circulating, selling, offering to sell, receiving for sale, advertising, exposing to public view, or having such a representation in his or her possession for any such purpose. This bill was not proceeded with either.

A number of attempts have been made since 1959 to strengthen the prohibitions against involving young people in sexually explicit conduct, and these are discussed below in the portion of this chapter dealing with young persons and prostitution. Only two bills have aimed specifically at involvement of young people in sexually explicit behaviour for the purpose of producing pornographic material. Bill C-53, introduced by the Minister of Justice and given first reading on January 12, 1981, would have made it an offence knowingly to induce, coerce or agree to use a person under 16 years to participate in any sexually explicit conduct for the purpose of producing, by any means, a visual representation of such conduct. The bill further provided that a person who at any material time appeared to be under the age of 16 would, in the absence of evidence to the contrary, be presumed to be under 16.

On February 8, 1983, Mr. Kilgour's bill C-673 received first reading. The bill created an offence for everyone who employs, uses, persuades, induces, entices, or coerces a person who is under 18 years of age to engage in sexually explicit conduct with the intent to disseminate any audio, visual or printed medium depicting such conduct. The bill also created the offence of being a parent, legal guardian, or person having the custody or control of a person under 18 years of age, and assisting or permitting such a person to engage in sexually explicit conduct with the intent to disseminate any audio, visual or printed medium depicting such conduct.

The recommendations of this Committee dealing with child pornography and the procurement of children to be in pornography are set out and discussed below. Included in this discussion are observations about how our proposals differ from the numerous attempts over the years to legislate on child pornography. At this point, it is appropriate to consider the other aspect of the pornography problem involving children, that is, their exposure to pornography.

1.5 Exposure of Children to Pornography

The exposure of youngsters to offensive or pornographic material is addressed in a number of ways in federal and provincial legislation.

In the *Criminal Code*, we find, again, the basic prohibition in section 159 against the distribution, circulation, selling, exposure to public view or possession for any of these purposes, of any obscene written matter, picture, model, phonograph record or other thing whatsover. A merchant keeping obscene materials for sale would be caught by this provision; and accordingly, one of the side effects of the provisions may be to encourage some commercial enterprises to restrict the type of material they have available.

Submissions at the public hearings of this Committee did, however, focus on a number of shortcomings of this criminal prohibition as a means of controlling what youngsters have access to, willingly or unwillingly. One such shortcoming is that the section reaches only those found with material within the definition of obscene. That definition, in the view of many, is not broad enough to include the sorts of material they would keep from young people, whatever may be the merits of the section where adults are concerned. Thus, many magazines, notices, posters or advertisements that would be considered inappropriate for young persons to see, are displayed with impunity.

Briefs at the public hearings also indentified enforcement of the *Criminal Code* provisions as a source of difficulty where material offensive to young people is on view. Community groups sometimes charged that material which they consider to be clearly within section 159 is left alone by local enforcement authorities. Many reasons are given, by community groups or police officials, for not responding to citizen complaints about this material. One, of course, is a difference of opinion between citizens and police about the applicability of section 159. The difficulties caused by the vague standards in subsection 159(8) have already been canvassed above. However, other reasons do not seem so reasonable. We have been told, for example, that some local authorities may believe that any publication which has entered Canada must have had clearance from Customs officials. Such clearance is not, however, a defence in law to a charge under section 159. We have also been told that unfortunately, some police authorities or Crown attorneys may not consider charges worth bringing, because of the high likelihood of acquittal. In some communities, too, citizens may be reluctant even to press for police action because of the size or closeness of the community and the prominence of the retailer whose conduct is offensive.

Because the criminal law sanctions against display of material are, for most purposes, of no practical use, more and more muncipalities have turned in recent years to the enactment of by-laws to control display of so-called adult materials. The central features of such by-laws will often be requirements that the merchant place "adult" material at a certain height from the floor, and ensure that it has an opaque cover or is displayed in such a way that only the title is visible.

This course of action was recommended by the Standing Committee on Justice and Legal Affairs in its 1978 Report. Its recommendation number 8 stipulated that:

> Provincial, regional, municipal and local authorities should adopt the necessary licensing, zoning, and child protection legislation, regulations, and by-laws to ensure that acceptable sexually explicit material is advertised, displayed, and sold discreetly to adults and under no circumstances to children or young people.[33]

The availability to young people of offensive records, audiotapes, record jackets, and videotapes was also cited in our hearings as the cause of difficulties. There are at present very few regulatory regimes which deal with any aspect of this problem. In fact, there are no controls, other than the criminal law, on audio recordings, and in only two jurisdictions, Nova Scotia and Ontario, have videotapes been brought under the aegis of a review board regime. These provinces require licensing of retail film exchanges which sell or lease material for private consumption. Details of the review scheme are outlined above.

We received many representations during the public hearings on the need for a good classification system for videotapes, so that parents wishing to do so could monitor their children's selections. In the absence of such a system, we were told, it is not always possible to determine from the title of a tape what its contents are likely to be, because titles of children's entertainments are sometimes also used for sexually explicit tapes. Similarly, we were told of young people unwittingly being subject to unpleasant material because of the difficulty of predicting from the title and cover what will be in the tape.

For the most part, parents who presented briefs at the public hearings did not expect the state to do the full job of protecting their youngsters from offensive or illegal material. These parents recognized willingly the role of the family in shaping the tastes and standards of young people, and in helping them to understand their developing sexuality. However, there was a distinct expectation on the part of parents that society should assist them in this endeavour. The film classification system now in operation in most jurisdictions was cited as a good example of how the state can provide information to parents. In some briefs, however, there were calls for greater particularity in descriptions of films, and for requirements that operators of movie establishments be more forthright about the classifications assigned by the authorities to movies they display.

Overall, however, the two methods of reviewing and classifying films and videotapes, and display restrictions for other adult material, received widespread and firm support as useful methods of helping parents monitor what young persons are to see. Interestingly, while there was some support at the hearings for the idea of segregating "adult only" movies and books to particular stores or enclaves in the city, such support was not uniformly strong. It appears that there is considerable confidence that properly administered systems of classification on the one hand, and display control on the other, can effectively handle the problems perceived by most.

Recommendation 68

> **Provincial and municipal authorities should continue their efforts to control the access of young people to offensive material by means of film and video classification systems and municipal by-laws regulating access to adult material.**

Some presenters at the public hearings drew to our attention the problem of young people gaining access to offensive material through adults or older children, and asked for measures specifically to deal with this problem. Where the material is provided by the parent, guardian or other person in charge of a child, then section 168 of the *Criminal Code* or child welfare legislation, may provide some recourse. However, where it is an adult who is not a parent, or an older child, who makes available the material, then there is no readily apparent direct recourse.

The availability problem and other issues related to the display of offensive material to youngsters, have been addressed in a series of bills introduced into federal Parliament in recent years to deal with pornography.

Bill C-210, introduced by Mr. Whiteway and receiving first reading in October, 1976, would have created for the provinces, classification boards which had jurisdiction over "any written matter, picture, model, phonograph record or other thing whatsover." The bill created an offence of knowingly, without lawful justification or excuse, selling, exposing to public view or having in possession for these purposes, any matter classified by the board as "restricted", in any outlet frequented by persons who are or appear to be under 18 years of age.

Mr. Whiteway's Bill C-281, receiving first reading in October, 1977, would have created a new offence of exposing minors to offensive publications or shows. The proposed new subsection 159(2.1) created the offence of knowingly, without lawful justification or excuse, exposing in a public place or in a place where persons under the age of 18 years are admitted, any matter or thing or live show that depicts or presents a person, whether or not in a state of undress, unduly displaying his or her body in a sexually suggestive manner, or engaging or participating in an act or a simulated act of masturbation or sexual intercourse, gross indecency, buggery or bestiality.

In Bill C-325, sponsored by Mrs. Appolloni in 1977, a new subsection 166.1(2) would have made it an offence for the proprietor or manager of premises open to the public to display, exhibit or advertise any matter or thing of a lewd or sexually suggestive nature. The section stipulated that the defence to a charge involved proof that no child has access to the premises, and that no child is exposed to the matter or thing from outside the premises, or proof that the matter or thing cannot harm a child morally or psychologically.

Mr. Kaplan's Bill C-411, which received first reading in December, 1977, made it an offence for the proprietor or manager of an adult bookstore, an adult motion picture theatre, an adult coin-operated entertainment establishment, an adult topless entertainment establishment, or an adult physical culture establishment, to display or describe a specified sexual activity or specified sexual area, as defined, on a sign, in an advertisement, in the window of the premises or by any means that attracts public attention outside the premises.

The Bill included specific definitions for the various "adult" outlets against which the offence was directed. It defined "specified sexual activity" as an act of sexual intercourse, sodomy or masturbation by a person; or fondling or erotic touching of the genitals, pubic region, buttocks or female breasts of a person; and specified "sexual area" as the naked genitals, pubic region or buttocks of a person, or that portion of a naked female breast located immediately below a point at the top of the areola.

Mr. Kilgour's Bill C-673 received first reading in February, 1983. It would have made it an offence to disseminate pornographic material to a person who is under 18 years of age, or to any person in a manner affording no immediately effective opportunity to avoid exposure to such material, or to commercially disseminate pornographic material to any person.

The recommendations of this Committee concerning availability of pornographic or offensive material to youngsters are set out and discussed below. We have not followed any particular bill described above, although there is some similarity between what is proposed by this Committee and some of the approaches experimented with by the Private Member's bills.

Now let us turn to an examination of the present law relating to prostitution.

2. Prostitution

2.1 Activities of the Child Prostitute

Section 195.1 of the *Criminal Code* provides that:

Every person who solicits any person in a public place for the purpose of prostitution is guilty of an offence punishable on summary conviction.

A young person may be charged under this section, and tried for the offence in a youth court pursuant to the *Young Offenders Act*.

The *Young Offenders Act* was proclaimed in force as of April 2, 1984. As mentioned above, a young person is defined in that *Act* as a person who is, or who, in the absence of evidence to the contrary, appears to be 12 years of age or more, but under 18 years of age. It is intended that by April 1, 1985, 18 will be the uniform upper age limit for this *Act* for all of Canada. In the transitional phase spanning the first year of operation of the *Act*, provinces are permitted to establish upper age limits lower than 18. In Newfoundland and British Columbia, the upper limit is now 17, and in Nova Scotia, New Brunswick, Prince Edward Island, Ontario, Saskatchewan, Alberta, the Yukon Territory and Northwest Territories, it is 16.[34]

A significant feature of the *Act* is that it does not apply to anyone under 12 years of age, defined in the *Act* as a "child".[35] Moreover, section 72 of the *Act* enacts a new section 12 for the *Criminal Code*, specifying that no person shall be convicted of an offence in respect of an act or omission on his part while he was under the age of 12 years. Formerly, sections 12 and 13 of the *Code* (repealed by the *Young Offenders Act*) had provided that no person while over the age of 7 and under the age of 14 years could be convicted of a criminal offence, unless he was competent to know the nature and consequences of his conduct and to appreciate that it was wrong.[36]

Certain important consequences flow from the fact that section 195.1 of the *Criminal Code* creates a summary conviction offence. These consequences arise whether the accused is subject to the *Young Offenders Act* or the *Criminal Code* procedures. By reason of subsection 452(2) of the *Criminal Code*, the arresting officer shall release from custody a person charged with a summary conviction offence, with the intention of compelling his appearance by way of a summons, or shall issue an appearance notice to the person, as soon as is practicable after an arrest. The officer may refrain from following this procedure if he or she has reasonable and probable grounds to believe that it is necessary in the public interest that the person be detained in custody, or that the person will fail to attend in court if released from custody. In making his or her determination about the public interest, the officer is entitled to have regard for the need to establish the identity of the person, secure or preserve evidence of the offence, or prevent the continuation or repetition of the offence or the commission of another offence.

Where the arresting officer does not release the accused pursuant to subsection 452(2), the officer in charge at the police station may do so. The officer in charge may compel the person's appearance by way of a summons,[37] or release him or her on a promise to appear[38] or on a recognizance not exceeding $500.[39] The officer in charge has the same mandate to consider the public interest in favour of keeping the person in custody as does the arresting officer. All of these provisions concerning release by police officers of someone charged with a summary conviction offence are in addition to the judicial interim release provisions of the *Code*.

Significantly, these release procedures are available in the case of a young person charged with soliciting under section 195.1. Both under the former *Juvenile Delinquents Act* and under the *Young Offenders Act*, a police officer might release a young person upon issuing a summons or appearance notice or upon his or her promise to appear on recognizance. The availability of these release procedures is explicitly recognized by subsection 9(2) of the *Young Offenders Act*.

We received many submissions about the difficulty caused by the so-called "revolving door" whereby a young person arrested for soliciting could be out on the street after a few hours. The existence of the revolving door was attributed by some witnesses to defects in provincial child protection laws, or to the scarcity of adequate resources for the detention pending trial of young people charged with soliciting.

Where the young person is charged with an offence under section 195.1, however, it would appear as if the root of the revolving door syndrome is in the release procedure set out in the *Code* for summary conviction offences. This procedure makes possible release without a judicial hearing, and without conditions about activities and associates being laid down for the young person. It seems as if police officers may give insufficient attention to their discretion to retain someone in custody, if to do so is in the public interest, having regard to the need to prevent the continuation or repetition of the offence or the commission of another offence. It may well be, of course, that the absence of appropriate detention facilities for young persons charged with soliciting contributed to some of the decisions to release them summarily.

Under the *Young Offenders Act*, subsection 9(2), notice of the summary release of a young person must be given to his or her parent. If the whereabouts of the parents are not known or it appears that no parent is available, the notice may be served on an adult who is known to the young person and likely to assist him. A youth court judge may dispense with this requirement of notice.[40]

A similar notice to the parent, guardian or relatives was required under the former *Juvenile Delinquents Act*,[41] and it had been held that lack of notice is a jurisdictional defect which prevents the court from convicting or acquitting.[42] Dismissal of the charge was apparently available at the instigation of defence counsel where the notice was defective.[43] We learned, at the public hearings and in our other research, that young persons sometimes gave false names upon being arrested for soliciting. Such practices may, of course, have led to the inability to proceed on some charges, but we have no information on the number of such cases. The provision in the *Young Offenders Act* that the youth court judge may dispense with notice altogether, may relieve against difficulties caused by the improper identification of young people charged with street soliciting. However, even under the *Young Offenders Act*, failure to give notice will still invalidate any subsequent proceedings where the notice requirement is not dispensed with, or where a parent does not actually attend the hearing.[44]

In addition to the prohibition against street solicitation, the young prostitute could face a charge under subsection 193(1) of the *Code* for keeping a common bawdy house. Under this provision, premises used by only one person for the purpose of prostitution or the practice of acts of indecency, can constitute a common bawdy house. Accordingly, even discreet use by a person of his or her apartment could attract the charge.

Being a keeper of a common bawdy house is an indictable offence. By reason of subsections 483(c)(vi) and 452(1) and 453(1) of the *Criminal Code*, a person arrested on this charge can be released by the arresting officer, or officer in charge, in the same summary way as can someone charged with a summary conviction offence.

The *Criminal Code* is not the only recourse available to law enforcement agencies if young people are found engaging in soliciting or acts of prostitution. They can be taken into care under the child welfare legislation of a province, as a child in need of protection, or a neglected child. It would appear that most provincial statutes include definitions of neglected child which are broad enough to include a child involved in prostitution. The explanation for the so-called revolving door syndrome in child welfare proceedings may depend to some extent on the wording of the individual provincial legislation. We suggest, however, that one underlying cause for the phenomenon in these proceedings, as in ones based on the criminal law, may be absence of adequate resources for the detention of the young person pending a hearing.

2.2 Using the Services of a Child Prostitute

There is no provision in the *Criminal Code* which specifically addresses the purchase by adults of the sexual services of the young. There are some sections which may, however, apply to particular sorts of conduct.

A male person who has sexual intercourse with a female person, not his wife, who is under the age of 14 is guilty of an indictable offence and liable to imprisonment for life.[45] The provision applies whether or not the person believes that the girl is 14 years of age or more. There is no requirement that the girl be "of previously chaste character", and the fact that the person consented to the commission of the offence is not a defence.[46]

It is an offence for a male to have intercourse with a female person, not his wife, who is 14 years of age or more, and under 16 years. However, the youngster must be "of previously chaste character."[47] Clearly, this requirement means that the provision would be inapplicable in the case of a juvenile prostitute. Also inapplicable for the same reason is section 151 of the *Code*, making it an offence for a male 18 years of age or more to seduce a female of previously chaste character who is 16 years or more of age, but under 18.

The limitations of the foregoing provisions are serious. To be protected by the *Code*, juveniles over 14 must have a previously chaste character, and even then, the *Code* protects only against intercourse. For example, a person could not be charged with requiring a 12 year old girl to masturbate him or perform fellatio on him. None of these provisions applies, in any event, to acts performed on young males, whether by males or by females.

The *Code* provides that everyone who commits buggery or bestiality[48] or an act of gross indecency with another person[49] is guilty of an indictable offence. Acts performed in private between husband and wife or between two consenting persons, each of whom is 21 or over, are not illegal.[50] A person can be charged with an offence of buggery or gross indecency even if the person with whom it is committed is not "of previously chaste character."

Turning now to the *Code* provision about soliciting, it should be noted that because of conflicting decisions from the Courts of Appeal of British Columbia and Ontario, it is unsettled whether a customer or potential customer of a prostitute can be charged with an offence under section 195.1. The B.C. Court of Appeal has ruled that a prospective customer cannot be charged,[51] but, in another case, the Ontario Court of Appeal refused to follow this ruling, and upheld the charge against the prospective customer.[52] Accordingly, the section offers no reliable protection against the solicitation of young persons.

2.3 Provisions Aimed at those Involving Young Persons in Prostitution

Section 166 of the *Criminal Code* provides that a parent or guardian of a female person who procures her to have illicit sexual intercourse with a person other than the procurer, or orders, is party to, permits or knowingly receives the avails of the defilement, seduction or prostitution of the female, is guilty of an indictable offence.

Section 167 provides that an owner, occupier or manager of premises, or person who has control of premises or assists in their management, who knowingly permits a female person under the age of 18 to resort to or be in or upon the premises for the purpose of having illicit sexual intercourse with a particular male person, or male persons generally, is guilty of an indictable offence.

Subsection 195(1) of the *Code* provides for an indictable offence for everyone who:

(a) procures, attempts to procure or solicits a person to have illicit sexual intercourse with another person, whether in or out of Canada,

(b) inveigles or entices a person who is not a prostitute or a person of known immoral character to a common bawdy house of assignation for the purpose of illicit sexual intercourse or prostitution,

(c) knowingly conceals a person in a common bawdy house or house of assignation,

(d) procures or attempts to procure a person to become, whether in or out of Canada, a prostitute,

(e) procures or attempts to procure a person to leave the usual place of abode of that person in Canada, if that place is not a common bawdy house, with intent that the person may become an inmate or frequenter of a common bawdy house, whether in or out of Canada,

(f) on the arrival of a person in Canada, directs or causes that person to be directed, or takes or causes that person to be taken, to a common bawdy house of assignation,

(g) procures a person to enter or leave Canada, for the purpose of prostitution,

(h) for the purposes of gain, exercises control, direction or influence over the movements of a person in such manner as to show that he is aiding, abetting or compelling that person to engage in or carry on prostitution with any person or generally,

(i) applies or administers to a person or causes that person to take any drug, intoxicating liquor, matter or thing with intent to stupefy or overpower that person in order thereby to enable any person to have illicit sexual intercourse with that person, or

(j) lives wholly or in part on the avails of the prostitution of another person.

Provincial child welfare legislation may also provide recourse against persons introducing children to prostitution or maintaining them in it, or using the services of child prostitutes. We have discussed above some of the shortcomings of provincial child welfare legislation, and here merely point out that those same shortcomings are evident in connection with use of the legislation to deal with child prostitution.

The principal advantage of such provincial legislation may be in enabling some severance of the connection between the child and the person creating the danger. The New Brunswick *Child and Family Services and Family Relations Act*, provides that the security or development of a child may be in danger when the child is physically or sexually abused, sexually exploited or in danger of such treatment.[53] The child may be taken into "protective care" in such a case. Within five days, unless the child is released, a court hearing ensues. At the hearing, one of the orders which may be made[54] is a "protective intervention order", directed to any person who, in the opinion of the court, is a source of danger to the child's security or development. Such an order may contain a direction to any person to refrain from any contact or association with the child. Violation of such an order is an offence.[55] Similarly, Québec's *Youth Protection Act* permits that parents and child may agree with youth protection authorities that certain persons refrain from coming into contact with a child; where there is no such voluntary agreement, a court application may produce an order to this effect.[56]

This Committee did not hear any evidence that would suggest that use of provisions like these is legally improper in the case of persons introducing juveniles to prostitution, keeping them in prostitution, or using their services. It would seem that the main determinants of whether the child welfare legislation will be used are the discretion of law enforcement officials, and availability of resources.

2.4 Previous Reform Attempts

A number of the bills introduced into the House of Commons in the last 10 years which have addressed the issue of involving young persons in sexual activities, have done so from the perspective of both pornography and prostitution. We have discussed above, Bills C-53 and C-673 which sought specifically to forbid the procurement of children to engage in the production of pornography. Other suggestions for reform have been much more broadly worded.

In 1977, Bill C-206, a Private Member's bill sponsored by Mr. Epp, proposed that it be an offence to procure a child to engage in or to assist any person to engage in a sexually explicit act, or to procure, to be party to, or knowingly receive the avails of the defilement, seduction or prostitution of a child. "Child" was defined as a person who is or appears to be under the age of 16 years. A "sexually explicit act" was defined as any act of masturbation, sado-masochism, or anal, oral, or vaginal intercourse, whether alone or with or upon another person, animal, dead body or inanimate object, and was said to include an attempted or simulated act.

This proposal to amend the present section 166 of the *Criminal Code* was aimed at every person, rather than just parents or guardians as the present section 166 is. It also would have protected young males as well as young females. These two features have characterized every attempt at legislative reform of this section since this bill.

The Standing Committee on Justice and Legal Affairs proposed in its 1978 report that section 166 of the *Code* be amended. The offence recommended by the Committee was identical to that in Mr. Epp's bill, with the exception of the Committee's definition of "sexually explicit act". The Committee proposed that the term encompass any act or simulated act of masturbation, sexual intercourse, gross indecency, buggery or bestiality, or the display of one's body in a sexually suggestive manner. The Committee proposed a slightly more restrictive definition of a "child", namely a person who is under the age of 16 years. Omitted from the definition was a person who appears to be under the age of 16.[57]

It is clear from the Committee's report that it considered that this reform of section 166 would reach the conduct of those who procure children to participate in the production of sexually explicit materials, as well as of those who procure children to engage in prostitution.[58] Mr. Whiteway introduced Private Member's Bill C-434 into the 1977-78 Session in order to implement this recommendation of the Standing Committee, but the bill was not passed.

Two government bills introduced after the Report of the Standing Committee also addressed the issue of procuring children.

Bill C-21, which received first reading on November 21, 1978, would have created two separate offences. The first involved the parent or guardian who procures a person to have illicit sexual intercourse with a person other than the procurer, or who orders, is a party to, permits or knowingly receives the avails of the defilement, seduction or prostitution of that person. Where the young person is under the age of 16 years, the offence was subject to a higher penalty than was the case when the young person was 16 years, but not more than 21 years.

The second offence was with respect to a person, not a parent or guardian, who procures a person under the age of 16 years. That offence carried a penalty similar to that imposed on a parent procuring a child under 16. In respect of both these offences, the bill provided that it is not material that an accused believed that the person in relation to whom the offence was committed was 16 years of age or more.

Bill C-53, which received first reading on January 12, 1981, made it an offence for the parent or guardian or person having the lawful care or charge of a person, or exercising authority over a person under 16 years of age, to engage in sexual misconduct with that person, or procure or knowingly permit sexual misconduct by that person. Similarly, it was made an offence for the owner, occupier or manager of the premises, knowingly to permit the premises to be used for the purposes of sexual misconduct involving a person under the age of 16.

The bill created offences involving third parties who were neither parents nor the managers of premises. A person who engaged in sexual misconduct with a person under the age of 14, or procured sexual misconduct by such a person, was guilty of an offence. Defences to this charge included the fact that the accused was under 14, or less than 3 years older than the complainant, but did not include the alleged consent of the victim, or a mistaken belief about the age of the victim. A comparable offence was created in respect of a person 14 years of age or more but under 16. Defences included the fact that the accused was under 16, or less than 3 years older than the victim, a mistaken belief about the age of the complainant, and the fact that the accused was less responsible than the victim for the sexual misconduct which took place. The bill did not provide a definition of "sexual misconduct".

In addition to these attempts to deal with procuring of a child, there has been one effort to address the issue of solicitation of a child by an adult. Bill C-360, introduced by Mr. Kaplan in 1974, would have added to the *Code* a new offence of inviting a person 14 years of age or under to engage in a sexual act.

This Committee's recommendations with respect to procuring are discussed below. Before proceeding to elaborate upon them, we will examine the activity at the international level, and in certain other jurisdictions, with respect to pornography and prostitution involving children.

Footnotes

[1] *Canada Post Corporation Act*, S.C. 1980-81-82-83, c.54.

[2] *R. v. Popert* (1981), 58 C.C.C. (2d) 505 (Ont. C.A.).

[3] *R. v. McDougall's Drug Store* (1982), 109 A.P.R. 463 (N.S. Co. Ct.) and *R. v. Cinema International* (1981), 13 M.R. (2d) 337 (Man. C.A.)

[4] *R. v. Penthouse* (1979), 96 D.L.R. (3d) 735 (Ont. C.A.).

[5] (1982), 69 C.C.C. (2d) 503 (Ont. C.A.).

[6] *R. v. Rioux* [1970], 3 C.C.C. 149, at p.169 (S.C.C.).

[7] *R. v. Harrison* (1973), 12 C.C.C. 26 (Alta. Prov. Ct.).

[8] *Customs Tariff Act*, R.S.C. 1970, c. C-41, s.14 and Schedule C.

[9] *U. of Manitoba v. Deputy Minister of Revenue for Customs and Excise* (1983), 24 Man. R. (2d) 198 (Man. Co. Ct.).

[10] (1981), 61 C.C.C. (2d) 287 (Ont. Co. Ct.).

[11] *Criminal Code*, s.151.

[12] *Ibid.*, s.153.

[13] *Ibid.*, s.155.

[14] *Ibid.*, s.157.

[15] *Ibid.*, s.166.

[16] *Ibid.*, s.167.

[17] *Ibid.*, s.23.

[18] *Ibid.*, s.22.

[19] *Ibid.*, s.423(1).

[20] *Ibid.*, s.423(2).

[21] *Juvenile Delinquents Act*, R.S.C. 1970, c.J-3.

[22] Section 33 of the *Juvenile Delinquents Act*, R.S.C. 1970, c. J-3 made it a summary conviction offence knowingly or wilfully to aid, cause, abet, or connive at the commission by a child of a delinquency, or to do any act producing, promoting or contributing to a child's being or becoming a juvenile delinquent or likely to make a child a juvenile delinquent. Subsection 2(1) defined juvenile delinquent as any child who violates any provision of the *Criminal Code* or of any federal or provincial statute, or of any by-law or ordinance of any municipality, or who is guilty of sexual immorality or any similar form of vice.

[23] *Child Welfare Act*, R.S.A. 1980, c. C-8.

[24] Badgley Report, Vol.1 at 548.

[25] R.S.A. 1980, c. C-8, s.40.

[26] Badgley Report, Vol. 1 at 549.

[27] The bills and their proposers were Bill C-207, 30th Parl., 3rd Sess., 1977 (Mr. McGrath); Bill C-239, 30th Parl., 3rd Sess., 1977 (Mr. Whiteway); Bill C-241, 30th Parl., 3rd Sess., 1977 (Mr. Dinsdale); Bill C-318, 30th Parl., 3rd Sess., 1977 (Mr. Epp); Bill C-325, 30th Parl., 3rd Sess., 1977 (Mrs. Appolloni); Bill C-348, 30th Parl., 3rd Sess., 1977 (Mr. Friesen), Bill C-399, 30th Parl., 3rd Sess., 1977 (Mrs. Appolloni); Bill C-400, 30th Parl., 3rd Sess., 1977 (Mr. Reid); Bill C-402, 30th Parl., 3rd Sess., 1977 (Mr. Lawrence).

[28] Bill C-206; 30th Parl., 3rd Sess., 1977 (Mr. Epp).

[29] House of Commons Standing Committee on Justice and Legal Affairs, Third Report, *Pornography*, (1978) Proceedings No. 18 at 18:4.

30 House of Commons Standing Committee on Justice and Legal Affairs, Third Report, *Pornography*, (1978) Recommendation 4, at 18:8.

31 Bill C-21, First reading November 21, 1978, s. 18.

32 The bill provided for a new subsection 159(10), stipulating that "where an accused is tried for an offence under this section, no opinion evidence is admissible with respect to community standards in order to prove that any matter or thing is or is not obscene, any law or practice to the contrary notwithstanding."

33 House of Commons Standing Committee on Justice and Legal Affairs, Third Report, *Pornography*, (1978) Recommendation 8, at 18:10.

34 *Martin's Criminal Code*, 1984, at 867.

35 *Young Offenders Act*, S.C. 1980-81-82, c.110, s.2(1).

36 *Ibid.*, s.72.

37 *Criminal Code*, s.453(1)(e).

38 *Ibid.*, s.453(1)(f).

39 *Ibid.*, s.453(1)(g).

40 *Young Offenders Act*, S.C. 1980-81-82, c.110, s.9(10)(b).

41 R.S.C. 1970, c. J-3, s.10(1).

42 *R. v. P.* (1979), 48 C.C.C. (2d) 390 (Ont. Prov. Ct.).

43 *R. v. Wowk* (1981), 61 C.C.C. (2d) 394 (Man. Prov. Ct.).

44 *Young Offenders Act*, S.C. 1980-81-82, c.110, s.9(9).

45 *Criminal Code*, s.146(1).

46 *Ibid.*, s.140.

47 *Ibid.*, s.146(2).

48 *Ibid.*, s.155.

49 *Ibid.*, s.157.

50 *Ibid.*, s.158.

51 *R. v. Dudak* (1978), 41 C.C.C. (2d) 31 (B.C.C.A.).

52 *R. v. DiPaola; R. v. Palactics* (1978), 43 C.C.C. (2d) 199 (Ont. C.A.).

53 S.N.B. 1980, c. 2.1, s.31(1)(e).

54 *Ibid.*, s.58(1).

55 *Ibid.*, s.58(6).

56 S.Q. 1977, c.20, s.54(6) and s.60, respectively.

57 House of Commons Standing Committee on Justice and Legal Affairs, *Pornography*, (1978) Proceedings 18, Recommendation 7, at 18:9-10.

58 *Ibid.*, at 18:9.

Chapter 44

International Obligations and Instruments

1. Pornography

The United Nations adopted the *Agreement for the Suppression of the Circulation of Obscene Publications* in 1910. In 1949, this Agreement was brought under the umbrella of the United Nations. The 1910 Agreement created duties on member states to centralize information in order to facilitate the tracing and suppression of actions of an international character which constitute infringement of states' domestic laws on obscene writings, drawings, pictures or articles. They are also to supply information on the importation of such publications or articles and to ensure or expedite their seizure. There is no definition in the Agreement of the term "obscene".[1]

A second agreement signed in 1923, and amended in 1947, is the *International Convention for the Suppression of the Circulation of and Traffic in Obscene Publications*. This Convention is concerned with the discovery, prosecution, and punishment by member states of those involved in a wide range of offences. All of these offences relate to "obscene writings, drawings, prints, paintings, printed matter, pictures, posters, emblems, photographs, films or other obscene objects", but neither does this Convention define the term obscene.[2]

Canada is a member of the Universal Postal Union, whose goals are to ensure the freedom of transit of mail throughout its territory; to secure the organization and improvement of postal services, and to provide technical assistance to member states. The *Universal Postal Convention* lays down detailed regulations as to how these goals will be attained. Article 33.2 of the Convention lists various articles prohibited for insertion into letter post items. "Obscene or immoral" articles are included as subsection (e) of the Article, and Article 33.4 provides that these "shall in no circumstances be forwarded to this destination, delivered to the addressees or returned to origin." Article 34 of the Convention authorizes postal administrations of the countries of origin and destination to submit to Customs control, according to the legislation of those countries, letter post items and, if necessary, officially to open them.[3]

Canada is also a member of the International Telecommunications Union. The first *International Telecommunications Convention*, signed in Madrid in

1932, set up the Union. It provided that the signing governments reserve the right to stop the transmission of any private telegram or radiotelegram which might appear dangerous to the safety of the state or contrary to the laws of the country, to public order, or to decency. This provision also applied to telephone communications. A second Convention was adopted in Montreux in 1965 and revised in Malaga-Torremolinos in 1973, an overhaul made necessary by the profound change in telecommunications methods and capacities. Whereas the provision for stoppage of telegrams described above was carried over into Article 19.1 of the new Convention, the provision relating to telephones was broadened to cover "telecommunications". Article 19.2 of the new Convention thus provides that members also reserve the right to cut off any private telecommunications which may appear dangerous to the security of the state or contrary to their laws, to public order or to decency.[4]

Canada adheres to these Conventions, so that they do not present the same problems of policy as do those in the area of prostitution. However, they do pose problems of interpretation, because the terms "obscene" and "decency" are not defined. This terminology problem becomes even more troublesome when one considers Resolution 1983/30 of the U.N. Economic and Social Council, passed in response to the Report of M. Jean Fernand-Laurent, Special Rapporteur on *The Suppression of the Traffic in Persons and the Exploitation of the Prostitution of Others.*

Clause 3(d) of Resolution 1983/30 recommends that member states draw up legislation and policies aimed at curbing the "pornography industry and the trade in pornography and penalizing them very severely when minors are involved". Interestingly, this is the first reference relating specifically to minors which can be found in the international instruments in this field. Unfortunately, there is no definition of "pornography" in this resolution. Turning to the Report of the Special Rapporteur, we find the following description of "pornography" involving children, in paragraph 30:

> In some industrialized countries, child prostitution has recently been organized to benefit the pornography industry, which produces photo albums, films and video cassettes. Children are photographed or filmed in indecent positions, and these pictures are sold for high prices through a clandestine network of persons interested in such things. This trade may be national or international.[5]

In discussing the role of UNESCO in combatting prostitution, the Special Rapporteur calls upon the General Conference of that body to invite member states:

> ...to recognize the necessary distinction between the erotic and the obscene, and to declare war on pornography at least, which is most likely to defile the female body and which, by separating sexual relations from affective relations, puts them at a less then human level.[6]

This commentary, while it assists the reader to understand the Special Rapporteur's position, really does little to clarify the problems of terminology in Resolution 1983/30.

U.N. General Assembly Resolution 38/107, passed in response to the Report of the Special Rapporteur, does not address the issue of pornography.

The 1959 *Declaration of the Rights of the Child* does contain a principle which has relevance to the issue of children and pornography. Principle 9 provides that the child shall be protected from all forms of exploitation, and shall not be the subject of traffic, in any form. The Principle also stipulates that the child shall in no case be caused or permitted to engage in any occupation or employment which would prejudice his health or education, or interfere with his physical, mental or moral development.

Once again, as in the case of prostitution, it would appear that Canada is missing a chance to assume a leadership role in international circles by not adopting the Universal Declaration.

2. Prostitution

Canada has signed and is a party to a number of international Conventions relating to aspects of prostitution (see Part III, Section II, Chapter 33). Here, however, it will be useful to focus on the provisions relating particularly to children and young persons.[7]

Canada is a party to the first international agreement on prostitution, signed in 1904. The *Agreement for the Suppression of the White Slave Traffic* was mainly concerned with the procuring of women or girls for immoral purposes abroad. It sets up a series of arrangements whereby governments will increase their surveillance at railway stations, ports and en route; arrange for the repatriation of prostitutes, and take a number of other measures aimed at curbing the international traffic.[8]

Canada is also a party to the *International Convention on the Suppression of the White Slave Traffic, 1910*, and the *International Convention for the Suppression of the Traffic in Women and Children, 1921*. The 1910 Convention states that whoever procured, enticed or led away, even with her consent, a woman or girl under age for immoral purposes shall be punished. The 1921 Convention established that the age limit for the purposes of the 1910 Convention would be 21 completed years. It also established that the protection of the 1904 Agreement and 1910 Convention would be extended to children of both sexes. Canada is also a party to the *Protocol to amend the Convention for the Suppression of the Traffic in Women and Children* of 1921, signed in 1947, transferring the powers in the Convention to the Secretary-General and participating countries of the United Nations.[9]

None of these Conventions actually addresses prostitution *per se*. Rather, they concentrate on "trafficking" in women and children. The first, and indeed only, U.N. Convention to deal with prostitution itself in a comprehensive way, is the *Convention for the Suppression of the Traffic in Persons and the Exploitation of the Prostitution of Others*. Adopted by the General Assembly in 1949, it came into effect on July 25, 1951. The preamble states that

...prostitution and the accompanying evil of the traffic in persons for the purpose of prostitution are incompatible with the dignity and worth of the human person and endanger the welfare of the individual, the family, and the community...[10]

Of significance in this Convention is the adoption of the word "person" rather than "women". It is recognized here, for the first time, that prostitution is not restricted to women, but applies to all persons, even though its practice and exploitation particularly afflict women. Importantly, the use of the word "person" includes children as well as adults. Articles 1 and 2 provide that the parties to the Convention agree to punish any person who, to gratify the passions of another, procures, entices or leads away, for purposes of prostitution, another person, even with the consent of that person; or exploits the prostitution of another person, even with the consent of that person. Further, the parties to the Convention agree to punish any person who keeps or manages, or knowingly finances or takes part in the financing of a brothel; or knowingly lets or rents a building or other place or any part thereof for the purpose of the prostitution of others.[11]

In these two articles and in articles 6 and 16, the signing parties agree to restrict repressive measures to those who "exploit the prostitution of others" (i.e., pimps and other procurers). While the Convention considers prostitution to be an evil, Article 6 recognizes that those who prostitute themselves should not be subject to special registration or to any exceptional requirements for supervision or notification. Furthermore, in Article 16 signatory states agree to take or to encourage, through their public or private educational, health, social, economic and other related services, measures for the prevention of prostitution and for the rehabilitation and social adjustment of the victims of prostitution.

No other Convention on prostitution has been developed by the international community since this one. Canada has not ratified the 1951 Convention.[12] Nor has Canada adopted the 1959 *Declaration of the Rights of the Child*.[13]

The Mexico World Conference of the International Women's Year in 1975 was the first of several U.N. forums that urged governments to adopt the 1951 Convention. As already noted, the U.N. Commission on the Status of Women persuaded, in 1982, the U.N. Secretary General to appoint a Special Rapporteur, M. Jean Fernand-Laurent, to examine the issues of suppression of traffic in persons and the exploitation of the prostitution of others. His report, submitted in March of 1983, focused on a number of issues of special relevance to the prostitution of young persons.[14]

In Chapter 1, the Special Rapporteur recites his findings concerning prostitution. In describing the activities of procurers, he points out that when it comes to the prostitution of children, it can be an older child who runs the business.[15] The Report discusses the various means that are used to recruit young people into prostitution. It should be noted that the Rapporteur was looking at the global scene when formulating these observations. However, the following remarks may be instructive for Canadians:

> There is no doubt that in the slum belts of certain large cities, children sometimes have no other choice in order to survive but to pick through garbage, beg, steal or become prostitutes. But adults - paedophiles or procurers - often take the initiative by offering money or gifts. In depressed rural areas, where the helpless peasant families are heavily in debt to a usurer, the children are sometimes bought or rented by a procurer from their parents, who may or may not be aware of their ultimate fate. If the child is an orphan, an abandoned child, a runaway or temporarily separated from his parents by some catastrophe, he is especially vulnerable and can simply be kidnapped. Paedophile tourists may be involved.[16]

The Report describes the phenomenon of the package "sex tour" in which the services of a prostitute are included in the price paid for the ticket; such phenomena are said to encourage the prostitution of young children, particularly in South-East Asia and Africa.[17]

The Rapporteur makes a number of recommendations for national governments and international organizations. The Report takes the position that a realistic goal is to combat procuring now and in the short term, while aiming in the long term at reducing actual prostitution.[18]

On the subject of child prostitution, the Report calls for dissemination of information and sensitization of public opinion as the most effective means of in-depth action. In particular, it recommends publicizing findings of physicians and medical associations on the lasting dangers to children's minds and bodies caused by sexual acts imposed on them by adults, and on the social cost of such traumas. The Report recommends that parents be informed of the risks associated with sexual abuse of youngsters, and that there be an increase in the number of teachers in what it calls "open environments" - youth clubs, sport clubs, and health clubs.[19]

M. Fernand-Laurent points out, however, that the campaign against prostitution and its physical and mental consequences, particularly among boys and girls, should not be restricted to the medical approach. It is also necessary to develop rehabilitative programs.[20] In this connection, particularly, he mentions the program of studies on "street children and street youth" sponsored by the International Catholic Child Bureau, begun in 1982, which should culminate in a publication proposing a program and methods for preventive action.[21]

The report highlights the position taken by the Secretariat of UNESCO that prostitution in general and the exploitation involved, are revealing of the image of women in the collective thinking of society. Accordingly, UNESCO is focusing attention on moral education, in order to arm children against manipulation of their minds by the media. Pointing out that "stereotypes that debase women and present them as being destined for physical pleasure of men are projected by magazines, advertising and the various cultural industries" the special Rapporteur cites the declaration of UNESCO's medium-term plan[22] that:

> It might henceforth be one of the essential functions of educational institutions to help young people to bring their critical faculty to bear in selecting and sorting the messages spread abroad by the communication media.[23]

On the legislative level, the Report calls for stiffer penalties for procuring. Specifically with regard to children, it urges that the exploitation of child prostitution should carry sanctions at least as severe as those applied to the crime of sexual abuse of a minor.

Following the presentation to it of the Special Report, the Economic and Social Council passed Resolution 1983/30, again inviting U.N. member states to ratify and implement the *1951 Convention for the Suppression of Traffic in Persons and of the Exploitation of the Prostitution of Others.*[24] The Resolution also recommended that states draw up legislation and policies in keeping with the report of the Special Rapporteur. Among those recommended were several with particular relevance to child prostitution. The Resolution recommended that states punish all forms of procuring in such a way as to deter it, particularly when it exploits minors, and that they aim at preventing prostitution through moral education and civics training in and out of school. In keeping with the emphasis of the 1951 Convention, and the report of the Special Rapporteur, Resolution 1983/30 recommended that states eliminate discrimination that ostracizes prostitutes and makes their reabsorption into society more difficult, and that states facilitate occupational training and reintegration into society of persons leaving prostitution.

The U.N. General Assembly referred to Resolution 1983/30 of the Economic and Social Council when it, in turn, passed a Resolution dealing with the prevention of prostitution. Resolution 38/107 of the General Assembly recites that:

> ...prostitution and the accompanying evil of the traffic in persons for the purpose of prostitution are incompatible with the dignity and worth of the human person and endanger the welfare of the individual, the family and the state ... and that women and children are still all too often victims of physical abuse and sexual exploitation.[25]

It urges member states to take all appropriate humane measures, including legislation, to combat prostitution, exploitation of the prostitution of others and all forms of traffic in persons, and appeals to member states to provide special protection directed towards rehabilitating victims of prostitution through measures including education, social guarantees and employment opportunities.

Canada, along with 24 other countries, abstained from voting on this Resolution. It seems that Canada's abstention was, in part, related to its view that the resolution dealt only with women and in part, because of concern over the issue of child prostitution.[26] While we find these reasons somewhat perplexing in the light of the text of the Resolution, we nevertheless believe that the thrust of the Resolution coincides very closely with the action that we think is appropriate with respect to children and prostitution.

Although Canada has not signed the 1951 Convention on prostitution, it is a party to the 1979 *Convention on the Elimination of All Forms of Discrimination Against Women,*[27] which provides in Article 6 that state parties shall take all appropriate measures, including legislation, to suppress all forms of traffic in women and exploitation of prostitution of women.

It seems unfortunate that Canada has not ratified the 1959 *Declaration of the Rights of the Child.* It would appear that national legislation does not diverge significantly from the position of this international instrument. Thus, formal adherence to it would not be burdensome for Canada, and would, moreover, permit Canada to take a stronger role in international forums addressing the issue of, for example, child prostitution. The timing for the assumption of a clear leadership role in this area is opportune.

Recommendation 69

Canada should ratify the 1959 Declaration of the Rights of the Child.

Footnotes

[1] House of Commons Standing Committee on Justice and Legal Affairs, *Pornography*, (1978), Proceedings 18, Recommendation 7, at 12.

[2] *Ibid.*, at 12-13.

[3] *Ibid.*, at 13.

[4] *Ibid.*, at 14.

[5] U.N. Economic and Social Council, Report of Fernand-Laurent, para. 30, p. 10 (in Sansfaçon, *op. cit.*, note 7, Appendix 4).

[6] *Ibid.*, para. 95, p. 32.

[7] This account of the international instruments is taken largely from D. Sansfaçon, *United Nations Conventions, Agreements and Resolutions on Prostitution and Pornography* W.P.P.P. #3.

[8] *Ibid.*, at 2 and 9.

[9] *Ibid.*, at 3 and 9.

[10] *Ibid.*, Appendix 1, at 19.

[11] *Ibid.*, at 4.

[12] *Ibid.*, at 4 and 9.

[13] The United Nations General Assembly adopted the Declaration unanimously on November 20, 1959.

[14] U.N. Economic and Social Council, Report of Mr. Jean Fernand-Laurent, Special Rapporteur on the suppression of the traffic in persons and the exploitation of the prostitution of others, March 17, 1983, Document E/1983/7. A portion of the Report is included in Sansfaçon, *op. cit.*, Appendix 4.

[15] Sansfaçon, *op. cit.*, Appendix 4 para. 19 at 7.

[16] *Ibid.*, Appendix 4, para. 29, at 9.

[17] *Ibid.*, Appendix 4, paras. 30 and 31, p. 10.

[18] *Ibid.*, Appendix 4, para. 63, p. 18.

[19] *Ibid.*, Appendix 4, para. 68.

[20] U.N. Economic and Social Council, Report of Mr. Jean Fernand-Laurent, Special Rapporteur on the Suppression of the traffic in persons and the exploitation of the prostitution of others, March 17, 1983, Document E/1983/7 para. 68 at 32.

[21] *Ibid.*, para. 102, at 35-36.

[22] 1984-89; adopted in November, 1982. U.N. Economic and Social Council, Report of Fernand-Laurent, para. 95, at 31 and fn 42.

[23] *Ibid.*

[24] The text will be found in Sansfaçon, *op. cit.*, Appendix 3 at 37.

[25] U.N. General Assembly, Thirty-eighth session, Resolution Adopted by the General Assembly: 38/107 Prevention of Prostitution, Document A/RES/38/107, February 3, 1984.

[26] Sansfaçon, *op. cit.* at 11.

[27] *Ibid.*, Appendix 2, at 27.

Chapter 45

Other Countries

The experience of other countries in the regulation and control of pornography and prostitution is discussed at length elsewhere in this Report. Here, we present for comparative purposes, the experience of the United States and the United Kingdom, in addressing these issues as they relate to children.

1. Pornography

1.1 United States

The *Child Protection Act*, Chapter 110 of Title 18 of the *United States Code*, is a federal statute dealing with the exploitation of children for pornography which is transported in interstate or foreign commerce, or mailed. Because the individual states possess the constitutional jurisdiction over the criminal law, the U.S. federal government's main initiative against involvement of children in pornography comes in this *Act*. In 1984, the *Act* was amended in the hope of increasing substantially its impact on what the amending *Act* described as "a highly organized multi-million dollar industry which operates on a nationwide scale".[1]

Paragraph 2251(a) of Chapter 110 is directed against any person who:

employs, uses, persuades, induces, entices, or coerces any minor to engage in, or who has a minor assist any other person to engage in, any sexually explicit conduct for the purpose of producing any visual depiction of such conduct.

Paragraph 2251(b) is directed against:

any parent, legal guardian or person having custody or control of a minor who knowingly permits such minor to engage in or to assist any other person to engage in, sexually explicit conduct for the purpose of producing any visual depiction of such conduct.

Because of the constitutional arrangement in the U.S., the offence consists of engaging in this conduct if the person knows or has reason to know that the visual depiction will be transported in interstate or foreign commerce, or mailed, or if such visual depiction has actually been transported in interstate or foreign commerce, or mailed.

On the first conviction, the person engaging in such conduct shall be fined not more than $100,000, or imprisoned not more than 10 years. Any organization committing a violation shall be fined not more than $250,000. The amendments of 1984 added for the first time this criminal liability for the organization; they also increased the fines for individuals from $10,000 to $100,000. The maximum fine for the second or subsequent conviction is $250,000. This fine, too, was increased from $15,000 by the 1984 amendments. The jail term for someone with a prior conviction under the section is not less than two nor more than 15 years.

Subject to the same penalties is any one who:

1) knowingly transports or ships in interstate or foreign commerce or mails any visual depiction, if:

    (A) the producing of such visual depiction involves the use of a minor engaged in sexually explicit conduct; and

    (B) such visual depiction is of such conduct; or

2) knowingly receives, or distributes, any visual depiction that has been transported or shipped in interstate or foreign commerce or mailed, or knowingly reproduces any visual depiction for distribution in interstate or foreign commerce or through the mails if:

    (A) the producing of such visual depiction involves the use of a minor engaging in sexually explicit conduct; and

    (B) such visual depiction is of such conduct;

A "minor" is any person under the age of 18 years, raised from 16 by the 1984 amendments. "Sexually explicit conduct" is defined as real or simulated sexual intercourse (including genital-genital, oral-genital, anal-genital, or oral-anal, whether between persons of the same or opposite sex), bestiality, masturbation, sadistic or masochistic abuse or the lascivious exhibition of the genitals or pubic areas of any person.

Added to chapter 110 by the 1984 amendments was a new section 2253 providing that any person convicted of any offence under sections 2251 or 2252, shall forfeit to the government the person's interest in any property constituting or derived from the gross profits or other proceeds obtained from the offence, and any property used, or intended to be used, to commit the offence. This provision for "criminal forfeiture", is matched by a provision for "civil forfeiture" in section 2254 of Chapter 110, also enacted by the 1984 amendments. The "civil forfeiture" section provides that the following kinds of material are liable to forfeiture: firstly, any material used, or intended for use, in producing, reproducing, transporting, shipping or receiving any visual depiction in violation of the chapter; secondly, any visual depiction produced, transported, shipped or received in violation of chapter 110, and thirdly, any property constituting or derived from gross profits or other proceeds obtained from a violation of the chapter.

In two decisions of the United States Supreme Court, important findings are made concerning the right of the state to deal with pornography and children.

At issue in *Federal Communications Commission* v. *Pacifica Foundation*[2] was the constitutional validity of an F.C.C. ruling that it was wrongful to broadcast over the radio, during the afternoon period, the George Carlin monologue "Dirty Words". The Commission cited four reasons why it believed broadcast messages deserved special treatment. One was that children have access to radios and in many cases are unsupervised by parents while listening to them. The Commission said this reason was "of special concern" to it and to parents.

The Commission placed a warning letter in the file of Pacifica Broadcasting as a result of the Carlin incident, and the Supreme Court held that this decision did not violate Pacifica's First Amendment rights. An essential element in the Court's holding was the proposition of American constitutional law that, of all forms of communication, it is broadcasting which has received the most limited First Amendment protection. One of the reasons for such limited protection, cited by Mr. Justice Stevens for the Court, was that broadcasting is uniquely accessible to children, even those too young to read.[3] The ease with which children may obtain access to broadcast material, coupled with the government's interest in the well-being of its youth and in supporting parents' claim to authority in their own household, were said by the Court amply to justify special treatment of indecent broadcasting.[4]

As mentioned previously, the states have jurisdiction over criminal law in the United States Constitution. A significant case dealing with the reach of permissible state action vis-a-vis children and pornography was *New York* v. *Ferber*.[5] In that case, the Supreme Court held that "the States are entitled to greater leeway in the regulation of pornographic depictions of children"[6] for five reasons. Firstly, the state's interest in protecting children from sexual abuse and exploitation is of surpassing importance. Secondly, the distribution of pornographic films depicting children is intrinsically related to the sexual abuse of children, because the materials are a permanent record of the abuse; the harm to the child is increased by their circulation, and because the distribution of such materials provides the impetus for the child abuse involved in producing them. Thirdly, the advertising and selling of pornographic material involving children provides an economic motive for the production of these materials. Fourthly, the value of permitting live performances or representations of children engaged in sexual activity is minimal. And fifthly, classifying child pornography as outside the First Amendment guarantee of freedom of speech is not inconsistent with prior Supreme Court decisions in the area.

In *Ferber*, the Court also addressed the standard to be met when determining whether material portraying children is obscene. It did so with reference to the test enunciated in *Miller* v. *California*,[7] a test which has now been adopted with some modifications in the criminal statutes of 43 states.[8] The Supreme Court declared in *Miller* that the basic guidelines for the trier of fact must be: (a) whether "the average person, applying contemporary community standards" would find that the work taken as a whole, appeals to the prurient interest; (b) whether the work depicts or describes, in a patently offensive way, sexual conduct specifically defined by the applicable state law; and (c) whether the work, taken as a whole, lacks serious literary, artistic, political, or scientific value.[9]

In *Ferber*, the Supreme Court noted that where pornography involving portrayals of children is under review, the *Miller* formulation is adjusted in the following respects:

> A trier of fact need not find that the material appeals to the prurient interest of the average person; it is not required that sexual conduct portrayed be done so in a patently offensive manner; and the material at issue need not be considered as a whole.[10]

However, the type of works to be prohibited by the statute must be adequately defined, as must the type of "sexual conduct" proscribed.

At issue in *Ferber* was the New York statute on sexual performance by a child,[11] first enacted in 1977. One provision of Article 263 criminalizes the use of a child less than 16 years of age in a sexual performance. A person is guilty of the offence if, knowing the character and content of the performance, he employs, authorizes or induces the child to engage in it, or being a parent, legal guardian or custodian of the child, consents to his or her participation. At issue in the *Ferber* case was a second provision of Article 263, providing that a person is guilty of promoting a sexual performance by a child when, knowing the character and content thereof, he produces, directs or promotes any performance which includes sexual conduct by a child under 16.

The definition of "promote" was very broad, including procure, manufacture, issue, sell, give, provide, lend, mail, deliver, transfer, publish, distribute, and a number of other activities. The definition of "sexual performance" was so wide as to include much material which would not have been regarded as obscene under the *Miller* test. It included actual or simulated sexual intercourse, deviant sexual intercourse, bestiality, masturbation, sado-masochistic abuse, or lewd exhibition of the genitals.

This decision was the first in which the Court examined a statute directed to depictions of sexual activity involving children. Its significance can be appreciated when one considers that at the time *Ferber* was heard, the Court observed that 20 states had prohibited the distribution of material depicting children engaged in sexual conduct, regardless of whether the material was obscene.

It is beyond the scope of this study to document the state laws in the various United States jurisdictions dealing with child pornography and dissemination of pornography to minors. The diversity of laws from state to state, and even within the various states makes such an undertaking difficult. What is striking to the observer of American law and policy in this area, is the wide discrepancy between what is alleged to be the problem in the area of child pornography, and what appear to be the inroads made in solving it.

Section 2 of the *Child Protection Act* of 1984[12] recites the Congressional finding that "child pornography has developed into a highly organized, multi-million dollar industry which operates on a nation wide scale" and "thousands of children including large numbers of runaway and homeless youth are exploited in the production and distribution of pornographic materials." By contrast, this Committee learned that in the fiscal 1978-79, the U.S. Department of Justice obtained the convictions of 24 defendants on obscenity charges, 13 of whom were distributors of child pornography. In 1979-80, 8 of the 20 defendants successfully prosecuted by the Department were distributors of child pornography, and in 1980-81, half of the 18 convicted defendants were convicted on charges involving child pornography.[13] These statistics, of course, cannot reveal the whole pattern of enforcement activity. What seems significant, however, is that while child pornography convictions represent about half of the total number of convictions, the total number of convictions is strikingly small.

1.2 United Kingdom

The general outlines of the laws of the United Kingdom relating to pornography have been given elsewhere in our Report (see Part II, Section III, Chapter 17). Here we examine certain features of that law which have particular reference to young persons.

The *Children and Young Persons (Harmful Publications) Act, 1955*,[14] was a reaction to the entry into Britain, especially in 1954, of a new wave of horror comics produced in the United States. The *Act* applies to any book, magazine or other similar work which is of a kind likely to fall into the hands of children or young persons, and which consists wholly or mainly of stories told in pictures, with or without the addition of written matter, portraying the commission of crimes, acts of violence or cruelty, or incidents of a repulsive or horrible nature, in such a way that the work as a whole would tend to corrupt a child or young person into whose hands it might fall.

The *Act* provides that a person who prints, publishes, sells, lets on hire or possesses, for any of these purposes, a work to which the *Act* applies, shall be guilty of a summary conviction offence. The penalty is imprisonment for up to four months, or a fine not exceeding '100, or both. The *Act* provides that a Justice of the Peace may issue a warrant authorizing the seizure of offending publications from the premises of one charged with an offence, and it further provides for the forfeiture of copies of the work, and any plate or film prepared for the purpose of making copies of it, which are in the possession of a person convicted under the *Act*. No prosecution may be brought except by, or with the consent of, the Attorney General. Although the *Act* provided that it was to have expired at the end of December, 1965, it was renewed by the *Expiring Laws Act* of 1969 and remains in force today.

The *Protection of Children Act, 1978*,[15] was passed to prevent children being involved in the production of pornography. The *Act* provides that it is an offence for a person to take, or permit to be taken, any indecent photograph of a child, to distribute or show such indecent photographs, to have in his possession such indecent photographs with a view to their being distributed or shown to himself or others, or to publish, or cause to be published, any advertisement likely to be understood as conveying that the advertiser distributes or shows such indecent photographs or intends to. "Child" means a person under the age of 16, and the *Act* makes it clear that distribution need not be for gain. A person is to be regarded as distributing an indecent photograph if he parts with possession of it to, or exposes or offers it for acquisition by, another person. Prosecution under the *Act* may be by way of indictment or by way of summary proceedings. If convicted on indictment, a person is liable to imprisonment for not more than three years, to a fine or to both. A person convicted summarily shall be liable to imprisonment for a term not exceeding six months or a fine not exceeding £1,000 or to both.

A Justice of the Peace may authorize seizure of articles which are, or are believed with reasonable cause to be, or include indecent photographs of children taken or shown on the premises, or kept there with a view to their being distributed or shown. The occupier of the premises must then show cause why the articles should not be forfeit.

In July, 1977, the Committee on Obscenity and Film Censorship, under the Chairmanship of Bernard Williams, was appointed by the Home Secretary to review the laws concerning obscenity, indecency and violence in publications, displays and entertainments and the arrangements for censorship in England and Wales. Excluded from the Committee's mandate was the field of broadcasting because the Annan Committee review of the whole field of broadcasting had been completed only the preceding February.

The *Protection of Children Act, 1978*, discussed above, was enacted by Parliament while the Williams Committee was sitting. It was introduced as a Private Member's bill and approved by Parliament, though with substantial amendments made by the government, to meet a public demand for action to prevent the use of children in pornography.[16]

The Williams Committee devoted very little of its report to a specific consideration of pornography and children. Although it had been set up at least, in part, as a response to public concern about an increasing use of children in pornography, it observed that no evidence was put before it that child pornography was a growing problem.[17] It observed that the new *Protection of Children Act, 1978* had been used in "only a very few cases" between the time of its passage and the publication of the Committee's report.[18]

The Committee records a certain caution about how susceptible children might be to the influence of pornography; its caution is predicated on the absence of experimental evidence, because for obvious reasons, children are not used in such experiments. Moreover, the Committee states that it heard no evidence of actual harm being caused to children.[19]

614

The Committee observed that it was clear from its discussions with witnesses that no very definite answer could be given about the age at which special protection of children is no longer necessary. It recorded that some witnesses declined to offer any view at all as to the age at which special protection should cease. The choice of others tended to hover between the ages of 16 and 18. The main determinant of the various views was the witness's idea about when individual sexual maturation might take place, so as to enable a young person to cope with exposure to pornography.[20]

The Committee is much more definite when it deals with the issue of the use of children to make pornography. Its report states:

> Few people would be prepared to take the risk where children are concerned and just as the law recognizes that children should be protected against sexual behaviour which they are too young to properly consent to, it is almost universally agreed that this should apply to participation in pornography.[21]

The Committee observes that participation in pornography will often involve the commission of offences like indecent assault, but recommends strongly that the problem of children's participation in pornography should not be left to the law of sexual offences. It observes:

> ...there are strong arguments that the prevention of this harm also requires the power to suppress the pornographic product as well as the original act, so as not to provide the incentive to pornographers to flout the sexual offence law, or to deal without inhibition in products which are imported from other legal jurisdictions.[22]

The Committee urges against a parochial approach to the prevention of harm to children, arguing "if English law is to protect children against offences in this country, it is hypocritical to permit the trade in photographs and films of the same activity taken overseas."[23]

The Williams Committee proposed an entirely new and comprehensive approach to the control of offensive material. The principles on which the scheme was structured were well defined. Firstly, the Committee argued that the law should rest partly on the basis of harms caused by, or involved in the existence of, the material. Only these harms could justify prohibitions. The law should also rest partly on the public's legitimate interest in not being offended by the display and availability of material. This interest, in the Committee's view, would justify restrictions designed to protect the ordinary citizen from unreasonable offence.[24] The Committee believed that the principal object of the law should be to prevent certain kinds of material causing offence to reasonable people or being made available to young people.

The Committee divided material into two classes, that subject to restrictions and that subject to prohibitions. Prohibited material includes photographs and films whose production appears to the court to have involved the exploitation for sexual purposes, of a person appearing from the evidence as a whole, to have been at the relevant time under the age of 16. The law should explicitly state that consent by a person under 16 is not a defence.[25] The

Committee recommended that it should be an offence to take any prohibited photograph or film, to distribute or show it, to have it with a view to its being distributed or shown, or to advertise it as being available for distribution or showing.[26] The offence would carry a maximum term of three years' imprisonment and an unlimited fine.

The Committee recommended[27] that the police have power to obtain a warrant for the seizure of material they believe to be prohibited, which is being kept in circumstances in which the police believe an offence is being committed. The court convicting a person of an offence involving prohibited material, should order that any material seized, which is in their view prohibited material, should be forfeited. However, the Committee recommended that there not be any procedure aimed at the forfeiture of prohibited material, separate from the criminal proceedings.

Prohibited material was to be prohibited from circulation in the post, and should be included in the list of goods prohibited from importation.

The Committee also considered that live performances, which involve the sexual exploitation of any person under the age of 16, should be prohibited. They recommend that it should be an offence to present, organize or take part in a performance which contravenes the prohibition. Although they do not specifically provide this exemption, it seems clear from the tenor of their remarks on this subject that the Committee would not be in favour of prosecuting the child participant himself or herself. The Committee does recommend, by way of exception, that the law should not be so framed as to apply to what is performed in a private house, so long as no person under 18 is present and no admission charge is made.

The Committee recommends that no prohibitions or restrictions should apply to the printed word. It proposes that restrictions should apply to matter other than the written word, and to a performance, whose unrestricted availability is offensive to reasonable people by reason of the manner in which it portrays, deals with or relates to violence, cruelty or horror, or sexual, faecal or urinary functions or genital organs.

Restriction is to consist in a ban on the display, sale, or hire of restricted material and on the presentation of restricted performances, other than in premises to which persons under the age of 18 are not admitted; to which access is possible only by posting a prominent warning notice in specified terms, and which make no display visible to persons not passing beyond the notice.

The Committee proposes that it be an offence to display, sell, or hire any restricted matter or to present a restricted performance in contravention of the restrictions laid down. Moreover, it would be an offence to send or deliver restricted material or advertisements for such material to a person who the sender knew, or ought reasonably to have known, was under the age of 18.

Interestingly, however, the Committee specifically provides that it should not be an offence for a person under the age of 18 to seek to gain entry to premises in which restricted material is being displayed, sold, or hired, or in which a restricted performance is being presented, or to order restricted material to be sent to him or her.

The Committee's proposals with respect to restricted material do not apply to films, because a separate film censorship regime is proposed. A Statutory Film Examining Board would take over the censorship powers of local authorities and the functions exercised by the British Board of Film Censors. The Board's examiners should allocate films to one of the following six categories: suitable for all ages; children under the age of 11 should be accompanied by a responsible adult; no person under the age of 16 to be admitted; no person under the age of 18 to be admitted; and for restricted exhibition (also forbidden to those under 18). A film would be refused a certificate altogether if it is unfit for public exhibition because it contains material prohibited by law, or is unacceptable because of the manner in which it depicts violence or sexual activity or crime, notwithstanding the importance of allowing the development of artistic expression and of not suppressing truth or reality.

The Committee recommends that in determining whether films are suitable to be shown to those under 18, the Board should take account of the protection of children and young persons from influences which may be disturbing or harmful to them, or from material whose unrestricted availability to them would be unacceptable to responsible parents. It would be an offence, punishable by fines of up to £1,000, to show an unclassified film or to show a film in a manner not in compliance with its classification. The Committee recommends, however, that it should not be an offence for a person under the age of 18 to seek to gain entry to a film designated as unsuitable for persons of that age.

The Williams Committee Report was delivered to the British government in November, 1979. The government largely ignored its recommendations, with the first legislative activity in relation to pornography coming in 1981, as a result of a Private Member's bill. The *Indecent Displays Control Act, 1981*,[28] provides that if any indecent matter is publicly displayed, the person making the display and any person causing or permitting the display to be made, shall be guilty of an offence. A display in a place for which the public must pay an admission fee, or in a shop to which access can be had only after passing by a warning sign, are not caught by the *Act*, provided that persons under the age of 18 years are not permitted to enter while the displays are continuing.

The most recent initiative of the British government is the *Video Recordings Act, 1984*.[29] This legislation establishes a classification regime for video works. The only such works exempt from the scheme will be those which, taken as a whole, are designed to inform, educate or instruct; or are concerned with sport, religion or music. Video games are also exempt.

However, even video works in these exempt categories are not exempt if they are works which, "to a significant extent", depict "human sexual activity or acts of force or restraint associated with such activity", "mutilation or torture of, or other acts of gross violence towards, humans or animals", or "human genital organs or human urinary or excretory functions." Video works in the exempt categories which are "designed to any significant extent to stimulate or encourage" human sexual activity, or acts of force or restraint associated with such activity, or are designed to any extent to stimulate or encourage "mutilation or torture of, or other acts of gross violence towards humans or animals", are also caught by the scheme.

The *Act* allows the Secretary of State to designate an authority to classify video works which will be viewed in the home. The *Act* contemplates three separate classifications for such video works. The first category is for works which are suitable for general viewing and unrestricted supply, with or without advice as to the desirability of parental guidance with regard to the viewing of the work by young children or as to the particular suitability of the work for viewing by children. The second category is for works suitable for viewing only by persons who have attained the age (not being more than 18) specified in the classification certificate. The third is suitable for supply only through a licensed sex shop.

The *Act* provides that where a classification certificate states that no recording containing the particular work is to be supplied to a person who has not attained the age specified in the certificate, a person who supplies or offers to supply the work to a person under that age commits an offence. The defence to the charge is to prove that the accused neither knew nor had reasonable grounds to believe that the person concerned had not attained the age.

The regulatory system contemplated by the legislation has not yet been implemented, although the British Board of Film Censors has been designated as the certifying authority.

2. Prostitution

2.1 The United States

Legislation relating to child prostitution exists at both the federal and state level in the United States.[30]

For many years, the sole federal statute was the *Mann Act*, enacted in 1910 by Congress in the midst of the "white slavery scare".[31] Section 2432 of that *Act* made it an offence to transport or finance the transportation of a person under 18 in interstate or foreign commerce for the purpose of engaging in prostitution or "prohibited social contact for commercial purposes." As might be expected with legislation of that vintage, the *Act* referred solely to the exploitation of female minors.

In the late 1970s, after considerable discussion in the media and congressional hearings, the *Protection of Children Against Sexual Exploitation Act* of 1977[32] was passed. The major purpose of the legislation was to extend the protection offered by the *Mann Act* to male minors.

Despite the extension of the federal criminal law protection in this way, doubts exist as to the efficacy of the legislation.[33] While it has been employed effectively in the case of female victims, who are often controlled by pimps who will move them around, it is not effective in the case of young males, who, if they travel across state lines, do so of their own volition. Even in the case of females, however, conviction rates are minimal: 14 in 1980, 16 in 1981, and 8 in the first 9 months of 1982.[34]

A second federal legislative initiative in the field of juvenile prostitution is the *Child Abuse (Prevention and Treatment) and Adoption Reform Act* of 1974, as amended in 1978.[35] The latter amendments were significant because they defined social exploitation as a form of child abuse.

After further amendment in 1977 the statutory definition now reads:

...the physical or mental injury, sexual abuse or exploitation, negligent treatment, or maltreatment of a child under the age of eighteen, or the age specified by the child protection law of the State in question, by a person who is responsible for the child's welfare under circumstances which indicate that the child's health or welfare is harmed or threatened thereby...[36]

Regulations under the *Act*, governing the eligibility of states for funds, define "social exploitation" as "allowing, permitting or encouraging a child to engage in prostitution, as defined by state law, by a person responsible for a child's welfare".[37] These regulations encourage the states to address "social exploitation", including juvenile prostitution.

A perceived weakness with this legislation, and in particular, the definitions under it, is that it focuses upon the involvement of parents and guardians in encouraging prostitution, but omits the influence of pimps for females and that of friends for males.[38] Moreover, in many instances, the decision by the young person to prostitute occurs only after he or she is "on the street". It is recognized, of course, that the legislation does have a vital role to play in allowing detection of child abuse by a parent or guardian, which may if not stopped lead to a drift into prostitution.[39]

A third piece of federal legislation which is relevant is the *Runaway and Homeless Youth Act*[40] which provides for the funding of shelters for runaway youths on a nationwide basis, and in the process, assists young prostitutes of both sexes who are runaways. Several runaway shelters with exemplary records have been funded under this program: especially *Bridge* in Boston, *The Shelter* in Seattle and *Huckleberry House* in San Francisco. The services provided include: attempts at family reunifications; short term residential care; medical screening; employment training; counselling for court referred youths; guidance on housing resources; counselling in self awareness, sociability, social identity, substance abuse and peer relations.[41] *Huckleberry House*, in particular, has developed a project related to an increase in prostitute clients, as well as those identified as gay or bisexual.[42]

This federal initiative in funding, which has helped to attract further public and private financial support, has both prevented runaways from turning to prostitution, and provided a crucial support system to those already engaged in it. Moreover, the educational and employment training programs have provided a way for young prostitutes to change their lifestyle and eventually, to leave the trade.[43] The level of funding for this program has been a matter of contention between the Reagan administration and Congress, but no appreciable cuts have been made.[44]

The fourth and final piece of federal legislation which bears on juvenile prostitution is the *Missing Children Act*[45] which establishes a national clearinghouse to facilitate identification of missing children, including runaways. As with the previous legislation discussed, the tracing of a child may prevent his or her induction into prostitution. It may also provide a means of finding young practising prostitutes and referring them to social service agencies, which can assist in assimilation back into the community.[46]

The legislation has some drawbacks, however, as far as juvenile prostitutes are concerned. In the first place, it involves a cumbersome and frustrating process for parents.[47] Secondly, it is of little value where, as is often the case with juvenile prostitutes, the runaways have been rejected by their families or have no stable family to worry about them. In these cases, they are all too often not reported as missing.[48] Finally, juveniles in this type of situation often tend to give false identification in order to cover their tracks.[49]

In the wake of the congressional hearings on the sexual exploitation of children in 1977, a proliferation of new or revised legislation on juvenile prostitution, both criminal and civil, emerged in the States. The criminal statutes are designed to punish adults who engage in acts of prostitution with young people, or pimps or procurers who exploit them.[50] The legislative provisions typically contain harsher penalties for those who patronize juvenile prostitutes, and the harshest penalties for pimps and procurers. Penalties are often increased where the exploiter uses force, threats or intimidation. The law also treats harshly those parents or guardians who promote prostitution by their own offspring or children in their custody.

In most state legislation, juveniles are characterized as victims and not penalized, although they may be subject to the penalties under juvenile delinquency statutes. There are also provisions which parallel the *Mann Act*, as amended, and are directed against transporting minors within the state for purposes of prostitution. Legislation diverges over whether a mistake of age is a valid defence, with some states adopting a strict liability approach, and others allowing the defence.

The civil enactments on juvenile prostitution typically relate to child abuse and the reporting of it. However, only a few states include sexual exploitation in their definition of child abuse.[51]

When it comes to enforcement, much of the potential in the wording of these state enactments remains unrealized.[52] Enforcement against pimps is woefully inadequate, despite the fact that the occasional vigorous exception proves that pimps can be neutralized by it.[53] The record of prosecuting customers is no better. As in the case of federal legislation, it is questionable how far it recognizes the differences in the social context between male and female prostitution. The defence of reasonable mistake, where recognized, is a very real impediment to successful prosecution. The civil legislation on the reporting of child abuse suffers from the limited focus on parent and guardian, which has already been discussed with regard to the equivalent federal legislation.

It is clear that a considerable amount of legislative activity in this area has taken place in the United States in the past 10 years. Progress has been made in clearly identifying juvenile prostitution as a serious social problem, and taking steps to combat it. However, with the exception perhaps of the federal legislation on runaways, which has generated some excellent lifetime programs, much of it is too narrow in ambit, or impervious to the social causes and context of prostitution to have a significant impact. It has been suggested by one writer that the States, in particular, need to commit themselves and their resources to identifying the causes of juvenile prostitution and the identification, prevention and treatment of sexual abuse.[54] The suggestion is also made that the parental rejection which causes many youths to run away should draw penalties, and that parental support obligations should be enforced, especially when parents refuse to take back a runaway.[55] Finally, the same writer calls for more inter- and intra-state co-operation on runaways and the provision of state funding for shelters, which are crucial to the welfare of runaways in general, and runaway prostitutes in particular.[56]

2.2 England and Wales

The process of discovering the law and practice in England and Wales on child prostitution requires an analysis of the criminal law, the law relating to juvenile delinquency and the child welfare system. The criminal provisions are stated quite simply in the *Street Offences* and *Sexual Offences Acts*.[57] Juvenile delinquency is the subject of the recent and controversial *Criminal Justice Act* of 1982.[58] Child welfare in general is governed by a system of local authority initiative and care under the aegis of the *Children and Young Persons Acts*.[59]

Assuming that a female child practising prostitution is above the age of criminal responsibility, which in England and Wales is set at 10 years, that person can be charged with soliciting or loitering as a common prostitute under section 1 of the *Street Offences Act*. A male would be subject to prosecution under the broader offence in section 32 of the *Sexual Offences Act* "to solicit or importune in a public place for immoral purposes".

It is a criminal offence under section 23 of the *Sexual Offences Act* to procure a female under the age of 21 "to have unlawful sexual intercourse in any part of the world with a third person".[60] "Unlawful sexual intercourse" presumably refers both to sexual acts, such as buggery, which are criminal with any person under 21, as well as to any sexual intercourse with a female under 16, with or without her consent (statutory rape).[61] The *Sexual Offences Act* also contains the offences of keeping a brothel and living on the earnings of a prostitute.[62] Neither offence limits its application to adult prostitution activity. Accordingly, the provisions must be taken as applying to juvenile prostitution as well. Moreover a child of over 10 and under 18 years could be charged with any of the "exploitation offences". While somewhat fanciful in the case of the brothel offence, it is not entirely unreal in the case of procuring and living on the earnings, especially in the case of 16 and 17 year olds.

The current system for responding to juvenile delinquency is one which is marked by conflicting philosophies. Until recently, the main philosophy of the system has been "treatment" rather than punishment. This type of regime is embodied in both the 1963 and 1969 *Child and Young Persons Act*.[63] The 1963 Act placed a duty on local authorities to provide services to families to prevent children being brought before a juvenile court.[64] The 1969 *Act* took this one step further by emphasizing that children were only to be brought to court when they could not be helped by other means.[65] For those brought to court, the Act specified, as the major means for dealing with them, a "supervision order" combined with what is called Intermediate Treatment (I.T.). Every area of the country is required to provide I.T. which is designed to provide positive guidance and activities for and stimulate new and beneficial attitudes in the subject of the supervision order.

Juvenile courts date from 1908 in England and Wales and are serviced by Magistrates (typically lay people). They are not open to the public. With some exceptions, they deal with juveniles up to and including the age of 16 years. A supervision order, prescribed by a juvenile court, places the juvenile under the supervision of the local authority, social worker or probation officer for up to three years.[66] Participation in I.T. may only be ordered if a scheme is locally available, and for a maximum period of 90 days during the currency of the supervision order.

An alternative to a supervision order is a care order committing the child to the care of the local authority which, after observation, decides where the juvenile should live and what treatment he or she should receive.[67] The options for care are: home; a foster home; a residential community home; or a secure community home.

For those who are considered in need of somewhat stiffer treatment, other options exist for the juvenile courts. In the case of a child between 10 and 17 who has been convicted of an offence which would be punishable by imprisonment in the case of an adult (including indecency between men, male soliciting and the exploitation offences), he or she may be ordered to attend, on a part-time basis, an attendance centre (where the emphasis is on physical fitness, citizenship training etc.).[68] Those between 14 and 17, who have committed such offences and are considered to need disciplinary treatment under a brisk, firm regime, can be sent to a custodial detention centre for 3 to 6 months.[69] Currently, these facilities are only available for males. In the case of an offence which is imprisonable for an adult, a juvenile may be fined, the parents usually be liable to pay. Moreover, parents or guardians may be bound over to take good care or exercise proper control of their offspring.

The *Criminal Justice Act* of 1982 reflects a somewhat different philosophy. It embodies the present British Government's view that more juvenile offenders need a "short, sharp shock". It makes it more attractive for magistrates to prescribe time in attendance at detention centres and these centres have been increased in number. Other changes include the extension to those 16 years old of a "community service order", previously confined to those of 17 years or more; and the investing of the courts with the power to specify the program of activities under a supervision order, including a "night restriction" or "curfew" order.[70]

Critics have pointed to the uneasy co-existence of elements of the former "welfare" regime and the new "law and order" philosophy.[71] While it is too early to assess the impact of the more draconian regime, it is clear that attendance at detention centre orders have increased. Based on past experience in which a recidivism rate of two thirds has been noted, the prognosis is said not to be good for these establishments.[72]

A juvenile, including a young prostitute, may of course not fall afoul of the criminal law, and yet may be the subject of the child welfare system.[73] A child of under 17 years of age, who is in need of care, may become the recipient of "voluntary" care by a local authority (voluntary because the parents may request the child's return); or of non-voluntary care, (where the judgment is made by the local authority that the welfare of the child already in care demands it and the parents or guardians are considered incapable of providing it); or be the subject of a "care order" sought by the local authority.[74] Among the reasons for granting such an order are that the child's proper development is being impaired or neglected or the individual is being ill-treated, or that he or she is exposed to moral danger. The latter typically involves moral danger in the sexual sense.

Law enforcement authorities in England and Wales do not see juvenile prostitution as a serious problem, although it undoubtedly exists to some extent. As in Canada, it is the runaway juveniles, who are close to 18 years old, who are the most problematic. The police are often of the view that it is pointless returning them to their homes. All they can do is to report the matter to the local authority, if they are concerned about the welfare of the child.[75]

Footnotes

[1] Public Law 98-292, May 21, 1984, s.2(1).

[2] 438 U.S. 1801 (1978).

[3] 438 U.S. 1801, at 749.

[4] 438 U.S. 1801, at 749-750.

[5] 458 U.S. 1113 (1982).

[6] 458 U.S. 1113, at 1122.

[7] 413 U.S. 15 (1973).

[8] D. Sansfaçon, *Pornography and Prostitution in the United States* W.P.P.P.#2 at 12.

[9] 413 U.S. 15, at 24.

[10] 458 U.S. 1113, at 1127.

[11] Penal Law, Article 263.

[12] See note 1.

[13] Sansfaçon, *op. cit.* at 23.

[14] U.K. 1955, c.28.

[15] U.K. 1978, c.37.

[16] Williams Report, para 2.28, at 19.

[17] *Ibid.*

[18] *Ibid.*

[19] *Ibid.,* para. 6.67 at 89.

[20] *Ibid.*

[21] *Ibid.,* para. 6.68 at 90.

[22] *Ibid.*

[23] *Ibid.*

[24] *Ibid.,* para. 9.7 and 10.2, at 114 and 130.

[25] *Ibid.,* para. 10.6, at 131-132.

[26] *Ibid.,* para. 10.13, at 134.

[27] For a summary of the Williams Report recommendations, see Chapter 13, at 159 ff.

[28] U.K. 1981, c.42.2

[29] U.K. 1984.

[30] This segment draws upon D. Weisberg, "Children of the Night: The Adequacy of Statutory Treatment of Juvenile Prostitution", (1984) 12 *Am. J. Crm. Law* 1.

[31] Ch. 395, 36 Stat. 825 (1910).

[32] 18 U.S.C. §§ 2251, 2253-2254 (1978).

[33] Weisberg, *op. cit.* at 50-51.

[34] *Ibid.*

[35] 42 U.S.C. § 5101 - 5106 (1974), as amended by *Child Abuse Prevention and Treatment and Adoption Reform Act*, 92 Stat. 205 (1978).

[36] 42 U.S.C. § 5102 (1977).

[37] 48 Fed. Reg. 3701, § 1340.2.

[38] Weisberg, *op. cit.* at 52.

39 *Ibid.*, 53.

40 Pub. L. No. 93-415, 88 Stat. 1109.43 (1974).

41 Weisberg, *op. cit.* at 54-55.

42 *Ibid.*, at 55-56.

43 *Ibid.*, at 56.

44 *Ibid.*, at 29.

45 28 U.S.C. § 534 (1982).

46 Weisberg, *op. cit.* at 57.

47 *Ibid.*

48 *Ibid.*, at 57-58.

49 *Ibid.*, at 58.

50 *Ibid.*, at 39-47.

51 *Ibid.*, at 47-49.

52 *Ibid.*, at 59.

53 *Ibid.*, at 60. Weisberg notes that in this research, the staff of a few law enforcement agencies (eg. Louisville, Kentucky; Minneapolis; Seattle) suggested that when police take time to be especially supportive of a prostitute, she is more willing to testify. He also notes "[s]ome progressive police departments now provide emotional and residential support services to prostitutes as well as protection from the pimp."

54 *Ibid.*, at 62-63.

55 *Ibid.*, at 63.

56 *Ibid.*, at 64-65.

57 *The Street Offences Act*, 1959. 7. 8 Eliz. 2, c.57; *The Sexual Offences Act*, 1956, 4 c. 5 Eliz. 2, c. 69. See generally on this topic M. Freeman, "The Rights of the Child in England" (1981-2). 13 *Columbia Human Rights L. Rev.* 601.

58 *The Criminal Justice Act*, 1982.

59 *The Children and Young Persons Act*, 1963, 17 Statutes, 669; *The Children and Young Persons Act*, 1969, 40 Statutes 843.

60 *Sexual Offences Act*, 1959, 7.8 Eliz.2, c.57.

61 *Ibid.*, s.6.

62 *Ibid.*, § 33, 30.

63 *The Children and Young Persons Act*, 1963, *The Children and Young Persons Act*, 1969.

64 *Children and Young Persons Act*, 1963, s.1.

65 *Children and Young Persons Act*, 1969, s.2.

66 *Ibid.*, § 11-13.

67 *Ibid.*, § 7, 20, 21.

68 *Freeman, op. cit.* at 668.

69 *Ibid.*, at 669.

70 For details, see J. McEwan, "In Search of Juvenile Justice - The Criminal Justice Act 1982" (1983) *J. of Social Welfare Law* 112.

71 *Ibid.*, at 116.

72 *Freeman, op. cit.* at 669.

73 *Ibid.*, at 629-30.

74 *The Children and Young Persons Act*, 1969, s.1(2).

75 *Freeman, op. cit.* at 606.

Chapter 46

Legal Recommendations

1. Introduction

In this section, we discuss our proposals for reform of the *Criminal Code* respecting prostitution involving youths, pornography involving youths, and access to pornography by young people. We also consider what reforms may be necessary to the criminal law in order to protect the young complainant or witness.

We recommend that all of these suggested reforms apply to persons below the age of 18 years.

Recommendation 70

All of the reforms to the criminal law and related statutes dealing with pornography and prostitution involving children and youths should be applicable to persons under 18 years of age.

This division between adult and youth corresponds to that which is found in the text of the *Young Offenders Act*. The scheme of the *Young Offenders Act* is, we note, one of the main reasons why we have departed from the thrust of previous law reform initiatives in this area, which used the age of sixteen as the boundary between adulthood and childhood. We consider that not only the correspondence with this major criminal procedure statute for young persons, but also the merits of the age, amply justify our selection. We are particularly interested in the reality that having 18 as the dividing line means that persons up to 17 are protected, whereas a dividing line of 16 includes only those up to 15 years of age. Evidence at the hearings, and gathered in the studies available to the Committee, place a substantial number of young prostitutes in the age range of 15 to 19. By choosing 18 as a cut-off point, we ensure that the provisions we have crafted will benefit those in half this range at least, instead of almost none of them.

Of course, this observation does point out that the dividing line is a somewhat arbitrary one. Some persons 18 and over may, in fact, be more vulnerable to exploitation than some under 18. We do not claim that the age we have chosen is perfectly appropriate. Yet we are reluctant to suggest that the age be higher, because of the restraints on personal autonomy which are inherent in providing "protection" for the vulnerable by means of the criminal law. At some point, society has to relinquish its protective instincts and trust that persons can look after themselves as adults. There is substantial social consensus that 18 is an acceptable point for this transition to occur.

We considered the possibility of using in the *Code* a flexible age for majority with respect to illegal activities. This approach is a feature of some European legislation.[1] It is, however, out of keeping with the way in which we commonly deal with young persons in Canadian law. Moreover, the flexible age leaves considerable vagueness in the criminal law, about which accused persons could properly complain. Although a fixed age limit may result in overprotection of some young people, we think that this risk is a very acceptable one, given the kinds of harms to which these recommendations are directed.

We have also noted that the Badgley Committee, in setting out offences, draws a line in its offences between those who are under 14, on the one hand, and on the other, those who are over 14 but under 18. The same distinction was featured in some of the bills we have reviewed, and, indeed, is found in some sections of the *Criminal Code*. We do not think that it would be useful to follow this pattern. It seems that the reason for it is to ensure that younger children get a level of protection which is high enough, while still accounting for the greater maturity to be found in those over 14. We are not sure that the results which may ensue from this approach justify its cumbersome nature, and we have declined to adopt it.

A note of caution must be sounded, however, about our choice of 18 as the significant age. While the text of the *Young Offenders Act* stipulates that a young person is one up to the age of eighteen, practice in the early phase of implementing the *Act* has resulted in a lower threshold age in many provinces. Pressure is building in some provinces to delay the date at which eighteen will be the uniform age across Canada for purposes of the *Young Offenders Act*.

We have recommended that persons under 18 be charged with the offences we have recommended be created only on the premise that the procedures of the *Young Offenders Act* will apply to their trial and the disposition of their cases. Should that *Act* not apply in some provinces after the effective date of any of our recommended reforms, then we would deplore the prosecution of a person between the age of eighteen and the upper age limit for the *Young Offenders Act* which is in effect in that province. We do not welcome the idea that a person of 17, or even sixteen, might be tried and incarcerated with adults, and like an adult, simply because of federal-provincial difficulties in the implementation of the *Young Offenders Act*.

Recommendation 71

   Trials of persons under 18, accused of any of the offences proposed in our recommendations should be conducted in accordance with the Young

Offenders Act. Accordingly, if the minimum age of 18 as provided in that Act is not fully implemented across Canada by the time these recommendations are in effect, no person under 18, who is not given the protection of the Young Offenders Act, should be charged.

Now we turn to a discussion of the recommendations in the areas of pornography and prostitution.

2. Pornography

This Committee is making a number of recommendations for reform of the *Criminal Code* in order specifically to address the use of young persons in the production of sexually explicit material, and the availability of such material to them. The overall scheme of our recommendations respecting pornography depends on classifying pornographic material into three categories or tiers. The sanctions attached to the material would depend on what category it is in and are described in detail in Part II, Section IV, chapter 20 of the Report. Here we will simply give an overview of the scheme so that the proposals we make about children can be seen in their proper context.

The first tier includes the material which we consider the most harmful. In this tier we have placed material which gives reason to believe that actual physical harm was experienced by the person or persons depicted in it. Such material is in this category because there is no doubt about the harm which has been experienced.

For the purposes of this Chapter, the more important components of tier one are those relating to the use of children in the production of pornographic material and the encouragement of sexual abuse of children. Thus, we subject to strong criminal sanctions both the production, distribution and possession of visual representations of the explicit sexual conduct of persons under 18 years of age, and the production and distribution of material that encourages sexual abuse of children.

We think that it will be apparent from our discussion of the principles underlying our view of children, why we consider it so essential to protect them from being used in the making of pornography. We consider any dissemination of such material to be harmful because it implies that children's sexuality can be exploited by adults. Clearly, to the extent that we can stop the production of such material and its distribution, then the problem of its possession and use by pedophiles becomes less significant.

The reason for prohibiting the production and distribution of material that encourages the sexual abuse of children, is equally clear. The harm to children that results if the message conveyed by such material is absorbed and acted upon by the viewer, is particularly serious.

For adult portrayals, we develop a second category of material which will be proscribed unless it can be shown to have genuine educational or scientific purpose or artistic merit. This tier, called "Sexually Violent and Degrading Pornography", contains material which we believe is extreme in its depictions and, for that reason, is harmful. Nevertheless, in the interest of striking a balance between competing values, we recommend that the material be available to consenting adults if it can be shown to have a scientific or educational purpose or artistic merit.

The third category of material is that which is sexually explicit but which lacks the violence or degradation of the sort we believe characterizes the tier two material. Consequently, we are recommending that this material not be prohibited, but be subject to regulation in terms of where it can be displayed and who can purchase it.

The relevance of tier two and tier three material for the purposes of children is that any material which is permitted under these categories, is subject to display and access restrictions. In all cases, a prominent warning notice must indicate that visual pornographic material is being displayed and that no one under 18 years of age can have access to the premises or part of the premises where the material is displayed. In addition, those under 18 will not be able to buy, rent or see the material in question. These provisions are, of course, designed to ensure that young people do not have access to material which we believe can be harmful to them.

The approach the Committee has adopted is to be as precise as possible in describing the kinds of material to be prohibited or subject to restrictions. In this way, the adjudication of the question of whether particular material falls within a particular tier, does not depend on discerning the community standards of tolerance for that material. For many reasons, we agree with those who have found this approach to be highly problematic. In fact, it is, in part, because we have to avoid the community standards of tolerance approach, that we have developed the system we have just described.

Let us turn now to an examination in more detail of the proposals relating to children.

2.1 Pornography Involving Children

Recommendation 72

Pursuant to recommendation 2 in this Part, the following new section of the Criminal Code should be enacted:

(1) Everyone who:
   (a) Uses, or who induces, incites, coerces, or agrees to use a person under 18 years of age to
   (i) participate in any explicit sexual conduct for the purpose of producing, by any means, a visual representation of such conduct;
   (ii) participate in any explicit sexual conduct in the context of a live show;

(b) **induces, incites, or coerces another person to use a person under 18 years of age to**
(i) participate in any explicit sexual conduct for the purposes of producing, by any means, a visual representation of such conduct;
(ii) participate in any explicit sexual conduct in the context of a live show;

(c) **participates in the production of a visual representation of or a live performance by a person under 18 years of age participating in explicit sexual conduct;**

(d) **makes, prints, reproduces, publishes or distributes, or has in his possession for the purposes of publication or distribution, a visual representation of a person under 18 years of age participating in explicit sexual conduct**

is guilty of an indictable offence and is liable to imprisonment for 10 years.

(2) For the purpose of subsection (1)

(a) a person who at any material time appears to be under 18 years of age shall in the absence of evidence to the contrary, be deemed to be under 18 years of age.

(3) Everyone who sells, rents, offers to sell or rent, receives for sale or rent, exposes to public view, or has in his possession for the purpose of sale or rent a visual representation of a person under 18 years of age participating in explicit sexual conduct, is guilty
(i) of an indictable offence and is liable to imprisonment for 5 years, or
(ii) of an offence punishable on summary conviction and is liable to a fine of not less than $1,000 and not more than $5,000 or to imprisonment for six months or to both.

(4) Every one who knowingly, without lawful justification or excuse, has in his or her possession a visual representation of a person under 18 years of age participating in explicit sexual conduct, is guilty of an offence punishable on summary conviction, and is liable to a fine of not less than $500 and not more than $2,000 or to imprisonment for six months or to both.

(5) For the purposes of subsections (1), (3) and (4) above,

(a) "explicit sexual conduct" includes any conduct in which vaginal, oral or anal intercourse, bestiality, masturbation, sexually violent behavior, lewd touching of the breasts or the genital parts of the body, or the lewd exhibition of the genitals is depicted;

(b) "sexually violent behavior" includes
(i) sexual assault, and
(ii) physical harm, including murder, assault or bondage of another person or persons, or self-infliction of physical harm, carried out for the apparent purpose of causing sexual gratification or stimulation to the viewer;

(c) "visual representation" includes any representation that can be seen by any means, whether or not it involves the use of any special apparatus.

This section would create a number of offences relating to the participation of a person under 18 in explicit sexual conduct, in two contexts: the production of a visual representation of such conduct, and the live show. The proposed section is intended to specify various offences relating to young persons and to that extent is a departure from the general style of the present section 159 dealing with obscenity.

The offences in our proposed section consist of using, inducing, coercing or agreeing to use a person under 18 to participate in any explicit sexual conduct for the purpose of producing a visual representation of the conduct, or in such conduct in the context of a live show. Also criminalized is the act of inducing, inciting or coercing another person to use a person under 18. The person who participates in the live show or the recorded performance with the person under 18 is subject to prosecution under paragraph (1)(c). A party who makes, prints, reproduces, publishes, distributes, circulates or has in his possession for such purposes a visual representation of a person under 18 engaged in explicit sexual conduct would be included within paragraph 1(d).

The penalty for the maker and the wholesale distributor is set at ten years imprisonment. By reason of section 646(2) of the *Code*, the court may in addition impose a fine, the amount of which would be in its discretion. The term of imprisonment cannot be imposed on the corporation, but paragraph 647(a) of the *Code* allows the court to impose a fine on the corporation in lieu of imprisonment.

The retailer is given somewhat different treatment. If convicted of an indictable offence, the retailer is subject to imprisonment for two years. Subsection 646(2) of the *Code* allows the court to impose a fine, the amount of which would be in its discretion, in lieu of imprisonment. Where the accused is a corporation, paragraph 647(a) of the *Code* provides for a fine, in the discretion of the court, but no period of imprisonment.

However, the Crown may also proceed against the retailer by way of summary conviction. In that event, we have provided that the retailer is liable to a fine of not less than $1,000 and not more than $5,000 or to imprisonment for six months or both. Unfortunately, these specially tailored penalties are available only where the accused is an individual, because paragraph 647(b) of the *Criminal Code* provides that a corporation cannot be fined an amount exceeding $1,000 where the offence is a summary conviction offence. We recognize that we are bound at this time by this general provision applying to corporations convicted of any summary conviction offence in the *Code*. However, in our view, the fine is very low, given the other penalties we are proposing, particularly those directed against individuals.

Recommendation 73

> **Paragraph 647(b) of the Criminal Code should be amended to provide a higher maximum penalty for a corporation convicted of a summary conviction offence; or the section should provide, as does subsection 722(1), that a higher penalty may be provided with respect to a particular offence.**

The rationale behind our creation of smaller penalties for sale of material lies in the position of the ordinary retailer. Although we are aware of the many cynical merchants who sell pornographic material fully knowledgable of what it is, yet we still think it necessary to preserve some flexibility to deal with the merchant who may be, if you will, a less cynical person. We are also concerned about the position of employees of such concerns, who are often those charged, but who may have little leverage to force a change in a situation they consider improper or illegal. In addition to a reduced sentence, we have provided, in our general provisions applicable to all of these suggested reforms, a defence for those who can demonstrate that they used due diligence in inspecting the material offered for sale to see that it did not contain illegal material.

Although the retailer is treated more leniently than the producer or wholesaler of such material, we have nonetheless provided for a minimum fine, to demonstrate that we view the offence as a serious one.

We have included in the draft section a summary conviction offence of possessing a visual representation of a person under 18 participating in explicit sexual conduct. We are aware of the argument that adults should be free to read whatever they wish in private surroundings. We have not dealt lightly with this principle in considering our recommendations. However, we are also mindful that private consumption is very frequently the method of using pornography involving juveniles. We know that youth pornography, like all pornography, has a long life, often circulating or being kept for some time after its original production or sale. Often, there will be no clue at all as to the original producer of the pornography.

We have been told that private production and use of such pornography occurs in circumstances where the only evidence of its production may be that of the child who was videotaped or photographed; for many reasons, that child may be unable or unwilling to testify. The recollection of the child may simply not be detailed enough to establish the requisite connection between the events he or she experienced and the accused's production through home photographic equipment of the representation in question. For these various reasons, the possibility of charging someone with possession of an offending representation is a desirable one. We believe that the availability of such a charge will act as some deterrent to the production and exchange of this material, particularly if convictions under the section are accompanied by publicity and offenders are sentenced to jail.

There is yet another reason for proposing a possession offence. We agree with the Williams Committee that a nation should not be isolationist, protecting only children who are its own nationals from use in pornography. The Report of M. Fernand-Laurent to the United Nations Economic and Social Council described the unfortunate circumstances which may involve children in other countries in pornographic productions. We believe that if creation of the possession offence could reduce, even a little, the international child pornography traffic, it would be well worth while.

We do not propose that persons under 18 years of age who themselves offend against this section should be given any immunity from prosecution. The provisions of the *Young Offenders Act* will provide for a trial procedure and sentencing options particularly designed to deal with the youthful offender. Within such a context, we are satisfied that a youthful offender against this, and the other recommendations we have made on pornography involving children, will be adequately safeguarded.

We have made the penalty for the offence a fine of not less than $500 nor more than $2,000, or six months imprisonment, or both. The minimum penalty is present to ensure that courts will treat the offence with at least some seriousness, but the maximum figure is high enough to deal with a situation where even a "first offender" may have a quantity or a type of material that is regarded as particularly serious. In the case of a repeat offender, of course, the penalty allows for either escalation of the fine or a sentence of imprisonment.

We have recommended provisions which address specifically the procurement of children to engage for reward in sexual acts, and the involvement of children in the production of pornography. These specific recommendations will, in our view, reduce the justification for retaining in the *Criminal Code* the present section 168.

Recommendation 74

Section 168 of the Criminal Code should be repealed.

Section 168 provides that everyone who, in the home of a child, participates in adultery or sexual immorality or indulges in habitual drunkenness or any other form of vice, and thereby endangers the morals of the child or renders the home an unfit place for the child to be in, is guilty of an indictable offence. As we mentioned above, this section has been used to prosecute a mother and her common law husband who took suggestive photographs of her eleven year old daughter.

We do not think that the section will continue to have much utility at all once the recommendations we have made have been implemented. We suspect that its main utility up to now, as in the case we mentioned, lay in the fact of its general wording; because there were no specific offences, section 168 might be pressed into service to cover particular instances of sexual exploitation.

However, the section presents enormous hazards. Its language is broad enough to cover, at least, the situation of two persons living common law, with the children of one or another, while awaiting the chance for one to secure a divorce from a former spouse. Such a couple would be participating in adultery in the home of a child. The use of the terms "sexual immorality", "other form of vice" endangering the morals, and rendering the home an unfit place, all contribute to the vagueness and elasticity of the section. That the administration of this section was seen even by its framers to present some difficulties is seen by the inclusion of a requirement that the Attorney General consent to any prosecution not brought by a recognized child welfare authority.

2.2 The Sexual Abuse of Children— Advocating or Encouraging

Recommendation 75

> A new section of the Criminal Code should be enacted to deal with production, dissemination and possession of material advocating, encouraging or presenting as normal the sexual abuse of children in the following form:
>
> (1) Everyone who makes, prints, reproduces, publishes, or distributes, or has in his possession for the purposes of publication or distribution material which advocates, encourages, condones or presents as normal the sexual abuse of children is guilty of an indictable offence and liable to imprisonment for 10 years.
>
> (2) It shall not be a defence to a charge under subsection (1) that the accused was ignorant of the character of the material, matter, thing or production.
>
> (3) Everyone who sells, rents, offers to sell or rent, receives for sale or rent, exposes to public view, or has in his possession for purpose of sale or rent material which advocates, encourages, condones or presents as normal the sexual abuse of children is guilty
> (i) of an indictable offence and liable to imprisonment for 5 years, or
> (ii) of an offence punishable on summary conviction and liable to a fine of not less than $1,000 and not more than $5,000 or to imprisonment for six months or to both.
>
> (4) Everyone who knowingly, without lawful justification or excuse, has in his or her possession material which advocates, encourages, condones or presents as normal the sexual abuse of children is guilty of a summary conviction offence and is liable to a fine of not less than $500 and not more than $2,000 or to imprisonment for six months or to both.
>
> (5) For purposes of this section "material" includes any written, visual or recorded matter.
>
> (6) For purposes of this section "sexual abuse" means any sexual activity or conduct directed against a person under 18 years of age which is prohibited by the Criminal Code.

In this provision, we have followed the same pattern as was established with the preceding section on pornography involving children. Everyone who makes, prints, reproduces, publishes, distributes or has in his possession for these purposes the offending material is guilty of an indictable offence punishable with 10 years imprisonment. An offence subject to lesser penalties is created for everyone who sells, offers to sell, receives for sale, advertises, exposes to public view, or has in his possession for these purposes the material. Simple possession, in turn, is made an offence punishable on summary conviction.

The material which will attract the sanction is that which advocates, encourages, condones or presents as normal the sexual abuse of children. We have not limited the sanction to material which consists of visual representations. Material which is entirely written will attract the sanction. We have seen, during the course of our research, a number of publications, entirely in prose, which focus on various aspects of sex with children. Many involve incestuous relationships. Often, the descriptions of sexual activities with young people will be explicit, if not lurid, in detail. The general tenor of such publications is that sexual relations with young persons is acceptable, or desirable, and indeed that young people themselves welcome such activities, whether incestuous or not. We did not want to create a criminal law scheme which would omit this type of material from its reach.

It has been drawn to our attention that there may well be a cultural dimension to material discussing or promoting sexual activities with young people. Spokespersons for the gay community in particular have cautioned us against measures which would make legitimate communication and exploration of sexual identity in that community a perilous activity. We are appreciative of the thoughtful and informed advocacy of this point of view which we received during our hearings.

We believe that we can respond to this interest in only a limited fashion, because of the other concerns which we must take into account in formulating our recommendations. Subsection (6) of this proposed section describes "sexual abuse" as any sexual activity or conduct directed against a person under 18 years of age which is prohibited by the *Criminal Code*. In discussing our recommendations on procuring, we have reviewed the offences which deal with sexual activity with young persons, and have noted that the upper age limit for prohibited acts is 21 with respect to buggery and gross indecency. We have recommended lowering that limit to "under 18" in order to rationalize these provisions with the other sections of the *Code* dealing with sexual offences involving young people. We have also recommended extending the protection of the *Code* which now is available only to young females to young males.

We think that this review of sections 140 to 157 of the *Code* should put treatment of sexual activity with young males on the same footing as that with young females; adults involved with young people should also be placed in the same position whether their activities are with young people of the same sex as they are or of a different sex. If that rationalization of the criminal law relating to sexual activity with young persons occurs, then we think that it is fair to incorporate the reformed sections into the definition of "sexual abuse" used in this proposed section.

We are not prepared to go further. We cannot, for whatever cultural reasons, accept that advocacy of sexual relations between adults and young people under 18 is a beneficial or even neutral act. The same observation applies to material encouraging, condoning, or normalizing such acts. We do not countenance such messages where the relations being advocated are heterosexual ones between adults and children. There has not been made out any special reason why it should be tolerated when the partners are of the same sex.

636

2.3 Live Shows

Recommendation 76

> Section 163 of the Criminal Code should be repealed and replaced by a new section which would include provisions dealing specifically with the presentation of a live show advocating, encouraging, condoning, or presenting as normal the sexual abuse of children, in the following form:
>
> (1) Everyone who, being the owner, operator, lessee, manager, agent or person in charge of a theatre or any other place in which live shows are presented, presents or gives or allows to be presented or given therein a performance which advocates, encourages, condones or presents as normal the sexual abuse of children is guilty of an indictable offence and liable to imprisonment for 10 years.

This provision with respect to live shows is a supplement to the subsections on live shows which are included in the section dealing with using children in pornography. The intent of the provision is to penalize advocacy, encouragement, condonation, or normalizing of sexual abuse of children when it occurs in a live show. The definitions applicable to this provision are the same as those which we use in conjunction with the subsections on the use of children in pornography.

2.4 Use of the Mails

Recommendation 77

> Section 164 of the Criminal Code should be repealed and a section enacted which includes provisions dealing explicitly with use of the mails to transmit material involving children or advocating the sexual abuse of children, along the following lines:
>
> (1) Everyone who makes use of the mails for the purpose of transmitting or delivering any material which:
>
> (a) depicts a person or persons under the age of 18 years engaging in explicit sexual conduct,
>
> (b) advocates, encourages, condones, or presents as normal the sexual abuse of children,
>
> is guilty of an indictable offence and liable to imprisonment for 10 years.

This section is intended to replace the present section 164 of the *Criminal Code*, which makes it an offence to use the mails for the purpose of transmitting or delivering anything that is obscene, indecent, immoral or scurrilous. In our proposed section, we have once again tried to be specific, and to directly refer to material involving children.

Distribution by mail of material which depicts a person or persons under the age of 18 engaged in explicit sexual conduct or which advocates, encourages, condones or presents as normal the sexual abuse of children is an indictable offence attracting a penalty of 10 years imprisonment. In addition to this penalty, the provision in the general section of our recommended provisions permitting forfeiture of such material applies to this section.

2.5 Pornography, Sale to and Access by Children

Recommendation 78

A new section should be included in the Criminal Code, to control display of visual pornographic material to persons under 18 years of age, in the following form:

(1) Everyone who

    (a) sells, rents or offers to sell or rent visual pornographic material to anyone under 18 years of age; or

    (b) displays for sale or rent visual pornographic material in such a manner that it is accessible to and can be seen or examined by anyone under 18 years of age; or

    (c) being the lessee, manager, agent or person in charge of a theatre, presents or gives or allows to be presented or given therein to anyone under 18 years of age any visual pornographic material

is guilty of a summary conviction offence and is liable to a fine not to exceed $1000 or to imprisonment for 6 months or to both.

(2) No one shall be convicted of an offence under subsection (1) who can demonstrate that

    (a) he used due care and diligence to ensure that there was no such visual pornographic material in the materials which he sold or rented, offered for sale or rent, displayed for sale or rent, or presented, gave or allowed to be presented or given; or

    (b) the visual pornographic material has a genuine educational or scientific purpose and was sold or rented, offered for sale or rent, or displayed for sale or rent, presented, given, or allowed to be presented or given, for that purpose; or

    (c) according to the classification or rating established for film or videotape material in the province or territory in which it is sold, rented, offered for sale or rent, displayed for sale or rent, presented, given or allowed to be presented or given, the film or videotape has been classified or rated as acceptable for viewing by those under the age of 18 years.

(3) For purposes of this section, "visual pornographic material" includes any matter or thing or live performances in which is depicted or described vaginal, oral or anal intercourse, masturbation, lewd touching of the breasts or the genital parts of the body, or the lewd exhibition of the genitals, but does not include any material prohibited by [offences involving portrayals of children and sexually violent or degrading material].

Recommendation 79

Subsections 159(2)(b), (c) and (d) of the Code should be repealed and replaced by a provision specifically directed at selling or displaying sex aids to a person under 18 years of age, in the following form:

(1) Everyone who

    (a) sells or offers to sell a sex aid to anyone under 18 years;

(b) **displays for sale sex aids in such a manner that they are accessible to and can be seen or examined by anyone under 18 years of age,**

is guilty of a summary conviction offence and is liable to a fine not to exceed $1000 or to imprisonment for 6 months or to both.

(2) **For the purposes of subsection (1) "sex aid" includes any device, apparatus or object designed solely to stimulate sexually the user of it.**

In the two draft sections set out above, we address the problem of access by children to pornographic material. The first section deals with the sale and availability to children of "visual pornographic material". This matter is broadly defined as including any material whether in the form of books, magazines, films or video-cassettes in which vaginal, oral or anal intercourse, bestiality, masturbation, sexually violent behaviour, lewd touching of the breasts or the genital parts of the body or the lewd exhibition of the genitals is depicted.

We have included in our recommendations a proposed section of the *Code* to prohibit display of visual pornographic materials generally. The thrust of that section is to prohibit the display of those materials so that they are visible to members of the public in a place to which the public has access by right or by express or implied invitation. The defence to the charge is to demonstrate that the material was displayed in a part of the premises to which access is possible only by means of passing a prominent warning notice advising of the display therein of visual pornographic material.

The section described above makes it an offence to sell or offer to sell visual pornographic material to anyone under 18 years of age. We do not recommend creation of a similar offence with respect to persons generally.

The section described above also creates an offence of displaying, for sale or rent, visual pornographic material in such a manner that it is accessible to and can be seen or examined by anyone under 18 years of age.

Because of the breadth of the definition of visual pornographic material, we have considered whether the section should provide any defences like those provided for the second tier of material, namely defences resting on artistic merit or on the scientific or educational purpose of the work. Alternatively, we have considered the possibility of lowering to 16 the age below which the young person cannot see the material.

We are not in favour of lowering the age in this one case. Upon close examination, the problem prompting consideration of these two options is the problem of the student of sixteen or seventeen, possibly at a CEGEP or university, whose curriculum may involve reading material which technically is within this definition. Or, consider too the case of the young married person who may be able to do some of the things described in the definition without fear of sanction but may not see representations of them. In either case, we think that the appropriate response to the dilemma is to provide exceptions, but not to lower the age. Even with the age at 18, it is likely that persons quite a bit younger than 18 will pass unchallenged into some premises. Were we to lower the limit, we think that we would, in reality, be lowering the effective age at which persons permit young people access to this material to a point quite a bit below 16. Accordingly, we have chosen to provide the artistic merit, and educational or scientific purposes, defences with regard to this offence. We have also provided a defence based on the due diligence of the proprietor in inspecting the material offered for sale or rent.

The provision with respect to sex aids is intended to replace, in part, the current offences in subsections 159(2)(b), (c) and (d). Paragraph (b) creates the offence of publicly exhibiting a disgusting object or show, and paragraphs (c) and (d) create offences relating to means, instructions, medicine, drugs or articles intended or represented as a method of causing abortion or miscarriage or of restoring sexual virility or curing venereal diseases or diseases of the generative organs.

We have framed a general definition of "sex aid" which we think will encompass the "disgusting object" now dealt with in paragraph 159(2)(b) and the materials claiming to restore virility described in paragraph 159(2)(d). The disgusting show covered in paragraph 159(2)(b) is, we think, adequately dealt with in our provisions respecting live shows. Medicines or agents aimed at curing diseases or procuring miscarriage are, in our opinion, more appropriately regulated by way of food and drug legislation, aimed at safety of product, accuracy of claims, and the social and medical desirability of the substance.

Our focus, in the recommendation concerning sex aids, is on the availability of such devices and substances to persons under 18 years of age. With some such mechanisms or substances, the concern of the criminal law is with actual safety, particularly when the youth who may get such a device or substance is quite young. In other cases, the concern is similar to that of the provision about accessibility of visual pornographic material: we desire to put out of the way of even a moderately curious young person, the chance of being unwittingly and unwillingly alarmed or upset by such materials. As it is certainly within the power of merchants to arrange their premises and displays so as to effect this object, we consider that it is quite reasonable to penalize failure or refusal to do so.

We propose to include in the foregoing sections the following definitions, which will be applicable to all of the provisions:

Recommendation 80

The following definitions should apply to the sections of the Code dealing with pornographic offences:

"sexually violent behaviour" includes
(i) sexual assault,

(ii) physical harm depicted for the apparent purpose of causing sexual gratification or stimulation to the viewer, including murder, assault or bondage of another person or persons, or self-infliction of physical harm.

"visual pornographic material" includes any matter or thing or live performances in which is depicted or described vaginal, oral, or anal intercourse, masturbation, lewd touching of the breasts or the genital parts of the body, or the lewd exhibition of the genitals.

2.6 Evidence

With respect to a number of the reform proposals we have made in the foregoing sections, it is apparent that law enforcement authorities will be relying on the evidence of young persons under 18 in order to proceed successfully with a prosecution. In some cases, only the evidence of the child or young person will be available.

We are not in favour of hedging the child's testimony with any requirement that it be corroborated, or that the court advise a jury that it is unwise to convict on the basis of such evidence alone. The Report of the Committee on Sexual Offences Against Children and Youths concluded, on the basis of its research, that young persons, even those young in years, can be reliable witnesses.[2] Persons who gave briefs at our hearings were in agreement that a child's testimony could be accepted without qualifications which would limit its probative value: we took the opportunity ourselves of probing this issue with those whose views we thought might assist us.

Recommendation 81

> **The Evidence Acts of Canada, the provinces and the territories should be amended to provide that every child is competent to testify in court and the child's evidence is admissible; the weight of the evidence should be determined by the trier of fact.**

Recommendation 82

> **There should be no statutory requirement for corroboration of "unsworn" child's evidence; this would entail repeal of section 586 of the Criminal Code, section 16(2) of the Canada Evidence Act and section 61(2) of the Young Offenders Act, and corresponding sections of provincial Evidence Acts.**

We think that it is in keeping with our approach to the dignity of the young person that no categorical restriction be placed on the reception or weight of a young person's evidence. It should be treated by a court according to the same principles as would be applied to the testimony of an adult.

We have included below some recommendations concerning protection from publicity which we think should be extended to the youthful witness and complainant. These protections should be available whether the accused is an adult being tried pursuant to the *Criminal Code* or a young person whose trial is governed by the *Young Offenders Act*. At present, the protections extended to the youthful complainant or witness are not as complete in a trial of an adult under the *Code* as are those available in a *Young Offenders Act* proceeding.

If the *Code* were amended to provide a more sheltered environment for the young complainant or witness, we do not think that further protections would be warranted. In particular, we would avoid any amendment or relaxation of the hearsay rules in order to permit a child's account of an act of sexual abuse to be presented to the court through the testimony of an adult to whom the child may have told the story on a previous occasion. We are not persuaded that such an adult, who will probably be quite close to the child in most cases, can in fact serve merely as a neutral conduit for the child's evidence. Neutrality in the initial reception of the story and in its subsequent retelling not being reliably predictable, we do not believe that a departure from the normal hearsay rules is warranted.

Recommendation 83

No alteration be made to the Evidence Acts of Canada or the provinces and territories to permit reception by a court of hearsay evidence of a child's account of the commission against him or her of a sexual offence.

This Committee is recommending that persons who involve young people in prostitution, or in the production of pornography, be subject to penalties. The creation of these new offences raises questions concerning the publicity to be given to the trials of accused persons, to convictions, and to the identity of youthful complainants, witnesses and accused.

There are at present provisions in both the *Criminal Code* and the *Young Offenders Act* which deal with these questions.

Subsection 442(1) of the *Criminal Code* states the general rule that proceedings against an adult accused shall be in open court. The subsection also provides, however, that where the presiding judge, magistrate or justice is of the opinion that it is in the interest of public morals, the maintenance of order, or the proper administration of justice to exclude all or any members of the public from the court room for all or part of the proceedings, he or she may so order.

In deciding whether to exclude the public under this section, a court is likely to bear in mind the principle enunciated by the Supreme Court of Canada that, as a general rule, the sensibilities of the individuals involved are not a basis for exclusion of the public from judicial proceedings.[3] As observed by Mr. Justice Brooke of the Ontario Court of Appeal:

> It is hard to imagine any trial, civil or criminal, where men or women, boys or girls, and particularly the latter have to testify as to sexual behaviour that the witness will not be embarrassed. But this alone is not reason to suppose that truth is more difficult or unlikely or that the witness will be so frightened as to be unable to testify.[4]

In one case arising under the section, the Crown's fear that teenaged girls who were being called as witnesses would be embarrassed to testify was held to be insufficient basis for an order excluding the public throughout the trial.[5] In another, it was ruled improper for a trial judge to have excluded from a trial on charges of keeping a common bawdy house a local reporter who refused to undertake to keep the names of found-ins out of the newspaper.[6] An order has also been refused in the case of the trial of a number of persons on gross indecency charges.[7]

This provision of the *Criminal Code* applies to the trials of accused persons who are eighteen years of age and over. Trials of persons under the age of eighteen years are governed by the *Young Offenders Act*. Section 39 of that *Act* contains a number of provisions dealing with exclusion of persons from the courtroom during the trial of a young person. Paragraph 39(1)(b) provides that where a court or justice is of the opinion that it would be in the interest of public morals, the maintenance of order, or the proper administration of justice to exclude any or all members of the public from the courtroom, any person may be excluded from the courtroom if the court or justice deems that person's presence to be unnecessary to the conduct of the proceedings.

It will be noted that this standard for excluding the public from a trial under the *Young Offenders Act* is quite similar to that in the *Criminal Code*, except that the *Young Offenders Act* imposes the further requirement that the presence of a person to be excluded must be "unnecessary" to the proceedings.

The *Young Offenders Act* includes, however, certain other provisions for the exclusion of persons from trials which are not found in the *Criminal Code*. Where the court or justice is of the opinion that any evidence or information would be seriously injurious or seriously prejudicial to the young person who is being dealt with in the proceedings, who is a witness in the proceedings, or who is aggrieved by the offence charged in the proceedings, then paragraph 39(1)(a) allows the court to exclude any person from all or part of the proceedings if it deems the person's presence to be unnecessary to the conduct of the proceedings.

The provisions of subsection 39(1)(a) were considered by Mr. Justice R.E. Holland of the Ontario High Court in *Southam Inc.* v. *Her Majesty the Queen*[8]. He held that it was valid under the *Canadian Charter of Rights and Freedoms*, as a reasonable limit on freedom of expression, demonstrably justifiable in a free and democratic society.

Subsection 39(1)(a) presumably allows the court to exclude a young person from the court while evidence is given which would harm him or her, or presumably to exclude another person from court while the young person is testifying. However, the *Young Offenders Act* provides that the court may not exclude the accused, his or her counsel, or parent from the trial pursuant to any power to exclude granted in subsection 39(2).

Differences between the *Criminal Code* and the *Young Offenders Act* may also be noted with respect to the court's power to forbid publication of details from the trial.

The *Criminal Code* provides in sections 246.4 and 442(3) that in cases of incest, gross indecency, sexual assault, sexual assault with a weapon and aggravated sexual assault, when an application is made by the complainant or the prosecutor, the presiding judge shall make an order directing that the identity of the complainant and any information that could disclose the identity of the complainant shall not be published in any newspaper or broadcast. Where there is no such application from the complainant or the prosecutor, the judge may still make this order, but is not bound to do so. Subsection 442(3.1) obliges the presiding judge to draw to the complainant's attention at the first reasonable opportunity the right to make an application for an order of non-publication.

The validity of those sections was considered recently by the Ontario Court of Appeal, in the case of *Canadian Newspapers Company Limited* v. *A-G Canada*.[9] Subsection 422(3.1) was upheld. However it was held that the mandatory element in subsection 442(3) was contrary to the *Charter of Rights*. The Court accepted that the social value to be protected, namely the bringing to justice of those who commit these kinds of sexual offences, is of superordinate importance and justifies a prohibition against publication of the victim's identity or of anything that could disclose it.[10] However, it ruled that making the order automatically, on the application of the complainant or the Crown, went beyond what could be considered a "reasonable limit" on the right to freedom of expression. This decision has the effect of removing this mandatory element, so that now, it is up to the court's discretion in every case whether an order of non-publication should issue, even if the victim applies for it.

The Chief Justice of Ontario, in coming to this decision, observed:

> The discretion given to the trial judge under s. 442(3) to make a prohibition order is a sufficient safeguard for the protection of the identity of the complainant. In most cases it will no doubt be made as a matter of course. However, in an exceptional case where it is not merited the presiding judge should have an opportunity to refuse to make it.[11]

As comforting as these words may be, one wonders if the courts will indeed be ready to grant non-publication orders all that readily. In *R.* v. *McArthur*[12] Mr. Justice Dupont granted an order refusing the publication of names of witnesses who were prison inmates and feared physical harm if other prisoners learned they testified. In the course of his reasons for doing so, he observed

> This case must be distinguished from those where the court is asked to restrain publication of names where not to do so would create embarrassment, humiliation or even financial loss. Under most of such circumstances, the rights [sic] of complete public disclosure is paramount.[13]

In cases where the grant of an exclusion order formerly was automatic, more judges may well now refuse them on the ground that potential embarrassment to the victim does not outweigh the public's interest in knowing her name. Unfortunately, it can be predicted that a few well-publicized decisions to this effect will have a negative effect on the willingness to report sexual assault.

Subsection 442(3) in the *Criminal Code* would protect a complainant who is an adult or a young person. There is, however, no provision to protect a witness from disclosure of his or her identity. Nor is there a provision to permit withholding the identity of an accused, and the case law shows an unwillingness to use the provisions of subsection 442(1) to achieve this purpose indirectly.

By contrast, subsection 38(1) of the *Young Offenders Act* prohibits the publication of a report of an offence allegedly committed by a young person or of any proceeding in connection with such an offence, in which the name of the accused young person, a child or young person aggrieved by the offence or a child or young person who appeared as a witness in connection with the offence is disclosed. It is also forbidden to publish any information which would serve to identify such child or young person. The protection against publication which is provided by subsection 38(1) of the *Young Offenders Act* is automatic; it does not depend on whether an application is made to the presiding judge. The validity of this provision was upheld in a decision of Mr. Justice Holland of the Ontario High Court, albeit before the decision of the Ontario Court of Appeal invalidating the mandatory element in subsection 442(3).

In our view, it is necessary to rationalize these provisions of the *Criminal Code* and *Young Offenders Act* if they are to be applied to the new offences we recommend. We note the following significant discrepancies between the protections afforded by the *Criminal Code* and those in the *Young Offenders Act*. Firstly, with respect to excluding persons from judicial proceedings, we note that the *Young Offenders Act* provides for an exclusion in order to protect a child or young person who is the complainant or witness from evidence or information which would be "seriously injurious" or "seriously prejudicial" to the young person. Similarly, where evidence is offered by a child or youth that may be seriously injurious or seriously prejudicial to a youthful accused, complainant or witness, the *Young Offenders Act* would allow exclusion of third parties during the taking of such evidence. The youthful witness or complainant in a trial involving an adult accused is not given similar protection, unless one can regard the possibility of an order under subsection 442(1) as equivalent.

It seems to this Committee that the position of the youthful witness or complainant should not depend on whether an accused is an adult or a young person. We recommend that provisions like those of subsection 39 of the *Young Offenders Act*, permitting exclusion of young complainants or witnesses, or of third parties, when the evidence will be seriously prejudicial or seriously injurious to the young witness or complainant should be inserted into the *Criminal Code*. We expect that judicial sensitivity to the dangers of having "secret" trials may cause courts to be sparing in their resort to such sections, but believe that the provisions should be there in the event that they are really needed.

Recommendation 84

> Subsection 442(1) of the Criminal Code should be amended to allow the court to exclude any person from the courtroom where any evidence or information presented to the court would be seriously injurious or seriously prejudicial to the complainant or witness who is under 18.

Turning now to the question of reports of trials, we note that while the identity of the youthful accused may not be published, that of the adult accused may be. We do not recommend changing that scheme. We have considered the position of the adult from two perspectives, that of the adult charged with an offence, but not convicted and that of the adult who has been convicted. In our view, publication of the names of an adult convicted of an offence involving use of young people in prostitution or pornography would serve an extremely valuable deterrent function. In fact, we would urge that as much publicity as possible be given to conviction and sentencing of these offenders, so that others may learn that such activites will not go unpunished. We would however, make an exception to this general principle in the case of those convicted of incest, where adverse consequences to the victim will ensue from publication of the perpetrator's name.

Recommendation 85

> As much publicity as possible should be given to the name of an accused who is convicted of an offence involving the child pornography or child prostitution offences we propose, and the sexual offences in the Code, with the exception of the name of a person convicted of incest.

In the case of adults accused and convicted of offences involving children, we see no compelling reason to extend to them the anonymity which now is given the youthful accused. There should be no ban on the publication of the names of such accused; however, mindful of the impact of publicity, we do not urge that accused persons' identities be publicized in the same way as we have urged that the names of the convicted be published.

With respect to the position of complainants and witnesses, we note that the protection afforded by the *Young Offenders Act* against identification of the youthful complainant or witness is better than that offered by the *Criminal Code*. The recent invalidation of the mandatory publication ban simply makes the position of the youthful victim of adult crime all the worse. Once again, we find it hard to justify providing better protection to a youthful witness or complainant where the accused is youthful than where the accused is an adult. The harm which can be done by publication of the identity is the same in both types of case. Accordingly, we would recommend that the youthful complainant, and youthful witnesses, be given, in the *Criminal Code*, the same automatic protection against publication of identity as provided now in subsection 38(1) of the *Young Offenders Act* to youthful complainants and witnesses.

Recommendation 86

Subsection 442(3) of the Criminal Code should be amended to provide for the complainant and witness under 18 years of age the same mandatory protection from publication of name or identifying information as is now extended to youthful witnesses and complainants in trials of young offenders by section 38 of the Young Offenders Act.

The question of course arises whether a mandatory provision protecting youthful complainants and witness in the *Criminal Code* would survive a challenge brought under the *Charter of Rights*. On the one hand, it is the decision of the Ontario Court of Appeal in *Canadian Newspapers* stating that the mandatory ban in subsection 442(3) is improper, but on the other hand, a decision upholding a similar mandatory ban in the *Young Offenders Act* in favour of protecting youthful complainants and witnesses.

One hopes that the philosophy of protecting youth and encouraging them to report sexual assault would prevail, to justify inclusion of a mandatory ban for youthful complainants and witnesses in subsection 442(3). If not, then there is a real prospect that a youthful complainant or witness in an adult proceeding will be denied "equality before the law" contrary to section 15 of the *Charter of Rights*. This is because the youth who is assaulted by an adult is, in the matter of protection of identity, treated less favourably than a youth assaulted by another youth. Given that aggression against children by adults is, arguably the more serious of the two situations, the discrepancy in protection is hard to justify.

It will be noted that section 442 is applicable to the offences described in section 246.4 of the *Code*. As a housekeeping matter, it will be necessary to include in section 442 reference to the offences which we have recommended be created, and we so recommend.

Recommendation 87

Subsection 442(3) of the Criminal Code should be amended so as to make it clear that section 442(3) applies to the offences recommended by this committee.

2.7 Defences

We have provided, in our draft legislation, for a due diligence defence in certain circumstances. With respect to the offence of sale of visual pornographic material to children, for example, we have provided that an accused may defend on the basis that he used due care and diligence to ensure that there was no such visual pornographic material in the materials sold or rented.

We propose that the due diligence defence be available in two other sections of our criminal law recommendations concerning child pornography. These two offences are the sale of child pornography and the sale of material advocating the sexual abuse of children.

Recommendation 88

A person accused of the offence of selling pornography containing sexually explicit portrayals of children, or of selling pornography advocating the sexual abuse of children, should be entitled to defend the charge on the basis that he had used due diligence to inspect the materials.

The draft section which we propose to make applicable to these offences is:

Nobody shall be convicted of the offences in sections—who can demonstrate that he used due diligence to ensure that there were no representations in the materials, matters or things which he sold, rented, offered for sale or rent, exposed to public view, or had in his possession for purposes of sale or rent, which offended the section.

Particularly at the retail level, there may well be situations where large volumes of material come from a wholesaler. We heard evidence at the public hearings that sometimes the retailer will not even inspect the material before it is put on the shelves. Often, the material will be shelved by young employees of a retail concern who would not, in any event, have the authority to prohibit display of improper material even if they detected it.

By making available a due diligence defence, we hope to encourage persons at the mangement level of retail enterprises to take an interest in what goes on the shelves, and to inspect the material for compliance with the law.

We have given considerable thought to the question of penalties for the proposed offences. The rationale for one particular choice of penalty is discussed above with the various recommendations.

2.8 Penalties and General Sections

In addition to the specific penalties for offences which are contained in the proposed sections, we note the impact of certain general sections of the *Criminal Code*.

Subsection 646(1) of the *Code* provides that an accused convicted of an indictable offence punishable with imprisonment for five years or less may be fined in addition to or in lieu of any other punishment that is authorized. Where the accused is convicted of an indictable offence punishable with imprisonment for more than five years, subsection 646(2) of the *Code* allows imposition of a fine in addition to any other punishment that is imposed. The size of the fine in either case is in the discretion of the Court.

Some of the offences we recommend are punishable upon summary conviction, rather than as indictable offences. Some of our proposals would permit the Crown to proceed either by indictment or by summary conviction.

Subsection 722(1) of the *Criminal Code* provides that, except where otherwise expressly provided by law, every one convicted of an offence at summary conviction is liable to a fine of not more than $500 or to imprisonment for six months or both.

As we have discussed above, we have departed from this minimum with respect to all the summary conviction offences which we recommend, because it is too low. By reason of paragraph 647(b) of the *Code*, a corporation convicted of a summary conviction offence may be fined, in lieu of imprisonment, an amount not to exceed $1,000. We view this provision as much too low. This statutory maximum fine provision would apply, for example, in the case of a corporation convicted, in summary proceedings, of selling a visual representation of someone under 18 participating in explicit sexual conduct. We do not think that a maximum fine of $1,000 adequately reflects society's opinion of the seriousness of this offence. It is true, of course, that in this instance, the Crown would have the option of proceeding by way of indictment, and thus securing a higher fine. However, this is not the case with some of the other summary conviction offences, like those involving display of visual pornographic material to children.

Paragraph 647(b) does not recognize the option that a higher fine may be attached to a particular crime, as does subsection 772(1). Accordingly, we cannot craft a penalty which we think appropriate for the corporate offender, in the case of a summary conviction offence. Such a change must come, as offences must come, as part of an across the board change, or not at all.

That is why we have recommended above that paragraph 647(b) be amended to raise the maximum fines for corporations convicted of a summary conviction offence, or to provide that the penalty can be individually suited to each offence enacted, as is the case with section 722(1).

There are, however, two other recommendations which will have a bearing on the corporate offender. The first of these is for forfeiture of the offending materials and copies of it in the event of a conviction under our proposed sections.

Recommendation 89

The Criminal Code should be amended to add a provision that:

In any proceedings in which a person is convicted of producing, distributing or selling pornographic material the court shall order the offending material or matter or thing or copies thereof forfeited to Her Majesty in the Right of the Province in which proceedings took place, for disposal as the Attorney General may direct.

This provision is not a free-standing section which would allow forfeiture proceedings to be brought whether or not a criminal charge had been laid against an individual or corporate accused, like the present section 160. Rather, it is an integral part of the penalty for the offence. It is some advance over the provisions which permit seizure only of the material before the court in the trial, because copies of that material may also be seized.

We believe that it is also important to have a section which addresses the criminal liability of the managers or directors of a company which offends the recommended provisions.

There are good reasons for wanting to go behind the corporate façade. Either in the notable case of a Bob Guccione or Hugh Hefner, or in the less grand case of a fly-by-night operator, the real advocate and purveyor of certain material will be an individual, but he will act through a corporation. The corporate structure may be such that he never can be said to be personally involved in the act of production, distribution or sale. In such a case, a section aimed at the director would help bring to account the person responsible for the behaviour.

Recommendation 90

> **A section should be added to the Criminal Code to provide for criminal liability of officers and directors, along these lines:**
>
> **Where an offence under this act committed by a body corporate is proved to have been committed with the consent or connivance of, or to be attributable to any neglect on the part of, any director, manager, secretary or other similar officer of the body corporate, or any person who was purporting to act in any such capacity, he, as well as the body corporate, shall be guilty of the offence and shall be liable to be proceeded against and punished accordingly.**

3. Prostitution

The Committee recommends that the sections of the *Criminal Code* dealing with soliciting, procuring, and bawdy houses be completely restructured, so that they address the contemporary reality of prostitution. The sections we have drafted to replace the present *Code* provisions deal with street nuisance, procuring, and prostitution establishments. The proposed provisions dealing with procuring and prostitution establishments contain special parts to address the situation of young persons. These parts are set out and discussed below. In addition, we create a new offence of engaging in, or attempting or offering to engage in sexual activity for money or other consideration with a person under 18. It, too, is set out and discussed in this part.

3.1 Procuring

Recommendation 91

> **Sections 166 and section 195(1)(a) to (i) of the Criminal Code should be repealed and replaced with a new prohibition on procuring, which would deal specifically with the procuring of those under 18. That section is:**

650

(1) **Everyone who**

    (a) **by force, by threat of force or by other coercive or threatening behaviour induces a person of 18 years or older to engage in prostitution with another person or generally, or**

    (b) **by force, by threat of force or by other coercive or threatening behaviour compels a person of 18 years or older to continue engaging in prostitution with another person or generally**

    is guilty of an indictable offence and liable to imprisonment for 14 years.

(2) **Everyone who**

    (a) **persuades, coerces or deceives a person under 18 years of age in order to induce that person to engage in sexual activity for money, or for any other consideration or reward, or in illicit sexual conduct with another person or generally, or**

    (b) **encourages, coerces or deceives a person under 18 years of age in order to induce that person to continue to engage in sexual activity for money, or for any other consideration or reward, or in illicit sexual conduct with another person or generally,**

    is guilty of an indictable offence and liable to imprisonment for 14 years.

(3) **For the purposes of subsection (2), "illicit sexual conduct" means any sexual behaviour or act which is prohibited by the Criminal Code, whether or not such prohibition is based upon the age of the parties to the act or of any one of them.**

These provisions about procuring are intended to replace the present procuring provisions of the *Criminal Code* which are found in paragraphs 195(1)(a) to (i). The procuring provisions relating to young persons which we recommend are found at subsections (2) and (3), outlined in heavy type. These provisions represent an innovation of sorts, because the *Code* does not now treat procuring of children any differently from procuring of an adult, except for the creation, in section 166 of the *Code*, of a prohibition against a parent or guardian procuring the defilement of a female child. Our provisions in (2) and (3) above would replace the present section 166.

Some important differences may be noted between subsection (1) of our procuring section, dealing with those 18 years and over, and subsection (2), dealing with those under 18. Firstly, the burden of the procuring offence vis-a-vis the adult victim is in the would-be procurer's use of force or threats. We have proceeded on the assumption that an acceptable degree of freedom of choice may be present in the decision of an adult to engage in prostitution, assuming that the element of coercion may be controlled. We do not make the same assumption about the decisions of those under 18. Accordingly, persuading or deceiving a person under 18 to engage in sexual activity is made a criminal offence, as is coercion of such a person.

It may well be argued that the distinction between the two cases is a somewhat artificial one. Someone over 18 may be persuaded or deceived into prostitution; some of those under 18 may be quite capable of realistically assessing efforts to "persuade" them to a particular course of conduct and of resisting such blandishments. We recognize that the distinction based on age in this way is not a perfect one. However, we believe that overall the greater harm may arise from underprotecting the younger person than from underprotecting the older one.

Secondly, the offence in regard to the older person consists of coercing him or her to engage, or continue to engage in prostitution. The definition of "prostitution" for purposes of this provision is "the provision of sexual services by one person to another in return for money". By contrast, the offence with regard to the younger person is to induce him or her to engage, or continue to engage, in sexual activity for money, or for other consideration or reward, or to engage or continue to engage in illicit sexual conduct. These types of activities are more extensive than "prostitution". The extension in the language is intended to cover the case where a young person receives no cash, but rather room and board, or presents, or other payment in kind in return for sexual activity. Sometimes, the young person may in fact receive nothing at all for his or her activities. We would prohibit procuring a child to engage in sex for no reward, just as we prohibit procuring of the child to engage in sex for reward. The prohibition against procuring the child to engage in "illicit sexual conduct" would, accordingly, cover this type of case.

The category of situations which would come within the definition of "illicit sexual conduct" must be carefully examined. Given the present wording of the *Criminal Code*, we believe that there are a number of problems arising from this formulation. For example, the "illicit sexual conduct" definition would encompass buggery and bestiality, as well as gross indecency. In order to escape prosecution for these offences, the acts have to be committed in private by two persons each of whom is 21 years of age or more. Unless this age limit is lowered to 18 years of age or more, the combination of our definition of illicit sexual conduct and these provisions will cause some awkward discrepancies. For example, a person could be charged with procuring a person to commit buggery only if the person were under 18, but it would still be illegal to commit buggery with someone between 18 and 21. Rather than extend our procuring recommendations to protect persons up to 21, we recommend dropping the upper age limit for the buggery and gross indecency offences to 18.

Recommendation 92

> **The age specified in section 157 of the Criminal Code should be lowered to 18 from 21, so that the prohibition against buggery in section 156 of the Code and against an act of gross indecency in section 156 will not apply to acts committed in private between persons who are 18 or over.**

Elsewhere, we have recommended that section 157 be repealed altogether. It may be thought that this leaves a gap in the protection afforded to young persons against certain kinds of assault. However, we consider that it is desirable for the sexual offences in sections 140 to 157 to be overhauled and brought up to date, and are satisfied that the protection afforded to young people by section 157 could be extended in a re-worked section which would not feature such vague and broad language as "gross indecency". Such an overhaul could, we recognize, also involve repeal of section 157 as we now know it.

A number of offences in the *Code* involve sexual intercourse with a female under a certain age, or in certain circumstances.[14] The prohibition does not extend to sexual intercourse with a male. Because we intend to prohibit procuring of young males for sexual activity just as surely as we intend to prohibit procuring of young females, we believe that these sections of the *Code*, to which the "illicit sexual conduct" definition applies should be rationalized, with their protection being extended to males as well as females.

Recommendation 93

> **Sections 146, 151, 152, and 153 of the Criminal Code should be amended in order to provide that the protection against sexual assault extended thereby to females is also available to males.**

Additionally, we note that many of the offences to which the "illicit sexual conduct" definition may refer require, as an element of the offence, that the victim be "of previously chaste character". It is not our intention to restrict the protection of the procuring provisions which we recommend; accordingly, we recommend that references to the previous chaste character be removed from the offences.

Recommendation 94

> **In offences involving sexual assault on young persons, the requirement that the victim be of "previously chaste character" should be removed from the Criminal Code.**

We have considered whether the problems raised by the use of our phrase "illicit sexual conduct" should require spelling out in our proposed section exactly what it is that we think is involved in illicit sexual conduct. Having considered this possibility, however, we have rejected it. We think that it is important for the procuring section to forbid procuring young people to perform acts which would themselves be illegal, whether the procuring had taken place or not. Thus, we want to maintain, in our procuring section, the reference to other *Code* offences.

We note with considerable interest that changes to this part of the *Code* have been recommended by the Committee on Sexual Offences Against Children and Youths.[15] Further, it would appear that extending the benefit of some of these *Code* provisions to males as well as to females may be mandated by the provisions of sections 15 and 28 of the *Canadian Charter of Rights and Freedoms*. Accordingly, we urge not only the enactment of the section on procuring of young persons which we have outlined above, but also the rationalization of sections 140 to 157 of the *Criminal Code* which appears to be required.

Recommendation 95

The offences involving young persons set out in Part IV of the Code should be reviewed with the aim of rationalizing them by repealing outmoded sections.

In our view, the proposed provisions on procuring will, when taken with our recommended provision on financial support from prostitution, substitute quite satisfactorily for the provisions of section 166 which are now, in our opinion, outmoded. The procuring proposal does not include the offence, now in section 166, of knowingly receiving the avails of the defilement, seduction or prostitution of the female child or ward, but our proposal to deal with financial support from prostitution will address this aspect of the conduct now dealt with by section 166.

We are mindful that previous reform attempts have all focused on trying to rework and broaden section 166, while leaving intact the basic approach of penalizing a parent, guardian or custodial adult more harshly for interference with children than is a third party. We also note, however, that attempts to follow this model have resulted in more and more complex proposals, in order to maintain the distinction between parents and third parties, as well as accommodate the various defences relevant to each separate offence. In our view, the basic offence created by our procuring proposal is one that can appropriately be applied to parents and guardians, as well as to third parties. The proposed penalty is serious enough to signal the gravity of the breach of social and emotional trust involved in a parent introducing his or her child to illicit sexual conduct. We do not think that a penalty of more than 14 years is required for parents committing such an offence. By the same token, we are not convinced that, given the seriousness of the offence, we should propose any lesser penalty for persons other than parents who engage in this conduct.

It may be noted that the proposed procuring provisions do not contain any term which replaces exactly the offence which is now found in section 167 of the *Criminal Code*. That section makes it an offence for the owner, occupier, or manager of premises, knowingly to permit a female person under the age of eighteen to resort to or be in the premises for the purpose of having illicit sexual intercourse with a particular male person or male persons generally. The harms aimed at by the offence are those of facilitating the sexual misconduct of a young female, and of facilitating male access to the young female. We note that the presence or absence of financial advantage to the manager of the premises is immaterial to the offence. In our view, this provision should be repealed altogether.

We acknowledge, of course, that previous efforts to rationalize the law in this area have included redrafted versions of this provision. However, we refrained from doing so because we think that the worst of the conduct reached by the section, namely facilitating sexual access to young persons, is addressed by the procuring provisions which we have recommended. We note that there have been very few reported cases under section 167 in this century. The section, as it now stands, could easily be used against friends or contemporaries of the young person who simply offer her the use of an apartment in which to engage in consensual sexual relations with a boyfriend of the same age. We consider such use inappropriate and recommend that this seldom used provision is better repealed than reformed.

Recommendation 96

Section 167 of the Criminal Code should be repealed.

We do not intend to suggest by the foregoing, however, that persons under 18 who procure the sexual activity for reward of other youths should escape the reach of the proposed section. In our opinion, a youth who preys on other youths does not deserve immunity from the law; such a person should be tried for the offence, pursuant to the procedures set out in the *Young Offenders Act*, in the same way as he or she would be charged and tried with any other offence he or she commits.

3.2 Financial Support from Prostitution

Recommendation 97

Section 195(1)(j) of the Criminal Code be repealed and replaced with a new prohibition against receiving financial support from prostitution, which would contain provisions dealing specifically with receiving support from the prostitution of those under 18. The section is:

(1) **Everyone who by force, threat of force or other coercive or threatening behaviour induces a person of 18 years or older to support him or her financially in whole or in part by acts of prostitution is guilty of an indictable offence and liable to imprisonment for 14 years.**

(2) **Everyone who is supported financially in whole or in part by a person under 18 years of age from the proceeds of sexual activities by that young person for money or for other consideration or reward is guilty of an indictable offence and liable to imprisonment for 14 years.**

(3) **For purposes of subsection (2), evidence that a person lives with a person or persons under the age of 18 who engage in sexual activity for money or for other consideration or reward is, in the absence of evidence to the contrary, proof that that person is supported, in whole or in part, from the proceeds of that activity.**

These provisions with respect to financial support from prostitution are intended to replace paragraph 195(1)(j) of the *Criminal Code*, which makes it an offence to live wholly or in part on the avails of the prostitution of another person. We have fashioned provisions which relate specifically to being supported from the proceeds of the activities of a juvenile prostitute. There are now no provisions of the *Code* addressing this issue separately, with the exception of the offence created by section 166 for a parent or guardian knowingly to receive the avails of the defilement, seduction or prostitution of a female person. We take the view that section 166 is too narrow because it relates only to female victims, and it does not reach the conduct of third parties who are receiving support from the activities of juvenile prostitutes. Accordingly, as we have done in other cases, we have given particular attention, in the drafting of our recommendations, to the situation of juveniles.

It will be noted that the offence involving adults depends on the presence of force, threat of force or other coercive or threatening behaviour being used. In all other situations, the conduct of the adult prostitute and his or her "dependents" is, in our view, no business of the criminal law. We must assume that an adult has the appropriate judgment to avoid being exploited, but, if he or she does not have that judgment, then we have concluded that the law must not interfere. As we argued in the case of the procuring provisions, regard for individual liberty and responsibility dictates that, at some point, societal protection against non-coercive behaviour must come to an end, however much protection may turn out to be needed in some individual cases.

By contrast, we think that society has an interest in protecting persons under 18. Society has an interest in their development free from what we regard as potentially harmful influences and activities, and society accordingly has a corresponding duty to shield them. Hence, we have made the offence of being supported from the proceeds of the sexual activities of a young person an offence which does not depend on the use of coercive behaviour. Even if the young person's contribution of support is voluntary, it would attract a charge under the proposed section.

Adult prostitutes told the Committee that the present provisions with respect to living on the avails of prostitution could jeopardize a person to whom the prostitute has an emotional attachment. They pointed out that a boyfriend with no job, or little income of his own, who lives with a prostitute or is supported by her, is liable to be charged under paragraph 195(1)(j) with living on the avails of prostitution. The risk extends, we were told, to other persons supported by the prostitute as part of her family or friendship network.

Our recommendations with respect to the person over 18 are intended to be responsive to this concern. Unless the support is exacted from the prostitute by coercive behaviour, then, in our view, society should not penalize the person who receives that support. We are not convinced that we should afford the same shelter for persons supported by the young person. The evidence before the Committee indicates that young people, particularly females, may be introduced to prostitution or maintained in it, by males with whom the young people believe they have an affectionate relationship. The creation of some sort of personal bond of this nature, being one of the methods of recruitment to prostitution, should not attract any comfort from the law, direct or indirect, to the unscrupulous who create such bonds.

The recommended offence, in the case of an adult, is that of coercing a person to support the accused financially "in whole or in part by acts of prostitution". In the case of the person under 18, the conduct generating the support is described as "sexual activites for money or for other consideration or

656

reward". We believe that young people who receive, and pass on to others, payment in kind for sexual activities should also be protected against exploitation, just as we protect those who support others by means of monetary proceeds of sexual activity. We do not wish to encourage a person to manipulate the type of reward for sexual activity received by juveniles in order to escape criminal sanctions for being supported from those proceeds.

As mentioned, we think that the proposed financial support section is broad enough to cover the activities of parents, guardians and other adults in charge of young people who may be receiving benefit from their sexual activities. Given the strength of the penalty which we have attached to this offence, we see no need to create a separate offence referable only to this one class of adult exploiter. This section is also broad enough to cover receipt of support by another person under the age of 18. There appears to be no special reason for specifically excluding these persons from the application of the section. The methods of trial and disposition provided for in the *Young Offenders Act* provide adequate protection to the youth charged.

Subsection (3) of our proposed provision is a reworking of the presumption which now appears in the *Code* as subsection 195(2). That subsection, drafted in language reflecting the other concepts in section 195, provides that evidence that a person lives with or is habitually in the company of prostitutes, or lives in a common bawdy house or house of assignation, is, in the absence of evidence to the contrary, proof that the person lives on the avails of prostitution. This presumption would apply to cases of living on the avails of the prostitution of the adult or the young person, because section 195 does not distinguish between these two types of case.

The presumption which we have created in the new subsection (3) applies only to the offence involving persons under 18. The offence dealing with adults depends on there being an actual showing of coercive behaviour. There is thus no need or justification for a presumption. The offence with respect to youths does not depend on this showing of violence or threat; the behaviour encompassed by the offence may present few outward, distinctive signs apart from the signal of residence. Thus, the effectiveness of law enforcement may well depend on the use of a presumption, that if certain facts are present, receipt of support from a young person's sexual activity can be assumed, in the absence of proof to the contrary.

In our opinion, living with a person or persons under 18 who engage in sexual activity for reward is a sufficiently distinctive characteristic to justify its use as a trigger for the presumption that a person is being supported from these proceeds. Maintenance of a common living place involves an element of shared decision making about the expenses of that living place. It is thus a characteristic rationally connected to the question of support. The "living with" test is more strict than the test in the present subsection 195(2) of being "habitually in the company" of prostitutes.

Once the element of "living with" has been established, we think that the state would be justified in calling upon the accused for an answer. The financial resources which the accused has at his or her command, the other calls on those resources, and an explanation of his or her sources of support are all particularly within the knowledge of the accused and of no one else. The provision that the presumption extend to someone who lives with "a person or persons" is intended to cover the situation of one who may be involved with more than one person and thus living full time with no one of them. We heard evidence at the hearings that a pimp may convince several people that he is their lover, spending some time with each, and telling none of his other involvements. We want the provisions with respect to financial support from sexual activity to reach this sort of person, as well as the person who is supported by only one young person.

3.3 Prostitution Establishments

We propose amendments to the existing provisions in section 193 of the *Criminal Code* relating to "common bawdy houses". We have replaced the historic terminology with the term "prostitution establishment" and have proposed that the sanctions against operating a prostitution establishment not apply to one or two persons over the age of 18 who perform acts of prostitution in their own homes. Moreover, we have recommended that the governments of the provinces consider development of programs whereby prostitution establishments could be licensed and regulated as other businesses are, such businesses to be exempt from the application of the *Criminal Code*.

We emphasize, however, that the person under 18 has no place in such an establishment. We do not intend by our proposals to create any enclave in which a young person may engage in prostitution, for to do so is merely to encourage the commercial instincts of any who would exploit that young person. It is clear to us that the exemption for one or two prostitutes operating from their own residence should be confined to persons 18 or over and that no provincial regulatory program should permit use of those under 18 in any licensed premises.

Recommendation 98

No person under 18 should be permitted to be employed in any prostitution establishment which might be set up pursuant to the exception for provincially regulated establishments provided in our proposal about prostitution establishments.

3.4 Sexual Activity for Reward with Juveniles

Recommendation 99

The following new section should be added to the Criminal Code:
(1) Everyone who engages in, or attempts or offers to engage in sexual activity for money or for other consideration or reward with a person under 18 years of age is guilty of an indictable offence and liable to imprisonment for five years.

(2) It is no defence to a charge under this section that the accused believed the other person to be 18 years or older.

We think that it is essential that the *Criminal Code* contain an offence specifically framed around sexual activity for reward with a person under 18. There is no provision now in the *Code* which adequately addresses this sort of behaviour. The usefulness of section 195.1, the soliciting provision, is seriously impaired by the doubt in some jurisdictions concerning its applicability to customers and by the attitude toward enforcement generated by judicial interpretation of its provisions. The section cannot be counted upon at all to curb the sexual exploitation of the young. The *Criminal Code* provisions respecting sexual assault would not apply to the majority of the ordinary commercial transactions involving young persons because of the young person's consent to the behaviour. The provisions of child welfare legislation, which we have considered, have too diffuse an impact on this conduct.

Accordingly, we recommend the creation of a specific offence aimed at those who engage in, attempt or offer to engage in sexual activity for money or other consideration or reward with persons under 18. We have not limited the types of reward to the monetary ones because of our understanding that youths may receive food, lodging, or presents for sexual activities rather than money. The attempt and the offer are prohibited in order to emphasize the seriousness with which the behaviour is viewed. In our opinion, a young person who is even approached by an adult should be able to invoke the law enforcement process. To await the completion of the sexual activity before triggering the criminal process is to lose a substantial portion of the deterrent value of this provision. Moreover, including attempt and offer offences means that law enforcement authorities will be able to use surveillance methods instead of relying exclusively on undercover officers or child complainants in order to enforce the law. Use of undercover operations presents tremendous difficulties in the context of this offence, ranging from finding a youthful appearing officer, to the problem of securing convictions based upon evidence of an undercover complainant who is actually over 18.

The section is directed toward the party whom we think is more likely to be the "aggressor" in the contacts between the user and provider of the sexual services of youths. Included in that group is the person under 18 who as the customer engages in, or attempts or offers to engage in sexual activity for reward with another young person. The behaviour aimed at by the section is the instigation, or attempted instigation, of commercial sexual activities with a young person. A would-be customer under 18 who engages in this conduct should be charged, and tried according to the procedure provided in the *Young Offenders Act*.

Recommendation 100

A young person who engages in sexual activity for reward as the provider of sexual services should not be subject to a criminal penalty.

There are many reasons for our decision not to create such an offence. It appears to us as if enforcement of such a provision presents two equally undesirable alternatives. The provision could be enforced by way of undercover police activity. The prospect that officers would actually approach persons under 18 and try to engage their sexual services, for purposes of effecting an arrest, is very distasteful to us, and we are sure that it would be equally repelling to most police authorities. Alternatively, one can consider the possibility that customers, or prospective customers, would complain to police authorities.

It is doubtful whether customers who had actually received sexual services for a consideration would complain, because of the prospect of being charged themselves. We doubt that police officials would welcome an adult's offer to give evidence against a child in order that the adult might secure immunity from prosecution. However, the adult customer could well use the threat of a report to the police in order to control the behaviour of the young person. Whether the threat were groundless would not matter if the youth believed that the customer would carry it through. The danger of blackmail is, in our view, real enough to merit caution about creating this offence.

Even if the customer or would-be customers were not inclined to blackmail, one wonders about the effectiveness of an enforcement system dependent to any significant degree on complaints. The most likely persons to bring complaints are persons who are offered but do not accept the services. Yet indifference, a desire to avoid involvement in the criminal justice system and even compassion may inhibit complaints from these individuals.

The question of the equity of our proposal must, of course, be faced. We have recommended penalizing one actor in a sexual transaction, or would-be transaction, while leaving the other outside the reach of the prohibition. Some have mentioned in the Committee hearings the possibility that youths will be the aggressors in these situations, and that a manipulative youth may well threaten to blackmail a customer. We must take those possibilities into account when assessing the impact and the fairness of our recommendation.

We point out that an adult prostitute suffers no criminal sanction for the straightforward activity of sale of sexual services, under our recommendations or, with one or two exceptions, under the present *Criminal Code*. We do not believe that there is any justification for penalizing in a young person what is not criminal when done by an adult. The rationale that is sometimes advanced for making sale of sexual services by a youth an offence is that it would have the beneficial effect of bringing the young person into contact with law enforcement officials and social agencies which would help break the links of the child to the life of prostitution. We have received little or no evidence of the efficacy of such intervention. In fact, the evidence we have received tends to show that this expected benefit will not arise, because young people are out on the street again within hours of arrest, and because effective rehabilitative programs are either seriously crowded or simply disappearing because of government restraint programs. Such a notional support system cannot possibly justify the criminalization of conduct by a youth which would not be criminal by an adult.

In fact, when one analyses the thrust of our recommendations, one sees that the difference in treatment under the law would be a difference between the customer of the adult prostitute and the customer or would-be customer of the youth. We think that there is ample justification for imposing sanctions on the customer of the youth. We heard arguments at the public hearings that penalizing the customer is an effective method of reducing the market for sexual services. We also heard complaints at the public hearings and in some private sessions that the penalties now applied to those who sexually exploit children are pitifully light, amounting to no sort of deterrent at all.

We consider use of children in commercial sexual activities to be a serious harm which should be deterred, because of what is often the imbalance of power and resources between perpetrator and victim, and the lasting interference with the child's personal integrity, both mental and physical. Accordingly, we consider it appropriate that a means which we have reason to believe will be effective as a deterrent, and which can be enforced by orthodox and acceptable law enforcement methods, should be employed to curb resort to children for commercial sex. We have considered it unnecessary to resort to punish the customers of adult prostitutes, because the social harm to adult prostitutes is arguably somewhat less than affecting children, and because we take the view that society can and should accord to adults more autonomy in their own lives and more responsibility for their own well being.

3.5 Disorderly Conduct, Indecent Exhibition, Loitering, Soliciting

It is not our intention to criminalize street soliciting *per se*. Rather, we have chosen to deal with the problem of street soliciting which presents itself to nearby residents and those who seek to use the streets and other public and private facilities, where prostitutes ply their trade. This problem is the nuisance created by some prostitutes, some customers, and sightseers, in any location which becomes a regular site of prostitution activity.

We have proposed the following revision of section 171 of the *Criminal Code:*

(1) Everyone who
    (a) not being in a dwelling house causes a disturbance in or near a public place,
        (i) by fighting, screaming, shouting, swearing or using insulting or obscene language,
        (ii) by using sexually offensive remarks or suggestions,
        (iii) by being drunk, or
        (iv) by impeding or molesting other persons,
    (b) openly exposes or exhibits an indecent exhibition in a public place,
    (c) loiters in a public place and in any way obstructs persons who are there,

(d) stands, stops, wanders about in or drives through a public place for purposes of offering to engage in prostitution or of employing the services of a prostitute or prostitutes and on more than one occasion
(i) beckons to, stops or attempts to stop pedestrians or attempts to engage them in conversation,
(ii) stops or attempts to stop motor vehicles,
(iii) impedes the free flow of pedestrian or vehicular traffic, or of ingress or egress from premises adjacent to that public place,

(e) disturbs the peace and quiet of the occupants of a dwelling house by discharging firearms, by any of the forms of conduct in paragraphs (a), (b), (c) or (d) of this subsection, or by other disorderly conduct in a public place,

(f) not being an occupant of a dwelling house comprised in a particular building or structure, disturbs the peace and quiet of the occupants of a dwelling house comprised in the building or structure by discharging firearms or by other disorderly conduct in any part of the building or structure to which at the time of such conduct, the occupants of two or more dwelling houses comprised in the building or structure have access as of right or by invitation, express or implied,

is guilty of an offence punishable on summary conviction.

We do not, as we have stated, recommend creating an offence which focuses on the sale of sexual services by young persons. However, we see no good reason why young persons who are using the streets and offend against any of the provisions of the redrafted section 171 should not be charged with that offence. The trial and disposition after conviction of any such youngster would be governed by the *Young Offenders Act*. We consider that this statute offers sufficient procedural protection to the young person.

Recommendation 101

Persons under 18 who are using the streets and commit any of the nuisances prohibited in our proposed section 171 of the Criminal Code should be prosecuted in accordance with that section.

Footnotes

[1] John S. Kiedrowski and Jan Van Dijk, *Pornography and Prostitution in Denmark, France, West Germany, The Netherlands and Sweden* W.P.P.P.#1 at 100.

[2] Badgley Report, Vol. I, at 67.

[3] *Attorney General of Nova Scotia et al* v. *MacIntyre* (1982), 132 D.L.R. (3d) 385 (S.C.C.), *per* Dickson, J. at 401.

[4] *R.* v. *Quesnel and Quesnel* (1979) 51 C.C.C. (2d) 270 (Ont. C.A.) *per* Brooke, J.A. at 274-5.

[5] *R.* v. *Quesnel and Quesnel*, (1979).

[6] *Re F.P. Publications (Western) Limited and The Queen* (1979), 108 D.L.R. (3d) 153 (Man.C.A.).

[7] *R.* v. *Several Unnamed Persons* (1983), 44 O.R. (2d) 81 (Ont.H.C.).

[8] 1984 Unreported (Ont.H.C.).

[9] *Canadian Newspapers Company Limited* v. *A.-G. for Canada; R.V.D.D.*, Feb. 1985 Unreported (Ont.C.A).

[10] *Canadian Newspapers* v. *A-G for Canada; R.V.D.D.* Feb. 1985 unreported at 30.

[11] *Canadian Newspapers* v. *A-G for Canada; R.V.D.D.* Feb. 1985 unreported at 38-39

[12] (1984), 13 C.C.C. (3d) 152 (Ont.H.C.).

[13] (1984), 13 C.C.C. (3d) 152 (Ont.H.C.).

[14] *Criminal Code*, ss. 146, 151, 152, 153.

[15] Badgley Report, Vol. I, at 46-48.

Chapter 47

Education and Social Services

The reform of the law with respect to child pornography and prostitution cannot be seen as the only action necessary to provide children and young people with better conditions in which to reach maturity. The law is not a particularly effective tool to bring about fundamental changes in the attitudes and behaviour of large numbers of people and organizations. While law clearly has role in defining the limits of acceptable behaviour, it is less likely to affect the more subtle aspects of the issues with which we are concerned. The law can and must state that activities, such as buying the sexual services of juveniles, or using them to make pornographic material, are unacceptable. But it is difficult to use the law to arrest a gradual shift towards acceptance of sexual relations between young children and adults or of the notion that the satisfaction of sexual desires justifies any and all indignities to one's partner.

Similarly, using the law may not be the most effective means of undermining long held and erroneous beliefs about sexual equality or sexual preference. Here it becomes evident that the need for education in the widest sense of the word is essential. This was a view expressed by many who made submissions to the Committee and one which we strongly endorse. Programs addressed to the public in general, specific professional groups in particular and to children and young people are needed.

It is assumed that, if programs are directed towards today's children, we will eventually have adults who are better informed about human sexuality and less likely to depend on misleading and erroneous material such as pornography. This is clearly a long term and slowly attained objective, but it is the core of any action to lessen the dependency on and effect of pornography. In addition, accurate information about the buying and selling of sexual services and the harms associated with such activities for young people should be available to counteract the partial and misleading information which is often contained in the media.

Although the focus of attention must be on children and young people, the integrity of the programs depends on the understanding of adults about such issues. It is important, therefore, that parents and adults with whom children come into contact in a professional way, for example, teachers, social workers and the medical profession, are informed and understanding of both adult sexuality and the developing sexuality of children. We do not believe that the education of children can or should be left just to the school system. Parents, religious groups and other organizations indicated their wishes for involvement in the process and this we consider entirely appropriate and to be encouraged. We need, however, to ensure that adults do have the requisite understanding of the issues and how the information can be given in a way appropriate to a child's level of comprehension.

More generally, we consider it important that the Canadian population as a whole be better informed about the rights of children and the developmental processes which are part of the child's growth towards maturity. If we have a better understanding of individual and societal responsibilities towards children, it is hoped that children can grow up free of exploitation and harmful interference. In order to achieve these objectives we believe that it is necessary to promote programs and make more widely available the necessary information rather than simply hope that, in some vague and unspecified way, young people and adults will learn what they think they need to know.

Educational programs for children and in relation to sex or family life education are not the only areas in need of attention. As we were often reminded, pornography is just one part of the mass media and shares many common elements with mainstream communications. Children using the media receive implicit if not explicit messages about such issues as the role of women, how to be successful in life, and the commodities necessary in order to be happy. Despite the overwhelming presence of the media in our lives, we do little to educate children about how they should interpret the messages they receive or how and why the programs on television, for instance, are constructed in a particular way. There is, therefore, a real need to increase children's awareness of these issues through what was sometimes referred to as media literacy programs.

As will be evident, the distinction between media literacy programs and sex education and family life programs is not necessarily clear. Rather they are inter-connected and inter-dependent since, in the final analysis, our concern is that children learn about the dignity and worth of human beings in all their variations and subtleties. The brief from the B.C. Teachers' Federation spoke to these issues and represents the concerns and interests of many groups who came before the Committee:

> The communications media have long been acknowledged as an important tool in the educational process. Video, films, records, magazines and other media have great influence on the values and behaviour of people, whether or not they have been designed as educational materials. Young people are particularly susceptible to this influence because they lack the analytical skills to evaluate the effects of the media upon them. Images present in the mass media have become ever more pornographic over the last decade. Society has increasingly allowed these images to become an acceptable and normal component of entertainment. The juxtaposition of 'sex' and overtly aggressive behaviour—from beatings to rape—is commonly found on prime-time television.

Children are impressionable. Their perceptions of the world and of the roles of men and women as sexual beings in the world are in an (sic) process of development. Children seek self-definition and strive to create individual and special identities, of which an important part is sexuality. The function or (sic) role models in this process is paramount. Children define themselves and learn to be 'attractive' and 'desirable' within externally established limitations. These limitations are set out by an adult-conceived and controlled 'teen culture' that provides role models which are strong determinants in the development of self-image, of personal sexuality and of the perception of others as sexual beings. Elements of that, 'teen culture', which begins with eight-year-olds, include advertising, rock music, rock videos, and television and film.

As the Canadian Teachers' Federation indicated, programs of media literacy should be designed, among other things:

(a) to decrease children's belief that TV programs depict real life;

(b) to increase children's tendencies to compare what they see on TV with other information sources;

(c) to decrease television's credibility by teaching children about economic and production aspects of television.

While the emphasis on educational programs is justifed with respect to the more long term goals, children in need of special care and protection have to receive immediate attention. As we do not believe that children should be regarded as criminals, it is essential that social services and programs be in place to meet the needs of young people. Our level of success to date in this regard is not satisfactory.

This lack of success is due in part to the need for specialized training for those working with children with problems; in part to the lack of specialized programs which address the specific needs of the children, and in part to the lack of commitment to fund social programs designed to assist children. Although we are emphasizing the needs of children, it is apparent that these needs often arise because of the failure of other units in society adequately to care for the young people. It is more than likely, therefore, that many of the needs of children cannot be addressed in isolation from the family or school.

Perhaps one of the most disheartening aspects of the whole phenomenon of child prostitution is the frequency with which young people have come into contact with social service agencies and the seeming inability of these agencies to be of real assistance. If we are indeed serious about protecting children from the exploitative and destructive aspects of our society, then we have to commit ourselves to a sustained effort in educating professionals, developing programs, and allocating the necessary resources. There are some examples of effective and innovative programs across the country, but all too frequently our efforts have been meagre and subject to the financial vagaries of govenment funding.

The leadership and assistance of governments at all levels will be needed to implement appropriate educational and social service programs. It is not expected, however, that governments will be the only or major presence in these activities. Indeed, many of those making submissions to the Committee indicated a clear preference for joint and collaborative action between governments and existing organizations and agencies. There are organizations which have developed expertise and programs in some of the areas of concern, and rather than ignoring this, it is necessary to learn of these efforts and support their further development and more widespread use whenever possible and appropriate. Organizations such as Media Watch and Planned Parenthood Associations can offer assistance in media literacy and sex and family life education programs as can religious organizations and provincial authorities. Their efforts should be encouraged and not duplicated.

Recommendations

Some of the recommendations in other parts of the Report, if implemented, will have an impact on children and the care we give them. In this section, however, we are making recommendations which are designed to have a specific effect on children and their environment. Although responsibility for many aspects of children's well-being is within provincial jurisdiction, it is our view that, in order adequately to address the needs of children, there must be co-operation, financial and other assistance among the federal, provincial and municipal governments and between governments and private agencies and organizations. There should be encouragement to develop new approaches and recognition that overly standardized programs may not be effective in meeting the different levels of need and the different experiences across the country.

Recommendation 102

Federal, provincial and territorial governments should reaffirm their commitment to providing an environment where all children have the opportunity to develop to the fullest extent, their intellectual, physical and spiritual attributes. To this end, the Secretariat proposed in this Report should give high priority to issues affecting children and young people.

Recommendation 103

The federal government should collaborate with and assist the provinces, territories and private organizations and agencies in the development of educational programs for children, and those with special responsibilties for the welfare of children, in the areas of family life, human sexuality and media literacy.

Recommendation 104

Provincial and territorial governments should give high priority to programs in family life, human sexuality and media literacy at all levels within the school system.

Recommendation 105

The federal government should collaborate with and assist the provinces, territories, and private organizations and agencies in assessing the effectiveness of social service programs designed to assist children and young people, in developing new programs and in implementing changes designed to better meet the needs and current realities of young people in the 1980s and 1990s.

Part V

Summary of Recommendations

Chapter 48

Recommendations on Pornography

1. Criminal Code

Recommendation 1

> The term "obscenity" should no longer be used in the Criminal Code, and the heading "Offences Tending to Corrupt Morals" should also be removed.

Recommendation 2

> New criminal offences relating to "pornography" should be created, with care being exercised to ensure that the definition of the prohibited conduct, material or thing is very precise.

Recommendation 3

> The federal government should give immediate consideration to studying carefully the introduction of criminal sanctions against the production or sale or distribution of material containing representations of violence without sex.

Recommendation 4

> There should be no sanctions introduced respecting material that is 'disgusting' even though our proposed repeal of section 159 would remove the existing offence related to a disgusting object.

Recommendation 5

> Controls on pornographic material should be organized on the basis of a three-tier system. The most serious criminal sanctions would apply to material in the first tier, including a visual representation of a person under 18 years of age, participating in explicit sexual conduct, which is defined as any conduct in which vaginal, oral or anal intercourse, bestiality, necrophilia, masturbation, sexually violent behaviour, lewd touching of the breasts or the genital parts of the body, or the lewd exhibition of the genitals is depicted. Also included in tier one is material which advocates, encourages, condones, or presents as normal the sexual abuse of children, and material which was made or produced in such a way that actual physical harm was caused to the person or persons depicted.

> Less onerous criminal sanctions would apply to material in the second tier. Defences of artistic merit and educational or scientific purpose would be available. The second tier consists of any matter which depicts or describes sexually violent behaviour, bestiality, incest or necrophilia. Sexually violent

671

behaviour includes sexual assault, and physical harm depicted for the apparent purpose of causing sexual gratification or stimulation to the viewer, including murder, assault or bondage of another person or persons, or self-infliction of physical harm.

Material in the third tier would attract criminal sanctions only when it is displayed to the public without a warning as to its nature or sold or made accessible to people under 18. In tier three is visual pornographic material in which is depicted vaginal, oral, or anal intercourse, masturbation, lewd touching of the breasts or the genital parts of the body or the lewd exhibition of the genitals, but no portrayal of a person under 18 or sexually violent pornography is included.

Recommendation 6

The provinces and the municipalities should play a major role in regulation of the visual pornographic representations that are not prohibited by the Criminal Code through film classification, display by-laws and other similar means. The provinces should not, however, attempt to control such representations by means of prior restraint.

Recommendation 7

Section 159 of the Criminal Code should be repealed, and replaced with the following provision:

PORNOGRAPHY CAUSING PHYSICAL HARM

159(1)(a) Everyone who makes, prints, publishes, distributes, or has in his possession for the purposes of publication or distribution, any visual pornographic material which was made or produced in such a way that actual physical harm was caused to the person or persons depicted, is guilty of an indictable offence and liable to imprisonment for five years.

(b) Everyone who sells, rents, offers to sell or rent, receives for sale or rent or has in his possession for the purpose of sale or rent any visual pornographic material which was made or produced in such a way that actual physical harm was caused to the person or persons depicted is guilty
(i) of an indictable offence and is liable to imprisonment for two years, or
(ii) of an offence punishable on summary conviction and is liable to a fine of not less than $500 and not more than $2,000 or to imprisonment for six months or to both.

(c) "visual pornographic material" includes any matter or thing in or on which is depicted vaginal, oral or anal intercourse, sexually violent behaviour, bestiality, incest, necrophilia, masturbation, lewd touching of the breasts or the genital parts of the body, or the lewd exhibition of the genitals.

SEXUALLY VIOLENT AND DEGRADING PORNOGRAPHY

159(2)(a) Everyone who makes, prints, publishes, distributes or has in his possession for the purposes of publication or distribution any matter or thing which depicts or describes:
(i) sexually violent behaviour;
(ii) bestiality;
(iii) incest, or
(iv) necrophilia

is guilty of an indictable offence and liable to imprisonment for five years.

(b) Everyone who sells, rents, offers to sell or rent, receives for sale or has in his possession for the purpose of sale or rent any matter or thing which depicts or describes:

    (i) sexually violent behaviour;
    (ii) bestiality;
    (iii) incest, or
    (iv) necrophilia

is guilty

    (i) of an indictable offence and is liable to imprisonment for two years, or
    (ii) of an offence punishable on summary conviction and is liable to a fine of not less than $500 and not more than $1,000 or to imprisonment for six months or to both.

(c) Everyone who displays any matter or thing which depicts

    (i) sexually violent behaviour;
    (ii) bestiality;
    (iii) incest; or
    (iv) necrophilia

in such a way that it is visible to members of the public in a place to which the public has access by right or by express or implied invitation is guilty of

    (i) an indictable offence and is liable to imprisonment for two years, or
    (ii) an offence punishable on summary conviction and is liable to a fine of not less than $500 and not more than $1000 or to imprisonment for six months or to both.

(d) Nobody shall be convicted of the offence in subsection (2)(a) who can demonstrate that the matter or thing has a genuine educational or scientific purpose.

(e) Nobody shall be convicted of the offence in subsection (2)(b) who can demonstrate that the matter or thing has a genuine educational or scientific purpose, and that he sold, rented, offered to sell or rent or had in his possession for the purpose of sale or rent the matter or thing for a genuine education or scientific purpose.

(f) Nobody shall be convicted of the offences in subsections (2)(a) and (2)(b) who can demonstrate that the matter or thing is or is part of a work of artistic merit.

(g) Nobody shall be convicted of the offence in subsection (2)(c) who can demonstrate that the matter or thing

    (i) has a genuine educational or scientific purpose; or
    (ii) is or is part of a work of artistic merit,
    and
    (iii) was displayed in a place or premises or a part of premises to which access is possible only by passing a prominent warning notice advising of the nature of the display therein,

(h) In determining whether a matter or thing is or is not part of a work of artistic merit the Court shall consider the impugned material in the context of the whole work of which it is a part in the case of a book, film, video recording or broadcast which presents a discrete story. In the case of a magazine or any other composite or segmented work the court shall consider the impugned material in the context of the specific feature of which it is a part.

DISPLAY OF VISUAL PORNOGRAPHIC MATERIAL

159(3)(a) Everyone who displays visual pornographic material so that it is visible to members of the public in a place to which the public has access by right or by express or implied invitation is guilty of an offence punishable on summary conviction.

(b) No one shall be convicted of an offence under subsection (1) who can demonstrate that the visual pornographic material was displayed in a place or premises or a part of premises to which access is possible only by passing a prominent warning notice advising of the display therein of visual pornographic material.

(c) For purposes of this section "visual pornographic material" includes any matter or thing in or on which is depicted vaginal, oral or anal intercourse, masturbation, lewd touching of the breasts of the genital parts of the body, or the lewd exhibition of the genitals, but does not include any matter or thing prohibited by subsections (1) and (2) of this section.

FORFEITURE OF MATERIAL

159(4) In any proceedings under section 159(1)(a) and (b), 159(2)(a) and (b), and 164, where an accused is found guilty of the offence the court shall order the offending matter or thing or copies thereof forfeited to Her Majesty in the Right of the Province in which proceedings took place, for disposal as the Attorney General may direct.

ABSENCE OF DEFENCE

159(5) It shall not be a defence to a charge under sections 159(1)(a) and 159(2)(a) that the accused was ignorant of the character of matter or thing in respect of which the charge was laid.

DUE DILIGENCE DEFENCE

159(6) Nobody shall be convicted of the offences in sections 159(1)(b) and 159(2)(b) who can demonstrate that he used due diligence to ensure that there were no representations in the matter or thing which he sold, rented, offered for sale or rent, or had in his possession for purposes of sale or rent, which offended the section.

DIRECTORS

159(7) Where an offence under this section committed by a body corporate is proved to have been committed with the consent or connivance of, or to be attributable to any neglect on the part of, any director, manager, secretary or other similar officer of the body corporate, or any person who was purporting to act in any such capacity, he as well as the body corporate shall be guilty of the offence and shall be liable to be proceeded against and punished accordingly.

DEFINITIONS

159(8) For purposes of this section, "sexually violent behaviour" includes

(i) sexual assault,

(ii) physical harm, including murder, assault or bondage of another person or persons, or self-infliction of physical harm, depicted for the apparent purpose of causing sexual gratification to or stimulation of the viewer.

Recommendation 8

Section 160 of the Code, allowing forfeiture proceedings to be brought, as an alternative to a criminal charge, should be retained in the Code but its application should be limited to tier one and tier two material.

Recommendation 9

> To clarify the law on this point, section 160 should be amended to make it clear that the onus rests on the Crown under this section to prove beyond a reasonable doubt that the material comes within either tier one or tier two.

Recommendation 10

> Section 161 of the Code should be amended as follows:

>> 161. Everyone who refuses to sell or supply to any other person copies of any publication for the reason only that such other person refuses to purchase or acquire from him copies of any other publication that such other person is apprehensive may offend section 159(1) or section 159(2) of the Code is guilty of an indictable offence and as liable to imprisonment for two years.

Recommendation 11

> Section 162 of the Code should be repealed.

Recommendation 12

> Section 164 of the Code should be repealed and replaced by:

>> MAILING PORNOGRAPHIC MATERIAL

>> 164(1) Everyone who makes use of the mails for the purpose of transmitting or delivering any matter or thing which:
>>> (a) depicts or describes a person or persons under the age of 18 years engaging in sexual conduct,
>>> (b) advocates, encourages, condones, or presents as normal the sexual abuse of children

>> is guilty of an indictable offence and liable to imprisonment for ten years.

>> (2) Everyone who makes use of the mails for the purpose of transmitting or delivering any matter or thing which:
>>> (a) by virtue of its character gives reason to believe that actual physical harm was caused to the person or persons depicted, or
>>> (b) depicts or describes:
>>>> (i) sexually violent behaviour,
>>>> (ii) bestiality,
>>>> (iii) incest, or
>>>> (iv) necrophilia

>> is guilty of an indictable offence and liable to imprisonment for five years.

>> (3) Everyone who makes use of the mails for the purpose of transmitting or delivering unsolicited visual pornographic material to members of the public is guilty of an offence punishable on summary conviction.

>> (4) Nobody shall be convicted of the offence in subsection (2)(b) who can demonstrate that the matter or thing mailed
>>> (i) has and is being transmitted or delivered for a genuine educational or scientific purpose, or
>>> (ii) is or is part of a work of artistic merit.

>> (5) It shall not be a defence to a charge under subsections (1) and (2) of this section that the accused was ignorant of the character of the matter or thing in respect of which the charge was laid.

(6) For purposes of this section "visual pornographic material" includes any matter or thing in or on which is depicted vaginal, oral or anal intercourse, masturbation, sexually violent behaviour, incest, bestiality, necrophilia, lewd touching of the breasts or the genital parts of the body, or the lewd exhibition of the genitals.

Recommendation 13

Section 165 of the Criminal Code should be repealed.

Recommendation 14

Section 163 of the Code should be repealed and replaced by:

LIVE SHOWS

163(1) Everyone who, being the owner, operator, lessee, or manager, agent or person in charge of a theatre or any other place in which live shows are presented, presents or gives or allows to be presented or given therein a performance which advocates, encourages, condones or presents as normal the sexual abuse of children is guilty of an indictable offence and liable to imprisonment for ten years.

(2) Everyone who, being the owner, operator, lessee, manager, agent or person in charge of a theatre or any other place in which live shows are presented, presents or gives or allows to be presented or given therein a performance which

(a) involves actual physical harm is being caused to a person participating in the performance, or

(b) represents:
    (i) sexually violent behaviour;
    (ii) bestiality;
    (iii) incest; or
    (iv) necrophilia

is guilty of an indictable offence and liable to imprisonment for five years.

(3) Everyone who, being the owner, operator, lessee, manager, agent or person in charge of a theatre or any other place in which live shows are presented, presents or gives, or allows to be presented or given therein without appropriate warning a performance in which explicit sexual conduct is depicted

is guilty of an offence punishable on summary conviction.

(4) It shall not be a defence to a charge under subsections (1) and (2) that the accused was ignorant of the character of the production.

(5) Nobody shall be convicted of the offence under subsection (2)(b) who can demonstrate that
    (i) the performance is or is part of work of artistic merit; and
    (ii) the performance was presented or given in a place or premises or a part of premises to which access is possible only by passing a prominent warning notice advising of the nature of the performance.

(6) For purposes of subsection 3 it shall be sufficient to establish that an appropriate warning was given that the performance was presented or given in a place or premises or a part of premises to which access is possible only by passing a prominent warning notice advising of the nature of the performance.

(7) For purposes of subsection 3 "explicit sexual conduct" includes vaginal, oral or anal intercourse, masturbation, lewd touching of the

breasts or the genital parts of the body, or the lewd exhibition of the genitals.

Recommendation 15

The provinces and the municipalities should play a major role in regulation of live performances involving sexual activity that are not prohibited by the Criminal Code, through licensing, zoning and other similar means.

Recommendation 16

Section 170 of the Criminal Code should be amended to add the following provision:

This section has no application to a theatre or other place licensed to present live shows

2. Canada Customs

Recommendation 17

The amendments we have proposed to the Criminal Code with respect to prescribed pornographic material should be incorporated by reference into the list of goods prohibited entry into Canada by Schedule C of the Customs Tariff and incorporated by reference into the Customs Act.

Recommendation 18

If, in administering the Customs Tariff, it becomes necessary for Customs to formulate descriptions of pornographic material more precisely than do our Criminal Code recommendations, Customs should put such formulations in the form of Regulations rather than internal policy guidelines or memoranda.

Recommendation 19

The Criminal Code should be amended to provide that it be an offence to import into Canada pornographic material proscribed by the Criminal Code.

Recommendation 20

Judges should be entitled to consider at the time of sentencing a person convicted of dealing in one manner or another with proscribed pornographic material that the person disclosed to law enforcement officers the source of the material in question.

Recommendation 21

The federal government should give higher priority than it now does to the control of the importation of pornography.

Recommendation 22

The basic 1977 policy guidelines on the interpretation of prohibited goods should be immediately revised to contain more precise and contemporary formulations of characteristics which must be present to make materials "immoral or indecent".

Recommendation 23

The jurisdiction to clear film and video recordings for importation into Canada should remain with Canada Customs. The jurisdiction to classify film and video recordings for sale or rent or public showing should remain with the provincial film classification boards.

Recommendation 24

Co-operation between Customs and provincial film classification boards should continue in order that the classification of film and video recordings can take place as part of a single, integrated administrative procedure.

Recommendation 25

Film or video recordings referred by Customs to provincial classification boards should remain in the continuous control of both agencies until the classification and clearance process is complete.

Recommendation 26

The management information services of Customs should be upgraded to provide an adequate central data base and the ancillary systems necessary to capture, store and retrieve information relating to the importation of prohibited material into Canada.

Recommendation 27

Customs should be adequately equipped to fulfill its responsibilities in contributing to the information flow required for an effective interface between the resources of Customs and law enforcement agencies.

Recommendation 28

Customs should investigate the practicality of charging appropriate fees for the filing and hearing of appeals from classification decisions.

Recommendation 29

Customs, as part of a combined project to be undertaken with the Department of Communications and the CRTC, should examine the Customs implications involved in trans-border telecommunication of pornographic material.

3. Canada Post

Recommendation 30

The Postal service should assign policy and administrative priority to the effective control of distribution of pornographic material by mail. We further recommend that the postal service actively participate with the RCMP and the Customs service in gathering and exchanging information and data in an effort to better co-ordinate effective investigation and enforcement techniques to control the distribution of pornographic material by mail.

4. Broadcasting and Communications

Recommendation 31

The amendments we have proposed to the Criminal Code with respect to proscribed pornographic material should be incorporated by reference into Regulations passed or to be passed by the CRTC pursuant to the Broadcasting Act with respect to all broadcast media.

Recommendation 32

> Canada should take the initiative to immediately open discussions on the international regulation of both public broadcasting signals and private signals emanating from fixed satellite services.

Recommendation 33

> The CRTC should conduct the appropriate research into and promote appropriate public discussion about technology capable of scrambling and descrambing satellite signals, in order that there can be a measure of practical control over the transmission and reception of satellite signals.

Recommendation 34

> Upon the issuing or renewal of a broadcast licence, a licensee should be required to post a bond in an appropriate amount to ensure compliance with the Regulations and conditions of licence relating to program content. In the event that a complaint about program content is upheld by the CRTC, the Commission should have the discretion to compensate the complainant for the costs incurred in presenting the complaint, such costs to be paid the licensee and secured by the aforesaid bond.

5. Human Rights

Recommendation 35

> Human rights commissions should vigorously explore the application of their existing legislation and jurisprudence to pornography issues, including exposure to pornography in the workplace, stores and other facilities. However, we do not recommend that a separate pornography-related offence be added to human rights codes at this time.

Recommendation 36

> Legislation along the lines of the Civil Rights Protection Act, 1981 of British Columbia should be enacted in all Canadian provinces and territories to provide a civil cause of action in the courts in respect of the promotion of hatred by way of pornography, and the existing British Columbia Act itself should be extended to cover the promotion of hatred by way of pornography.

Recommendation 37

> Even if legislatures decide to include in human rights codes a specific pornography-related provision, we recommend that the civil cause of action described in Recommendation 36 be provided as an alternative.

6. Hate Literature

Recommendation 38

> The definition of "identifiable group" in subsection 281.1(4) of the Criminal Code should be broadened to include sex, age, and mental or physical disability, at least insofar as the definition applies to section 281.2 of the Code.

Recommendation 39

> The word "wilfully" should be removed from section 281.2(2) of the Code, so as to remove the requirement of specific intent for the offence of promoting hatred against an identifiable group.

Recommendation 40

> The requirement in s.281.2(6) that the Attorney General consent to a prosecution under s.281.2(2) should be repealed.

Recommendation 41

> The text of subsection 281.2(2) should be amended to make it clear that graphic representations which promote hatred would be covered by the provision. The subsection could prohibit "publishing statements or visual representations or any combination thereof, other than in private communications" which promote hatred against any identifiable group.

7. Film Classification and Censorship

Recommendation 42

> Canada should not opt for a national film review system, but rather maintain the existing arrangement whereby review is done on a province by province basis.

Recommendation 43

> Those provinces and territories which have not implemented a film review system should consider doing so.

Recommendation 44

> Film review boards and Customs authorities should not enter into arrangements whereby local film review boards have de facto control over what enters Canada; we further recommend that the 60-day clearance period allowed by Customs to films entering by way of Québec ports be discontinued.

Recommendation 45

> Provincial film review boards should have an explicit statutory mandate to refuse to permit exhibition in the province of films which are contrary to the Criminal Code. Provincial film review boards should not be empowered to prohibit or cut films which are not contrary to the Criminal Code.

Recommendation 46

> Provincial film review legislation or regulations should contain explicit standards to govern the boards' activities in classifying and, where these powers exist, in prohibiting and cutting films.

Recommendation 47

> The provinces should not exercise a power of prior restraint over advertising of films; however, the power to require that film classifications be included in an advertisement should be kept.

Recommendation 48

Clearance for exhibition by a provincial authority should not constitute a defence or a discretionary bar to a prosecution under the Criminal Code, with the exception that a film classification permitting a film to be shown to persons under 18 will constitute a defence to a charge of displaying visual pornographic material to a person under 18.

Recommendation 49

Each province should establish a system of review and classification for video recordings intended for private use in the province. Under such a system, the review board should be given an explicit statutory mandate to refuse to classify video recordings which are contrary to the Criminal Code but not be empowered to prohibit or cut video recordings which are not contrary to the Criminal Code.

Chapter 49

Recommendations on Prostitution

Recommendation 50

The government of Canada in conjunction with the governments of the provinces and territories should strengthen both their moral and financial commitment to removing the economic and social inequalities between men and women and discrimination on the basis of sexual preference.

Recommendation 51

The government of Canada in conjunction with the governments of the provinces and territories should ensure that there are adequate social programs to assist women and young people in need.

Recommendation 52

The government of Canada in co-operation with the provinces and territories, should provide financial support for both research into and the implementation of sensitive and relevant educational programs on human sexuality for use in the country's schools; in particular the governments should jointly fund a National Centre and Program in Sexuality and Life Education to bring together the leading scholars and clinicians in the field to conduct research and formulate program and pedagogical models.

Recommendation 53

The government of Canada in conjunction with the governments of the provinces and territories should undertake the direct funding or indirect financial support of community groups involved in the care and welfare of both practising and reformed prostitutes, so that adequate social, health, employment, educational and counselling services are available to them.

Recommendation 54

The Government of Canada in co-operation with the governments of the provinces and territories should commission further research on prostitution as a means of informing attempts to address it as a social phenomenon, and to deal effectively with its adverse impact on those who are or who have been involved in it.

Recommendation 55

The prostitution related activities of both prostitutes and customers should be removed from the Criminal Code, except insofar as they contravene non-prostitution related Code provisions, and do not create a definable nuisance or nuisances.

Recommendation 56

In the Criminal Code provisions dealing with exploitative conduct other than running a prostitution establishment, the concern of the criminal law should be confined to conduct which is violent or which threatens force; special police details or units should be established, and adequately funded, where required, to investigate and prosecute violent and abusive procurers and pimps; any prostitution business which operates without contravening the Criminal Code should be subject to municipal regulation.

Recommendation 57

The criminal law relating to prostitution establishments should be drawn so as not to thwart the attempts of small numbers of prostitutes to organize their activities out of a place of residence, and so as not to prevent provinces from permitting and regulating small-scale, non-residential commercial prostitution establishments employing adult prostitutes.

Recommendation 58

STREET PROSTITUTION

1. Repeal section 195.1 of the Criminal Code.

2. Amend section 171 of the Criminal Code as follows:

SECTION 171(1): DISORDERLY CONDUCT, INDECENT
EXHIBITION, LOITERING,
SOLICITING, ETC.

(1) Everyone who
   (a) not being in a dwelling house causes a disturbance in or near a public place,
      (i) by fighting, screaming, shouting, swearing or using insulting or obscene language,
      (ii) by using sexually offensive remarks or suggestions,
      (iii) by being drunk, or
      (iv) by impeding or molesting other persons,
   (b) openly exposes or exhibits an indecent exhibition in a public place,
   (c) loiters in a public place and in any way obstructs persons who are there,
   (d) stands, stops, wanders about in or drives through a public place for purposes of offering to engage in prostitution or of employing the services of a prostitute or prostitutes and on more than one occasion
      (i) beckons to, stops or attempts to stop pedestrians or attempts to engage them in conversation,
      (ii) stops or attempts to stop motor vehicles,
      (iii) impedes the free flow of pedestrian or vehicular traffic, or of ingress or egress from premises adjacent to a public place
   (e) disturbs the peace and quiet of the occupants of a dwelling house by discharging firearms, by any of the forms of conduct in paragraphs (a), (b), (c) or (d) of this subsection, or by other disorderly conduct in a public place,
   (f) not being an occupant of a dwelling house comprised in a particular building or structure, disturbs the peace and quiet of the occupants of a dwelling house comprised in the building or structure by discharging firearms or by other disorderly conduct

684

in any part of the building or structure to which at the time of such conduct, the occupants of two or more dwelling houses comprised in the building or structure have access as of right or by invitation, express or implied,

is guilty of an offence punishable on summary conviction subject to a maximum fine of $1,000.

(2) In the absence of other evidence, or by way of corroboration of other evidence, a summary conviction court may infer from the evidence of a peace officer relating to the conduct of a person or persons, whether ascertained or not, that a disturbance described in paragraph (1)(a), (d), (e) or (f) was caused or occurred.

3. Remove definition of "public place" from section 179(1) of the Criminal Code, and revise the definition of "public place" in section 138 of the Code to read:

'public place' includes any place to which the public have access as of right or by invitation, express or implied, doorways and hallways of buildings adjacent to public places and to vehicles situated in public places.

Recommendation 59

PROCURING

1. Substitute for the existing section 195(1) the following:

Everyone who
   (a) by force, threat of force or by other coercive or threatening behaviour induces a person of 18 years or older to engage in prostitution with another person or generally,
   (b) by force, threat of force or by other coercive or threatening behaviour compels a person of 18 years or older to continue engaging in prostitution with another person or generally is guilty of an indictable offence and liable to imprisonment for 14 years.

2. Repeal subsections (3) and (4) of section 195.

Recommendation 60

FINANCIAL SUPPORT FROM PROSTITUTION

1. Substitute for section 195(1)(j) (living on the avails) the following:

Everyone who by force, threat of force or other coercive or threatening behaviour induces a person of 18 years or older to support him financially in whole or in part by acts of prostitution is guilty of an indictable offence and liable to imprisonment for 14 years.

2. Repeal subsection (2) of section 195(1).

Recommendation 61

PROSTITUTION ESTABLISHMENTS

1. Replace existing section 193 of the Criminal Code with the following provision:

(1) Everyone who operates or aids in the operation of any place which is used in whole or in part for purposes of prostitution is guilty of an indictable offence and is liable to imprisonment for two years.

(2) Everyone who as owner, landlord, lessor, tenant, occupier, or otherwise having charge or control of any place, knowingly permits it to be let or used for purposes of prostitution is guilty of an offence punishable on summary conviction, subject to a maximum fine of $5,000.

(3) This section does not apply to:
    (a) a place of residence in which two residents of 18 years or more of age of that place engage in acts of prostitution;
    (b) a prostitution establishment licensed and operated in accordance with a regulatory scheme established by the provincial or territorial legislature in that jurisdiction.

(4) Where a person is convicted of an offence under subsection (1) the court shall cause a notice of the conviction to be served on the owner, landlord, or lessor of the place in respect of which the person is convicted or his agent, and the notice shall contain a statement to the effect that it is being served pursuant to this section.

(5) Where a person upon whom a notice is served under subsection (4) fails forthwith to exercise any right he may have to determine the tenancy or right of occupation of the person so convicted, and thereafter any person is convicted of an offence under subsection (1) in respect of the place, the person on whom the notice was served shall be deemed to have committed an offence under subsection (1) unless he proves that he has taken all reasonable steps to prevent a recurrence of the offence.

(6) For purposes of this section "place" includes any place, whether or not
    (a) it is covered or enclosed,
    (b) it is used permanently or temporarily, or
    (c) any person has an exclusive right of user with respect to it.

2. Repeal definition of "common bawdy house" in section 179(1) of the Criminal Code.

3. Repeal clauses (a) and (d) of section 180(1) of the Criminal Code.

Recommendation 62

1. Amend section 155 and 157 of the Code, so that they no longer extend to consensual acts between those of 18 years or older.

2. Repeal section 158 of the Criminal Code.

Recommendation 63

In view of the uncertainty which surrounds the meaning and purpose of section 176 of the Criminal Code, and the confusion over the relationship between the nuisance provisions in the Code and the power of an Attorney General of a province to seek a civil injunction to restrain a common nuisance, the federal Minister of Justice and his provincial counterparts should, if necessary, make a reference of this issue to the Supreme Court of Canada, or seek a legislative solution to the problem.

Recommendation 64

Repeal section 253 of the Criminal Code.

Recommendation 65

Canada should review its position on its failure to become a party to the 1951 United Nations Convention for the Suppression of the Traffic in Persons and the Exploitation of the Prostitution of Others and its low profile international stance on prostitution and how to deal with it, in general; in particular, if it takes issue with some of the prescriptions of the Convention, or future resolutions of international bodies on prostitution, then it should be on grounds of principle rather than expediency.

Chapter 50

Recommendations on Children

1. The Present Law

Recommendation 66

> Provincial child welfare authorities are encouraged to review their response to child sexual abuse, as recommended by the Committee on Sexual Offences on Children and Youths (at pp. 548-549). We recommend that the issue of children's involvement in the production of pornography should be on the agenda of any such review. However, we caution that not every child involved in the production of pornography may be a neglected child within the philosophy of child welfare legislation. Accordingly, we recommend that a balance be struck between recognizing the autonomy and capacity of the family to deal with exploitation of its own children and the provision of state assistance where that is needed.

Recommendation 67

> We recommend the enactment of criminal sanctions for the production, dissemination, and possession of "child pornography".

Recommendation 68

> Provincial and municipal authorities should continue their efforts to control the access of young people to offensive material by means of film and video classification systems and municipal by-laws regulating access to adult material.

2. International Obligations and Instruments

Recommendation 69

> Canada should ratify the 1959 Declaration of the Rights of the Child.

3. Legal Recommendations

Recommendation 70

> All of the reforms to the criminal law and related statutes dealing with pornography and prostitution involving children and youths should be applicable to persons under 18 years of age.

Recommendation 71

Trials of persons under 18, accused of any of the offences proposed in our recommendations should be conducted in accordance with the Young Offenders Act. Accordingly, if the minimum age of 18 as provided in that Act is not fully implemented across Canada by the time these recommendations are in effect, no person under 18, who is not given the protection of the Young Offenders Act, should be charged.

Recommendation 72

Pursuant to recommendation 2 in this Part, the following new section of the Criminal Code should be enacted:

(1) Everyone who:
    (a) Uses, or who induces, incites, coerces, or agrees to use a person under 18 years of age to
        (i) participate in any explicit sexual conduct for the purpose of producing, by any means, a visual representation of such conduct;
        (ii) participate in any explicit sexual conduct in the context of a live show;
    (b) induces, incites, or coerces another person to use a person under 18 years of age to
        (i) participate in any explicit sexual conduct for the purposes of producing, by any means, a visual representation of such conduct;
        (ii) participate in any explicit sexual conduct in the context of a live show;
    (c) participates in the production of a visual representation of or a live performance by a person under 18 years of age participating in explicit sexual conduct;
    (d) makes, prints, reproduces, publishes or distributes, or has in his possession for the purposes of publication or distribution, a visual representation of a person under 18 years of age participating in explicit sexual conduct

is guilty of an indictable offence and is liable to imprisonment for 10 years.

(2) For the purpose of subsection (1)
    (a) a person who at any material time appears to be under 18 years of age shall in the absence of evidence to the contrary, be deemed to be under 18 years of age.

(3) Everyone who sells, rents, offers to sell or rent, receives for sale or rent, exposes to public view, or has in his possession for the purpose of sale or rent a visual representation of a person under 18 years of age participating in explicit sexual conduct, is guilty
        (i) of an indictable offence and is liable to imprisonment for 5 years, or
        (ii) of an offence punishable on summary conviction and is liable to a fine of not less than $1,000 and not more than $5,000 or to imprisonment for six months or to both.

(4) Every one who knowingly, without lawful justification or excuse, has in his or her possession a visual representation of a person under 18 years of age participating in explicit sexual conduct, is guilty of an offence punishable on summary conviction, and is liable to a fine of not less than $500 and not more than $2,000 or to imprisonment for six months or to both.

(5) For the purposes of subsections (1), (3) and (4) above,

(a) "explicit sexual conduct" includes any conduct in which vaginal, oral or anal intercourse, bestiality, masturbation, sexually violent behavior, lewd touching of the breasts or the genital parts of the body, or the lewd exhibition of the genitals is depicted;

(b) "sexually violent behavior" includes

(i) sexual assault, and

(ii) physical harm, including murder, assault or bondage of another person or persons, or self-infliction of physical harm, carried out for the apparent purpose of causing sexual gratification or stimulation to the viewer;

(c) "visual representation" includes any representation that can be seen by any means, whether or not it involves the use of any special apparatus.

Recommendation 73

Paragraph 647(b) of the Criminal Code should be amended to provide a higher maximum penalty for a corporation convicted of a summary conviction offence; or the section should provide, as does subsection 722(1), that a higher penalty may be provided with respect to a particular offence.

Recommendation 74

Section 168 of the Criminal Code should be repealed.

Recommendation 75

A new section of the Criminal Code should be enacted to deal with production, dissemination and possession of material advocating, encouraging or presenting as normal the sexual abuse of children in the following form:

(1) Everyone who makes, prints, reproduces, publishes, or distributes, or has in his possession for the purposes of publication or distribution material which advocates, encourages, condones or presents as normal the sexual abuse of children is guilty of an indictable offence and liable to imprisonment for 10 years.

(2) It shall not be a defence to a charge under subsection (1) that the accused was ignorant of the character of the material, matter, thing or production.

(3) Everyone who sells, rents, offers to sell or rent, receives for sale or rent, exposes to public view, or has in his possession for purpose of sale or rent material which advocates, encourages, condones or presents as normal the sexual abuse of children is guilty

(i) of an indictable offence and liable to imprisonment for 5 years, or

(ii) of an offence punishable on summary conviction and liable to a fine of not less than $1,000 and not more than $5,000 or to imprisonment for six months or to both.

(4) Everyone who knowingly, without lawful justification or excuse, has in his or her possession material which advocates, encourages, condones or presents as normal the sexual abuse of children is guilty of a summary conviction offence and is liable to a fine of not less than $500 and not more than $2,000 or to imprisonment for six months or to both.

(5) For purposes of this section "material" includes any written, visual or recorded matter.

(6) For purposes of this section "sexual abuse" means any sexual activity or conduct directed against a person under 18 years of age which is prohibited by the Criminal Code.

Recommendation 76

Section 163 of the Criminal Code should be repealed and replaced by a new section which would include provisions dealing specifically with the presentation of a live show advocating, encouraging, condoning, or presenting as normal the sexual abuse of children, in the following form:

(1) Everyone who, being the owner, operator, lessee, manager, agent or person in charge of a theatre or any other place in which live shows are presented, presents or gives or allows to be presented or given therein a performance which advocates, encourages, condones or presents as normal the sexual abuse of children is guilty of an indictable offence and liable to imprisonment for 10 years.

Recommendation 77

Section 164 of the Criminal Code should be repealed and a section enacted which includes provisions dealing explicitly with use of the mails to transmit material involving children or advocating the sexual abuse of children, along the following lines:

(1) Everyone who makes use of the mails for the purpose of transmitting or delivering any material which:
  (a) depicts a person or persons under the age of 18 years engaging in explicit sexual conduct,
  (b) advocates, encourages, condones, or presents as normal the sexual abuse of children,

is guilty of an indictable offence and liable to imprisonment for 10 years.

Recommendation 78

A new section should be included in the Criminal Code, to control display of visual pornographic material to persons under 18 years of age, in the following form:

(1) Everyone who
  (a) sells, rents or offers to sell or rent visual pornographic material to anyone under 18 years of age; or
  (b) displays for sale or rent visual pornographic material in such a manner that it is accessible to and can be seen or examined by anyone under 18 years of age; or
  (c) being the lessee, manager, agent or person in charge of a theatre, presents or gives or allows to be presented or given therein to anyone under 18 years of age any visual pornographic material

is guilty of a summary conviction offence and is liable to a fine not to exceed $1000 or to imprisonment for 6 months or to both.

(2) No one shall be convicted of an offence under subsection (1) who can demonstrate that
  (a) he used due care and diligence to ensure that there was no such visual pornographic material in the materials which he sold or rented, offered for sale or rent, displayed for sale or rent, or presented, gave or allowed to be presented or given; or
  (b) the visual pornographic material has a genuine educational or scientific purpose and was sold or rented, offered for sale or rent, or displayed for sale or rent, presented, given, or allowed to be presented or given, for that purpose; or

(c) according to the classification or rating established for film or videotape material in the province or territory in which it is sold, rented, offered for sale or rent, displayed for sale or rent, presented, given or allowed to be presented or given, the film or videotape has been classified or rated as acceptable for viewing by those under the age of 18 years.

(3) For purposes of this section, "visual pornographic material" includes any matter or thing or live performances in which is depicted or described vaginal, oral or anal intercourse, masturbation, lewd touching of the breasts or the genital parts of the body, or the lewd exhibition of the genitals, but does not include any material prohibited by [offences involving portrayals of children and sexually violent or degrading material].

Recommendation 79

Subsections 159(2)(b), (c) and (d) of the Code should be repealed and replaced by a provision specifically directed at selling or displaying sex aids to a person under 18 years of age, in the following form:

(1) Everyone who
(a) sells or offers to sell a sex aid to anyone under 18 years;
(b) displays for sale sex aids in such a manner that they are accessible to and can be seen or examined by anyone under 18 years of age,

is guilty of a summary conviction offence and is liable to a fine not to exceed $1000 or to imprisonment for 6 months or to both.

(2) For the purposes of subsection (1) "sex aid" includes any device, apparatus or object designed solely to stimulate sexually the user of it.

Recommendation 80

The following definitions should apply to the sections of the Code dealing with pornographic offences:

"sexually violent behaviour" includes
(i) sexual assault,
(ii) physical harm depicted for the apparent purpose of causing sexual gratification or stimulation to the viewer, including murder, assault or bondage of another person or persons, or self-infliction of physical harm.

"visual pornographic material" includes any matter or thing or live performances in which is depicted or described vaginal, oral, or anal intercourse, masturbation, lewd touching of the breasts or the genital parts of the body, or the lewd exhibition of the genitals.

Recommendation 81

The Evidence Acts of Canada, the provinces and the territories should be amended to provide that every child is competent to testify in court and the child's evidence is admissible; the weight of the evidence should be determined by the trier of fact.

Recommendation 82

There should be no statutory requirement for corroboration of "unsworn" child's evidence; this would entail repeal of section 586 of the Criminal Code, section 16(2) of the Canada Evidence Act and section 61(2) of the Young Offenders Act, and corresponding sections of provincial Evidence Acts.

Recommendation 83

No alteration be made to the Evidence Acts of Canada or the provinces and territories to permit reception by a court of hearsay evidence of a child's account of the commission against him or her of a sexual offence.

Recommendation 84

Subsection 442(1) of the Criminal Code should be amended to allow the court to exclude any person from the courtroom where any evidence or information presented to the court would be seriously injurious or seriously prejudicial to the complainant or witness who is under 18.

Recommendation 85

As much publicity as possible should be given to the name of an accused who is convicted of an offence involving the child pornography or child prostitution offences we propose, and the sexual offences in the Code, with the exception of the name of a person convicted of incest.

Recommendation 86

Subsection 442(3) of the Criminal Code should be amended to provide for the complainant and witness under 18 years of age the same mandatory protection from publication of name or identifying information as is now extended to youthful witnesses and complainants in trials of young offenders by section 38 of the Young Offenders Act.

Recommendation 87

Subsection 442(3) of the Criminal Code should be amended so as to make it clear that section 442(3) applies to the offences recommended by this committee.

Recommendation 88

A person accused of the offence of selling pornography containing sexually explicit portrayals of children, or of selling pornography advocating the sexual abuse of children, should be entitled to defend the charge on the basis that he had used due diligence to inspect the materials.

Recommendation 89

The Criminal Code should be amended to add a provision that:

In any proceedings in which a person is convicted of producing, distributing or selling pornographic material the court shall order the offending material or matter or thing or copies thereof forfeited to Her Majesty in the Right of the Province in which proceedings took place, for disposal as the Attorney General may direct.

Recommendation 90

A section should be added to the Criminal Code to provide for criminal liability of officers and directors, along these lines:

Where an offence under this act committed by a body corporate is proved to have been committed with the consent or connivance of, or to be attributable to any neglect on the part of, any director, manager, secretary or other similar officer of the body corporate, or any person who was purporting to act in any such capacity, he, as well as the body corporate, shall be guilty of the offence and shall be liable to be proceeded against and punished accordingly.

Recommendation 91

Sections 166 and section 195(1)(a) to (i) of the Criminal Code should be repealed and replaced with a new prohibition on procuring, which would deal specifically with the procuring of those under 18. That section is:

(1) Everyone who

(a) by force, by threat of force or by other coercive or threatening behaviour induces a person of 18 years or older to engage in prostitution with another person or generally, or

(b) by force, by threat of force or by other coercive or threatening behaviour compels a person of 18 years or older to continue engaging in prostitution with another person or generally

is guilty of an indictable offence and liable to imprisonment for 14 years.

(2) Everyone who

(a) persuades, coerces or deceives a person under 18 years of age in order to induce that person to engage in sexual activity for money, or for any other consideration or reward, or in illicit sexual conduct with another person or generally, or

(b) encourages, coerces or deceives a person under 18 years of age in order to induce that person to continue to engage in sexual activity for money, or for any other consideration or reward, or in illicit sexual conduct with another person or generally,

is guilty of an indictable offence and liable to imprisonment for 14 years.

(3) For the purposes of subsection (2), "illicit sexual conduct" means any sexual behaviour or act which is prohibited by the Criminal Code, whether or not such prohibition is based upon the age of the parties to the act or of any one of them.

Recommendation 92

The age specified in section 157 of the Criminal Code should be lowered to 18 from 21, so that the prohibition against buggery in section 155 of the Code and against an act of gross indecency in section 156 will not apply to acts committed in private between persons who are 18 or over.

Recommendation 93

Sections 146, 151, 152, and 153 of the Criminal Code should be amended in order to provide that the protection against sexual assault extended thereby to females is also available to males.

Recommendation 94

In offences involving sexual assault on young persons, the requirement that the victim be of "previously chaste character" should be removed from the Criminal Code.

Recommendation 95

The offences involving young persons set out in Part IV of the Code should be reviewed with the aim of rationalizing them by repealing outmoded sections.

Recommendation 96

Section 167 of the Criminal Code should be repealed.

Recommendation 97

Section 195(1)(j) of the Criminal Code be repealed and replaced with a new prohibition against receiving financial support from prostitution, which would contain provisions dealing specifically with receiving support from the prostitution of those under 18. The section is:

(1) Everyone who by force, threat of force or other coercive or threatening behaviour induces a person of 18 years or older to support him or her financially in whole or in part by acts of prostitution is guilty of an indictable offence and liable to imprisonment for 14 years.

(2) Everyone who is supported financially in whole or in part by a person under 18 years of age from the proceeds of sexual activities by that young person for money or for other consideration or reward is guilty of an indictable offence and liable to imprisonnement for 14 years.

(3) For purposes of subsection (2), evidence that a person lives with a person or persons under the age of 18 who engage in sexual activity for money or for other consideration or reward is, in the absence of evidence to the contrary, proof that that person is supported, in whole or in part, from the proceeds of that activity.

Recommendation 98

No person under 18 should be permitted to be employed in any prostitution establishment which might be set up pursuant to the exception for provincially regulated establishments provided in our proposal about prostitution establishments.

Recommendation 99

The following new section should be added to the Criminal Code:

(1) Everyone who engages in, or attempts or offers to engage in sexual activity for money or for other consideration or reward with a person under 18 years of age is guilty of an indictable offence and liable to imprisonment for five years.

(2) It is no defence to a charge under this section that the accused believed the other person to be 18 years or older.

Recommendation 100

A young person who engages in sexual activity for reward as the provider of sexual services should not be subject to a criminal penalty.

Recommendation 101

Persons under 18 who are using the streets and commit any of the nuisances prohibited in our proposed section 171 of the Criminal Code should be prosecuted in accordance with that section.

Recommendation 102

Federal, provincial and territorial governments should reaffirm their commitment to providing an environment where all children have the opportunity to develop to the fullest extent, their intellectual, physical and spiritual attributes. To this end, the Secretariat proposed in this Report should give high priority to issues affecting children and young people.

Recommendation 103

The federal goverment should collaborate with and assist the provinces, territories and private organizations and agencies in the development of educational programs for children, and those with special responsibilities for the welfare of children, in the areas of family life, human sexuality and media literacy.

Recommendation 104

Provincial and territorial governments should give high priority to programs in family life, human sexuality and media literacy at all levels within the school system.

Recommendation 105

The federal government should collaborate with and assist the provinces, territories, and private organizations and agencies in assessing the effectiveness of social service programs designed to assist children and young people, in developing new programs and in implementing changes designed to better meet the needs and current realities of young people in the 1980's and 1990's.

Chapter 51

General Recommendations

There are a number of recommendations in this Part which also appear in other Parts of this Report. They are repeated here because they are of a general nature and are applicable to the areas of pornography and prostitution involving both adults and children as addressed in this Report.

Recommendation 50

> The government of Canada in conjunction with the governments of the provinces and territories should strengthen both their moral and financial commitment to removing the economic and social inequalities between men and women and discrimination on the basis of sexual preference.

Recommendation 51

> The government of Canada in conjunction with the governments of the provinces and territories should ensure that there are adequate social programs to assist women and young people in need.

Recommendation 52

> The government of Canada in co-operation with the provinces and territories, should provide financial support for both research into and the implementation of sensitive and relevant educational programs on human sexuality for use in the country's schools; in particular the governments should jointly fund a National Centre and Program in Sexuality and Life Education to bring together the leading scholars and clinicians in the field to conduct research and formulate program and pedagogical models.

1. Education

There was recognition throughout the public hearings that pornography is just one part of our entire communications media. While it was argued that pornography is often the most extreme material with respect to its depiction of dehumanized sex and sexual violence, it shares many common elements with other media content. What starts as sex-role stereotyping in much of the mainline content, ends as obscene violence and degradation. Pornography, therefore, cannot be separated from other aspects of our communications industry and dealt with in complete isolation. Nor can we expect that legal remedies alone will be successful in dealing with such a complex issue.

The Toronto Task Force on Public Violence Against Women and Children expressed this common view:

> Law reform will not eliminate pornography from our society. Neither will the disappearance of pornography eliminate the problems that pornography has caused. The problems in our society and the violence to which women and children are subjected go far beyond imagery. People's attitudes must change and in the long run this will only evolve through positive depictions in all forms of the media.

The views on why pornography will not be adequately addressed through legal channels alone are summarized very succinctly in the following statement:

> For centuries, perhaps always in civilization as we know it, this inequality, this power imbalance has existed. As many pornographers rightly point out, pornography has long been with us; as they neatly omit, so has sexual inequality, sexism and misogyny ... pornography mirrors and celebrates this inequality.
> New Brunswick Advisory Council Status of Women

Such a view suggests, of course, that pornography is not just an issue relating to the mass media, but that its roots are deep within our society. Long term solutions to the display of dehumanized sexual activities will, therefore, require sustained efforts towards achieving greater equality of opportunity for all people in society, and an new consciousness on the part of Canadians about the detrimental impact of sex-role stereotyping and the role the media plays in maintaining inequalities between women and men.

Arguments such as these, led many organizations appearing before the Committee to call for wide ranging educational and informational programs to be addressed to the public in general, and to specific groups such as parents, teachers, judges, police and social workers, and other professionals who work with children or young people. The objectives of such programs would be to increase public understanding about human sexual relations and the ways in which the media, and pornography in particular, present distorted images of human behaviour. Related to such a program is the aim of encouraging positive media images of women and men and a corresponding elimination of the traditional sex-role stereotyping which is still all too common in programming.

While acknowledging that the magnitude of such public education programs would require the leadership (and financial support) of federal government departments such as Health and Welfare Canada and the Department of Communications, many briefs stressed the importance of government funding to encourage the participation of community groups, many of which are already providing sex education and information on sex role stereotyping, usually on a shoe-string budget or a voluntary basis.

One of these groups, the Vancouver Status of Women, strongly urged that financial support be provided to existing groups which are: doing research and public educational work in the area of pornography; providing adults and teenagers with accurate and positive information regarding sex, including birth control and health matters (Planned Parenthood, for example); doing research and public educational work in the area of female sexuality; and producing alternative media imagery which engages in an exploration of sexuality and sexual issues from a woman's point of view.

They also recommended that financial support be provided for research and implementation of projects aimed at counteracting the persistent media acceptance and legitimization of violent behaviour towards women, with the goal of prevention of violent and sexual crimes against women and girls.

A similar point was made by the the Anglican Church of Canada, Diocese of New Westminster, which urged that funds be directed to such groups as Media Watch and Status of Women groups to monitor and control stereotyping of women in the media.

Other groups urged that the Federal Government reinstate funding that had been cut from existing programs:

> [The] Federal Government [should] take serious consideration of the recent cutbacks to federal programs re: sexuality and family planning education and health services and ... this funding [should] be markedly increased. Further ... the federal government [should] develop a strong policy statement in favour of sexuality and family planning education and health services and [should] set financial policy which will encourage every province to support these areas, both through policy and through financial assistance ....
> Planned Parenthood of Nova Scotia, Halifax

It was also suggested to the Committee that the support and funding of Women's Studies Programs in educational institutions should be recognized as a fundamental necessity in creating broader educational awareness of the questions of issues and sexuality.

Many organizations believed that an inextricable part of the public education program should be a campaign to combat the sex-role stereotyping of women in the news media. Media Watch, Vancouver, a national women's organization dedicated to improving the portrayal of women and girls in the media, has taken the lead on this issue. Its objective is to eliminate sexist and pornographic images and to encourage the creation of images that reflect the changing and diverse roles of women in Canadian society.

Media Watch defines sex role stereotyping as:

> failure to represent women in their full variety of ages, shapes, sizes and colours;
>
> failure to reflect the increasing diversity of women's lives;
>
> failure to portray a representative range of the occupations that women hold;
>
> invisibility of women in discussion of many issues;
>
> portrayal of women as sexual lures and decorative objects;

invisibility of female experts and decision makers;

language which assumes that everyone is male unless identified otherwise.

Media Watch considers sex-role stereotyping to be harmful to women because it dehumanizes, misrepresents and degrades them. The extreme form of this distortion is, of course, pornography.

Media Watch, Calgary, in its presentation to the Committee, described the stereotyped portrayal of women in the media.

> Media images reflect and magnify the prevalent ways that our culture defines women, and illustrates how limiting and offensive these stereotypes are ... In the media men are identified by occupations in the public sphere. Women are shown performing household and child care tasks and this work is constantly trivialized ... They have to be perfect mothers, perfect wives, perfect employees, and perfect bed partners. In short, women are defined by their relationship to men, they are not shown to have a legitimate identity that is separate from men ....

> In the media women are rarely portrayed as gainfully employed. Their contribution to the work world is either systematically ignored or distorted ... their value is judged according to their ability to perform a given task ... it doesn't matter what the woman's occupation is, she is supposed to be occupied by a continual concern about whether or not her body is beautiful or sexually attractive enough ....

> Media Watch considers that sex role stereotyping of woman creates an environment that encourages the dehumanization, misrepresentation and degradation of women. The extreme form of this attitude is pornography. Presently our environment is polluted with messages that tell us women are powerless, feebleminded, submissive, victims, and only valuable if they are young, beautiful and white ....

> Male dominance and female submissiveness are at the very heart of the stereotype of men and women. Pornography is the extreme portrayal of dominance-submissiveness, the objectification and the abuse of women. Media Watch views sex role stereotyping and pornography as a continuum which must be uprooted from our culture.
> Media Watch, Calgary

In order to reduce or eliminate sex-role stereotyping and pornography from the news media, several national organizations, among them the Canadian Teachers' Federation, the Canadian Coalition Against Media Pornography, Media Watch, and the Canadian Congress for Learning Opportunities for Women, proposed that guidelines on sex-role stereotyping and pornography should be established for the CRTC, The Canadian Film Development Corporation, the Department of Communications, the Canada Council and all other government-funded communications and cultural agencies.

The Committee found many of the suggestions made at the public hearings compelling and persuasive. As will have been apparent throughout our Report, we do not believe that legal action alone can deal with the disturbing and pervasive nature of many aspects of the media and of pornography in particular. Most clearly, of course, legal remedies cannot address the lack of understanding about human behaviour and specifically human sexual relations which appear to lead some people into believing that media and pornographic representations are truthful and accurate depictions of people. Accordingly, the Committee is making a series of recommendations about public educational programs.

Recommendation 106

> The federal government in conjunction with the provincial governments should initiate and supporto public education programs designed too
>> (a) increase the general understanding of human sexual relations;
>> (b) promote a fuller appreciation of the impact of the mass media in creating or maintaining beliefs and attitudes about human behaviour.
>
> In implementing such programs, the governments should fund and assist the work already being carried out by numerous voluntary, community or religious organizations.

Recommendation 107

> The federal government should ensure that all its departments and agencies which have responsibility for research, culture and communications, e.g., the CRTC, the Canadian Film Development Corporation, the Canada Council, the Social Sciences and Humanities Research Council, the Department of Communications, develop guidelines designed to reduce or eliminate sex-role stereotyping in the programs or work for which each is responsible.

Chapter 52

Implementation of Recommendations

Recommendation 108

(1) A Secretariat should be set up under the aegis of the federal Departments of Justice, of the Solicitor General and of Health and Welfare:
  (a) To stimulate and co-ordinate efforts at the federal level to deal with pornography and prostitution as social phenomena;
  (b) To stimulate discussions and co-operation with the governments of the provinces and territories, and with social, education and charitable organizations in the private sector, on ways and means of dealing with these two problems;
  (c) To monitor and inform public opinion and seek public input on these two problems.

(2) The Secretariat should as priorities:
  (a) Canvass all levels of government to determine what social and educational programs relating to the problems surrounding pornography and prostitution are presently in place;
  (b) Establish federal-provincial task forces on various elements of the social problems associated with pornography and prostitution to develop working papers on those problems and approaches to them.

We have made a number of recommendations which will require effective and co-ordinated effort by all levels of government to ensure their implementation.

Our recommendations are directed to a wide variety of government departments and their agencies which have a coincidental interest in both the causes and effects of pornography and prostitution. There is currently such a diffusion of interest and effort that one of our tasks has been simply to identify who is involved and in what role.

A number of federal government departments are concerned with the social, legal and remedial aspects of both problems. The Department of Justice and the Ministry of the Solicitor General share the principal responsibility for the enactment and enforcement of laws. The Departments of National Revenue, Communications and the Ministry responsible for the Canada Post Corporation administer legislation which regulates the flow and distribution of material and electronic communication into and throughout Canada. The regulatory agencies they use include Canada Customs, the Canadian Radio-

Television and Telecommunications Commission, and Canada Post Corporation. The following other federal departments are interested in both the social causes and consequences of pornography and prostitution:

The Department of National Health and Welfare
The Ministry Responsible for the Status of Women
The Department of Employment and Immigration
The Department of Labour
The Department of Youth
The Secretary of State

At various places in this Report we have described both the specific and integrated roles played by these several federal departments and agencies. We have described what we have been able to find out about areas where there has been and continues to be inter- and intra-departmental co-operation. With some exceptions, we have found that the diffusion of interests has led to an almost complete decentralization of response at the federal level.

The departments and agencies of the provinces and their municipalities are also currently involved in the effort to deal with the social phenomena of pornography and prostitution. During our public hearings we were told about various local initiatives taken by both concerned governments and citizens. The programs are so numerous and so disparate that we will not attempt to describe them. Suffice it to say that we found the same decentralization that exists nationally to be present in the provinces and municipalities.

Agencies and organizations in the private sector play an important role in the educational and remedial aspects of the problems associated with pornography and prostitution. It is essential not only that new initiatives in the private sector be encouraged, but also that the development of those private organizations already established, be fostered.

If we are going to have any chance for real progress in dealing with both the causes and effects of pornography and prostitution, it will be because all members of the Canadian community want there to be progress. It will be necessary to include all members of the community in the work that must be done to find solutions. If some members of the community are excluded or are allowed to excuse themselves from the debate, an opportunity will be lost. One way of involving the community is to encourage private foundations, trusts and charities to play a larger role in providing services.

These charitable institutions have already made distinguished contributions to our country. They have undertaken projects and have supplied services and facilities that governments either cannot or will not. Private charitable institutions have a long history of helping children.

It is fine for a committee such as ours to recommend increased government funding for what we are convinced is an urgent cause. But, we can hardly expect that our commitment to these issues soon become the commitment of government. Not because the government is mean or will refuse to listen, but because the public purse is limited and there are many calls on the public list of priorities.

For all of these reasons we are of the view that tax incentives and concessions to those of our private and corporate citizens who may be eager to help fund the kind of effort we recommend will result in more happening and sooner.

There will always, of course, be a primary obligation on all levels of government. It is, of course, to be expected that all those concerned with the problems have so far responded to the acknowledged need for action in a way that reflects their particular interest. Because of the community of interest that exists, however, there has been some sensible sharing of information and effort. Nevertheless, it is apparent that much more can and should be done to strategically plan and co-ordinate efforts by all those who clearly have a stake in both understanding the need for concerted action and in designing programs and initiatives.

Canadians are clearly expecting as much. Many of the hundreds of people who came to the Committee's public discussions, expressed an animated urgency about both these subjects. They wanted better co-operation within government, better organization of effort and better execution and results. There were the inevitable, although genuine, complaints about lack of funding and misdirected government priorities, but what is more important, they complained about hesitation and inertia in both law enforcement and remedial treatment, two areas where governments have the principal roles to play. These complaints were usually accompanied by the suggestion that the purpose of government needs to be better understood and that the efforts of the various departments could be much better co-ordinated.

How can these complaints, concerns, and suggestions be translated into accomplishment?

First and most obvious is the requirement that there be actual consultation between governments. That may seem a benign suggestion, but the fact is that there has not been much consultation so far in these areas. It may be true that Canadians have an almost unparalleled belief in the consultative process. If that is so, it is because we have learned to talk and to listen to one another. That is how we have tried to manage both the duality and plurality of this country, and it is the only way that we have been able to make sure that our regional and cultural diversity helps to unite the country rather than divide it. Increased formal consultation about pornography and prostitution clearly must take place, early and often.

Talking and listening are only a prelude to effective ultimate action. While there is a continuing need for decentralized effort, there must be some better centralization of planning and purpose. We think, therefore, that a Secretariat should be established to ensure that urgent steps are taken to consider and to co-ordinate the various interests involved.

In our view, the Secretariat should be established under the joint aegis of the federal Departments of Justice, the Solicitor General and Health and Welfare. While the Secretariat should report to these three sponsoring departments, we think that it should include representatives from other relevant federal and provincial governments and agencies, as well as interested members of the public. Such broad membership is necessary not just to ensure that all interests are represented, but also to make sure that there is a broad base of both support and response.

We expect that separate task forces would have to be created to deal with particular aspects of the Secretariat's work. Some examples of the wide variety of activity to be undertaken are services for young people, co-ordinated investigation techniques, and education and employment opportunities for those wanting to join the work force.

The Secretariat could quickly begin its work by canvassing all levels of government to determine what relevant programs are presently in place where information and experience either is being or could usefully be shared. The Secretariat could then determine its priorities for the first two years of its operation and ensure that those priorities are published and understood across the country.

We would hope that by publishing annual reports, the Secretariat could maintain contact with the public and promote response. We also think that from time to time, the Secretariat would benefit from public participation at well structured symposia where its work and continuing priorities could be reviewed and critically assessed.

It is our hope that the Secretariat will be a co-ordinating vehicle accountable for specific programs, rather than the random arrangements that now exist. Canadians are anxious to have not only a better understanding of what problems we face and why, but also to know that something is actually being done to achieve tangible progress.

Recommendation 102

Federal, provincial and territorial governments should reaffirm their commitment to providing an environment where all children have the opportunity to develop to the fullest extent, their intellectual, physical and spiritual attributes. To this end, the Secretariat proposed in this Report should give high priority to issues affecting children and young people.

Recommendation 103

The federal government should collaborate with and assist the provinces, territories and private organizations and agencies in the development of educational programs for children, and those with special responsibilities for the welfare of children, in the areas of family life, human sexuality and media literacy.

Recommendation 104

Provincial and territorial governments should give high priority to programs in family life, human sexuality and media literacy at all levels within the school system.

Recommendation 105

The federal government should collaborate with and assist the provinces, territories, and private organizations and agencies in assessing the effectiveness of social service programs designed to assist children and young people, in developing new programs and in implementing changes designed to better meet the needs and current realities of young people in the 1980's and 1990's.

Appendix

The Committee received submissions both at the public hearings and by mail. The following is a list of those groups and individuals who submitted briefs. The list is presented in the order in which the public hearings were held. Non-appearing submissions are listed in accordance with their place of origin and are shown below the names of those who made presentations at the hearings.

Many other people sent letters to the Committee. We are not able to acknowledge all of those correspondents here, and can only thank them as a group for their interest.

APPENDIX

EDMONTON, ALBERTA

January 9, 1984

Presentation by:

Every Woman's Place	Christine Kulyk
The Ukranian Catholic Women's League of Canada (Edmonton Eparchy)	Catharine Chickak Adlynn Hewitt, Q.C.
University Women's Club of Edmonton	Tammy Irwin
Herbert Presley Mark Pickup	
Across-Canada	Shirley Krause
Ross Olsen	
Ukranian Women's Association of Canada	Helen Raycheba
Dave Billington (The Edmonton Sun)	
The Ecumenical Women's Group of Edmonton	Jean Armstrong
City Centre Association	Maury G. Van Vliet, Chairman
Roy Piepenburg	
Concerned Citizens on Pornography and Prostitution	Manfred Lucat
Alberta Human Rights Assoc.	Allan Welsh
Pornography Action Committee	Tina Rogers Chairperson

Edmonton Local Council of Women	Olga Cylurik, President
Mair Smith, "Violent Response to a Violent Issue", Webspinner, December, 1983	
Alberta MacKenzie Council of the Catholic Women's League of Canada	Rose-Marie McCarthy
Alberta Federation of Women United for Families	Jean Takahashi Joanne Lewicky Kathleen Higgins
Il Nuovo Mondo	Janak Advani, Editor
Women's Section, Alberta NDP	Starr Curry Terry Hatrichuk
Alliance Against Sexual Harassment	Mary Hickmore

Non-Appearing Submissions:

Alberta Women's Institutes	Kay Rowbottom, President Aileen Kritzinger Beryl Ballhorn Olive Meyer
Alberta Association of Registered Nurses	Beverly Anderson Arnette Anderson Jeanette Boman Joyce Relyea An Ad Hoc Committee of the A.A.R.N. Provincial Council
Laurence Decore, Mayor	Supported by: City of Edmonton Police Local Board of Health Edmonton Social Services Edmonton Public Library Edmonton Separate School Board Edmonton Public School Board
Don Burdego President, Board of Directors Boys' and Girls' Clubs of Edmonton	
Edmonton Women's Shelter Ltd.	Mary F. Weir, President
La Fédération des femmes cana-diennes-françaises	Églande Mercier President

| Edmonton Federation of Community Leagues | Arlene Meldrum, Chairman Ad Hoc Committee |

CALGARY, ALBERTA

January 9, 1984

Presentation by:

Calgary Police Commission	Brian E. Scott, Chairman Inspector Frank Mitchell Staff Sergeant Boiteau
Calgary Media Watch	Dr. Maria Ericksen
Calgary Y.W.C.A.	Felicia Melnyk Pat Cooper Janice Sich-Thompson Prof. Kathleen Mahoney Lee Kasdorf
J.W.S. Smyth	Private Citizen (former member of R.C.M.P.)
Brothers & Sisters in Christ	Bart Craig
Calgary Status of Women	Lynne Fraser Cheryl Kehoe
Darwin Cronkhite	
Dr. John Heintz	Philosophy Department University of Calgary

CALGARY, ALBERTA

January 10, 1984

Presentation by:

Calgary Local Council of Women	Dorothy Groves Donalda Vine
Fred Wagner "Your Choice" Video Service	
Kathleen Gilbert	
Susan Morgan	

Deborah Carnat

University Women's Club of Calgary   Lois Cummings
                                          Janice Hecht

Gordie Lagore
Calgary Christian Centre

Calgary Free Presbyterian Church   Thomas Tice — Minister
                                          Darrell Urushi

Henry Nielsen

Calgary Evangelical   Rev. Alan Dunbar
Ministerial Association

Annette Lengyel

Darrell Uruski

Gary Duffy

Non-Appearing Submissions

Hugh Jones

Council for the Family   Ardis Beaudry

Laura Henkel

Family Resource Centre
of the Roman Catholic
Diocese of Calgary

VANCOUVER, BRITISH COLUMBIA

January 11, 1984

Presentation by:

Rental Housing Council of B.C.   J.L. Hayes, Executive Director

City of Vancouver —   May Brown
Submission by Alderman   Terry Bland, City Solicitor
May Brown

The West End Seniors' Network   Catherine B. Jensen

St. Andrew's - Wesley Church   Bob Shank, Senior Minister
                                          George Balfour, Board Chairman

Vancouver Archdiocesan Council   Rose Kamm
Catholic Women's League

714

W.E.D.N.E.S.D.A.Y. (West End Dedicated Neighbours Emphasizing Solutions Designed Around You)	Howard Faulkner
Vancouver Multicultural Women's Association Chris J. Garside	Deletia Crump Mary Lakes
Pat Carney, M.P.	Donna MacKie, President Vancouver Centre Riding Association
C.R.O.W.E. (Concerned Residents of the West End)	Gerry Stafford Davis & Company Elliott Myers Glen Tynan Howard La Favor Heinz Brett Barbara Brett
West End Community	Gordon Price
Gordon Neighbourhood House	Richard P. Morley

VANCOUVER, BRITISH COLUMBIA

January 12, 1984

Presentation by:

British Columbia Hotels' Association	Virginia Engel Boughton & Co., Barristers
Group of Concerned Social Workers	David Butcher
Cecilia von Dehn	Private Citizen
Eleanor Hadley	Private Citizen
N.D.P. Women's Rights Committee	Joan Smallwood, Chairman Margaret Birrell
Women Against Pornography (Victoria)	Jan Boudelier Teresa Sankey Pam Blackstone
B.C. Civil Liberties Association	Dr. Alister Brown Dr. David Copp Non-written brief

First United Church	Barry Morris
	Linda Irvin
	Alan Alvare
	Leslie Black
Sam Campbell	Street Worker
Nancy Morrison (Lawyer)	
Hospital Employees Union, St. Paul's Unit	Raimo Hietakangas
	Marie Hietakangas
West End Community Advisory Council	Peter Westlake
	Carole McIntyre
West End Traffic Committee	Carole Walker
Terrence Bland, Vancouver Corporation Counsel	

Non-Appearing Submissions:

Mary Lakes

Raymond Lee

B.C. Conference of the
United Church of Canada

VANCOUVER, BRITISH COLUMBIA

January 13, 1984

Presentation by:

West End Tenants' Association	Greg Richmond, Project Director
	Anna Snelling, Treasurer
Tom Vikander	
Amelia Alvarez	
Nancy Tillson	
Georgia Hotel	Lee Cusak, General Manager
Vancouver Status of Women	Lorri Rudland, Researcher

Group of Clergy	Rev. Jeremy Bell Endorsed by: — 7 Signatures of Concerned Individuals
Frederick Gilbertson Content Co-ordinator of "Angles" Magazine	
Nona Thompson Founder of "Step Up" School	
Arleigh Haynes	
R. Burda	
Vic Redmond	
Vancouver Council of Women	Margaret Piggot
Larry Splanna	
Rick Smith	
Harry Rankin	Vancouver Alderman; former head, L.S.B.S.

Non-Appearing Submissions:

Brig Anderson and Concerned Women	
Alliance for the Safety of Prostitutes (A.S.P.)	Marie Arrington Sally de Quadros

TORONTO, ONTARIO

February 6, 1984

Presentation by:

Mayor Art Eggleton City of Toronto	Mary Lunch, Executive Director Patricia McCarney Research Associate
Roman Catholic Archdiocese of Toronto	Dr. Suzanne Scorsone, Office of Catholic Family Life
Glad Day Bookshop	Paul Jenkins and Jerald Moldenhauer
Canadians for Decency	Nancy Pollock

Canadian Organization for the Rights of Prostitutes (Toronto Chapter)	Peggy Miller
National Action Committee on the Status of Women	Doris Anderson Kathy Coffin Jillian Riddington
Libertarian Party of Canada	Paul Vesa
The Pentecostal Assemblies of Canada	Rev. Hudson T. Hilsden On behalf of: —Members and adherents 155,000 in 970 local congregations and Pentecostal Assemblies of Canada with additional 30,000 members and adherents in 160 churches
David Crombie, M.P.	

P.O.I.N.T. (People and Organizations in North Toronto)	Freda Finlay
	Marion Langford
	Roberta McFadden
	  Members:
	  Ann Barrett
	  Marilyn Cullum
	  Anne Gordon
	  Mandy Macrae
	  Roberta McFadden
	  A. Cecila Pope

Toronto Area Caucus of Women and the Law	Reva Landau Stephanie Holbik Marla S. Kelhorne Mary Lou Fassel

Esther Harshaw with 176 Supporting Signatures	Esther Harshaw, Trustee
	Ward 10, Toronto Board of Education
	Co-Sponsored by:
	  North Rosedale Ratepayers' Association
	  Rosedale United Church with support and co-operation of other local concerned groups

Non-Appearing Submissions:

P. van Lammers, Chairman
Advocacy Committee, Ontario Association of Family Service Agencies

Jean Fenton (Oakville)

Fred Light (Nepean)

John Mascotto (Geraldtown)

James Savage (Kendal)

TORONTO, ONTARIO

February 7, 1984

Presentation by:

Helen Porter

Right to Privacy Committee	George W. Smith
Canadian Federation of University Women, Metro Toronto Clubs	Elizabeth Tugman Shirley Sims Carolyne Keene (Representatives of nine Metro Toronto University Women's Clubs with combined membership of approximately 2,500 women).
United Church of Canada, Division of Mission	Joanne Fairhart Liz McCloy Rev. Peter Wyatt Jean Westney Ruth Evans
Rosedale Church Group and Public Health Nurses Group	Patricia Fenton President, UCW Rosedale United Church Petition of 95 names in support. 11 Public Health Nurses Signatures
Alderman, Ward 6, Jack Layton	
Elizabeth Fry Society of Toronto	Nina Quinn
Metro Toronto Board of Commissioners of Police	N. Jane Pepino Membership: Doris Anderson John Bousfield Inspector Jean Boyd Austin Cooper Trudy Don

Norm Gardner
Jo-anne Grayson
Mary Hall
Sgt. Jackie Hobbs
Burthe Jorgenson
Dr. Pat Kincaid
Pat Marshall
Debbie Parent
Judith Ramirez
Dr. Gail Robinson
Marlaina Sniderman
Jan Tennant

Task Force on Public Violence
Against Women and Children

Jane Pepino
Marilou McPhedran
June Rowlands
Stephen Watt

Alderman June Rowlands

Pink Ink

Gary Kinsman

Film and Video Against Censorship
Statement

Varda Burstyn

Y.W.C.A. of Metropolitan Toronto

Denise Gardian
Francis Hogg
—Metro Task Force on Public Vio-
   lence Against Women and Children
—Toronto Area Caucus of Women
   and the Law
—Judy Campbell
—Wendy King
—Lisa Freedman
—Marilou Fassel
—Reva Landau
—Stephanie Holbick
—Linda Patton

Dahn Batchelor, Criminologist

Carl E. Beigie
Ellen G. Shapiro

The Body Politic

Christine Bearchell, Co-Editor

Non-Appearing Submissions:

Candace Woolley, M.S.W.
Eganville, Ontario

720

The Ontario Film & Video Appreciation Society	Malcolm Dean
Freedom of Expression Committee	Catharine Wismer, Chairman
Y.W.C.A. of Canada	Vera de Bues
Alan V. Miller	

TORONTO, ONTARIO

February 8, 1984

Presentation by:

Alderman Ann Johnston	Ward 11 — Toronto — "Comments reflecting views expressed to [her] by people who [she] has been elected to represent"
A.C.T.R.A.	Alex Barris, V.P. Paul Siren Arden Ryshpan Colleen Murphy Michael Mercer Ronald Lieberman
Ontario Liberal Party	David R. Peterson, M.P.P. Terry Kirk
Toronto Residents on Street Soliciting (T.R.O.S.S.)	Christopher Bolton Haney Tom Morris L. Castonquay Shirley Krause (spokesperson for Alliance of Concerned Residents on Street Soliciting A.C.R.O.S.S.) —over 80 names of representatives and organizations; and private and public companies
David Scott	Action Group on Media Pornography Canadian Coalition against Violent Entertainment National Coalition on Television Violence
R.E.A.L. Women of Canada	Jean Murphy Gwen Landolt

Susan Cole

Evangelical Fellowship of Canada	Rev. Brian C. Shiller
The Anglican Diocese of Toronto	Rev. Arthur Brown, Bishop
Girl Guides of Canada	Joan Howell Sheila Crosby
Salvation Army, Toronto	Major Russell Hicks Major Ruth Meakings Major Maxwell Ryan J. Ellery
Seneca College Women's Caucus	Sarah Kelley
B'Nai Brith Women of Canada	Sharron Tenhouse Selma Sage

John Lee
Prof. of Scarborough College

TORONTO, ONTARIO

Non-Appearing Submissions:

Ontario Committee on the Status of Women	Helen Findlay Lee Grills for the Steering Committee
Viking Houses	David M. Aird, M.E.D. Executive Director
Federation of Women Teachers' Associations of Ontario	Representing 31,000 women who teach in Ontario

Mary Brown, Director,
Ontario Film Review Board

Rev. Brad Massman

Rose Dyson

St. John's Prayer Group Community, Newmarket	—Endorsed by 16 signatures

Wilma Voortman

Harold Backer

Valerie M. Perkins

Mike van Dyke (Brockville)

Joan B. Getson (Dryden, Ontario)

B.L. Lavieille (Willowdale)

Leslie Lawlor
Board of Directors,
Education Wife Assault
Margaret Smith
Barbara Waisberg

Frank G. Sommers, M.D.

The Action Learning Group on
Pornography
Jon Arnold
Michael Bach
Adrienne Braitmann
David Hunwicks
Shirley Perry
Sue Wilson

The Board of Directors of Catholic
Family Services of Toronto
William Howlett, President

Réseau des femmes du sud de
l'Ontario,
Sous-comité sur la violence

Toronto Spokespersons for Commit-
tee Against Pornography
Reva Landau
Jean Westney
Denise Gardian

Stephen G. McLaughlin, Commis-
sioner
City of Toronto
Planning & Development Department

The Writers' Union of Canada
Penny Dickens, Executive Director

Additional Ontario Submissions:

Dr. J. Lamont
McMaster University

Council of Christian Reformed   Rev. A.G. Van Eek
Churches in Canada

D. L. Valentine

Chris Asseff
Executive Director
Ontario Separate School
    Trustees' Association

Diana Cherry

Women of Halton Action Movement
Helen Vaccaro

Prof. T.C. Jarvie
York University

Prof. L. Groake
Philosophy Dept.,
Sir Wilfred Laurier University

John Osborne
Campaign "P"

Tony Matrosous

F. Schultz-Lorentzen

LONDON, ONTARIO

February 9, 1984

Presentation by:

The National Council of Women of Canada	Margaret McGee
Marc Emery, Publisher of London Metro Bulletin	
Clarke Leverette (Librarian and Small Press Publisher)	
The Catholic Women's League of Canada, London Diocesan Council	Muriel Murphy
The Executive of London Conference of the United Church of Canada	Susan Eagle
Robert Metz, President of Freedom Party of Ontario	

724

Students from the Faculty of Law, University of Western Ontario	Elaine Deluzio Sharyn Langdon Barbara Boake Michele Dodick Susan Sleman (Non-Appearing Co-Authors Jasmine Belis Helen Brooks)
Prof. Constance Backhouse Faculty of Law, University of Western Ontario	
London Status of Women Action Group	Erin Hewitt, M.A. Gail Hutchinson, Ph.D Marion Gerull, B.A.A. Peggy Jurimae, B.A.
Citizens for Decent Literature	J.K. MacKenzie Various written comments from concerned citizens from London and area —Signatures totalling 1,069 names
Citizens Concerned for Community Values	Rev. J. Kirk Rev. Alan Ahlgrim S. Blanken Rev. L.D. Campbell Rev. J. Crumpler Monty Lobb Rev. Clyde Miller Rev. Hugh Rosenberg Rev. Harold Russell Rev. E.O. Thomas Cathy Woods
Central Committee of Catholic Women's League of Canada, London	Sheila M. Coughlan (Representing approximately 1,719 women)
Prof. W.K. Fisher, Department of Psychology, University of Western Ontario	
Stephen Males	
Donald Huffman, Jr. Port Elgin, Ontario	
Anglican Diocese of Huron	John J. Robinson (on behalf of 90,000 active members of Anglican Diocese of Huron)

Uniondale Women's Institute	Irene Robinson, President
	Robert Smith, Secretary
St. Mary's (Ont.) Coalition	Margaret McBride
Against Pornography	Kathy Monks-Leason
B.H. Barrett	
Nancy Muller and	
S. Muller	

Non-Appearing Submissions:

The Church in Society Committee of the Middlesex Presbyterial United Church Women	Joan Mitchell
	Bernice Santor
	Marie Campbell
	Phyllis Hanna
	Endorsed by a Petition
	totalling 143 signatures
D.B. Andrews, Superintendent Criminal Investigation Division	
Doris Moore for P.C. McNorgan City Clerk	

NIAGARA FALLS, ONTARIO

February 9, 1984

Presentation by:

Catholic Women's League of Canada	Jacqueline Herman
	Janice DesLauriers
	Verna Morgan
	Vivian Malouin
	Joan Bell
	Barbara Telesnicki
Social Planning Council of Niagara Falls	John Walker
	Study Group:
	John Carson
	Isabelle Boild
	Gary H. Enskat
	Dr. Keith Knill
	Dianne Sheppard
	Emma Spironella
	Stacey Schmagala

Positive Action Committee	Michael Halle
Downtown Board of Management	Mark McCombs
C.A.R.S.A. Inc., Niagara Region Sexual Assault Centre	Cindy Davis
Ed Mitchelson	
Patrick Cummings, Acting Mayor of Niagara Falls	Endorsed by: Donald Harris, Chief of Police
Superintendent of Police	James Moody Also Brief by: Sgt. George McGloin Cst. Kenneth Conhiser
Local Council of Women	Margaret Harrington
Thomas Prues League	
Chamber of Commerce	Bill Thompson, President
Joe Hueglin, M.P.	Michael Halle
The Federal Progressive Conservative Women's Caucus of Niagara Falls	Bonnie Gillings

Non-Appearing Submissions:

Lioness Club of Georgetown	Endorsed by: Signatures of 23 members

WINDSOR, ONTARIO

February 10, 1984

Presentation by:

The Salvation Army	Capt. William Blackman Capt. Neil Watt Lt. Aldo Di Giovanni
Windsor Coalition Against Pornography	Anne McIntyre Rose Voyvodic Sheelagh Conway Lenore Langs Maryellen MacGuigan
Students for the University of Windsor School of Social Work, Human	Rose De Rosa Antoinette De Troia

Sexuality Course of Dr. Kumar Chatterjee

Michelle Goudreau
John Loewen
Kathy Moran
(Including 158 additional
University of Windsor
Students, Non-Appearing)

James Meredith

Rev. Donald Bardwell
(Chalmers United Church)

The Elizabeth Fry Society
of Kingston

Felicity Hawthorn
Liz Elliot

The Catholic Women's League of
Canada (London Diocese)

Betty Scherer

Ian Benson (Law Student)

MONTRÉAL, QUÉBEC

February 27, 1984

Presentation by:

Concordia (University)
Women's Collective

Dame Maria Peluso
Students:
   Isabel Bliss
   Joanne Poirier
   Leeanne Francine
   Catherine Easels

Denis Côté

Service de police de la Communauté
urbaine de Montréal

André DeLuca, directeur
Guy LaFrance, avocat

Centre de services sociaux
Ville-Marie

Laurier Boucher
Mike Godman
Kathy Faludi

Suzanne de Rosa

Rassemblement des citoyens et
citoyennes de Montréal

Jean Doré, President
Cathleen Verdun
John Gardiner
Barbara Carie

Centre de recherche — Action sur les
relations raciales

Fo Niemi,
Executive Director
Kevin Cadloff, Legal Counsel

Ben Wilson-Williams

Normand Montminy

Judith Dobbie

Non-Appearing Submissions:

Le Comité de la protection de la jeunesse	Tellier Béranger
Mayor Drapeau, Mᶜ Allard, Mᶜ Laliberté for City of Montreal	
Canada Customs from Montréal	Vital Marin Roger Barron
Montreal Citizenship Council	Margaret A. Dvorsky, President
Eastern Orthodox Clergy Association	Archpriest Antony Gabriel, President
La Fédération des Unions de familles Inc.	André Buhl Président

Marielle Landry, Présidente
Comité d'Information et d'action
anti-pornographie

MONTRÉAL, QUÉBEC

February 28, 1984

Presentation by:

Bruno Tousignant Proprietor of Club Video Fantastique	
Regroupement féministe contre la pornographie	Diane Bronson Élise Massicotte
Dame Monica Matte	
La Fédération des femmes du Québec	Ginette Busque Suzanne De Rosa Noëlle-Dominique Willems
Conseil de la Famille Richelieu - Yamaska	Helen Petit Pierrette Perreault

729

Le Conseil des femmes de Montréal	Emily Dubé Aimée Williams
Fraternité des policiers de la Communauté urbaine de Montréal Inc.	Réal Déry Gilles Massé Président
Association nationale de la femme et le droit	Suzanne Boivin

Sabrina Vézina

Jacques Cimon

Le centre des services sociaux du Montréal métropolitain	Thérèse Wiss Thérèse Johnson Denis Ménard
L'Association féminine d'éducation et d'action sociale	Lise Paquette Lise Houle Johanne Des Rosiers Alice Buttel

Eric Johnson

Diane De Rase Bonne

MONTRÉAL, QUÉBEC

February 29, 1984

Presentation by:

Deborah Seed
Department of Humanities
John Abbott College
	Endorsed by:
	  Alan Silverman
	  Renée Lallier
	  Patricia McGraw
	  Sharon Rozen-Aspler
	  Marcia Kovitz
	  Bert Young
	  Carolyn Henderson

Collectif masculin contre le sexisme	Alan Besré Denis Laplante
Emergency Committee of Gay Cultural Workers Against Obscenity Laws	Thomas Waugh Jose Arroyo

Elana Medicoff

Montreal Actra Women's Caucus

Linda Lee Tracy
Ardyn Rishpan
Kelly Ricard

Comité des ex-détenues

Marcelle Grondine

Jean-François Larose

Fernand Tremblay

Marcelle Brisson
Professeur au C.E.G.E.P. Ahuntsic

Non-Appearing Submissions:

Comité contre la pornographie à
Ripon

Dame Nathalie Duetam
El Mascotto

L.S. Jayasooriya

Women's Collective to Overthrow the
Patriarchy

Cécile Richard
Adjointe administrative

André Guérin
Président du Bureau de surveillance
du cinéma et directeur de l'Office du
film du Québec

Stuart Russell

Germain Trottier
Prof., Laval University

Women Against Pornography

Beabea Jones

Comité de lutte
contre la pornographie
de Châteauguay

Alice Herscovitch
Nicole Ladouceur
Marjolaine Dufort
Christine Poirier
Denise Filion
Louise Dufort
Patricia Gauthier
Michelle Lalonde

SHERBROOKE, QUÉBEC

March 1,1984

Presentation by:

Lennoxville and District   Rina Kampeas
Women's Centre

L'Escale de L'Estrie Inc.   Danielle Houle
                                   Dominique Gagné

Le Centre d'Aide et de Lutte contre   Diane Lemieux
les agressions à caractère
sexuel, au nom du Regroupement
québécois des Centres d'Aide et de
lutte contre les agressions à caractère
sexuel

L'Association féminine   Pauline Paradis
d'éducation et d'action sociale,
région de Sherbrooke

Pierre Gagné
Head of Psychiatry,
Sherbrooke Hospital

Arlene and Pierre Schiettekatte

Professor René Turcotte
Faculty of Law
University of Sherbrooke

VAL D'OR, QUÉBEC

March 1, 1984

Presentation by:

Les femmes de Senneterre   G. Trudel
                                  Martine Gendron
                                  (No Written Brief)

La cause d'elle   A.M. Bebard
                                  M. St-Germain

Knights of Columbus   Ivan Boucher
                                  Edgar Wait

Le Collectif "Alternative   Mychèle Balthazard
pour elles" de Rouyn-Noranda   Chantal Genesse

	Carole Bouffard
	Denise Stewart
	Marie Brunelle
	Louise Delisle
U.Q.A.T. La Sarre	Serge Tessier
	Suzanne Baril-Lavigne
	Ghislaine Camirand
	Solange Morin-Lavoie
	Michel O'Dowd
	Madeleine Paré
	Danielle Simard-Gagnon
Pétition des femmes de l'Abitibi-Témiscamingue	Endorsed by:
Madeleine Lévesque	Signatures of 432 Concerned Citizens
Mission Pentecôte	Bruce Muirhead
Groupe Renaissance	Normand Tremblay

QUÉBEC CITY, QUÉBEC

March 2, 1984

Presentation by:

Le regroupement des femmes de la région de Québec contre la pornographie	Diane Grenier
Le groupe d'hommes contre la pornographie et l'exploitation sexuelle	Jean Lemarre
La Fédération des femmes du Québec, Conseil régional Saguenay Brief and Annexes	Marthe Vaillancourt Antoinette Dubé
Paul Beaulé	
L'Armée du Salut de la Ville de Québec	Major Stuart Booth Major S.W. Booth Joy Rennick Arthur R. Pitcher
Le Réseau d'Action et d'Information pour des femmes (R.A.I.F.)	Marcelle Dolment

Pierre Maranda
Nicole Coquatrix
Laval University

Le groupe d'hommes contre   Geoffrey Edwards
la pornographie et
l'exploitation sexuelle

Roger Delorme

Camil Aubin

Non-Appearing Submissions:

Fran Shaver
Research Consultant
Laval, Quebec

Robert Dufault

CHARLOTTETOWN, PRINCE EDWARD ISLAND

May 7, 1984

Presentation by:

Media Watch, P.E.I.	Margaret Ashford
Canadian Congress for Learning Opportunities For Women (C.C.L.O.W.)	Bea Mair John MacFarlane Heather Orford (Director C.C.L.O.W.)
Transition House Association	Joanne Engs
P.E.I. Women's Liberal Association	Dorothy MacKay
Canadian Federation of University Women	Daphné Dumont
Charlottetown Business and Professional Women's Club	Evelyn Matheson
Federated Women's Institute of P.E.I.	Doris Worth
Ad Hoc Committee on Pornography	Janice Devine
The Advisory Council on the Status of Women of P.E.I.	Delores Crane Ruth Power

734

Catholic Women's League	Mona Doiron
	Rev. Wendell MacIntyre
	Phyllis Quinn
	Elaine Gallant
	Helen Macisaac

Non-Appearing Submissions:

Beth Percival, Ph.D.
University of P.E.I.
Charlottetown, P.E.I.

VICTORIA, BRITISH COLUMBIA

April 2, 1984

Presentation by:

Rosemary Brown, M.L.A., Brief

| City of Victoria | Alderman Gretchen Brewin |
| | Georgene Glover |

| Canadian Federation of University of Women - and - | Margaret Strongitharm |

| The University Women's Club of Victoria | Sharon Vipond |
| | Victoria Pitt |

Prof. Charles B. Daniels,
Philosophy Dept.,
University of Victoria

People Opposed to Pornography	Janet M. Baird
	Lynne McFarlane
	Pat Webber
	Endorsed by 7 Signatures of Concerned Citizens

Anglican Diocese of B.C., Diocesan Program Committee	Gregg Perry
	Dianne Taylor
	Maureen Franks
	Endorsed by:
	H.J. Jones, Bishop and Executive Council of the Anglican Diocese of B.C.

Women Against Pornography	Susan Isomaa
	Pam Blackstone
	Rebecca Pazdro

735

Laurence E. Devlin
Brishkai Luna

Victoria Status of Women Action Group	Avis Rasmussen Diana Butler Josephine Adams Shirley Avril Office Coordinator
B.C. Public Interest Research Group	Alison LeDuc Mercia Stickney
Vancouver Island Co-Operative Pre-School Association	Jack Dorgan
Concerned Citizens Action Group Against Pornography	Murray and Rita Coulter

Dorothy Smith

B.C. Association of Social Workers	Chris Walmsley Jocelyn Gifford

Non-Appearing Submissions:

Catholic Women's League
Sacred Heart Council
Victoria, B.C.

Police Perspective on Prostitution and Soliciting	Supt. D.E. Richardson

Anthony Burke
Victoria Civil Liberties Association

Raymond Lee

B.C. Conference of the United
Church of Canada

VANCOUVER, BRITISH COLUMBIA

April 3, 1984

Presentation by:

City of Vancouver	Mayor Mike Harcourt Alderman Libby Davies Chris Warren, Social Planning Council

B.C. Civil Liberties Association	Dr. John Dixon Dr. Bob Rowan
Red Hot Video Ltd.	Mark Dwor, Counsel
Working Group on Sexual Violence	Francis Warrerlein Kate Andrew
British Columbia Teachers' Association	Jane MacEwan Marcia Toms
Jancis Andrews	Brief Sponsored by: 16 additional names and addresses of concerned citizens
Vancouver Status of Women	Pat Feindel
Vancouver Association of Women and the Law	Heather Holmes Linda King Laura Parkinson Deborah Strachan
Anglican Church of Canada, Diocese of New Westminster Task Force on Pornography	Margaret Marquardt
University Women's Club of Vancouver	Catherine A. Stevenson
Port Coquitlam Area Women's Centre	Karen Phillips
North Shore Women's Centre	Donna Stewart
United Citizens for Integrity	Rev. Bernice Gerard
West Kootenay Women's Assn.	Surindar Dhaliwal Rena Armstrong
Daryl Nelson C.R.O.W.E. (Concerned Residents of the West End)	Richard J. MacKinnon
Knights of Columbus, B.C. and Yukon State Council	
Vancouver Council of Women	Helen Totarek Margaret Pigott Pat Hutcheon Bernece Williams Doris Mellish
Vancouver Archdiocesan Council Catholic Women's League	Rose Kamm

737

University Women's Club of South
Delta

Media Watch

British Columbia Provincial Women's   Ruth Fenner
Institute

The Corporation of the District of   F.B. Durrand
Central Saanich

B.C. NDP Women's Rights
Committee

P. Condie

R. Moeliker

R.L. Stirling
Dept. of Consumer Affairs

National Watch on Images   Lucy Alderson
of Women in the Media Inc.   Project Coordinator

Brian D. Robertson

P. Susan Penfold
Assoc. Prof.
Division of Child Psychiatry

Linda King

REGINA, SASKATCHEWAN

April 4, 1984

Presentation by:

City of Saskatoon   Mary Cliff Wright
                                      Mayor Clifford

Alderman Donna Birkmaier,
Saskatoon

The Feminist Research Group   Mary Wilson
                                      Sally Chaster

Saskatchewan Action Committee on   Palma Anderson, President
the Status of Women   Arlene Franko
                                      Susan Duzl

Regina Council of Women	Marion Beck
	Jacquie Hogan
	Rita Labiola
Saskatoon Committee Against Pornography	Pat Lorje
Saskatchewan Federation of Women	Sally Hitchins
	Betty Lepke
Christian and Missionary Alliance Churches	Rev. Richard Sipley
Y.W.C.A. of Saskatoon	Ruth James
	Marie Dunn
	Gwen Anderson
	Marie Kiskchuk
Swift Current Council of Women et al	Jean E.M. Read
	Marlene Hoffert

Non-Appearing Submissions:

Ukranian Catholic Women's League of Canada	Adeline Dudar
	Jean Saran Chuk

WINNIPEG, MANITOBA

April 4, 1984

Presentation by:

Manitoba Action Committee on the Status of Women	Lydia Giles
	Caroline Garlich
	Penny Mitchell
	Pam Jackson
	Sherry Dangerfield
Y.W.C.A. of Winnipeg	Georgia Cordes
	Dale Unruh
	Bernice Sisler
Thunder Country Jaycees	Nancy Doetzel
The Children's Home of Winnipeg	Sel Burrows
	Vera Steinberger
	Linda Trigg
	(Social Policy Committee)
Catholic Women's League of Canada, National Council	Evelyn Wyrzykowski
Concerned Morality League	Bernadette Russell

Manitoba Advisory Council on the Status of Women	Jennifer Cooper Roberta Ellis
Men Against Sexism	Bruce Wood
Manitoba Women's Institute Brief prepared by:	Gwen Parker Louis Neabel
University Women's Club of Winnipeg	Susan Currie Nina C. Phillips, President
Communist Party of Canada	Paula Fletcher Manitoba Provincial Leader D. Davis Paul Madock
Inter-Agency Group	Clark Brownley Endorsed by: 18 Signatures from Concerned Citizens

Non-Appearing Submissions:

T.L. Coles, Instructor
Anthropology Dept.
University of Winnipeg

Don Mills, President
Manitoba Library Association

Elsie Jawolik

Robert Ellis, Chairperson
Manitoba Advisory Council
on the Status of Women

Stella Carson

Judy Holden
Public Affairs Chairman
Junior League of Winnipeg

REGINA, SASKATCHEWAN

April 5, 1984

Presentation by:

Regina Women's Centre and Sexual Assault Line	Abby Ulmer

740

Regina Evangelical Ministerial Association	Rev. Wayne Kerr Rev. Ross Ingram
Catholic Women's League of Canada, Saskatchewan Provincial Council	Claire Heron Fern Foster
Ernest Lyon Estevan, Saskatchewan	
Saskatchewan Human Rights Commission	Ron Kruzinski, Chief Commissioner Shelagh Day, Executive Director
Steve Selenski	
City of Regina	Mayor Larry Schneider Raymond Tessier
L.R.S.	Ron Richmond, Associate Prof. of Education University of Regina
Government of Saskatchewan	Hon. Pat Smith Hon. Gary Lane Hon. Gordon Dirks

Non-Appearing Submissions:

Jean Baptiste John L. de Bruyne	
Jean E.M. Reid	Endorsed by: List of 642 signatures from various organizations
Miron Balych	
Saskatchewan Women's Institutes	Margaret E. Peterson, Executive Secretary
Catholic Women's League of Canada	Evelyn Wyrzykowski
L.A. Copeland	
University of Regina Dr. Agnes Groom	
Lorraine Samborsky Canadian Federation of University Women	

741

WINNIPEG, MANITOBA

April 5, 1984

Presentation by:

Réseau — Janick Belleau

Wayne Sowden

Klinic, Inc. — Brenda L. Johnson

Manitoba Teacher's Society — Audrey Burchuk, Chairperson, Status of Women in Education Committee

ACTRA — Alice Porper
Edward Ledson
Brief by: Margaret Allan

Ukranian Canadian Women's Committee — Dorothy Cherwick, President
Vera Werbeniuk, President

Mother's Union of the Anglican Church of Canada — Marion Lepinsky, President

P. Snowdon

Non-Appearing Submissions:

Council of Women of Winnipeg — Rosemary Malahar, President

Seven Oaks School Division #10 — N.P. Isler

Manitoba Association for Rights and Liberties — J.J. van der Krabben, President

OTTAWA, ONTARIO

April 6, 1984

Presentation by:

Canadian Civil Liberties Association — Alan Borovoy General Counsel;
Prof. Louise Arbour, Board Member

City of Ottawa — Mayor Marion Dewar

Canadian Advisory Council on the Status of Women	Lucie Pepin, President; Jennifer Stoddart, Director of Research Merilee Stephenson, Chief Researcher
Periodical Distributors of Canada	Gerald Benjamin, President Ron Thomas, Counsel Tobi Levinson, Ontario Advisory Committee
Canadian Association of University Teachers	Dr. Sarah Shorten, President Dr. Donald Savage, Executive Director
Ontario Advisory Council on the Status of Women	Sheila Ward, Vice-President Gail Hutchinson
Dianne Kinnon Cynthia Manson	
Canadian Library Association	Paul Kitchen Lois M. Bewley, President
Canadian Conference of Catholic Bishops	Bishop James MacDonald
Public Service Alliance of Canada	Pierre Samson, President Bonnie Carroll Susan Kilpatrick Steven Chilkenny
Lynn McDonald, M.P.	
Video Retailers' Association	James Sintzel Kathleen Curry

Non-Appearing Submissions:

Mary Nickson, President Council of Women of Ottawa and Area	
The Canadian Home Economics Association	Diana Smith Executive Committee
Editorial Advisory Board Goodwin's Magazine	Donna Balkan

OTTAWA, ONTARIO

April 7, 1984

Presentation by:

Comité contre la pornographie à
Ripon

Nathalie Duhamel Mascotto

Federated Women's Institutes of
Canada

Alice McLaggan
Bernice B. Noblitt, President

Canadian Coalition Against
Media Pornography

Cynthia Wiggins, President
Rose Potvin

Canadian Teachers Federation

Brian Shortall, President
Dr. Stirling McDowell
Sylvia Gold

The Hastings-Prince Edward
County Roman Catholic
Separate School Board

Gerald Bibby, Chairman
Principals' Association
Sister Mary Joan

Gays of Ottawa

Blair Johnston
Barbara McIntosh

Group of Concerned Parents in
Ottawa

Bruce Pringle

Roots and Wings

Inez Berg

Non-Appearing Submissions:

Ottawa Women Fight Pornography
(OWFP)

Ottawa Council for Low Income
Support Services

Randal Marlin

Associate Prof. Carleton University

ST. JOHN'S, NEWFOUNDLAND

May 7, 1984

Presentation by:

Provincial Advisory Council
on the Status of Women,
Newfoundland and Labrador

Ann Bell, President
Dorothy Robbins
Jennifer Mercier

The Newfoundland Teachers' Association	Grace Howlitt Barbara Lewis
Citizens' Coalition Against Pornography	Dr. John Lewis Judy Facey
Community Against Pornography	Sharon Parsons-Chatman Cynthia O'Toole Joanne Cranston Kathy Porter
Dorothy Inglis Vice President N.A.C.	
Archdiocesan Pastoral Council Roman Catholic Diocese of St. John's Newfoundland	Sister Lorraine Michael Brian F. Furey

Newfoundland and Labrador
Women's Institutes
	Angela Sullivan —
	    1st Vice President
	Jennifer Perry —
	    Executive Director
	Patty Martin — Convener

The Salvation Army Newfoundland	Major Margaret Hammond
The Canadian Catholic School Trustees' Association	Molly Boucher Frank Furey
The Newfoundland Status of Women Council	Pauline Stockwood Beth Lacey

Newfoundland Provincial Council
Catholic Women's League of Canada
	Val McNiven
	    Catherine Power
	    J.W. Allen
	    Iris Kendall

Archdiocese of St. John's Family Life Bureau	Margaret Bruce Tom Milla

Non-Appearing Submissions

Cornerbrook Satus of Women Council	Marie Furlong-Bass
St. John's Status of Women Council	Judith Skidmore
Newfoundland and Labrador Women's Institutes	Jennifer Perry Executive Administrator

| Newfoundland Assoc. of Social Workers | Nancy Forsey
Wanda Lundrigan
Pres. N.A.S.W. |
| Newfoundland & Labrador Assoc. of Youth Serving Agencies | D. Paul Althouse, President |

FREDERICTON, NEW BRUNSWICK

May 8, 1984

Presentation by:

St. John and District Ministerial Association	Rev. Ramon Hunston Rev. Mel Norton Malcolm Berry Rev. Roy Campbell
Max M. Wolfe	
People Opposing Pornography	Timothy Johnson
La Fédération des dames d'Acadie	Rachel Guérette
Federation Clergy Council	Eleanor Johnson
Kathy Royama	
New Brunswick Advisory Council on the Status of Women	Madeline Le Blanc, Presidente Myrna Richards, Vice President Elspeth Tullock, Researcher
Carlton-Victoria Association of the United Baptist Churches	Rev. N.W. MacKenzie, Chairman Pastor Steven Mullin Margaret McIsaac
Saint John Deanery of the Anglican Diocese of Fredericton	Archdeacon Harry Quinn Rev. Christopher Pratt Endorsed by: Harold J. Nutter, Archbishop
Association des enseignants franco-phones du Nouveau-Brunswick	Rosemarie Coule, President Nicole Dupéré
Saint John Chapter, Canadian Federation of University Women	Jane Barry
Catholic Women's League New Brunswick	Rita Milner Kay Robinson

Arthur Standing

Tom Evans

Lea Robichaud

Non-Appearing Submissions:

Women's Institute   Bernice Noblitt, President
New Brunswick

Board of School Trustees   Anne Marie McGrath
School District Number 20   Assistant Superintendent

Asst. Superintendent   Dale Horncastle
Board of School Trustees

HALIFAX, NOVA SCOTIA

May 9, 1984

Presentation by:

Mayor Ron Wallace, Halifax

Atlantic Provinces Library   Terry Paris
Association   Andre Guay
                                            Elinor Benjamin
                                            Gerard Lavoie
                                            John Mercer
                                            Janet Phillipps

Prof. Richard Beis

Voice of Women of Nova Scotia   Elizabeth Mullaby

P.C. Women's Association of Nova   Gloria Marshall, President
Scotia

Nova Scotia Advisory Council on the   Francene Cosman, President
Status of Women

Downtown Halifax   Mila Riding
Residents' Association   Elizabeth Pam Piers
                                           Howard McNutt

Lloma Jane Chase

Le Conseil des Acadiennes   Alphosine Saulnier
de la Nouvelle-Écosse   Denise Sancon

747

Social Action Committee
Antigonish Women's Association

Donna Wallaver
  Lucille Sanderson
  Pat Halper

Non-Appearing Submissions

John Poag

St. John The Evangelist
Mothers' Union, Lower Sackville
Nova Scotia

Geraldine Connors

North End Area Council
Halifax

Family Life Council

Diocese of Nova Scotia
Rev. Lewis H. How

Dalhousie Legal Aid Service
C. Birnie

Gerald B. Freeman

J.W. Clattenberg
Municipal Clerk (Pictou)

Gilles G. LeBlanc

Dale Godsoe, President
Y.W.C.A.

Prof. John Fraser
Department of English
Dalhousie University

HALIFAX, NOVA SCOTIA

May 10, 1984

Presentation by:

R.C. Archdiocese of Halifax
Nova Scotia

Archbishop James M. Hughes

Pictou County Branch,
Canadian Federation of
University Women

Penny Mott
  Pamela MacDonald

Libby Fraser
Charmaine Wood

Endorsed by:
  Session J. Wesley
  Smith United Church
  Halifax

Robert Bean
Grant MacDonald
Neil Purcell
Ken Ward
Jim Drobnick
Jim McCalla Smith
Michael Welton
George Peabody
Doug Meggison
John Bouris
Steve Campbell

Student Union Women's Committee
Nova Scotia College of Art and
Design

Karen Fainman
Barbara Lounder
Liz MacDougall

Nova Scotia Association of Social
Workers

Freda Bradley
Norma Jean Profitt

Francene Cosman

Nova Scotia Branch
Canadian Research Institute for the
Advancement of Women

Barbara Cottrell
Adele McSorley
Susan Shaw

Prof. Clare F. Beckton

Planned Parenthood of Nova Scotia

Katherine McDonald, President
Mary Hamblin,
Executive Director
Endorsed by:
  Marilyn R. Peers
  C.A.S. of Halifax

Group from Atlantic School of
Theology

Gordon MacDermott
Joyce Kennedy
Endorsed by:
  The Signatures of
  49 Citizens

Jill Robinson

Non-Appearing Submissions:

Nova Scotia Provincial Council of the
Catholic Women's League

Doreen MacDonnell
Msg. J. Niles Theriault,
Spiritual Director

749

Peter Clark
Anthony Davis
(Dalhousie University)

P.C. Women's Association of Nova   Gloria Marshall
Scotia

Public School Responsibility Unit of   Rev. Lewis How
the Program Committee — Diocese
of Nova Scotia

Mount Saint Vincent University   Christine Ball
Re: The Institute for the
    Study of Women

Donald J. Weeren
(Associate Prof. of Education at Saint
Mary's University)

William Morse, M.D., C.M.
F.R.C.P.(C)
Jean M. Morse, B.Sc., M.S.W.

THUNDER BAY, ONTARIO

June 19, 1984

Presentation by:

The Northwestern Ontario   Fiona Karlsteot
Women's Centre   Margot Blight
— Thunder Bay   Endorsed by:
                                    —Social Action Committee,
                                      Cambrion Presbytery, The United
                                      Church of Canada
                                    —The Faye Peterson Transition
                                      House
                                    —Crisis Homes Inc.
                                    —Northwestern Ontario Women's
                                      Decode Council

Lakehead Evangelistic Association   Rev. Roy Kemp
                                    Rev. Ron Ashton

City of Thunder Bay   Inspector John Boulter
Police Force

Dr. Ruth Kajander, Psychiatrist

Thunder Bay Council of Clergy   Kerry Craig

Rev. Richard Darling
Anne K. McLaughlin,
Director of Communications
Roman-Catholic Diocese of
Thunder Bay

Murray R. Gadica

Joan Skelton (Chairperson, Committee Against Harmful Pornography

Endorsed by:
—Petition of 5,068 signatures
—City Council of Thunder Bay
—Lakehead District Separate School
  Board
—Lakehead Board of Education
—Federation of University Women of
  Thunder Bay
—C.U.P.E. Local 2486
—Lakehead Women Teacher's Association
—Office & Professional Employees
  International Union
—Ontario Federation of Home and
  School Assoc.
—Ontario Public School Teachers'
  Federation
—Ontario Secondary School Teachers' Federation

Blake Kurisko, Law Researcher
Lakehead Board of Education

Susan Braun, Chairperson
Dr. Riley Moynes
Mel MacLachlan

Committee on Outreach and Social
Action, United Church of Canada

Non-Appearing Submissions:

Thunder Bay Public Library

Gerry Meek
Lois M. Bewley, President
Canadian Library Association

The United Church of Canada
Cochrane Presbytery

Rev. William Ferrier,
Secretary

Jack Masters, M.P.
(Thunder Bay, Nipigon)

J.A. MacDonald
Secretary-Treasurer,
Northwestern Ontario
Municipal Association

751

YELLOWKNIFE, NORTHWEST TERRITORIES

June 19, 20, 1984

Presentation by:

Y.W.C.A. of Yellowknife	Michele Boon
	Eya Lewycky
	Lynne MacLean
	Lynn Saunders
Dennis Patterson	Member of Legislative Assembly, N.W.T.
Sheila Keete	Co-Ordinator, Women's Bureau, N.W.T.
Media Watch, N.W.T.	Jean Wallace
Bob MacQuarrie Member of Legislative Assembly	
Native Women's Association	Violet Erasmus
Foster Family Association of Yellow-knife	Nancy Harrison
Anglican Church of Canada — N.W.T.	Bishop John Sperry
Rev. Henry Barch	
Yellowknife Catholic School Board	Paul Driscol

WHITEHORSE, YUKON

June 21, 1984

Presentation by:

Yukon Status of Women Council Media Watch	Sharon Hounsell Vera Blackwell
Whitehorse United Church Social Justice Committee	Trevor Martin
	Helen Bebak
	Blair Kirby
	Rosemary Cormie

Hopkins
(N.A.C. Executive Member)

Government

Chris Pearson,
Government Leader
Bill Klausen,
Health & Human Resources
Lorrie McFeeters,
Women's Bureau
Bob Cole,
Acting Administration Justice
Pat Harvey,
Corporate and Consumer
   Relations
Jill Thomson,
Intergovernmental Relations
   Officer

Official Opposition

Tony Penikett, Leader
Roger Kimmerley, MLA